WARSHIP BUILDERS

STUDIES IN NAVAL HISTORY AND SEA POWER
Christopher M. Bell and James C. Bradford, editors

Studies in Naval History and Sea Power advances our understanding of sea power and its role in global security by publishing significant new scholarship on navies and naval affairs. The series presents specialists in naval history, as well as students of sea power, with works that cover the role of the world's naval powers, from the ancient world to the navies and coast guards of today. The works in Studies in Naval History and Sea Power examine all aspects of navies and conflict at sea, including naval operations, strategy, and tactics, as well as the intersections of sea power and diplomacy, navies and technology, sea services and civilian societies, and the financing and administration of seagoing military forces.

WARSHIP BUILDERS

AN INDUSTRIAL HISTORY OF
U.S. Naval Shipbuilding, 1922–1945

THOMAS HEINRICH

Naval Institute Press
Annapolis, Maryland

Naval Institute Press
291 Wood Road
Annapolis, MD 21402

Library of Congress Cataloging-in-Publication Data
Names: Heinrich, Thomas R., (date)– author.
Title: Warship builders : an industrial history of U.S. naval shipbuilding, 1922–1945 /
    Thomas Heinrich.
Other titles: Industrial history of U.S. naval shipbuilding, 1922–1945
Description: Annapolis, Maryland : Naval Institute Press, [2020] | Series: Studies in Naval
    History and Sea Power | Includes bibliographical references and index.
Identifiers: LCCN 2020035555 (print) | LCCN 2020035556 (ebook) | ISBN 9781682475379
    (hardback) | ISBN 9781682475539 (ebook) | ISBN 9781682475539 (epub)
Subjects: LCSH: Shipbuilding industry—United States—History—20th century. |
    Warships—United States—History—20th century. | Shipyards—United States—
    History—20th century.
Classification: LCC VM299.6 .H453 2020 (print) | LCC VM299.6 (ebook) |
    DDC 338.4/7623825097309041—dc23
LC record available at https://lccn.loc.gov/2020035555
LC ebook record available at https://lccn.loc.gov/2020035556

⊗ Print editions meet the requirements of ANSI/NISO z39.48-1992 (Permanence of Paper).
Printed in the United States of America.

28 27 26 25 24 23 22   9 8 7 6 5 4

To Felix, Luka, and Fritz

CONTENTS

ILLUSTRATIONS

CHARTS

FIGURES

ACKNOWLEDGMENTS

Over the past decade, I have accumulated a vast debt of gratitude to the people who have supported this project. Emma Raub at the Baruch College Newman Library patiently processed my innumerable interlibrary loan requests. Research staffers at the National Archives in College Park, Maryland, who helped me unearth a treasure trove of U.S. Navy records include Marci Bayer, Michael Bloomfield, Paul Cogan, Susan Gillett, Jacob Haywood, Russell Hill, Jacob Lusk, Haley Maynard, Amy Morgan, and Lauren Theodore. Special thanks to Nate Patch and Alicia Henneberry. At the regional branches of the National Archives, archivists Gail Farr and Stephen Charla in Philadelphia and Kelly McAnnaney in New York provided invaluable research advice, as did Sandra Fox at the Navy Department Library at the Washington, DC, Navy Yard, Elizabeth McGorty at the Brooklyn Navy Yard Development Corporation Archives, Tiffany Charles at the Wisconsin Maritime Museum, and Craig Burns at the Independence Seaport Museum Archives in Philadelphia. Thanks also to German archivists Marion Alpert, Jörn Brinkhus, Imke Brünjes, and Konrad Elmshäuser at the Bremen State Archives and Christian Böse at the Krupp Historical Archives in Essen. In Britain, I received helpful guidance from Sam Maddra and Emma Yan at the University of Glasgow Archives; Nerys Tunnicliffe and Barbara McLean of the Glasgow City Archives; Zoe Walter of the Tyne & Wear Archives in Newcastle; and Will Meredith of the Wirral Archives in Birkenhead.

Gerry Krieg did a masterful job with the shipyard maps.

My fellow historians have my gratitude for their comments and criticisms, especially Bob Batchelor, Christian Ebhardt, David Edgerton, Jeff Kerr Ritchie, Eike Lehmann, Chris Madsen, Chris Miller, William D. O'Neill, Nathan Okun, Donna Rilling, Jürgen Rohweder, Neil Rollings, Philip Scranton, Amy

Slaton, Heinrich Walle, and David Winkler. Special thanks to my friends and colleagues in the Baruch College History Department and participants in our roundtable: Jed Abrahamian, Carol Berkin, Anna Boozer, Charlotte Brooks, Stan Buder, Ana Calero, Yolanda Cordero, T. J. Desch-Obi, Julie Des Jardins, Vincent DiGirolamo, Zoe Griffith, Johanna Fernandez, Elizabeth Heath, Martina Nguyen, Kathy Pence, Mark Rice, Tansen Sen, Andrew Sloin, Clarence Taylor, Randolph Trumbach, and Cynthia Whittaker. Over the years, I was fortunate to present my research at meetings of the Business History Conference, the Association of Business Historians, the Hagley Museum & Library Research Seminar Series, Yale University's Technology and Strategy Workshop, the International Maritime Economic History Association Conference, the National Museum for the Royal Navy, the New York Military Affairs Symposium, the German Society for Seafaring and Maritime History (Deutsche Gesellschaft für Schiffahrts- und Marinegeschichte), the Maritime Heritage Conference, the National Iron and Steel Museum, and the Gilder Lehrman Institute of American History. Many thanks to the organizers and my fellow panelists. The deans of Baruch College's Weissman School of Arts and Sciences Jeff Peck and Aldemaro Romero generously provided research and travel funding, as did the PSC-CUNY Research Foundation and the American Philosophical Society.

Rudolf Boch, Michael Frisch, Thomas Childers, George Iggers (†), Mike Katz (†), Jürgen Kocka, Reinhart Koselleck (†), Walter Licht, and Hans-Ulrich Wehler (†) apprenticed me to the historian's craft at the University of Bielefeld in Germany, SUNY Buffalo, and the University of Pennsylvania.

Thanks also to my editors at the Naval Institute Press who guided the manuscript safely from proposal to publication, especially David Bowman. I also thank Drew Bryan, my copy editor, as well as my production editor Caitlin Bean, Laura Davulis, Glenn Griffith, and Paul Merzlak. Anonymous manuscript reviews saved me from potentially embarrassing errors. Any remaining ones are of course mine.

My family and friends have given me their unfailing support, especially my father Heinz (†), my mother Siglinde (†), my brothers Gottfried (†) and Michael, my sisters Marianne and Irene (†), my sister-in-law Ulli Sottmar, my brother-in-law Herrmann Toewe, and my nieces and nephews Anne, Christian, Heike, Jonas, Lara, Maren, Moritz, and Nora. I cherish my friendships with the Angelero family, the Baker family, the Ives family, the Jehan family, Simon Middleton, Kerry Miller, Markus Mohr, the Petrinic family, Sivan Pliskov, the Rados family, Sarah Spry, and Tony and Sandra Ciko. Special thanks to Lorie Heinrich. This book is dedicated to our sons Felix, Luka, and Fritz, our pride and joy always.

Introduction
The Workshop of American Sea Power

T his book examines the history of naval construction from the early 1920s to the end of World War II, when American builders produced a fleet that was instrumental in defeating the Axis in the war at sea. A colossal undertaking that cost billions and employed virtual armies of workers, warship building mobilized the nation's most prominent shipyards to construct combatants whose size and complexity dwarfed that of most other weapons platforms. During the war, American builders delivered eight million tons of naval combatants, more than their British, Japanese, and German counterparts combined (see chart 0.1).

The wartime public was largely unaware of the sheer scope and scale of naval shipbuilding, in contrast to cargo shipbuilding under the auspices of Henry Kaiser, who was widely celebrated as a hero of wartime entrepreneurship for delivering hundreds of Liberty ships. Accolades heaped on Kaiser, a publicity-savvy construction magnate without longstanding shipbuilding experience, rankled veterans of the trade like Homer Ferguson of Newport News Shipbuilding, who told naval architects and marine engineers at midwar:

> We have had a great deal of talk and publicity about the new ships, the Liberty ships and other types. . . . But nothing, practically, has been said of the old shipyards. . . . They have built more ships, higher-grade ships and finer ships, and on account of the secrecy surrounding our war movements, no one has been able to say anything about it. These people who are unpublicized, who don't get their pictures in the papers, have forgotten more about shipbuilding than most of the new people have ever learned or ever will learn, and they are building real fighting ships that require design and knowledge and experience.[11]

1

Though the government-mandated veil of secrecy that shielded naval construction from prying eyes was gradually lifted after the war, the industry has largely remained a black box. A handful of exceptions notwithstanding, most studies of the wartime Navy have focused on combatant design and the war at sea without paying much attention to the naval shipbuilding industry.[2] Shining a light into the box reveals the vast, multifaceted, and fascinating workshop of American naval dominance. Its vibrant core consisted of three dozen yards like Bethlehem Shipbuilding Fore River in Massachusetts, the Philadelphia Navy Yard, and other little-known organizations whose significance for the war effort rivaled that of household names of industrial mobilization like Kaiser and General Motors. In naval construction, "most of the work was performed and the greatest investment was made in the nucleus of 28 private yards and 8 Navy yards," according to the Bureau of Ships, the Navy's premier procurement organization. "In these plants alone could the necessary

Chart 0.1. Naval Shipbuilding, 1940–1945

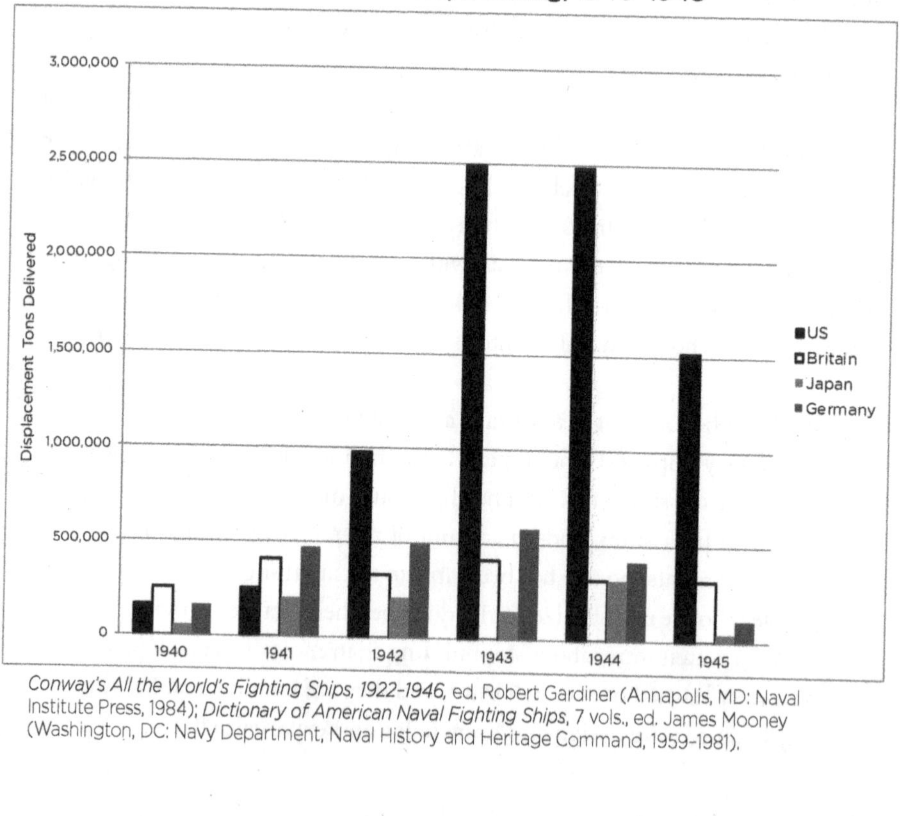

Conway's All the World's Fighting Ships, 1922-1946, ed. Robert Gardiner (Annapolis, MD: Naval Institute Press, 1984); Dictionary of American Naval Fighting Ships, 7 vols., ed. James Mooney (Washington, DC: Navy Department, Naval History and Heritage Command, 1959-1981).

management and facilities be combined to do the tremendously complex work required for the construction of major combatant types."[3] *Warship Builders* examines their history.

In addition to documenting and analyzing the industrial underpinnings of American sea power, this study contributes to a revisionist analysis of industrial mobilization in World War II. Conventional narratives posit that the United States lacked weapons production capability worth mentioning before the war. According to this interpretation, the Roosevelt administration relied on private industry to convert from the production of civilian goods to military hardware starting in 1940, when U.S. entry into the war became a distinct possibility. The mobilization of big business and its vaunted mass-production capabilities on behalf of the war effort enabled the armed forces to bury the Axis under a virtual avalanche of weaponry that rolled off the assembly lines, or so the story goes. Usually substantiated with references to the Kaiser shipyards and the Ford bomber plant in Willow Run, Michigan, which produced 4,600 B-24 Liberators using production techniques borrowed from the automobile industry, this portrait fits well with grand narratives of business and technology history that emphasize the pivotal role of large-scale corporations and mass production in American industrial development.[4]

Warship Builders argues that this understanding of industrial mobilization requires substantial rethinking to include batch formats, flexible specialization, disintegrated production, and skilled labor. Manufacturing systems that featured some or all of these characteristics have often been portrayed as distinctly European, but revisionist historians of American business and technology have documented their existence in industries as diverse as Philadelphia's nineteenth-century textile manufacture and World War II aircraft production.[5] Strengthening the revisionist case, this book documents similar structures and dynamics in warship building. Batch formats were particularly evident in the construction of heavy combatants, which were rarely built in series exceeding a dozen units. Flexible specialization, notably general-purpose production equipment suitable for diverse projects, enabled shipyards and their subcontractors to build a large variety of combatants. Disintegrated production formats involving hundreds of specialty firms was the norm in an industry where no single corporation built under one roof the many subsystems that made up a complex naval weapons platform, including armor plate, fire control systems, guns, and propulsion systems, all of which were manufactured by outside suppliers. Skilled labor played a pivotal role on shop floors and slipways, where seasoned shipfitters and machinists performed tasks that required extensive craft training and practical experience. Design freezes, which were the name of the game in Liberty ship construction, proved difficult to achieve in warship building because the Navy often changed blueprints and specifications while the ships were already under construction to ensure that designs incorporated recent combat experience.

The technical and organizational imperatives of naval construction, in short, were often incompatible with task simplification, design freezes, and other Fordist practices. "One reason for the inability to achieve so-called mass-production methods in building fighting ships is that labor tasks on such ships cannot be made so specialized and repetitive as is possible in the production of merchant ships," a Harvard study explained after the war. "A yard which produces fighting ships must inevitably develop a more versatile labor force with more skills per man than a yard which builds merchant ships exclusively . . . because fighting ships must have finer workmanship."[6] Technical and managerial know-how acquired over years if not decades was critical. "A shipyard that has never built a destroyer . . . is simply lost in trying to do it," an admiral summed up the procurement philosophy of the Navy, which entrusted the construction of battleships, fleet carriers, cruisers, and other combatants to managers and workers well-versed in the trade.[7]

In addition to investigating the salient features of naval shipbuilding, each chapter revisits interpretive questions raised by historians of industrial mobilization: How did prewar developments shape the American war economy? Were the armed services instigators of technological innovation or mere beneficiaries of civilian initiatives, as some scholars have argued? What was the role of the state in industrial mobilization?

Written for readers interested in the history of the U.S. Navy, business, technology, labor, and industrial mobilization, *Warship Builders* examines naval work with an emphasis on shipyard management and shop floor practices. Straddling naval and industrial history, it also explores the broader economic, political, and strategic contexts of the interwar period and World War II. The story begins in the wake of the Great War, when builders laid the groundwork for wartime naval work and when they launched most of the ships that fought in the opening phases of World War II. Chapter 1 investigates the profound challenges that confronted the industry in the 1920s, when orders dried up as a result of overbuilding in World War I and postwar naval arms control agreements. The Great Depression resulted in further hardship, followed by slow recovery during the New Deal, when the Roosevelt administration's National Industrial Recovery Act provided funds for warship construction, enabling builders to weather the Depression and hone construction capabilities critical to naval rearmament in the late 1930s. Technological change that transformed combatant construction between the wars is the subject of chapter 2, which documents the development of welding techniques, prefabrication methods, and propulsion systems that had major implications for production systems and industrial organization.

In 1940, the Roosevelt administration tasked industry with the construction of a two-ocean navy, the origins of which are examined in chapter 3 in the context of political controversies, strategic developments, and major reforms of U.S. Navy procurement policies. Chapter 4 focuses on warship building and repair in government-owned and -operated navy yards, which were among the nation's best-equipped shipbuilding facilities as a result of major investments before and during the war. The chapter also examines the shipbuilding process in workshops and on slipways during the construction of *Iowa*-class battleships to provide insights into design routines, project administration, and worker skills at the point of construction. Chapter 5 turns to the private sector, which received direct Navy investments into facilities to equip yards for a massive expansion of tonnage output during the war. Following a discussion of management and industrial relations, the chapter investigates subcontracting networks made up of specialty firms that supplied everything from ship steel to steam valves, calling attention to the prevalence of disintegrated production formats in naval shipbuilding. All chapters include comparisons with British, German, and Japanese naval construction policies and practices to pinpoint the distinct features of U.S. warship building.

A few notes on nomenclature are in order. In the pages that follow, Britain's navy is referred to as the "Royal Navy," its Japanese counterpart as the "Imperial Navy," and the German navy as the "Reichsmarine" until 1935 and as the "Kriegsmarine" afterward. Warship tonnage is reported in full load displacement, defined by the U.S. Navy as the weight of water displaced by a ship "ready for service in every respect, with liquids in machinery at operating level; authorized complement of officers, men and their effects; full allowances of ammunition; full complement of airplanes (fully loaded); full supply of provisions and stores for the period specified in the design characteristics; 60 gallons per man of potable water; fuel in amount necessary to meet endurance requirements; all other liquids in tanks to full capacity." Where indicated, displacement is reported in "standard tons," defined under the Washington Naval Treaty of 1922 similar to full-load displacement "but without fuel or reserve feed water on board."[8] Merchant ship tonnage is measured in gross tons, defined as a vessel's carrying capacity. Corporate names reflect industry parlance. For example, the New York Shipbuilding Corporation of Camden, New Jersey, is referred to as "New York Ship," the Bethlehem Steel Corporation's Fore River Shipyard in Quincy, Massachusetts, as "Fore River," and John Brown & Company of Clydebank, Scotland, as "Browns." The New York Navy Yard was officially called just that by naval authorities, but the designation never caught on among New Yorkers, who still refer to it as the "Brooklyn Navy Yard," a convention followed in this book.

1

"A Highly Specialized Art"

The Decline and Recovery of
Interwar Shipbuilding

American shipbuilders confronted daunting challenges from the end of World War I well into the 1930s. Emerging from the Great War with expanded facilities and bulging order backlogs, they fell on hard times in the 1920s, when a postwar maritime recession coupled with naval arms control left slipways empty and builders' finances in disarray. The industry recovered slowly later in the decade thanks to improving demand for merchantmen, but the Great Depression brought new hardships. At the start of his presidency in 1933, Franklin Roosevelt approved a multimillion-dollar naval program under a public works scheme to reduce unemployment in shipbuilding, followed in his second term by a more ambitious naval rearmament effort in the context of growing crises in the Far East and Europe. In addition to contracting with private shipyards, the peacetime Navy relied heavily on government-owned navy yards, which played a critical role in American warship building.

On the eve of World War II, the United States boasted one of the world's largest warship-building industries, which served as a launch pad for wartime construction. This notion, which will be elucidated in the pages that follow, is at odds with conventional narratives of American industrial mobilization. "The United States had no tradition of military industry," historian Richard Overy has claimed; "the strengths of the American industrial tradition—the widespread experience with mass production, the great depth of technical and organizational skill, the willingness to 'think big,' the ethos of competition— were . . . needed to transform American production in a hurry" at the start of the war.[1] Suggestions that American industrial mobilization relied primarily on civilian businesses without defense-related production experience that converted quickly to weapons manufacture during the war is inapplicable to combatant construction, where seasoned contractors with long records of naval work took center stage. Homer Ferguson of Newport News posited that "shipbuilding is a highly specialized art that cannot be played except by people who know how. In my judgement, it takes just about 20 years before a man can know the business and know the design end of it."[2] The interwar shipbuilding crisis took a heavy toll on the major firms, some of which succumbed, but the vital core remained intact thanks largely to government patronage. Leading builders, many of which were highly defense-dependent, exhibited behavior familiar to students of the military-industrial complex, whose origins long predated the war.

THE POSTWAR SHIPBUILDING CRISIS

World War I precipitated phenomenal growth in American shipbuilding, whose output exceeded that of all other nations except Britain. An industry that consisted of only a handful of yards in 1914 added dozens of new ones during the war to construct vessels on foreign and domestic accounts. Government orders for cargo ships, oil tankers, and later troop transports were issued by the federal government's Emergency Fleet Corporation, which provided funds for facility improvements at existing yards and for the construction of new ones. Naval work became the responsibility of established builders who delivered some 500,000 tons under the Naval Act of 1916, which was intended to produce a "navy second to none" but was only partially implemented. Between the declaration of war in April 1917 and the Armistice, the number of slipways in American steel shipyards more than doubled to 461, with the Hog Island yard near Philadelphia alone featuring fifty ways to accommodate standardized cargo ships, most of which were completed after the war.[3]

Wartime shipbuilding and a short-lived postwar boom saturated markets for years. Builders more than replaced merchant ships lost as a result of the war, fueling a 30 percent expansion of worldwide carrying capacity from forty-nine million gross tons in 1914 to more than sixty-five million in 1923, even though seaborne trade had posted only minor gains. In the United States, the continuation of merchant construction well into 1921, ordered by the Emergency Fleet Corporation in hopes of invigorating the structurally weak U.S. merchant marine with a massive infusion of cheap tonnage, created a buyers' market, leaving the expanded shipbuilding industry with a smaller customer base than before the war. Similar trends were evident in naval work, where the extension of wartime programs after the Armistice produced vast amounts of excess tonnage. More than half of all 162 *Clemson*-class destroyers were laid down after November 1918, and only six were canceled, leaving a virtual armada of these so-called four-stackers. The U.S. Navy did not order another destroyer for almost a decade after the last *Clemson* had been delivered in 1921. "In a very real sense the United States compressed most of its shipbuilding activity for the next twenty years into the seven-year period 1914–1921," maritime historian John Hutchins commented after World War II, concluding that these developments were "basically bad for the industry."[4]

Naval arms control dealt a further blow to yards equipped for warship building. The construction of battleships and battlecruisers ceased in 1922 after the U.S. Senate ratified the Washington Naval Treaty, a landmark agreement that was consistent with public demands for drastic reductions in taxes and

Chart 1.1. U.S. Merchant Shipbuilding, 1921–1939

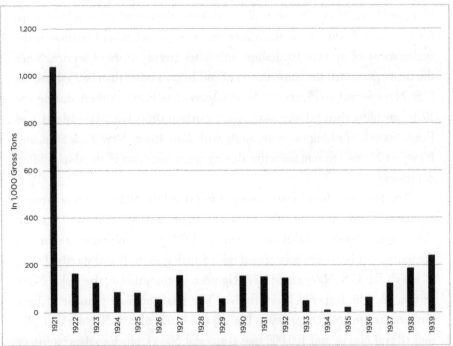

Includes only self-propelled merchant steel ships of two thousand tons and over.
H. Gerrish Smith, "Shipyard Statistics," in The Shipbuilding Business of the United States of America, vol. 1, ed. F. G. Fassett Jr. (New York: Society of Naval Architects and Marine Engineers, 1948), 78

arms spending, coupled with President Warren Harding's desire for a major foreign policy initiative to be implemented by Charles Hughes, his pragmatic secretary of state. At the Washington Conference of November 1921, Hughes traded major cutbacks in the vast and ongoing U.S. naval shipbuilding program and nonfortification of American bases in Western Pacific for reductions of British and Japanese construction and the dissolution of the Anglo-Japanese naval alliance, regarded by many American policymakers as a potential threat to U.S. strategic interests in the Pacific. Supplemented by the Nine Power Agreement that cemented the U.S. Open Door Policy in China, the Washington Treaty limited the maximum total tonnage of battleships and aircraft carriers to 660,000 standard tons (Britain), 660,000 (United States), 396,000 (Japan), 235,000 (France), and 235,000 (Italy), impelling the signatory powers to dispatch dozens of capital ships to the breakers. The U.S. Navy alone canceled eleven battleships and battlecruisers whose keels had been laid at the navy yards in Brooklyn; Mare Island, California; Norfolk, Virginia; and Philadelphia, and at the private yards of Newport News Shipbuilding, New York Ship, and Fore River. The treaty also suspended the construction of battleships for ten years, limited their main armament to 16 inches, and permitted the replacement of overage battleships only after twenty years of service. Since the treaty permitted the construction of combatants other than battleships, the U.S. Navy issued contracts for *Northampton*-class heavy cruisers during the 1920s, enabling their builders—the navy yards in Brooklyn, Mare Island, and Puget Sound, Washington State, along with Fore River, New York Ship, and Newport News—to remain active during the worst years of the shipbuilding depression.[5]

The Hoover administration sought to extend the 10:10:6 ratio of American, British, and Japanese battleships agreed upon at Washington to all warship classes at the London Naval Conference of 1930. The resulting treaty limited the tonnage of heavy cruisers armed with 8-inch guns to 10,000 standard tons, of which the U.S. Navy could have eighteen in commission, the Royal Navy fifteen, and the Imperial Navy twelve. The total standard tonnage of light cruisers carrying 6-inch guns was limited to 143,000 tons (U.S. Navy), 192,000 tons (Royal Navy), and 100,000 tons (Imperial Navy), much to the chagrin of U.S. Navy leaders and anglophobe congressmen who felt that American negotiators had been outfoxed by the British. The signatory powers also agreed to extend the battleship building holiday until 1936 in a blow to naval builders and armor producers who had expected battleship construction to resume in the early 1930s. Unlike the Washington Treaty, the London accord dealt exclusively with naval matters and did not include political agreements to curb Japanese ambitions. From 1922 to 1933, the United States laid down only 330,000 standard tons of warships, a smaller amount than any of the other signatory powers except Italy (300,000 tons), trailing Japan (480,000), France (500,000), and Britain (520,000). Austerity budgets became the norm in the United States during the early 1930s, when annual naval shipbuilding expenditures rarely exceeded $40 million (compared to an average of $100 million during the New Deal). By 1933, actual U.S. fleet tonnage was only 65 percent of the maximum allowed under the treaty regime, in contrast to Japan, whose tonnage approached the treaty limits, leaving the Imperial Navy with de facto parity with its American counterpart.[6]

The combination of excess shipbuilding capacity, oversupply of merchant tonnage, and decline in naval orders ravaged the industry for years. Competition for the preciously few contracts that came available increased sharply, often because shipbuilding novices were determined to elbow their way into the industry even at the cost of staggering losses. When Inter-Island Steam Navigation of Honolulu invited tenders on the passenger steamer *Haleakala* in 1922, it received thirteen bids ranging from $1.46 million to $1.03 million, and the winner, Sun Shipbuilding of Chester, Pennsylvania, completed the ship at a 39 percent loss. Sun survived, but many others did not. Of the fifty-four yards that commenced steel shipbuilding between 1914 and the Armistice, a mere six remained active during the interwar period. Much of this vast capacity reduction came as little surprise because many new yards erected during the war were government-financed emergency facilities and were not expected to remain active in the long term, but the downturn also uprooted well-established firms. Almost half of all yards that had constructed steel ships before 1914 abandoned new construction, converted to ship repairs or nonmarine work, or closed their doors.[7]

Naval armor and gun production also declined sharply from its World War I peak. Made up of Midvale of Philadelphia, Bethlehem Steel of Bethlehem, Pennsylvania, and the U.S. Steel subsidiary Carnegie-Illinois at Homestead, Pennsylvania, the armor industry had expanded during the war under the Naval Act of 1916. The same year, Congress had authorized and funded the construction of the Naval Ordnance and Armor Plant in South Charleston, West Virginia, which opened only at the end of the war and was soon mothballed. After the Great War, private firms deactivated most of their armor plants except those required to produce modest amounts for *Northampton*-class cruisers. The government-owned Naval Gun Factory at the Washington Navy Yard, which had been massively enlarged in World War I, kept busy during the 1920s relining battleship guns, crafting antiaircraft batteries for *Nevada*-class battleships undergoing modernization, and producing 8-inch guns for six *Northampton*- and two *Pensacola*-class heavy cruisers, the only major combatants laid down at the time.[8]

The much-publicized downfall of William Cramp & Sons of Philadelphia, one of the nation's most prestigious builders, sent shock waves through the industry and remained a reference point of policy debates for years. Having launched more than half of the fleet that fought in the Spanish-American War, it laid down forty-six destroyers in World War I and booked contracts for five *Omaha*-class cruisers, all which were completed after the Armistice. Among the most diversified firms in the industry, with a brass foundry, extensive repair facilities, and a steel plant, Cramp & Sons seemed well-positioned to weather the postwar crisis. Its fortunes dipped after 1919, however, when it was acquired by financier Averell Harriman, who extracted exorbitant dividends to prop up American Ship & Commerce, his tottering maritime empire. In addition to Cramp, Harriman controlled steamship lines, a large shipyard in Bristol, Pennsylvania, and a smaller one in Chester, Pennsylvania, to repair and overhaul his fleet of former German liners. The poorly conceived venture drained Cramp & Sons of precious financial reserves and forced the closure of the Bristol and Chester yards. At Cramp & Sons, completion of the last *Omaha* cruiser contract (which was delayed by a disastrous strike in 1921) and the passenger liner *Maolo* left the yard empty. In April 1927, Cramp & Sons terminated shipbuilding after nearly a century in the business and consolidated the engineering subsidiaries under a separate corporate entity. Most of its shop floor equipment was sold for bargain prices, and the physical plant deteriorated for more than a decade until the yard reopened in 1940 (chapter 5).[9]

Across the Delaware River in Camden, New Jersey, New York Ship avoided Cramp & Sons' fate by a hairbreadth. In World War I, it delivered

Wickes-class destroyers and troop transports, in addition to preparing for the construction of the 38,000-ton battlecruiser *Saratoga*, the largest vessel in the history of the U.S. Navy, whose keel was laid in 1920. Though the Washington Treaty required the elimination of all battlecruisers, it permitted the conversion of several into carriers, providing New York Ship with a much-needed source of income as markets contracted. With *Saratoga* largely complete at mid-decade, the workforce shriveled from 5,200 to 1,600 and the yard was acquired by American Brown Boveri, the U.S. subsidiary of a Swiss electrical engineering firm, which planned to convert the facilities to the production of transformers and electric locomotives. New York Ship "abandoned shipbuilding in 1925 and only was concerned in the completion of contracts then on hand," the firm's treasurer recalled. "Certain additional shipbuilding work was taken in the period of 1925 and 1928 merely to occupy the facilities not otherwise useful."[10] Makeshift work included completion of the heavy cruiser *Salt Lake City* awarded to Cramp & Sons prior to its demise, but New York Ship struggled to finish the contract. Diversification into electrical equipment, "together with the change of management which had taken place, resulted in the serious demoralization of . . . the shipbuilding organization and further resulted in such a falling-off in the quality and character of the work that the corporation and its officers were subjected to very severe criticism and condemnation by the Navy Department for the work which was then in progress," company president Clinton Bardo explained.[11] The shipyard's future was uncertain at best.

Newport News Shipbuilding of Virginia survived the 1920s in better shape than the Delaware Valley yards. Founded in the late nineteenth century by the railroad magnate Collis Huntington, it competed vigorously with Cramp & Sons and New York Ship for first-class tonnage prior to World War I. Having completed its wartime contracts for the battleships *West Virginia* and *Maryland,* twenty-four destroyers, and several cargo ships, Newport News scrapped the partially complete *Lexington*-class battlecruiser *Constellation* on the slipway in accordance with the Washington Treaty. The yard kept most of its 5,200-strong workforce employed during an overhaul of the passenger liner *Leviathan* (ex-German *Vaterland*) but lost $1.4 million on the $8 million contract. Led by Homer Ferguson, Newport News survived the doldrums with contracts for garbage barges, yachts, dredges, tugs, and the occasional passenger liner. Operating a pair of dry docks, it was equipped for overhauls and repairs,

Launch of the heavy cruiser *Salt Lake City* at New York Ship, January 23, 1929.
The covered slipways in the background are empty, as is the wet dock on the left,
indicating the lack of ship work that nearly cost the yard its existence.
Special Collections, J. Willard Marriott Library, University of Utah

unlike New York Ship, whose lack of such facilities limited its ability to stake
a claim in this profitable business. Newport News also made more successful
forays into general engineering than New York Ship, building railroad rolling
stock, paper machines, and hydroelectric power equipment, including stationary turbines for the Dneprostroi Dam in the Soviet Union. After-tax losses
totaled $2.5 million during the first three years of the shipbuilding crisis, but
the firm managed to recover as early as 1925 and accumulated profits there-
after. Though the turnaround was partly attributable to the growth of nonmarine business, Ferguson was eager to return to shipbuilding. "I suppose it
is fortunate that we can do something else," he remarked. "We can build turbines and box cars; we can beat swords into ploughshares and pruning hooks;
but no man born and bred to the business of building ships can get enthusiastic
about it."[12]

Chart 1.2. Newport News Shipbuilding Profits in Dollars, 1920–1934

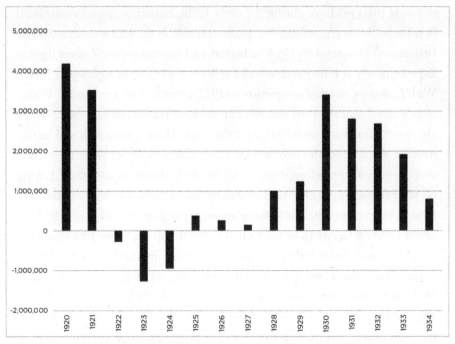

Munitions Industry, Part 20: Naval Shipbuilding: Newport News Shipbuilding and Dry Dock
Company. Hearings Before the Special Senate Committee Investigating the Munitions Industry,
74th Cong., 1st Sess., 1935, 5646 and 5655

Bethlehem Shipbuilding, a subsidiary of Bethlehem Steel Corporation with
eleven shipyards in the early 1920s, adopted a multifaceted survival strategy
of yard closures, facility conversions, diversification, and consolidation of new
construction in a select group of shipyards. Vice President of Operations Joseph
Powell, the driving force behind these initiatives, axed the Harlan Plant in
Wilmington, Delaware, the Alameda Yard in California, and the Moore Plant
in Elizabeth, New Jersey, with a combined total of sixteen slipways. In Maryland, Powell converted two yards to repair work and consolidated new merchant construction at the Sparrows Point Yard southeast of Baltimore, where
Bethlehem also operated the world's largest steel mill. Fore River remained the
vital core of its shipbuilding operation and was responsible for most of the division's interwar naval work. Founded in the late nineteenth century and acquired
by Bethlehem shortly before World War I, Fore River operated seven major
slipways, the largest of which could accommodate capital ships. Conversion

of the lead ship of the *Lexington* class from a battlecruiser into an aircraft carrier kept the yard busy during the early 1920s, but other work proved hard to come by. Most repairs and overhauls available in the area were handled by Bethlehem's Simpson Dry Dock in Boston, and nonmarine work never figured as prominently at Fore River as it did at New York Ship and Newport News. With *Lexington* nearing completion in 1927, general manager Samuel Wakeman warned that the yard was fast approaching the end of its tether. "There are two car floats and an oil barge on the ways. These contracts should be finished in about a month or six weeks. There is practically no work in our tool shop, mold loft, or machine shop, which are the backbone of our plant." Laying off workers and placing the yard on standby status was not a viable option. "We have, at the present time, the best organization that Fore River has ever had, . . . and it would be a pity to be compelled to break this up, as we find that good men leave our shipyards they get positions in other lines and are very reluctant to come back into a business which has such wild fluctuations in its output."[13] Wakeman's woes underscored a dilemma that plagued the entire industry: shipbuilding required a core workforce of highly experienced men, but the interwar crisis often made it impossible to procure enough contracts to keep them employed. Some firms took loss-making work just to keep a skeleton workforce busy, as Sun Ship and Newport News did when they built or overhauled ships at a cost that far exceeded contract prices. Since Wakeman was unable to convince Bethlehem Steel executives of the necessity to swallow financial losses in order to provide steady employment, Fore River's workforce expanded and contracted at a breathtaking rate, raising disturbing questions about the yard's ability to maintain its technical expertise.[14]

The postwar crisis that decimated American shipbuilding wrought similar havoc in Britain, still the world leader. Wartime expansion raised the number of slipways suitable for oceangoing ships from 450 (1914) to 650 (1920) and employment rose from 200,000 to more than 300,000. During the war, responsibility for government-financed merchant construction was transferred from the Admiralty to the Ministry of Shipping, which encouraged builders to produce cargo vessels in large series. In 1920, yards launched an unprecedented two million gross tons, but the boom collapsed in autumn of that year. The subsequent decline in domestic orders was partly attributable to long-term problems facing merchant ships under the Red Ensign, notably the takeover

Chart 1.3. Bethlehem Fore River Yard Workforce, 1927–1934

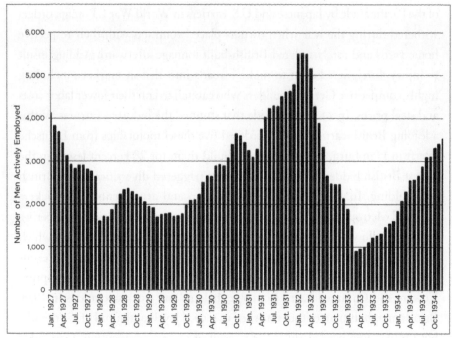

Exhibit 1649, U.S. Senate, Munitions Industry, Part 21: Naval Shipbuilding: Bethlehem Shipbuilding Corporation. Hearings Before the Special Senate Committee Investigating the Munitions Industry, *74th Cong., 1st Sess., 6108 (1935).*

Aircraft carrier *Lexington* outfitting at Bethlehem Fore River, April 7, 1927.
19-LC-23-L-2, C&R # CV2/S85, Serial 18824, Box 23, RG 19, Entry LCM Construction and Launching of Ships, 1930–1955, BB-58 through BB-60, National Archives and Records Administration, College Park, MD.

of the Pacific trade by Japanese and U.S. carriers in World War I. Foreign orders withered during the war when owners placed contracts with their respective home yards and rarely ordered British-built tonnage afterward. Adding insult to injury, foreigners began to make inroads into British markets, including highly competitive German builders who capitalized on their lower labor costs and steel prices. In a telling episode that stunned the industry, Furness Withy, a leading British carrier, in 1925 ordered five diesel motorships from Deutsche Werft in Hamburg, which offered to build them for 28 percent less than the lowest British bidder. These developments triggered diversification in British shipbuilding. In 1919, the naval construction and armaments giant Vickers acquired Metropolitan Carriage, which included a major electrical engineering business, followed by Cammell Laird, a naval and merchant builder, which staked a claim in railroad and subway car production. Like the maritime economy, the railroad industry stagnated during the 1920s, however, prompting Vickers and Cammell Laird to merge their rolling stock operations in 1928. British merchantman output returned to record levels at the end of the decade, but profits often proved elusive as a result of intense competition. Harland & Wolff, whose cost structure left much to be desired, lost 20 percent on $6.8 million worth of contracts in 1927, and Fairfield posted losses on twelve out of sixteen ships laid down from 1924 to 1929. On the Clyde alone, nine shipyards ceased operations during the 1920s.[15]

The decline of warship construction in the wake of the Washington Treaty contributed to further corporate restructuring. Until 1926, Vickers controlled a majority share in Beardmore, whose Naval Construction Yard at Dalmuir on the Clyde had been specifically designed for naval work. Retooling for merchant work saddled the firm with enormous debt, convincing Vickers of the need to liquidate its holdings, followed by Beardmore's collapse in 1930. Armstrong Whitworth, one of Britain's largest industrial employers, which produced armor, guns, ships, and locomotives, operated the Low Walker yard at Tyneside near Newcastle. The yard completed *Nelson*, the last battleship commissioned into the postwar Royal Navy, in 1927 at a loss while the parent company embarked on an ill-fated diversification strategy into papermaking. On financial life support from the Bank of England, Armstrong Whitworth agreed to sell its shipbuilding and armament operations to a new corporate entity controlled by Vickers, which mothballed the Low Walker yard.[16]

Chart 1.4. British Merchant Shipbuilding, 1921–1939

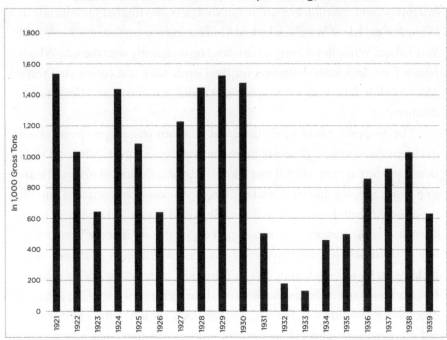

Lloyds Register of Shipping, Appendix to Lloyds Register Book 1947-48 (*London: Lloyd's Register, 1947*).

Faced with shrinking demand for heavy combatants, big yards competed with medium-sized ones for destroyer contracts, which in contrast to the United States remained available during the 1920s. Browns and Scotts on the Clyde, the Vickers yard at Barrow, Cammell Laird at Birkenhead, and Swan Hunter on the Tyne booked a trickle of destroyer work. Destroyer specialist Thornycroft retained a foothold in the trade with an innovative design for the proto-type destroyer *Amazon*, followed by five destroyers for the Royal Navy, in addition to six *Serrano*-class destroyers for the Chilean navy. Yarrow on the Clyde, by contrast, failed to defend its position as the Royal Navy's leading destroyer builder and relied increasingly on exports, in contrast to U.S. yards, which failed to stake a claim in warship building for foreign navies between the wars, except the submarine builder Electric Boat of Groton, Connecticut. After developing the prototype destroyer *Ambuscade*, Yarrow was unable to secure follow-up orders from the Admiralty and instead used the design to build a pair of Portuguese destroyers and licensed it to Dutch builders for the *Admiralen*-class, laid down in the Netherlands. The Colombian and Yugoslav navies issued contracts for new builds, but the Royal Navy did not order Yarrow destroyers until the mid-1930s. Foreign contracts also figured prominently at Whites on the Isle of Wright, which had built twenty-seven destroyers in World War I alone. While Royal Navy orders dried up completely after the war, Whites rebuilt four *Aetos*-class destroyers for the Greek navy and constructed three *Mendoza*-class destroyers for Argentina, in addition to ferries and Great Lakes steamers.[17]

The disappearance of major firms and problems plaguing survivors raised questions about industry's ability to sustain British sea power. Admiral David Beatty warned as early as 1920 that "skilled labour, accustomed to special warship work, is being dispersed, and the longer warship construction is put off, the more difficult it will be to find suitable skilled labour."[18] Director of naval construction Sir Eustace D'Eyncourt agreed, predicting that the "total cessation of construction would involve us in a serious deficiency of trained shipbuilding staffs and mechanics."[19] The Admiralty managed to pry some funds for new builds out of the governments and parliaments of the 1920s, partly in order to keep builders in business, but contracts for a handful of destroyers did not pay nearly as much as battleship orders (the battleship *Nelson*'s hull and machinery cost $6.7 million compared to $1 million for a D-class destroyer exclusive of guns).[20]

Browns, Britain's largest shipyard, which had concentrated on naval work in World War I, maintained a profitable marine engine business thanks partly to a contract with Kawasaki to construct turbines and gears for steamers under construction at that company's Kobe yard. Browns' shipbuilding operations, however, became a stop-and-go affair as vessel orders were suspended, contributing to mediocre profits on fifteen steamship contracts and steep losses on eight. In the late 1920s, a Royal Australian Navy contract for the heavy cruisers *Australia* and *Canberra* yielded a profit, but four Royal Navy destroyers produced losses. The launch of the last in the series in September 1930 left the slipways virtually empty, "a condition I have never known before during my 44 years at Clydebank," managing director Sir Thomas Bell told the board of directors.[21] Bell breathed a sigh of relief when the Union Bank of Scotland renewed a $970,000 line of credit, but the yard's future appeared bleak.[22]

Firms that weathered the 1920s in better financial shape included Swan Hunter of Newcastle in the northeast of England. Half of the 460,000 gross tons of merchant shipping launched over the course of the decade were cargo vessels, Swan Hunter's long-standing specialty, plus oil tankers and a handful of liners. In the late 1920s, it netted Royal Navy orders for three destroyers and three sloops, which offset a decline in merchant construction. Most shipbuilding contracts and the firm's extensive repair business produced respectable profits, which enabled the board to distribute 3 percent in dividends annually and accumulate $8.3 million in reserves by 1930.[23]

The fate of postwar German shipbuilding resembled that of its American and British counterparts. Expecting a postwar boom in merchant construction, wartime builders doubled construction capacity to reach 600,000 gross tons, leaving Germany with thirty-nine major yards and two hundred ways at the end of the war. In the early 1920s, builders booked contracts to replace merchant ships for British and French owners who had lost tonnage during the war. The versatile Bremer Vulkan yard alone completed sixteen cargo ships totaling 138,000 gross tons for foreign owners. The loss of the Reich's merchant fleet under the Versailles Treaty prompted German carriers to order replacement tonnage the construction of which was partially funded by a public compensation scheme enacted in 1921. Major yards that played a key role in rebuilding the merchant marine included Germaniawerft in Kiel, a wholly owned subsidiary of Krupp Steel, which had built U-boats during the war and during the early 1920s constructed tankers and cargo ships. Since private firms were barred from most naval work under the Versailles Treaty, the limited amount of warship building permitted went to the Wilhelmshaven Navy Yard and the government-owned Deutsche Werke in Kiel.[24]

Originally expected to last ten years, the reconstruction of the German merchant marine under the replacement program fizzled out in 1923, when the worldwide oversupply of carrying capacity and the central bank's restrictive monetary policy in the wake of hyperinflation forced shipowners to cancel contracts. Well-managed yards that survived the slump in good shape included Bremer Vulkan, which remained active with innovative diesel motorships for German and Canadian owners. Other yards reached the end of their tether when financier Johannes Schröder, like Harriman, merged several yards into the Deutsche Schiff- und Maschinenbau Aktiengesellschaft (Deschimag), which sterilized 25 percent of German shipbuilding capacity, including the venerable Stettiner Vulcan yard and Tecklenborg in Wesermünde, in order to sustain its

Chart 1.5. German Merchant Shipbuilding, 1921–1939

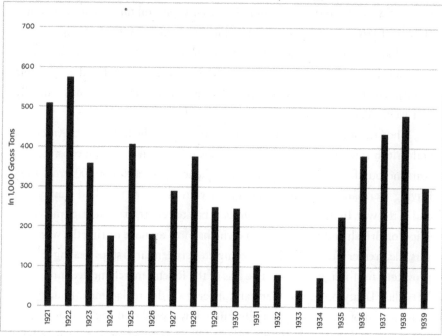

Lloyds Register of Shipping, Appendix to Lloyds Register Book 1947–48 *(London: Lloyd's Register, 1947).*

core operations at AG Weser in Bremen. The latter secured an order for the majestic *Bremen,* a superliner that became the pride of the Weimar Republic, but the $14 million contract produced a substantial loss. A $12 million federal fund that loaned shipowners up to 50 percent of construction costs benefited only a handful of builders and petered out quickly.[25]

Japanese shipbuilding developed along similar trajectories. World War I had witnessed a major expansion from six to forty-five steel shipyards to meet the Imperial Navy and merchant marine's skyrocketing demand for new tonnage. Ishikawajima of Yokosuka, Uraga in Yokosuka, Uchida at Yokosuka, and other independent builders were joined by zaibatsu like Suzuki Shoten, which acquired Harima Zosensho at Aioi. While output capacity grew during the war, however, "the quality was on a low level, due to the fact that during the war, under the influence of haste, only simplified standard types of vessels were being built," the U.S. Office of Naval Intelligence concluded. "On an especially low level was the technique of production on the new wharves and shipbuilding works."[26] The industry began to feel the effects of commercial market saturation in late 1921, when orders dried up. Yard utilization declined to only 15 percent of capacity, prompting builders to lay off workers, mothball slipways and workshops, close their doors, or diversify into nonmarine work. Fujingata of Osaka and Asano Shipbuilding near Tokyo closed temporarily, but Mitsubishi, Kawasaki, Uraga, Ishikawajima, and Harima of Kobe remained in business thanks in part to the Imperial Navy's efforts to expand the fleet to Washington Treaty limits in the late 1920s.[27]

Mitsubishi, Japan's largest shipbuilder, invested a sizable share of its World War I profits ($300,000) in facility improvements at its main works in Nagasaki to prepare for the construction of the battleship *Tosa*, laid down in February 1921. Though *Tosa* was canceled and broken up a year later in accordance with the Washington Treaty, Mitsubishi put the new facilities to use during the construction of *Furutaka*, Japan's first heavy cruiser, and two other ships of the same type. Mitsubishi's smaller Kobe yard acquired a specialty in submarines, twelve of which were built during the 1920s. In addition to constructing

Chart 1.6. Japanese Merchant Shipbuilding, 1921–1939

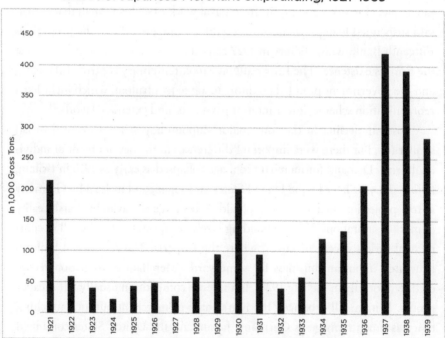

Lloyds Register of Shipping, Appendix to Lloyds Register Book 1947-48 *(London: Lloyd's Register, 1947).*

profitable surface combatants, Mitsubishi Nagasaki delivered passenger liners to Nihon Yūsen, Osaka Shosen, and other Japanese carriers. In the mid-1920s, the technologically versatile builder staked a claim in diesel technology, which attracted the attention of economy-minded owners who placed orders for motorships. After accumulating considerable reserves during the short-lived postwar boom, Mitsubishi managed to remain profitable until 1932, when it posted the first loss in the company's history.[28]

Kawasaki of Kobe, the nation's second-largest private builder, experienced greater difficulties. Work on the *Tosa*-class battleship *Kaga* ceased after the Washington Treaty went into effect and the ship was converted into an aircraft carrier. Unlike the U.S. Navy, however, which assigned the conversion of two comparable *Lexington*-class battlecruisers to New York Ship and Fore River, the Imperial Navy had the unfinished *Kaga* towed to the government-owned Yokosuka Navy Yard for completion as a carrier. The firm's remaining work-load included five cruisers, two destroyers, and thirteen submarines, as well as freighters for its shipping subsidiary Kawasaki Kisen, but it failed to gain the patronage of independent carriers. Payments to the loss-making shipping division depleted reserves and profits from naval work to such an extent that Kawasaki suspended loan payments to its creditors, dragging down the prestigious Fifteenth Bank, whose failure in 1927 caused a financial panic and nearly cost the firm its existence. The Imperial Navy took temporary control of the yard, and the government prodded creditors to agree to a bailout, which included a reorganization scheme, lower interest payments, and extensive layoffs.[29]

Postwar decline in the four major shipbuilding nations evinced broad similarities, but there were important differences in the development of individual firms. Demand for merchant tonnage collapsed as early as 1920 in Britain, followed a year later by the United States and Japan, and in 1923 by Germany as rosy projections of a postwar shipbuilding boom gave way to the harsh reality of market saturation. Warship building rarely compensated for the fall in commercial orders except in Japan, where the Imperial Navy's gradual buildup generated important business for some yards. Merchant construction recovered temporarily in the late 1920s, but intense competition usually left meager profits. Britain still produced the lion's share of merchant output, launching twice as much tonnage as Germany, Japan, and the United States combined from 1921 to 1930. By the latter year, American shipbuilders laid down less merchant tonnage than their German and Japanese counterparts. National trends tell only part of the story, however. Poorly conceived corporate strategies were evident at Cramp & Sons, Armstrong Whitworth, AG Weser, and Kawasaki. Firms that maintained their financial viability against great odds included Newport News, Swan Hunter, Bremer Vulkan, and Mitsubishi. While some of these successes were the result of clever business strategies, others were attributable to shady deals and collaborative schemes hatched behind closed doors in the netherworld of the naval-industrial complex.

THE CARTELIZATION OF NAVAL SHIPBUILDING

In the United States, Fore River, Newport News, and New York Ship embarked on a legally questionable course of cartelization to survive the doldrums (cartels are defined as producer agreements to maintain high prices by limiting competition). After Cramp & Sons' demise, the Big Three were the only U.S. firms equipped to build heavy surface combatants, and they exploited that ability for all it was worth. In 1927, when the navy invited bids for six *Northampton*-class heavy cruisers in the largest naval program since the war, executives of the Big Three secretly coordinated their bids to ensure that each would receive at least one of the contracts and reap hefty profits. Proposing to build each ship at highly inflated prices, the yards' internal estimates of actual construction costs were significantly lower. Fore River, for example, expected to spend $7.5 million to build the lead ship *Northampton* but submitted a $10.7 million bid to the Navy, while the Puget Sound Navy Yard at Bremerton, Washington, spent only $7.4 million building the comparable *Louisville* thanks largely to efficient management (see chapter 2). Big Three profits on *Northampton*s totaled more than $12 million, with Fore River netting 25 percent of the contract price, Newport News 35 percent, and New York Ship 37 percent.[30]

The builders added another twist to the scheme during subsequent bidding rounds that resulted in a division of contracts according to combatant type, with major consequences for naval work. When the Navy asked for bids on a pair of *Portland*-class heavy cruisers in 1929, Newport News intentionally submitted an unrealistically high bid on both ships, having informally agreed to leave cruiser construction to New York Ship and Fore River. The latter two returned the favor a year later by bidding high on the carrier *Ranger*, which was built by Newport News at a 23.1 percent profit. The distribution of contracts initially had little to do with extant capabilities. Newport News had never built a carrier before it laid down *Ranger* in 1931, unlike New York Ship and Fore River, which had converted the battlecruisers *Saratoga* and *Lexington*, respectively, into carriers. *Ranger*'s design was fraught with problems but taught Newport News a great deal about the new type, facilitating the acquisition of highly specialized expertise in aircraft carrier design and construction. In the short run, rigged bidding in 1933 enabled Newport News to book contracts for the carriers *Yorktown* and *Enterprise*, predecessors of the *Essex* class, the construction of which became the yard's mainstay in World War II.[31]

These machinations were brought to light in 1935 during the Senate inquiry into the munitions industry headed by Republican Gerald Nye, who sought to prove in the so-called "merchants of death" investigation that lobbying by arms dealers was responsible for the U.S. entry into World War I. Though the Nye committee failed to achieve its main objective, it managed to document the sheer extent of secret collaboration among naval builders during the late 1920s and early 1930s. Their secret deals exuded the unmistakable stench of illegal cartelization but also produced undeniable benefits. First, rigged bidding facilitated the survival of important firms at a time when many others recorded staggering losses. From 1927 to 1934, Newport News' annual earnings exceeded 10 percent while New York Ship accumulated $6 million in profits, reduced its debt by $1.5 million, and quadrupled its reserves to $6.8 million. Builders bereft of profitable naval work that succumbed included the Bath Iron Works and the Lake Torpedo Boat Company, a major submarine builder. Second, the cartelization of naval work set the Big Three on a course of yard specialization, which produced tangible benefits for wartime shipbuilding. Like Newport News in carriers, New York Ship and Bethlehem carved out a niche in cruisers, enabling them to accumulate know-how that proved invaluable during the war (see chapter 5).[32]

Cartelization was also evident in Britain, where firms equipped for naval work formed the secretive Warshipbuilders' Committee in 1926.[33] When the Admiralty issued a call for tenders, the committee's coordinator collected realistic cost estimates from member firms, calculated the mean, added 10 percent, and determined the "winning bid" based on a rota. Each member firm then submitted doctored bids to the Admiralty, which awarded the contract to the yard that had been secretly preselected by the committee's coordinator, ensuring that group members booked the orders they desired from the limited pool available. Though the arrangement did not produce exorbitant profits in the early 1930s, it contributed to the survival of hard-pressed firms by limiting financial losses in British naval contracting and by keeping core workforces employed. When a commission uncovered the committee's existence in 1935, Sir Charles Craven of Vickers argued cogently, "Without such arrangements it is obvious that, in view of the comparatively small volume of work available, the weaker of the firms would have disappeared from business, and the stronger firms would have had their resources considerably depleted by the effect of accepting work at unremunerative prices."[34]

NAVY YARDS

In the United States, suspicions were that the Big Three had taken unfair advantage of their privileged position in naval work, which had contributed to the revitalization of navy yards. Like yard specialization under the cartel scheme, the extensive use of government-owned shipyards became a salient feature of American warship construction, creating industrial assets that played an important role in naval rearmament during the 1930s and beyond.

With almost all new construction of surface combatants performed by private firms during the 1920s, most navy yards had to survive on a slim diet of fleet maintenance, occasional bookings for naval auxiliaries, and orders from the U.S. Coast Guard, which needed fast cutters to enforce Prohibition. The navy yards were also responsible for battleship modernizations, for example *New York* and *Texas*, whose coal-fired boilers were replaced with oil-fired ones and whose fire-control systems and antiaircraft batteries received upgrades at the Norfolk Navy Yard. Private builders and ship repairers, eager to perform such work in their own yards, constantly demanded the mothballing or outright closure of the government-owned facilities. The Navy Department occasionally pondered deactivating major navy yards but in the end deactivated only a small facility in New Orleans.[35]

While most representatives and senators opposed closures simply in order to secure jobs in their home districts, some of the navy yards' congressional allies viewed government-owned and -operated shipyards in a broader political context. Representative Frederick Dallinger, for example, was a Republican from Massachusetts whose district included the Boston Navy Yard. Though unaware of the behind-the-scenes dealings of the Big Three, Dallinger suspected as early as 1928 that private firms reaped enormous profits on combatants that could be constructed cheaper in the navy yards, as Puget Sound had demonstrated when it delivered *Louisville* for far less than what the Navy paid for her sister ships. To rectify this situation, Dallinger proposed an amendment to a 1928 authorization of heavy cruisers stipulating that half of all new ships be built in navy yards. In the course of congressional hearings, he mocked private builders' claims of navy yard inefficiencies. Paving the way for an anticorporate rhetoric that proliferated during the Nye committee hearings, Dallinger noted that if private contractors were so much better equipped than the government to handle defense work, "why not abolish the War Department and the Navy Department, and make a contract with the United States Steel Corporation or some other big corporation to take care of national defense for us?" It was sheer folly for the Navy to rely on private contractors, who were not only likely to fleece the government but were exposed to the whims of the free market, as evidenced by Cramp & Sons' demise. If "these private corporations go to the wall, as they have been going to the wall in spite of the Government business which they enjoyed, a war may occur and you have no Government plants that are capable of producing one of these battleships or cruisers," Dallinger warned, coupling his call for arms production in government plants with a searing indictment of corporate warmongers. "I believe one of the principal causes of war among nations to-day is the existence of private munitions plants," he posited. "In order to sell their goods they have got to have a war going on somewhere; and one of the provisions in the League of Nations covenant, you will remember, was to the effect that in time of peace all military and naval supplies should be manufactured by the governments and not by private corporations."[36] Dallinger and his supporters understood that implementation of the amendment required substantial facility upgrades at the navy yards. Major investments were needed to bring slipways and workshops at Norfolk and Philadelphia up to date, and even the better-equipped plants at Brooklyn and Mare Island required substantial sums.

Private builders were predictably outraged. "I think it will be better for the Government and for the shipbuilding industry to kill the [cruiser] bill entirely rather than use it for building up further Government competition with the shipbuilding industry," a Newport News executive confided to his opposite number at New York Ship.[37] Wakeman of Fore River told the House

Committee on Naval Affairs that Cramp & Sons' fate was a portent of what was in store for other firms if the amendment passed. "What has happened to the Cramp Shipbuilding Co. will happen to some of the other yards if they do not receive more work than they have had in the last two or three years."[38] The concomitant loss of naval architecture and marine engineering skills would deal a crushing blow to the Navy, warned Charles Wetherbee, engineering superintendent of the Bath Iron Works: "These staffs, representing the result of many years of trial and elimination of men to build them up, would be disbanded if the private shipyards are obliged to close through lack of naval work.... Without these technical staffs, our Navy would be limited to duplicating ships already built, whose plans had already been made. Progress would stop."[39]

When Congress included the Dallinger amendment in the authorization of cruiser construction for 1928, the Navy Department requested funds for facility improvements at the four navy yards slated to build heavy cruisers. Philadelphia and Mare Island each had a slipway rebuilt and Puget Sound added a new warehouse. At Brooklyn, the Navy Department established the Central Drafting Office, the single most important innovation to emerge from the cruiser program. Prior to its establishment in 1929, the navy yards lacked draft offices that could compare to the design organizations of the Big Three, and the formation of the Central Drafting Office rendered the Navy to a degree independent of private builders. Moreover, the $1.4 million in facility improvements associated with the cruiser program marked a turning point in the development of interwar shipbuilding because they represented the first significant investments into yard facilities since the early 1920s. The beginning of the Great Depression prompted an economy-minded Congress to delay appropriations for the construction of *New Orleans* and her six sister ships, but Puget Sound managed to lay the first keel in September 1930, followed shortly by Brooklyn and Philadelphia.[40]

THE GREAT DEPRESSION

American shipbuilding weathered the early Depression years in surprisingly good condition. Merchant construction recovered as a result of the Jones-White Act of 1928, which authorized the accelerated sale of wartime tonnage at rock-bottom prices, increased mail subsidies to American carriers that serviced international routes, and established a $250 million fund to provide loans for new builds and overhauls. The act sparked a flurry of activity as carriers ordered forty-one passenger liners and cargo ships. Shipyards spent the next three years churning out tonnage at a respectable rate while profiting from the rapid deflation of steel prices and sharply lower labor costs, which unexpectedly boosted financial performance. New York Ship, which had booked a $41 million United States Lines contract for the passenger liners *Washington* and *Manhattan*, recorded $507,000 in profits for 1931 and $645,000 for 1932. When the twin liners approached completion, however, executives rang the alarm bells in a letter to President Herbert Hoover. "Unless new work is made available promptly [our workforce] will be reduced [from 5,520] to approximately fifteen hundred men by the end of [1932]," they warned. "Our engineering force of two hundred fifty indispensable technical men is now working on half time basis. A substantial number of these men will be totally relieved within a short time, if new work cannot be had."[41] The Navy's chief constructor, Rear Adm. George Rock, told Congress, "Most of the yards will be without any merchant shipbuilding work by the end of the present calendar year [1932]." Like Beatty and D'Eyncourt in Britain, Rock worried about industry's ability to sustain the Navy long-term. "When work thus dies down, the skilled workmen and the members of the technical staffs must and do seek employment elsewhere, and when these men have once settled in new work they are not easily enticed back."[42]

Similar predictions became commonplace as the industry reached its interwar nadir. Output of merchantmen plummeted from 155,000 gross tons in 1933 to a paltry 16,000 a year later. Private-sector payrolls fell by almost half from 1930 to 1933, when yards employed only 33,800 workers. Industrywide, net losses exceeded profits from 1931 to 1935. Remarkably, however, no major American shipyard capitulated for good. In Britain, by contrast, yard closures proliferated under the auspices of National Shipbuilders Securities, formed by shipbuilders in collaboration with the Bank of England to acquire and sterilize excess capacity. Entire plants that ceased to build ships included Beardmore's enormous Naval Construction Yard, Harland & Wolff's Greenock works on the Clyde, and Palmers of Newcastle (the latter was barred from building ships until "21 years after the death of descendants of King George V then born"[43]). National Shipbuilders Securities also conducted partial sterilizations, notably four slipways at Fairfield, a major builder on the Clyde that was technically insolvent when shipbuilding magnate James Lithgow acquired it for a nominal sum in 1935. In Germany, the Depression claimed the yards of Stocks & Kolbe of Kiel, Ostseewerft at Stettin, and Klawitter in Danzig. AG Weser teetered on the brink of collapse in 1931, when orders dried up completely, followed by a bailout by the Reich and the city of Bremen that turned the firm into government property in all but name. Like the United States, Japan reported no permanent closures of major firms, partly as a result of state subsidy programs.[44]

American shipbuilders benefited from public policies enacted by the New Deal administration of President Roosevelt, who was familiar with the industry as a result of his eight-year stint as President Woodrow Wilson's Assistant Secretary of the Navy. In 1915, he had assisted New York Ship and Fore River in negotiating the delivery of two battleships to the Argentinian navy, and a year later he took charge of the largest naval program in American history to that date. After leaving Washington for his home in Hyde Park, New York, Roosevelt agonized over the Navy's decline under Republican tutelage during the 1920s and blamed the proliferating shipyard crisis on Hoover's "pacifism," a verdict that was widely shared by shipbuilders, who supported Roosevelt's 1932 election campaign. Arthur Homer, who had served as Roosevelt's special assistant in World War I and chaired the Marine Committee of the Democratic National Campaign Committee in 1932, told shipbuilders, "It is apparent that if we are to have a treaty strength Navy, we must have someone other than a pacifist in the White House. As a treaty strength Navy is of vital importance to you shipbuilders, we believe that the best interest of the industry will be served by the election of Governor Roosevelt, who has full knowledge of the Navy's problems, having been intimately acquainted with the troubles which came from unpreparedness in the World War."[45] After the election, the president picked Claude Swanson, a sickly seventy-year-old, for Navy Secretary because Roosevelt wanted to manage the Navy Department himself from the Oval Office. "I am my own Secretary of the Navy," he remarked.[46] Throughout his first two terms, Roosevelt was deeply involved in the department's administrative affairs, intervened in personnel decisions and shipyard labor relations, and selected the names of all naval vessels built during the New Deal. He also reviewed warship designs and revised construction blueprints, to the alarm of professional naval architects and marine engineers, who found it difficult to rein in the president's enthusiasm for elegant curves and extra funnels without technical purpose. Though keen to avoid breaches of the interwar naval arms limitation agreements, Roosevelt favored efforts to build the fleet closer to the limits of the Washington and London treaties than his predecessor, who saw peacetime naval spending as inherently wasteful.[47]

NAVAL SHIPBUILDING AS PUBLIC WORKS

New Dealers launched their first major attempt to revitalize the industry in 1933, when they included funds for naval construction in the National Industrial Recovery Act. Plans to label warship building as public works had originated a year earlier in the Navy Department, where officials were looking for money to pay for the construction of combatants that had already received congressional authorization but no funding. The idea had fallen on deaf ears in the last year of the Hoover administration but was revived in 1933 by U.S. Representative Carl Vinson (D-GA) and Rear Adm. Emory Land, chief of the Navy Department's Bureau of Construction & Repair, who told Navy Secretary Swanson in March 1933: "The private shipbuilding yards in the United States are close to the starvation point, so far as shipbuilding is concerned. These shipbuilding plants are a great national asset and worthy of the fullest consideration. Work at the east coast Navy yards is at a low ebb. . . . This means that workmen at the east coast yards will have to be discharged during the coming year. A shipbuilding program will not only avoid this, but will permit increases from the ranks of the unemployed."[48] The Vinson-Land proposal elicited political support even from Republicans. U.S. Representative George Darrow (R-PA) commented in April 1933: "Such a program for construction of new ships would greatly stimulate the shipbuilding industry, which has been allowed to stagnate in recent years, and a revival of this industry means an increase in employment."[49] As a result, the Public Works Administration (PWA) allocated $238 million to naval shipbuilding and, equally important, more than $30 million to navy yard improvements, supplementing the meager regular appropriations. Roosevelt, aware that selling the measure as a one-off "unemployment relief" initiative was critical to its success because regular naval appropriations of this size would have been rejected by Congress, told Swanson, "Claude, we got away with murder."[50]

Under an administration that was committed to the spirit of the Dallinger amendment—which technically covered only the *New Orleans* class—the navy yards booked a sizable share of the new orders. In 1933, the Navy Department entrusted them with two *Brooklyn*-class light cruisers, ten *Mahan*-class destroyers, a pair of *Porpoise*-class submarines, and two *Erie*-class patrol gunboats, the construction of which was financed by the PWA. To prepare shipbuilding facilities under the cognizance of the Navy Department's Bureau of Yards &

Docks, the PWA financed a variety of plant improvements at the eight navy yards tasked with the construction of these ships. Mare Island, California, received $180,000 to complete a power plant for electric arc welding of destroyer hulls and superstructures. Philadelphia replaced a rotted timber slipway with a $350,000 concrete structure that could accommodate the light cruiser *Philadelphia*. Brooklyn, responsible for the construction of the light cruiser *Brooklyn* and the patrol craft *Erie*, built a pair of fifty-ton traveling cranes at a cost of $300,000. The Naval Gun Factory at the Washington Navy Yard netted $250,000 for machine tools. Though small compared to the vast facility improvements undertaken in World War II, these additions not only enabled the navy yards to complete their New Deal–era orders, but also performed important duties in wartime naval work (see chapter 4).[51]

The Big Three claimed the lion's share of PWA naval shipbuilding, netting contracts worth $92 million. "The size of this program created a situation where the Navy needed the use of every private and navy yard instead of the private and navy yards needing the Navy work to keep themselves going," congressional investigators recorded. "The usual picture was completely reversed. It was no longer a buyer's market as it was from 1927 through 1932. It was now a seller's market."[52] Emboldened by the National Recovery Administration's tacit endorsement of cartels, the Big Three once again coordinated their bids in order to carve the program into profitable slices. Newport News, which was busy putting the finishing touches on *Ranger* at the time, booked a $38 million contract for a pair of *Yorktown*-class carriers. Fore River secured four *Mahan*-class destroyers for $15.5 million, and New York Ship landed the largest share with two *Brooklyn*-class cruisers and four *Mahan*-class destroyers. Such prospective business attracted speculators even before the Navy awarded the bids, prompting American Brown Boveri to sell New York Ship to automobile magnate Errett Cord on August 1, 1933. "Next day the Navy Department dished out its New Deal contracts and Mr. Cord's shipyard got the biggest slice of all—a $38,450,000 order," *Time* magazine reported.[53] Investigations revealed that New York Ship expected to spend only $28.3 million to build the six ships, leaving potential profits exceeding $10 million.[54]

In addition to building two *Brooklyn*s, New York Ship was responsible for drafting detailed plans and specifications for the entire class of light cruisers, a complex undertaking that required technical as well as organizational skills.

Aircraft carrier *Enterprise* outfitting at Newport News, April 1, 1937. Note the hammerhead crane with a sixty-foot reach and a maximum lifting capacity of 120 tons, one of the largest in American industry. Similar cranes were installed during and after World War I at the navy yards in Philadelphia and Brooklyn and at New York Ship.
Commandant Fourth Naval District, "History of Naval Administration, World War II," vol. 1, Navy Department Library, Rare Book Room, Washington Navy Yard, Washington, DC

This presented major challenges because New York Ship—unlike Newport News and Fore River—no longer operated a full-fledged design department. After firing most of its naval architects and marine engineers, the firm had outsourced blueprint preparation to the Marine Engineering Corporation of Philadelphia, a consultancy staffed by naval architects, marine engineers, and draftsmen formerly employed by Cramp & Sons and New York Ship itself. The firm was headed by John Metten, Cramp & Sons' former chief naval architect, who had designed many of that yard's passenger liners and naval vessels and who controlled valuable patents for marine turbines and valves. After Cramp & Sons' demise in 1927, Metten's consultancy had designed *Northampton*-class heavy cruisers and the passenger liners *George Washington* and *Manhattan*, built by New York Ship. In 1933, the Cord group that took control of New York Ship recruited Metten to rebuild the yard's design department, put him in charge of the *Brooklyn*-class project, and a year later made him president of the yard. Metten dissolved Marine Engineering Corporation and brought its staff from Philadelphia to Camden, raising the number of naval architects, marine engineers, and draftsmen employed by New York Ship from a mere handful to 350.[55]

Metten's arrival marked a turning point in the history of the shipyard and laid the foundations for important cruiser and carrier work in World War II. The *Brooklyn*-class design process was initially fraught with problems, partly as a result of management's inability to integrate the design organization into the shipyard, and partly because the cruiser design itself differed radically from its predecessor, necessitating a great deal of basic technical work. New York Ship's tardy submissions of plans for review infuriated the Navy Department because the delays made it impossible for the navy yards in Brooklyn and Philadelphia to lay their cruiser keels as originally scheduled. The late start of navy yard cruiser construction in spring 1935 defeated the primary purpose of the PWA shipbuilding program to provide swift unemployment relief. Simultaneously, however, the onboarding of some of the nation's most experienced naval architects and marine engineers created a major asset for New York Ship, whose design organization came to rival that of Newport News and Fore River. In the course of the *Brooklyn*-class design process, Metten's men also acquired highly specialized technical expertise, which proved useful for later light cruiser projects, notably the *Cleveland* class constructed in World War II (see chapter 5).[56]

In addition to the Big Three and the navy yards, PWA-financed naval work involved several smaller yards, all of which played a major role in warship building during the 1930s and beyond. The Bath Iron Works, which had built destroyers in World War I, closed in 1925 after undertaking fruitless attempts to diversify into paper machines, steel plows, and other nonmarine products. The firm was resuscitated by a group of naval architects and investors headed by Peter Newell, New York Ship's former general manager. Re-equipped with machine tools scavenged from Cramp & Sons, Bath Iron Works built luxury yachts and in 1931 won a navy contract for a *Farragut*-class destroyer, which marked its return to naval work. In 1933, it submitted a successful $6.9 million bid for a pair of *Mahan*-class destroyers. Two ships of the same class went to the Federal Shipbuilding & Dry Dock Company of Kearny, New Jersey, a subsidiary of U.S. Steel formed in 1916 to provide an outlet for its parent company's steel output. During the shipbuilding crisis, "[s]ix of [Federal's] original ways were abandoned, and the company undertook other types of activities in order to avoid closing the yard entirely," a post–World War II investigation revealed.[57] The yard delivered barges, car floats, and small merchant ships but did not engage in naval construction until it received two destroyer contracts under the PWA program. Another pair of *Mahans* went to United Shipyards of Staten Island, whose predecessor organization Staten Island Shipbuilding had built minesweepers and Navy tugs in World War I. In addition to its main business in merchant ship repairs and overhauls, United Shipyards constructed ferries, towboats, and barges in the 1920s and submitted its first bid for naval work in 1933. United Shipyards, Federal Ship, and Bath Iron Works were collectively known as the "Little Three" of American naval shipbuilding.[58]

Lastly, in 1933 the Navy Department issued a $5.4 million contract for two submarines to Electric Boat of Groton, Connecticut, a pioneer of submarine construction. Formed in 1899 to develop inventor John Holland's design of the first viable submersible, Electric Boat initially concentrated on the design of submarines assembled in other shipyards. Its entry into shipbuilding dated to the turn of the century, when it erected a boatyard at Bayonne, New Jersey, to build electric-powered boats and small vessels fitted with diesel engines manufactured by Electric Boat at a facility in Groton. Control of valuable patents generated considerable revenue from European licensees, notably Vickers, which shared its submarine profits with Electric Boat. After World War I, the poor performance of its S-class submarine design soured relationships with the U.S. Navy, which established its own submarine design and construction activity at the Portsmouth Navy Yard. Portsmouth built all seven submarines commissioned into the U.S. Navy during the 1920s except one constructed by the Mare Island Navy Yard. Electric Boat, which retooled its Groton facility for hull construction in 1924, built submarines for the Peruvian and Brazilian navies, overhauled the S-class for the U.S. Navy, constructed motorboats and yachts at Bayonne, branched out into textile machinery and locomotive repair during the shipbuilding crisis, and suspended dividends. In 1931, the Navy returned with a contract for the V-boat *Cuttlefish*, followed two years later by a pair of *Porpoise*-class submarines, the construction of which was financed by the PWA.[59]

The sheer size of the program and the scarcity of properly equipped slipways necessitated a phased implementation of PWA-financed naval construction. In August 1934, when most destroyers and submarines awarded the previous year had been laid down, the Navy Department opened bids for a second round of contracts totaling $50 million. There were some nasty surprises, but the Navy was now better prepared to deal with them. When Fore River and Federal Ship submitted outrageously inflated bids for the heavy cruiser *Wichita*, for example, the department summarily rejected them and allocated the ship to the Philadelphia Navy Yard, which was well-equipped to build heavy combatants as a result of recent facility improvements. The administration's adherence to the spirit of the Dallinger amendment ensured that the navy yards expanded their role in destroyer construction, with a total of eight allocated to Boston, Mare Island, Norfolk, and Puget Sound. Portsmouth and Mare Island also booked orders for three submarines. Though the second round of PWA-financed naval shipbuilding was only half the size of the first, it kept the government-owned and private shipyards running for the time being.[60]

Roosevelt's attempts to stabilize the industry with naval contracts had few parallels overseas, where policymakers stimulated merchant shipping, though some of these programs were formulated to benefit navies. Japan did so as early as 1932 under the Ship Improvement Plan, which provided $5 million in subsidies for the replacement of 400,000 gross tons of overage merchant vessels with 200,000 tons of new builds. Merchant shipbuilding output tripled over the next three years as a result, including ships suitable for conversion into naval auxiliaries, notably a pair of fast tankers built at the initiative of the Imperial Navy, which planned to repurpose them as fleet oilers in the event of war. In 1937, the navy subsidized the construction of passenger ships of the *Nitta Maru* class laid down by Mitsubishi Nagasaki, designed from the outset for conversion into escort carriers. Naval work forced builders to build better ships, the U.S. Office of Naval Intelligence observed. "The naval ministry, placing its orders with private enterprises, to a large degree . . . contributed to their qualitative growth on the strength of the fact that this required great technical equipment on the part of the enterprises and training of personnel."[61]

The German government subsidized the scrapping of 400,000 gross tons, which benefited primarily AG Weser of Bremen and Blohm & Voss at Hamburg, followed in 1934 by a more ambitious $120 million aid package to shipowners and builders, which boosted new merchant construction to the point of recovery. Some of the ships built under the program were later converted into auxiliary cruisers and served during the war, including several of the *Ehrenfels* class of freighters laid down at AG Weser and Bremer Vulkan in the late 1930s. British policymakers, habitually suspicious of direct subsidies, did little to cushion the Depression's impact. Cunard netted limited government assistance to have the superliner *Queen Mary* laid down at Browns, but her construction was suspended in 1932 due to a lack of private funds and was resumed only in 1934 thanks to a special subsidy, which also supported the building of her half-sister *Queen Elizabeth*. A year later, the government finally adopted a more general policy under the British Shipping Act, which provided a meager $17 million for a scrap-and-build program. Combined, the sums expended by the Japanese, German, and British governments to aid merchant shipping and shipbuilding amounted to half of what the United States expended on naval work under the PWA program alone.[62]

In 1936, Congress boosted merchant shipping and shipbuilding with the passage of the Merchant Marine Act, which generated important contracts for some builders. At the time, the U.S. merchant marine was "one of the slowest in the world," *Fortune* reported. "Oldest of any of the [world's big] fleets, 88 per cent of its decrepit ships are fourteen years or more. . . . It is more expensive to operate than any fleet in the world."[63] The Merchant Marine Act encouraged overage tonnage scrapping and created the U.S. Maritime Commission, which issued vessel contracts directly to builders and then leased or sold the government-owned merchantmen to private operators. The act also provided subsidies to close the cost gap between American and foreign tonnage. In the shipbuilding industry, the act's primary beneficiaries included Fore River, which booked contracts for eight freighters and three combination passenger and cargo liners totaling 84,000 gross tons. Newport News laid down more than 150,000 gross tons in Maritime Commission ships, including the passenger liner *America*, the most prestigious contract in prewar merchant construction. From 1936 to 1939, the commission ordered 141 vessels at a cost of $345 million, by far the largest sum expended by any government on merchant shipbuilding between the wars.[64]

The Merchant Marine Act, whose subtitle included the phrase "to aid in the national defense," had important implications for the U.S. Navy, which like its foreign counterparts planned to convert merchantmen into naval auxiliaries in the event of war. The legislation instructed the Maritime Commission to "cooperate closely with the Navy Department as to national-defense needs and the possible speedy adaptation of the merchant fleet to national-defense requirements."[65] Specifically, the commission was required to submit all plans and specifications for merchantmen built under the act to the Navy Department for review and approval. Further cementing its relationship with the Navy, Roosevelt appointed as chair of the Maritime Commission the recently promoted Vice Admiral Land, a trained naval architect with a specialty in submarine design and former chief of the Bureau of Construction & Repair. Land, a proponent of building up the fleet supply train, encouraged the construction of tankers suitable for conversion into oilers, a vessel type that received low priority in the Navy itself.[66]

NAVAL REARMAMENT

From the start of naval arms control until 1933, Japan commissioned nearly 350,000 standard tons, significantly more than America's 245,000 tons, producing the world's most modern fleet, which included fast and heavily armed cruisers as well as destroyers. Japan's quest for ships that could outperform their foreign counterparts conformed the Imperial Navy's doctrine to "use a few to conquer many," which was based on the assumption that though America's and Britain's greater industrial capabilities enabled them to construct more combatants, Japan could build better ones.[67] Operationally, the Imperial Navy secured the army's rear during the invasion of Manchuria in 1931, which marked the beginning of Japanese aggression in the Far East. The same year, the Japanese Diet passed the First Naval Armament Replenishment Plan, which expended $70 million on four *Mogami*-class cruisers, twelve destroyers, and twenty-three other vessels over a period of five years. While many Western observers downplayed the significance of these developments based on beliefs that Japanese technology was derivative and inherently inferior, others worried that the U.S. Navy was in fact insufficiently equipped to defeat its Japanese counterpart in accordance of War Plan Orange, the U.S. blueprint for a Pacific war. The General Board of the U.S. Navy, a senior committee that advised the Navy Secretary on strategy, naval policy, and shipbuilding, warned in 1932 that "the present relative inferiority of the American Navy is so great . . . as to be provocative of a national emergency."[68] The board's assessment was shared by Roosevelt, who argued that pitting the American Navy against a Japanese adversary that enjoyed both qualitative and—in carriers and modern destroyers—quantitative superiority was not a viable scenario, privately acknowledging in August 1933 that the U.S. Navy "was and probably is actually inferior to the Japanese navy."[69]

Through much of his first term, Roosevelt sought tighter naval arms controls to curb Japanese capabilities and ambitions. In February 1934, efforts by Big Navy proponents in Congress to expand the fleet to full treaty strength resulted in the Vinson-Trammell Act, which authorized the Navy to request funding for a 15,000-ton carrier to replace the aging *Langley*, six cruisers for a total of 60,000 standard tons, sixty-five destroyers aggregating 99,500 tons, and thirty submarines totaling 35,530 tons. Once fully implemented by 1942, the program would equip the Navy with the maximum tonnage allocated to the United States in the London Naval Treaty. Importantly, the act authorized but did not appropriate funds for such a program. In every congressional budget process, the Senate and House committees on naval affairs first had to empower the Secretary of the Navy to ask for funds with an authorization before he could request money from the appropriation committees. Roosevelt, keen to mollify

Table 1.1. Ships Laid Down or Appropriated For, 1922–1932

	United States	Japan	Britain
Battleships	0	0	2
Carriers	1	1	1
Cruisers	16	20	25
Destroyers	11	63	54
Submarines	6	42	30

Harvard Graduate School of Business Administration, *The Use and Disposition of Ships and Shipyards at the End of World War II* (Washington, DC: Government Printing Office, 1945), 169

Table 1.2. Naval Vessels in Commission, 1932

	United States	Japan	Britain
Battleships	11	10	14
Carriers	3	4	3
Cruisers	20	39	42
Destroyers	72	104	84
Submarines	42	62	42

Secretary of the Navy, *Annual Report Fiscal Year 1932* (Washington, DC: Government Printing Office, 1932), 6 isolationists, pacifists, and the Japanese, went out of his way to stress the preliminary nature of the Vinson-Trammell authorization, explaining that—like all authorizations—it was "not a law for the construction of a single additional United States warship." The act "appropriates no money for such construction and the word 'authorization' is, therefore, merely a statement of policy of the present Congress. Whether it will be carried out depends on the action of future Congresses."[70] In the same breath, Roosevelt reiterated his commitment to arms control: "It has been the policy of the Administration to favor continued limitations of naval armaments. . . . It is my personal hope that the Naval Conference to be held in 1935 will extend all existing limitations and agree to further reductions."[71]

At the time, Tokyo was already determined to torpedo the 1935 naval arms talks and abrogate the Washington and London treaties. This debilitating blow to the international order was the handiwork of the radical Fleet Faction in the Imperial Navy, which had opposed the Washington Treaty from the beginning and had nearly succeeded in derailing the 1930 London Treaty. The ratification of that treaty was regarded as outright treason because it allegedly relegated Japan to an inferior status vis-à-vis the Western powers. After a treaty opponent had assassinated Prime Minister Hamaguchi Osachi in 1931, the Fleet Faction purged moderate officers and took control of the Navy General Staff. The Diet approved the Imperial Navy's $123 million Second Naval Replenishment Plan of 1934 to build the fleet to full treaty strength with the construction of two *Hiryu*-class carriers, a pair of *Tone*-class cruisers, fourteen destroyers, and twenty-nine smaller vessels. Shortly after Congress had passed the Vinson-Trammell Act of 1934, Japan notified the other signatory powers that it would not renew the Washington Naval Treaty upon its expiration. Moreover, the Japanese delegation walked out of the second London negotiations in 1936, followed shortly by the signing of the Anti-Comintern Pact, which aligned Japan with the Third Reich and eventually fascist Italy.[72]

Tokyo's abandonment of the treaty system made it more difficult for other powers to develop accurate threat assessments. The Imperial Navy, hardly a model of transparency during the treaty era, went out of its way to conceal the size and nature of its shipbuilding plans, in some instances literally: The battleship *Musashi*, laid down at Mitsubishi Nagasaki in 1938, was covered during construction by a four-hundred-ton rope curtain (its production caused hemp shortages throughout the country). To safeguard against intelligence leaks, the navy placed technical information on a strict need-to-know basis. Referring to the battleship *Yamato* armed with 18-inch guns, a Japanese gunnery officer told American interrogators after the war, "In the Navy College we were not permitted to talk about these ships. The guns were listed as '40 Special.'"[73] Japanese officials often prevaricated in public. Asked whether the latest generation of battleships displaced 45,000 standard tons, a rear admiral told the *New York Times* that reports to that effect constituted "entirely groundless rumor" (*Yamato* actually displaced 70,000 tons).[74] Though the U.S. Office of Naval Intelligence occasionally managed to collect bits and pieces of data, Japan's effective information management generally left American authorities in the dark about key aspects of Tokyo's rearmament program. When a congressman asked chief of naval operations William Leahy point-blank, "Is Japan building a 45,000-ton battleship?" the admiral admitted that naval intelligence "has been unable to get that information."[75] Well into the Pacific War, American sources routinely referred to *Yamato* and *Musashi* as 35,000 tonners armed with 16-inch guns.[76]

Lack of reliable information notwithstanding, the United States markedly increased its naval shipbuilding expenditures at mid-decade. In fiscal year 1936, big-ticket items included the $20 million carrier *Wasp* built by Fore River and a pair of *St. Louis*-class cruisers laid down at New York Ship and Newport News for $13 million each. Battleship construction resumed in 1937 with *North Carolina*, followed in 1938 by her sister ship *Washington*.

Expectations that the battleships would be awarded to private yards proved premature. When the Navy Department opened the bids on June 17, 1937, it found that Fore River offered to build one for $60 million and New York Ship the other for $56 million (Newport News' tender failed to meet certain technical requirements). The department asked the navy yards in Philadelphia and Brooklyn for their estimates, which came in at $36.6 million and $37.2 million, respectively, for the hulls exclusive of armor and armament. Roosevelt dropped a bombshell during a press conference on June 22, when he declared that both battleships would be allocated to the navy yards. Industry reactions were not slow in coming. New York Ship's chief naval architect Thomas Bossert wrote to Roosevelt, "I request, I entreat that before you award both of these ships to Navy Yards, that you MR. PRESIDENT grant New

Chart 1.7. U.S. Naval Shipbuilding Expenditures, 1933–1939

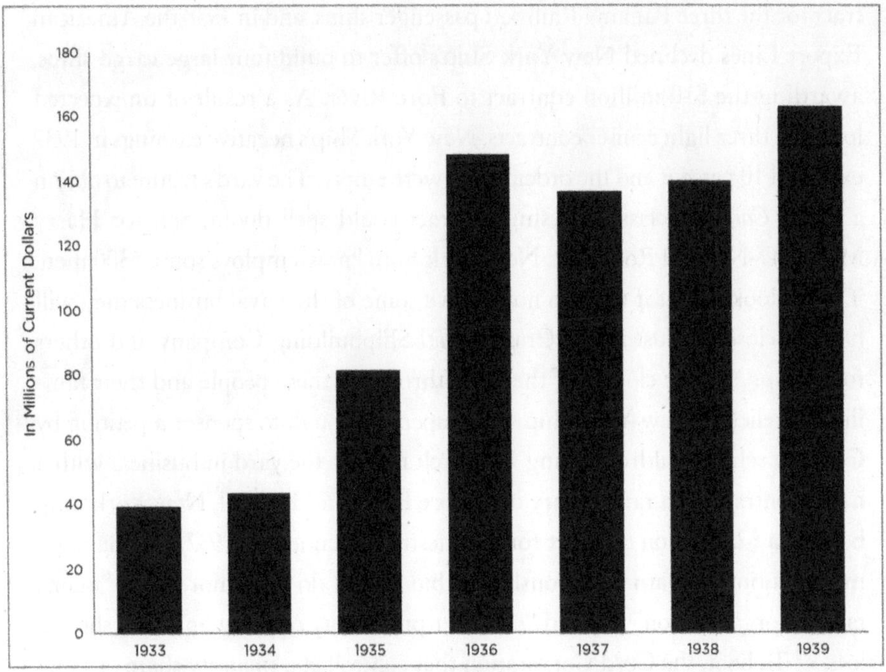

Navy Dept. Bureau of Supplies and Accounts, Naval Expenditures, 1933-1939.

York Shipbuilding Corp. a hearing and determine the equity of its bid" on *North Carolina*, which all things considered was equal to or better than that of the Brooklyn Navy Yard estimate, or so he claimed.[77] (Roosevelt responded matter-of-factly that since "considerable comparative data are available," he considered it "in the best interests of the United States to have the vessel constructed at a Navy Yard."[78]) *Marine Engineering*, the industry's leading mouthpiece, relegated the decision "to the limbo of all things tainted with politics."[79] Local interests quickly joined the fray. The Camden County Chamber of Commerce told the president that it had confidently expected New York Ship to "receive a contract for one of the battleships on which it submitted one of the lowest bids," blaming its failure on "the apparent attitude of the Federal Government" toward private enterprise.[80]

New York Ship was eager for a battleship contract because it once again found itself in financial trouble due to a lack of commercial orders. In 1936, it suffered a defeat when it submitted an unsuccessful bid for a pair of large cargo ships, followed a year later by failure to obtain an order for the superliner

America. Fore River prevailed in a bitterly fought contest for a $12 million con-
tract for the three Panama Railroad passenger ships, and in 1938 the American
Export Lines declined New York Ship's offer to build four large cargo ships,
awarding the $10 million contract to Fore River. As a result of unexpected
losses on three light cruiser contracts, New York Ship's negative earnings in 1937
exceeded 10 percent and the order books were empty. The yard's failure to obtain
a *North Carolina*–class battleship contract could spell doom, Senator Harry
Moore (D-NJ) told Roosevelt. New York Ship "now employs some 5300 men.
The outlook is that if they do not receive some of the naval business they will
have to close up, just as the Cramps [*sic*] Shipbuilding Company and others
folded up. . . . The closing of the Yard throws all these people and their families on relief."[81] New York Ship was desperate enough to sponsor a petition by
Camden school children asking Roosevelt to keep the yard in business with a
naval contract. In a rare victory over Fore River and Federal, New York Ship
booked a $23 million contract for two destroyer tenders in 1937, but manage-
ment cautioned that its perilously low bid would do little more than "maintain the organization" and did "not offer probability of profit and may show a
loss."[82] To boot, the Cord Corporation that controlled a majority share of New
York Ship's stocks was in dire financial straits as a result of steep losses in its
luxury automobile lines, precipitating a buyout by a banking consortium, which
phased out the car business and reorganized what was left into the Aviation &
Transportation Company. The latter retained control of the shipyard, which
earned a 4.8 percent net margin in 1938.[83]

Roosevelt meanwhile urged an acceleration of naval construction after the
Japanese invasion of China in July 1937, which marked a major escalation of
Japanese aggression in the Far East. In the "Quarantine Speech" of October
1937, he raised the possibility of international collaboration to "make a concerted
effort to uphold the laws and principles on which alone peace can rest assured."[84]
Contrary to claims that the Quarantine Speech was little more than a flash in
the pan, Roosevelt pursued the matter behind closed doors. His interest in naval
options was piqued by a confidential memorandum written in November 1937
by Adm. Harry Yarnell, the commander in chief of the Asiatic Fleet, who
proposed a naval blockade of Japan in the event of war. Yarnell posited that
Japan "is becoming an increasing and intolerable menace to the peace and
security of the many nations vitally interested in the future of the Orient."

Explaining that the Empire's dependence on raw material imports rendered it vulnerable to a blockade, the memorandum stressed that "such an economic, and therefore economical war, must be one of strangulation, in short, *an almost purely naval war in the Pacific as far as we are concerned*." Yarnell deemed such a strategy feasible if the U.S. Navy collaborated with British, Dutch, and even Soviet forces to create a "naval superiority in the Pacific [that] would enable us to conduct the naval war in the Pacific in the manner largely of our own choice, which would mean complete severance of Japanese lines of commerce to the rest of the world, excepting China from the Yangtze north."[85] The president, having studied the plan carefully, told Leahy, "Yarnell talks a lot of sense in that confidential memorandum about the Oriental situation."[86] Warming up to the idea, FDR instructed the Navy in November 1937 to study the requirements for an Allied naval blockade of Japan. The navy's War Plans Division responded with suggestions to initiate Anglo-American staff talks but stressed that extant American capabilities were insufficient to institute an effective blockade, arguing that more shipbuilding was necessary to augment American capabilities.[87]

Demands for fresh naval programs proliferated after mid-decade, when Japanese, Italian, and German warship construction increased substantially. In 1937, the Imperial Navy embarked on an ambitious construction effort under the Third Naval Replenishment Plan, which earmarked $230 million for naval construction. In addition to two *Yamato*-class battleships and two *Shōkaku*-class carriers, it called for eighteen *Kagero*-class destroyers, which were among the largest and fastest vessels of this type, armed with the Type 93 torpedo that was to wreak havoc during the opening phases of the Pacific War. Simultaneously, the Third Reich doubled its naval shipbuilding budget from $117 million in 1935 to $243 million in 1937 to finance the construction of two *Bismarck*-class battleships, five *Admiral Hipper*–class heavy cruisers, and twenty-two destroyers. Together with a similarly ambitious Italian program, the future Axis powers built almost as much naval tonnage as the United States and Britain combined. Though Chief Leahy was uncertain about the exact size, cost, and characteristics of these programs, he warned in January 1938 that Japan, Italy, and Germany were "engaged in an extravagant naval building program, particularly in battleships which are the backbone of naval power; and there is now in existence an Italio-German-Japanese 'Anti-Communist Protocol' [Anti-Comintern Pact] which must be taken into consideration by America's sea defense."[88]

Roosevelt responded in early 1938 with a call for substantial increases in naval appropriations. In January, he told Congress that "our national defense is, in the light of the increasing armaments of other nations, inadequate for purposes of national security and requires increase for that reason. . . . We cannot assume that our defense would be limited to one ocean and one coast and that the other ocean and the other coast would with certainty be safe."[89] As a result of this sobering assessment, Roosevelt raised his original naval shipbuilding request for fiscal year 1939 and asked Congress to authorize a 20 percent increase in naval tonnage over then-current levels. Tellingly, the threat assessment that justified the raise was largely derived from newspaper articles because U.S. naval intelligence remained unable to provide data on Japanese construction plans from other sources. During the testimony of Charles Edison, Assistant Secretary of the Navy, before the House Committee on Naval Affairs, a congressman asked, "You realize that we are embarking upon quite a program perhaps, based entirely upon newspaper reports?"[90]

Roosevelt meanwhile urged the timely completion of existing projects. In March 1938, he told Edison, "On looking over the January tenth report of progress on vessels under construction, it looks to me as if the Newport News Shipbuilding Company is lagging. Will you lightly convey the message that I wish they would speed it up a bit?"[91] Irate about other construction delays, he instructed Edison the next day, "In the case of the three cruisers, the Philadelphia Navy Yard and to a less degree, the New York Navy Yard need to be told that the Commander-in-Chief is much dissatisfied."[92] These and similar episodes demonstrated not only Roosevelt's close monitoring of naval shipbuilding, but also his growing concern about the speed of rearmament in the context of the worsening international situation after the Japanese invasion of China.

An additional fleet expansion program sponsored by Vinson and Trammell in 1938 further accelerated naval rearmament. The so-called Second Vinson-Trammell Act authorized (but did not fund) three *Iowa*-class battleships, two carriers, nine cruisers, twenty-three destroyers, and nine submarines. Separate legislation appropriated funds for the construction of four *South Dakota*-class battleships, the carrier *Hornet*, four cruisers, eight destroyers, and six submarines. Shortly after its passage, the Navy Department solicited bids from the builders, whose tenders were more reasonable than in previous years. By early 1939, it had signed contracts for the entire program. The Norfolk Navy Yard and each of the Big Three netted one *South Dakota*–class battleship, while Fore River and Federal Ship booked two *Atlanta*-class light cruisers each.[93]

The program's impact on the shipbuilding industry varied. For New York Ship, which had recorded a $1.4 million loss in 1937, the $50 million order for the lead ship of the *South Dakota* class was a much-needed shot in the arm and contributed to the financial recovery of this most defense-dependent of the Big Three (profits exceeded $920,000 in 1939). Other builders were less enthusiastic about naval work. Fore River was busy with merchant contracts that produced larger financial rewards at a time when the 1934 Vinson-Trammell Act's 10 percent cap on profits in naval contracting remained in place. By the late 1930s, Fore River not only generated sufficient profits to prop up Bethlehem Steel, its Depression-stricken corporate parent, but it also enabled Bethlehem's shipbuilding division to acquire the Staten Island facilities of United Shipyards, which went bankrupt in 1938. The same year, Newport News Shipbuilding netted a 4.8 percent margin on account of its extensive merchant work, followed in 1939 by 6.6 percent. Private builders' eagerness for naval contracts diminished further because prewar naval work required plant modernizations and tool replacements specifically tailored to meet the needs of combatant building. Since turret shops, facilities to store and process naval armor, and heavy cranes that could lift gunhouses were unnecessary for merchant construction, builders tried to include expenses for these items in the cost of a ship. The U.S. Treasury Department frequently raised objections, leaving private builders stuck with exceedingly large bills for plant improvements. Fore River, for example, spent $640,000 of its own money in 1939 alone to develop facilities for naval work in the largest plant improvement program since the Great War. Facility financing remained unresolved until 1940, when the Navy Department and the Reconstruction Finance Corporation developed a variety of schemes to provide funds for upgrading private shipyards (chapter 3). In 1939, the Navy had to confront the uncomfortable truth that two of the nation's largest shipyards not only bulged with merchant work that left little physical space for naval work, but were also reluctant to bid for profit-limited warship contracts whose fulfillment required substantial investments. As a result, private industry raised few objections when the Navy Department announced in February 1939 that two 58,400-ton battleships of the *Iowa* class appropriated the year before would be allocated to the navy yards in Brooklyn and Philadelphia.[94]

Similar dynamics were evident in Japan, where naval rearmament coincided with a merchant shipbuilding boom that stretched industrial capabilities to the limit, prompting the Imperial Navy to rely heavily on navy yards. Implementation of the Second and Third Naval Replenishment Plans of 1934 and 1937, respectively, fell behind schedule partly because shipowners ordered new builds to take advantage of merchant shipbuilding subsidies. Like their American counterparts, Japanese builders were not keen on naval work because it required large investments in facilities and machinery rarely used in merchant construction. Mitsubishi, for example, whose Nagasaki yard was responsible for the construction of the battleship *Musashi*, had to build a new mold loft for the project, acquire two giant floating cranes, and rebuild its largest slipway, which had to be extended into a mountain slope to accommodate the 862-foot hull. For navy yard upgrades, the Imperial Diet approved $19 million under the Third Naval Replenishment Plan of 1937, primarily to equip the Kure yard for the construction of *Yamato* and Yokosuka for the carrier *Shōkaku*.[95]

German warship construction was tightly restricted by the Versailles Treaty until 1935, when its provisions were superseded by those of the Anglo-German naval agreement.[96] Naval rearmament initially proceeded slowly because the buildup of the army absorbed enormous resources. Private builders were busy with merchant work and lacked sufficient naval construction capabilities because they had not built warships since the end of World War I. The handful of firms eager for naval work included AG Weser, whose commercial orders dried up in 1935, when it booked two heavy cruisers and four destroyers. The naval contracts enabled the firm—like New York Ship—to resolve its financial problems and issue its first dividend of the decade in 1936. Other private yards were more reluctant to take naval work because lucrative commercial orders proliferated, notably British and Scandinavian contracts, which were paid for in Sterling and other hard currencies. Encouraged by economic policymakers who sought to replenish the Reich central bank's perilously low foreign currency reserves, ship exports were frowned upon by the navy because they rendered slipways unavailable for warship construction. To the navy's chagrin, the Bremer Vulkan yard neglected the acquisition of naval construction capabilities and remained focused on merchant work on British and Norwegian accounts until 1939. Blohm & Voss, Germany's largest yard, continued to build merchantmen but also took a prominent role in naval rearmament with the construction of the battleship *Bismarck*, the heavy cruiser *Admiral Hipper*, and four destroyers at an aggregate cost of $62.5 million. Like other German firms, Blohm & Voss was even less prepared for naval construction than its American, British, and Japanese counterparts because it had not built combatants in almost two decades. To grease the skids, the navy provided Blohm & Voss with a $2.8 million no-interest loan for yard upgrades and tacitly allowed the firm to exceed an official 5 percent limit on profits. The Krupp subsidiary Germaniawerft in Kiel received similar inducements to equip the yard for the construction of the heavy cruiser *Prinz Eugen*, four destroyers, and twenty-five submarines. Most of the remaining heavy combatants built during the period of naval rearmament were assigned to the Wilhelmshaven Navy Yard, which laid down the battleships *Scharnhorst* and *Tirpitz*, and to Deutsche Werke, which was responsible for the battleship *Gneisenau*, the heavy cruiser *Blücher*, and the aircraft carrier *Graf Zeppelin*.[97]

In Britain, large-scale naval rearmament commenced in 1937 after the cabinet had approved an ambitious building program to equip the Royal Navy for simultaneous wars in Europe and the Far East. British war planning had previously focused almost exclusively on the Japanese threat, but German rearmament after mid-decade raised the possibility of a parallel conflict closer to home; the Defence Requirements Subcommittee of the Committee of Imperial Defence warned in 1935: "We should be able to send to the Far East a Fleet sufficient to provide 'cover' against the Japanese fleet; we should have sufficient additional forces behind this shield for the protection of our territories and mercantile marine against Japanese attack. . . . [A]t the same time we should be able to retain in European waters a force sufficient to act as a deterrent to prevent the strongest European power Naval Power from obtaining control of our vital home terminal areas while we make the necessary redispositions."[98] The Admiralty estimated that meeting a triple threat required the construction of five *King George*–class battleships, nine carriers, forty-seven cruisers, and a variety of smaller combatants at an annual cost exceeding $500 million.[99]

In 1937, British yards commenced the construction of 350,000 tons of warships, almost triple the amount laid down the previous year. Mobilizing industrial capacity proved difficult because facilities to produce armor, ordnance, and other items were scarce. Shipbuilders, "even if their apparent capacity was more than adequate, were not geared to undertake a suddenly increased amount of work," a postwar review explained. "Besides this, changes in Naval requirements and especially the steadily growing amount of electrical engineering and instrument work required, meant that even moderate programmes of peace time were too much for the producers concerned and that delays had to be accepted while new capacity of a highly specialised type was created."[100] In *King George V*–class battleship construction, Cammell Laird required a $500,000 facility upgrade before it could lay down *Prince of Wales*, and Swan Hunter spent $350,000 rebuilding its largest slipway in preparation for *Anson*. Even Fairfield, financially drained as a result of its brush with insolvency in 1935, invested moderate amounts in new machinery before it commenced *Howe*. In addition to battleships, the Admiralty's 1937 building program included *Illustrious*-class carriers, three of which were built by Vickers and one by Harland & Wolff of Belfast, the world's largest shipbuilder, which had heretofore played a negligible role in naval construction. In contrast to the American and Japanese navy yards, the prewar Royal Dockyards built nothing larger than light cruisers and instead concentrated on modernizations of capital ships, including several of the *Queen Elizabeth* class, two of the *Renown* class, and *Hood*.[101]

Cartelization and the lack of profit limitations ensured that British naval shipbuilding was generally more lucrative than its American and German counterparts. Fairfield, for example, realized a 30 percent profit on *Howe* alone. From 1936 to 1939, when the firm devoted itself almost exclusively to naval work, Admiralty contracts netted it $7.5 million in profits, which bolstered Fairfield's ability to distribute 6 percent in annual dividends while also increasing its reserves, much as New York Ship and AG Weser had done during the prewar years. Swan Hunter realized more than 12 percent in profits on *Anson* while hull and electrical equipment netted Browns 20.4 percent on *Duke of York* and Cammell Laird 25 percent on *Prince of Wales*. Their ability to realize large profits set British naval contractors apart from merchant builders, whose returns were often less than satisfactory even as order backlogs swelled during an upswing in commercial demand in 1937. On the eve of war, the trade journal *Fairplay* noted in its survey of eighteen leading firms, "Considering the large amount of capital which is invested in the Companies included in the list, and the value of the work which they turn out, it cannot reasonably be suggested that the dividends paid are sufficient, especially when regard is had to the number of lean years which have gone before."[102] The profitability of navy work was partly attributable to the behind-the-scenes activities of Warshipbuilders' Committee, which remained active during rearmament. Unlike the American naval cartel of the late 1920s and early 1930s, however, the Warshipbuilders' Committee did little to foster yard specialization. Scotts, for example, built destroyers, cruisers, and submarines, as did Cammell Laird, which also constructed *Prince of Wales* and the carrier *Ark Royal*.[103]

Cost comparisons are difficult because navies differed in terms of accounting procedures and equipment included in contract prices, but rough estimates of battleship prices reveal that the U.S. Navy paid significantly more per ton than its foreign counterparts. While British and Japanese prices were about equal, Germany paid 30 percent more, and the United States almost three times as much. The cost differential was partly attributable to higher American engineering standards, more expensive equipment, and better habitability of U.S. Navy ships compared to their foreign counterparts, which often lacked adequate bathrooms and other comforts that made onboard life more bearable for American crews. Moreover, British and Japanese warship builders achieved cost savings by relying on riveted construction, which was cheaper than welding (see chapter 2).[104]

Rearmament confronted the leading navies with similar challenges that provoked a range of responses. Faced with growing demand for both warship and merchant tonnage that created bottlenecks in private industry, the American and Japanese navies relied more heavily on government-owned shipyards than the Royal Navy and Germany's Kriegsmarine, which incentivized naval work through subsidies for yard improvements. America's prewar navy yards played a particularly important role in battleship construction, which involved

Table 1.3. Comparative Cost of Battleships

Name	Tons standard	Approximate total cost including armament in U.S. dollars	Approximate per-ton cost
North Carolina	34,000	$76,000,000	$2,200
King George V	38,031	$29,900,000	$790
Bismarck	41,700	$45,800,000	$1,100
Yamato	65,000	$51,000,000	$780

Calculated from Ian Buxton and Ian Johnston, *The Battleship Builders: Constructing and Arming British Capital Ships* (Barnsley, UK: Seaforth Publishing, 2013), 42; Christopher Thiel, *Der Deutsche U-Bootkrieg im 2. Weltkrieg* (Berlin, Germany: Epubli, 2016), 11; Victor Davis Hanson, *The Second World War: How the First Global Conflict Was Fought and Won* (New York: Basic Books, 2017), 106. Exchange rates calculated as £1:$4.80; Reichsmark 1:$0.40; ¥1:$0.20, using the historical currency converter available at "Portal for Historical Statistics," https://www.historicalstatistics.org, edited by Rodney Edvinsson, Swedish Collegium for Advanced Study, accessed May 14, 2019; see also William D. O'Neil, "Interwar U.S. and Japanese National Product and Defense Expenditure," CNA Analysis & Solutions, Center for Naval Analyses, 2003, available at https://apps.dtic.mil /docs/citations/ADA596762, accessed May 14, 2019 some of the industry's most sophisticated production equipment, in contrast to Britain, whose dockyards focused largely on overhauls. The trend continued in World War II, when U.S. navy yards performed a disproportionate share of heavy combatant construction (see chapter 4).

CONCLUSION

In April 1940, Roosevelt summed up the interwar history of American ship-building as follows: "During the period of 16 years following the close of the wartime building program not a single ocean-going cargo vessel had been built in this country, and but a few shipbuilding yards were kept alive by tanker orders and such naval construction as the greatly curtailed Navy program permitted. Lately, great strides have been made in rehabilitating this industry by build-ing up the Navy to its authorized strength and by rebuilding our merchant marine through the Maritime Commission."[105] Though self-serving, Roosevelt's account was not too far off the mark. Wracked by a postwar overproduction crisis that coincided with a sharp decline in warship construction during the 1920s, the industry contracted as major yards closed and surviving ones reduced their workforces to the bare minimum. While the Big Three weathered the doldrums via product diversification and cartelization, the navy yards remained afloat as a result of political pressure, which netted important cruiser work along with congressional appropriations for yard improvements. The Depression brought merchant construction to a standstill, but yards that were equipped to build naval combatants soon recovered as a result of the New Deal public works program, which tidied them over with warship contracts until the onset of naval rearma-ment at mid-decade sparked a general recovery.

Disputing claims that the United States lacked a tradition of military pro-duction prior to World War II, this chapter has documented that a vital core of experienced combatant builders existed long before Pearl Harbor and weath-ered the interwar years with government work, particularly naval work. Studies of the aircraft industry have documented similar trends in fighter and bomber production between the wars, when firms like Boeing, Grumman, and Doug-las survived in no small measure thanks to a trickle of military contracts from the U.S. Army Air Forces. During the 1930s, most of these firms combined military with civilian production while acquiring highly specialized design and production expertise, which laid the groundwork for industrial mobiliza-tion in World War II.[106]

2

"An Unending Effort to Satisfy the Needs for High Speed and Great Strength"

Warship Design, Welding, and Marine Engineering between the Wars

The interwar years marked an era of rapid change in combatant design and construction. Taking advantage of technical breakthroughs, naval architects and marine engineers devised warships that were faster, more fuel-efficient, and equipped with more effective armament and fire control than their predecessors of World War I vintage. This would make it difficult for older ships to prevail over modern ones in battle, as wartime experience would demonstrate. In workshops and on slipways, naval builders introduced electric arc welding and prefabrication, speeding the construction process and laying the groundwork for some of the industry's wartime achievements.

Some students of industrial mobilization have claimed that American wartime production was based on shop floor technologies that originated in the civilian sector. Political economists Gregory Hooks and Gregory McLauchlan contend that "World War II era tanks, planes, and ships were constructed with technologies and components adapted from civilian products."[1] In truth, the design of warships and merchantmen differed considerably. "A cargo ship, by its very nature, has wide empty spaces in its hold for carrying freight," a postwar Harvard study pointed out. "In contrast, a fighting ship packs machinery, armament, shell-handling equipment, radio and radar installations, and many other types of accessory equipment into every possible space which is not necessary for housing the men or for the storage of supplies, oil, or ammunition. The fighting-ship structure is also complicated by an unending effort to satisfy the needs for high speed and great strength."[2] As a result, commercial designs were often incompatible with Navy standards. To keep combatant displacement within treaty-mandated tonnage limits, moreover, warship designers launched a quest for weight savings that was unparalleled in the commercial sector. Technology transfers were evident in some areas, but their dynamics were often the exact opposite of what Hooks and McLauchlan have claimed. Electric arc welding, for example, originated in warship design and construction and was only later adopted in merchant shipbuilding, and even then important differences remained, as the present chapter explains.

NAVAL ARCHITECTS AND MARINE ENGINEERS

The development of warship plans and specifications was primarily handled by naval architects responsible for overall ship design and by marine engineers who devised propulsion systems. Most were seasoned professionals who had undergone extensive training in a variety of settings, and many joined professional organizations to discuss recent advances in their respective fields. Though naval architects and marine engineers were close observers of general engineering practices, their professions required highly specific expertise in seaborne technology that guided their design philosophies. Designers of seaborne technology "are necessarily more conservative in their designs than need be the case ashore," one observer remarked. "The problems of space, weight, steaming radius, reliability and accessibility for repair and also the motion of a ship at sea, are all factors that require very serious consideration." Systems reliability received closer attention than in land-based applications, this author stressed. "A break down of machinery in a land power plant may be inconvenient, but in a few minutes a 'hook up' with some other plant may be readily made and power is then available again. Of course this is impossible at sea, where a serious break down of the ship's power plant may endanger the safety of the ship."[3]

In the U.S. Navy, so-called naval constructors received their initial training in both naval architecture and marine engineering at the Naval Academy in Annapolis, Maryland. Select ensigns who had completed their regular coursework at the academy spent two years at sea to become eligible for advanced training at the Naval Postgraduate School in Annapolis. After two years of postgraduate coursework, the aspiring naval constructor enrolled in a naval architecture program at the Massachusetts Institute of Technology (MIT), which taught theoretical mechanics, advanced mathematics, the theory and practice of warship design, and marine and electrical engineering. Students spent their summers performing manual labor at one of the navy yards to "develop managerial judgment through contact with the yard labor as a colleague" and to acquire "mechanical skill and knowledge of shipyard trades and methods," an instructor explained.[4] Upon completion of a summer course in management at the General Electric works in Schenectady, New York, the student graduated from MIT with a master of science degree and spent six weeks at the Navy Department's Bureau of Construction & Repair before being assigned as an assistant to the Construction Corps, a bureau branch made up of staff officers (abolished in 1940 and merged into the Civil Engineer Corps). Here, the student often worked with ship carpenters of warrant officer rank who had been recruited as temporary assistant naval constructors in World War I and had completed abbreviated MIT courses in naval architecture and marine engineering. Full-fledged naval constructors held officer rank and often joined professional organizations, which held annual meetings to discuss technical papers, notably the American Society of Naval Engineers and the Society of Naval Architects and Marine Engineers. Many also developed industrial management expertise, which made them prime candidates for senior positions in navy yards and the Navy Department.[5]

The careers of several high-profile naval architects and marine engineers illustrate the contributions of their respective professions to naval shipbuilding. Allan Chantry, who graduated at the head of his class from the Naval Academy in 1906, served on board ship for two years and then studied naval architecture at MIT, where he received a master of science degree in 1910. An assignment to the Norfolk Navy Yard, a teaching position at the Naval Academy, and a tour of duty as fleet constructor of the Pacific Battleforce were followed in 1929 by an appointment to the Bureau of Construction & Repair at the rank of captain. As head of the bureau's Preliminary Design Section during the 1930s, Chantry supervised the *South Dakota*–class battleship design for which he developed an innovative interior armor system, later adopted in the *Iowa* class (see chapter 4). Promoted to rear admiral, he was appointed industrial manager of the Philadelphia Navy Yard in 1939, where he remained until his retirement from active service in 1946.[6]

The Naval Academy's class of 1906 also included Harold Bowen, perhaps the U.S. Navy's most tenacious marine engineer. During his early career, he served as executive officer on board a *Bainbridge*-class destroyer, whose troubled propulsion system piqued Bowen's interest in marine engineering, prompting him to return to Annapolis in 1911. At the time, "There was a great deal of dry rot and stagnation in the Naval Academy," he later opined. "The Academic Board apparently had no contact with the outside world, academic or otherwise"—though Bowen granted that institutional culture began to change with the establishment of a new program in marine engineering taught by more resourceful faculty members.[7] After completing a master's degree in mechanical engineering at Columbia University in 1914, he served as chief engineer on board several battleships during the Great War, was appointed battle fleet assistant engineer, and became production manager of the Puget Sound Navy Yard, which was at the time notorious for its failure to complete projects on time and on budget.[8] Never one to hide his light under a bushel, Bowen took credit for introducing merit-based promotions, requiring shop supervisors to submit daily progress reports, and tightening inspection routines during the construction of the heavy cruiser *Louisville*, which in the end cost substantially less than its sister ships built in private yards (see chapter 1). In 1931, Bowen reported for duty as assistant chief of the Bureau of Engineering and four years later was promoted to chief of the bureau, a position that enabled him to advocate aggressively on behalf of major improvements in propulsion technology. As head of the Naval Research Laboratory from 1939 to 1941, he sought to exclude civilians from Navy weapons research, an attempt that backfired in what Bowen later described as a "painful process originated by politicians and admirably perfected by college professors."[9] Confrontations with Vannevar Bush, the head of the Office of Scientific Research and Development, resulted in Bowen's ouster from the Naval Research Laboratory and the Navy's exclusion from the Manhattan Project. During the war, he was responsible for seizing troubled private shipyards on behalf of the government in his capacity as special assistant to Undersecretary of the Navy James Forrestal (see chapter 5).[10]

Samuel Robinson shared Bowen's background but not his temper. After graduating from the Naval Academy in 1903, he served as gunnery officer on board ship for six years, during which time he realized that "I was not a good ship handler," he later admitted.[11] Upon his return to Annapolis, he enrolled in the Academy's new postgraduate engineering program and became interested in turboelectric propulsion technology developed by General Electric for the experimental coal ship *Jupiter*. Like Bowen, Robinson graduated with a master's degree in mechanical engineering from Columbia, and he served on board *Jupiter* during her shakedown cruise, in the course of which his adept handling of an electric power failure prevented the ship from running aground. Assigned to the Bureau of Engineering in World War I, he became a member of a battleship design team and during a stay in Britain acquainted himself with recent developments in Royal Navy engineering. Rising through Bureau of Engineering ranks during the 1920s, Robinson became "cognizant of the necessity for an engineer to be well informed on the elements of the design of the hulls of ships. For this reason, I spent a great deal of time in the drafting room of the Bureau of Construction and Repair"—an experience that served him well in later stages of his career, when he was responsible for integrating marine engineering with naval architecture.[12] From 1927 to 1931, he served as industrial manager at Puget Sound, where he supervised the construction of *Louisville*. More willing to share laurels than was Bowen, who worked under him at Puget Sound, he recalled that "we established a record for the economical building of a cruiser, saving about 25 percent over that which had been expended by any other shipyard or Navy Yard."[13] Promoted to rear admiral in 1931, Robinson became chief of the Bureau of Engineering, where he was instrumental in the development of turbine technology and of high-speed diesel-electric engines for submarines. More controversially, he was a vocal critic of long-range research at the Naval Research Laboratory, proposed draconian staff cuts, and threatened to reduce the organization to a mere adjunct to corporate research. Succeeded by Bowen as bureau chief in 1935, Robinson opted for a less prestigious position as inspector of machinery at General Electric in Schenectady, New York, explaining that he was eager to investigate engineering research at GE's renowned research facility. "I spent a great deal of my time in that laboratory, and very reluctantly returned to Washington, at Admiral Bowen's request, because he was having trouble with carrying on the high pressure, high temperature steam which I had instituted."[14] When Bowen left in 1939 to head the Naval Research Laboratory, Robinson returned to his old job as chief of the Bureau of Engineering, organized its merger with the Bureau of Construction & Repair into the Bureau of Ships in 1940, and served as its first chief. After Pearl Harbor, he was appointed director of the Office of Procurement & Material (see chapter 3).[15]

The U.S. Navy's combination of academic and practical experience evident in these careers resembled other navies' training regimes. In Britain, talented midshipmen served four-year apprenticeships in the dockyards. A successful apprentice enrolled in the Royal School of Naval Architecture and Marine Engineering at Greenwich for three years before spending twelve months at sea, then joined the Royal Corps of Naval Constructors at assistant rank. There the apprentice performed design calculations and became eligible for promotion after several years. Japanese practice, which in many respects emulated the British model, combined hands-on training at navy yards with coursework in Tokyo University's naval architecture program before a full-fledged naval constructor became a member of the Navy Technical Department responsible for combatant design. The career of an aspiring German naval constructor began at the naval technical schools in Stralsund or Kiel, and the candidate subsequently attended the technical universities of Charlottenburg or Danzig to pursue a degree in naval engineering. Following two years of practical training at the Reichsmarine's Wilhelmshaven Navy Yard, a demanding examination had to be passed before the aspiring naval constructor could be hired by the Naval Construction Office in Berlin. Like their American counterparts, graduates of these programs usually joined professional organizations like Britain's Royal Institution of Naval Architects, the Society of Naval Architects of Japan, and the German Society for Maritime Technology.[16]

In the civilian sector, American naval architects and marine engineers underwent training in a variety of settings. The Webb Institute of Naval Architecture in Bronx, New York, offered mostly technical lectures on naval architecture, general and marine engineering, physics, and chemistry. Lehigh University in Pennsylvania, by contrast, developed a more innovative approach by combining technical education with courses in industrial management, business administration, and economics. Lehigh professor Lawrence Chapman, who had gained shipyard management experience at Electric Boat in World War I, explained, "If the engineering student is given a broad training in the fundamentals of engineering, applied economics and business management, then spends several years following his graduation in practical work and in engineering designing and construction, and at the same time keeps in touch with the problems of management and economics, he will not hesitate to assume the larger responsibility of executive work when opportunity offers."[17] Naval architecture and marine engineering programs at MIT and the universities of Michigan, California, and Cornell adopted similarly broad curricula to prepare graduates for technical and business careers.[18]

Institutionally, American combatant design involved both Navy-run and private organizations. The former included the Preliminary Design Section in Washington and draft offices at several navy yards. The most important was the Central Drafting Office established at the Brooklyn Navy Yard as part of the 1929 heavy cruiser program (see chapter 1). Staffed by naval architects and marine engineers transferred from the Bureaus of Construction & Repair and Engineering, respectively, as well as draftsmen from other navy yards, the Central Drafting Office was responsible for the preparation of detail plans and material orders for *New Orleans*–class heavy cruisers, *Farragut*-class destroyers, and *North Carolina*–class battleships. In 1937, it was dissolved and the staff transferred to the Brooklyn Navy Yard's local design division, which produced detail plans and specifications for *Iowa*-class battleships (see chapter 4). The Portsmouth Navy Yard established a similar activity for submarines, and the Boston Navy Yard did so for destroyer designs. In the private sector, Newport News and Fore River maintained integrated design departments while New York Ship outsourced the preparation of blueprints and specifications to the Marine Engineering Corporation until 1934 (see chapter 1). United Shipyards, the lead builder of *Mahan*-class destroyers, lacked an adequate design staff and recruited the Gibbs & Cox consultancy. Cofounder William Gibbs, who had a good rapport with Roosevelt, Robinson, and Bowen, agreed to organize the United Design Department staffed by two hundred naval architects and marine engineers to develop the *Mahan*-class design for United Shipyards and for the follow-on builders Bath Iron Works and Federal Shipbuilding.[19]

Design relied increasingly on models. Emulating British practices, the Bureau of Construction & Repair established an experimental model basin at the Washington Navy Yard at the end of the nineteenth century to test different hull forms prior to construction by crafting wooden models and attaching them to a movable carriage "to tow the model at uniform speed and to measure in pounds the resistance offered by the water to the passage of the model. The resistance is measured by means of a graphical recorder which shows the speed and pounds resistance at that speed," a naval constructor explained.[20] Model basin staff members cooperated with their colleagues at the Engineering Experiment Station in Annapolis, established after the turn of the century to conduct experiments with propulsion systems in areas such as propeller cavitation. During the interwar years, basin staff tested models of cruisers of the *New Orleans* and

Brooklyn classes, destroyers of the *Porter, Farragut, Mahan,* and *Sims* classes, and the carriers *Ranger* and *Wasp.* Hull models were launched from miniature slipways to forecast a hull's launch path as it entered the water. Basin models were primarily designed to test hydrodynamic resistance but did not show a ship's interior. This changed in the 1930s, when Gibbs & Cox pioneered scale models showing the detailed layouts of decks, armament, and interior spaces according to blueprints and specifications the firm developed for *Mahan*-class destroyers. This resulted in major changes in design and construction practices. "The models were so accurate that it was safe for a draftsman to obtain dimensions from them, and it was much easier for the pipe shop to lay out its piping from the model than to construct it by laying templates in the actual vessel," Bowen later recalled. "The Navy Department was so impressed with this approach that it finally stipulated in its contracts that the shipbuilder must supply a model in addition to the ship he was building. It was hoped that this would result in the widest possible use of models with all the attendant improvements in planning design."[21]

The design of American warships proceeded in complex routines, which differed significantly from commercial practices. In the latter, a shipowner told the builder what size, speed, and carrying capacity he wanted, negotiated the price, reviewed a few dozen blueprints in collaboration with ship and engine designers, and took possession of the final product after the trial trip. A combatant's general characteristics, by contrast, were first defined by the General Board, which sketched the ship's military purpose, speed, protection, and armament in light of strategic circumstances and war plans. Upon review of the proposal by the Navy Secretary, naval constructors at the Bureau of Construction & Repair's Design Section drafted preliminary plans in collaboration with the Navy Department's other technical bureaus (principally engineering and ordnance), which showed various combinations of speed, armament, and other characteristics. A British observer pointed out that "a great deal more time is spent in preliminary studies and in the development of the design before going out to Contract than is the case in the British Service."[22] After reviewing the various alternatives and model tests, the Bureau of Construction & Repair selected a specific draft as the basis for the so-called contract design of several dozen blueprints. "These plans consist in general of the lines, which are laid down, faired up, and traced from the data furnished by the Model Basin; the midship section which shows in the greatest detail the construction, of the ship, with the scantlings of the different parts of the structure, the type of riveting, and the details of special features of construction; the outboard and inboard profiles, and the general arrangement plans of deck, sometimes called joiner plans, which show the general layout of the ship on each deck and in the hold." The Bureau of Engineering developed separate contract plans, which "generally show in as much detail as possible, the arrangement and location of the boilers, main engines, propellers, shafting, all auxiliaries and the steam, exhaust and feed water piping."[23] The bureaus also issued written specifications for the hull, ordnance, engines, boilers, and electrical systems. Contract plans and specifications were made available to shipbuilders so they could prepare their bids. Once a bid had been accepted, the contractor's naval architects drafted thousands of blueprints that constituted the so-called "working plans," which were reviewed by the Bureau of Construction & Repair and other bureaus prior to their implementation. Bowen pointed out that "No piece of equipment or member of the hull was installed until the drawings were approved by the appropriate Bureau of the Navy Department."[24] Such close customer involvement in the design process was unheard of in merchant construction, where owners left the detail development of blueprints and specifications to professional naval architects and marine engineers.[25]

ELECTRIC ARC WELDING AND PREFABRICATION

Prewar naval architects and shipbuilders experimented with a variety of new designs and shop floor techniques, notably electric arc welding and prefabrication. Compared to riveting, welding reduced the ship's weight, a critical variable in both merchant and naval construction because it affected fuel consumption. Some private shipowners preferred lightweight welded hulls because they required less engine power and lowered fuel oil bills, but many remained wary because the American Bureau of Shipping, Lloyd's Register, and other classification societies often did not approve the technique for commercial work, citing safety concerns. Builders generally disliked welding because it involved expensive retooling of slipways and workshops. Though interwar navies were likewise cost conscious, they were generally more willing to consider welded construction because it helped them deal with treaty-related design problems. A cruiser's displacement, for example, could not exceed ten thousand standard tons under the

Washington and London agreements, presenting formidable challenges to naval architects. The French navy's director of naval construction told Britain's Royal Institution of Naval Architects in 1931 that "Displacement, which was formerly the final conclusion, now becomes the point of departure" in the design process.[26] The low weight of welded hulls compared to riveted ones enabled designers to allocate more weight to protection (armor), offensive capabilities (guns), and other heavy equipment.

Welding and riveting differed in important areas. A riveted joint required an overlap between two adjoining plates, each of which received rows of oval punched holes in the shop. On the ways, shipfitters aligned the joint and drillers finish-bored the holes, each of which received a rivet, which was hammered flat on one side. Proponents of welding argued that riveting was too labor-intensive, hole punching weakened the structural integrity of steel members, and overlaps and rivets added weight. The added weight consumed precious engine power and fuel, increased the hull's hydrodynamic resistance, and wasted space, which could be used for ammunition compartments and fuel bunkers. Electric arc welding involved fewer shop floor skills because it eliminated the need for punching and drilling, dispensed with heavy overlaps, and reduced a member's structural integrity only marginally if at all. During the welding process, "the operator brings one end of the electrode into contact with the base metal and then withdraws the electrode about an eighth of an inch," MIT professor of naval construction Henry Rossell explained. "Electrons flow along the arc and impinge upon the base metal. Sufficient heat is generated by this bombardment to raise the base metal locally to a temperature of about 2,300° C. and to form in it a hollow or crater. At the same time the end of the electrode is raised to a temperature of about 2,000° C. As the end of the electrode melts small globules or drops of metal from it are projected along the arc to the crater."[27] Enthusiasts predicted that a welded ship, compared to a riveted one of identical size, "will contain about 15 percent less steel, will take 40 percent less labor, will take 25 percent less time for construction, will take 2 percent less power for propulsion, will be cheaper to maintain, and be of 5 percent greater capacity."[28]

Critics objected that the disadvantages of welded construction outweighed its benefits. First, it produced difficult-to-predict distortions when the seam cooled from its original temperature of about 4,000° Fahrenheit, causing it to

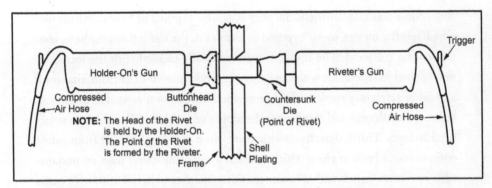

Figure 2.1. Driving a button-head countersunk rivet. On the left, the holder-on's gun holds the rivet in place while the pneumatic riveting gun hammers the rivet flat. *Shipbuilding Division, Bethlehem Steel,* An Introduction to Shipbuilding *(Washington, DC, 1942), 30.*

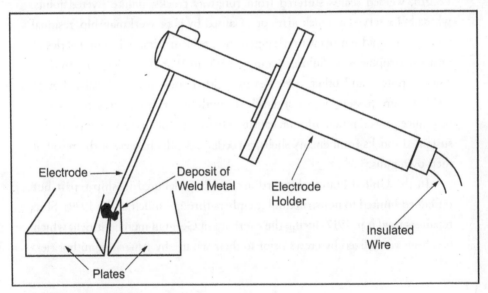

Figure 2.2. Electric arc welding. The coated electrode heats the plate edges to melting temperature and fuses them. *Shipbuilding Division, Bethlehem Steel,* An Introduction to Shipbuilding *(Washington, DC, 1942), 34.*

contract and warp the parent metal, which often resulted in noticeable deviations from blueprints. Naval architects tried to address the problem with complicated designs in which contractions offset each other. More successful solutions were developed on shop floors, where shipfitters used strongbacks and jack clamps to correct distortions. Second, welded hulls were more rigid than riveted ones and their flexible joints relieved longitudinal stresses that ensued when the ship rode a wave. Insufficient ductility was a by-product of bare electrode use, which left the molten metal exposed to nitrates in the natural atmosphere, contaminating the weld. The problem was eventually tackled with the introduction of shielded metal arc welding using electrodes coated in calcium, titanium, and other refractory oxides, which prevented nitrification as well as oxidation, reducing brittleness and improving the ability of welded hulls to absorb structural stresses. Third, defective welds were often indistinguishable from intact ones, unlike a broken rivet, which emitted a different sound than an undamaged one when struck with a hammer. Their inability to perform reliable quality controls prompted many builders to eschew welded construction until the introduction of radiographic inspection permitted the detection of poor welds. Fourth, welded seams suffered from runaway cracks, unlike riveted joints, whose holes served as crack arrestors. Caused by poor workmanship, residual stresses, or rapid temperature changes, the problem persisted until a series of near-catastrophic weld failures prompted World War II builders to introduce crack arrestors and other remedies in welded construction. Lastly, though welded seams possessed greater tensile strength than riveted joints, their shock resistance proved much inferior, causing obvious problems in warships, which sustained shocks from enemy shells, torpedoes, depth charges, or the recoil of their own guns.[29]

In the United States, shipyard arc welding debuted in ship repair but remained limited to nonstructural members through much of the 1920s. Ship repairers used it in 1917 during the overhaul of German merchantmen, which had been vandalized by crews prior to their seizure by American authorities.

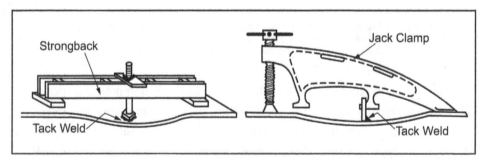

Figure 2.3. Strongback and jack clamps used to remove bulges in plates.
Pennsylvania Department of Public Instruction, Division of Industrial Education, Shipbuilding Shop Fabrication—Bulletin 345-C *(Harrisburg, PA: Department of Public Instruction, 1943), 38.*

These emergency repairs, performed at the initiative of the U.S. Navy, were not authorized by the classification societies, which imposed tight restrictions on welded parts permissible in merchant new builds. In 1919, Lloyd's allowed welded decks and nonstructural members, but excluded strength members from the list of weldable ship steel. It granted exceptions in particular cases, notably for the British coastal steamer *Fullagar*, the world's first all-welded ship, launched by Cammell Laird in 1920.[30]

In new construction, designers experimented with welded hull designs to keep warship displacement in compliance with treaty-mandated tonnage limits. The first to do so were the Germans, who under the Versailles treaty could not build light cruisers exceeding six thousand tons. This forced them to make even more strenuous efforts to save weight than their counterparts elsewhere, who designed light cruisers according to the Washington treaty's ten thousand standard ton limit. Their efforts resulted in the light cruiser *Emden*, laid down in 1921 at the Wilhelmshaven Navy Yard, whose hull featured a welded inner bottom and bulkheads. Unfortunately, the seams suffered cracks throughout her service career because welders had used bare electrodes, which yielded insufficient ductility. Moreover, *Emden*'s real displacement exceeded treaty limitations by some one thousand tons, prompting the Reichsmarine to doctor the official data. Similar problems plagued the follow-on light cruiser *Königsberg*, laid down in 1926 at Wilhelmshaven.[31]

Naval architects in the U.S. Navy Department's Bureau of Construction & Repair, close observers of German practices, first experimented with welded designs in garbage barges laid down at navy yards in the 1920s. "Some German shipyards have had considerable experience in electric welding of ships, and several German shipbuilders have published excellent articles on the general problem," a design team reported from the Mare Island Navy Yard. "The total information collected, however, was not sufficient to serve as more than a very general guide."[32] The garbage barge project confirmed that the technique resulted in substantial weight reductions because it dispensed with the attachment angles and box corners that were staples of riveted construction. In welded construction, "a surprisingly simpler design is inherently possible with fewer parts, requiring less time and effort on the part of the designer and ship fitter," one observer recorded.[33] Many naval architects initially failed to exploit such benefits because they used principles of "orthodox riveted construction, simply substituting welding in place of rivets, and therefore not making appreciable savings in weight and only slight increase in strength," a frustrated engineer commented.[34] Most of these shortcomings were eventually tackled, but practical problems remained because naval architects rarely considered shop floor conditions. "Although the average draftsman may be well versed in welding theory, his knowledge of the actual welding technique is apt to be very limited, since in many cases he has never seen a welder at work," one observer complained. "He has never gone down into a double-bottom tank and watched the contortions of a welder trying to work under conditions which a little thought and foresight on his part would have eliminated or at least eased considerably."[35] Prewar naval architects learned to avoid some of these mistakes by enrolling in instructional programs, attending the meetings of professional societies, and reading trade publications that stressed the need for designs that could be executed by welders. Extensive welding research and development was undertaken by the navy yards to investigate design problems, shop floor techniques, and welding equipment, particularly at the Brooklyn Navy Yard's Material Laboratory, which was instrumental in developing specifications.[36]

Welding in new builds moved past the experimental stage in the early 1930s to become an important fixture of American warship building. The U.S. Naval Institute's *Proceedings* observed in 1931, "While the Navy was not the first to apply electric welding to industrial work, it was a pioneer in applying it to practical shipbuilding. There are now building at the various navy yards three all-welded seaplane wrecking derricks, two all-welded tugs, one all-welded freight lighter, all of them being self-propelled. As a still further evidence of this development for the Navy, the forward eighty-eight feet of the four light cruisers now under construction at the navy yards are to be practically all-welded construction."[37] At Newport News, naval architects preferred welded to riveted engine foundations. "When the power plant is laid out and machine locations determined, it is unnecessary to arrange the parts so that existing rivet holes will line up with the foundation members," according to one account.[38] Electric Boat applied the technique extensively during the construction of the 1,100-ton submarine *Cuttlefish*. At the Brooklyn Navy Yard, naval architects incorporated welded transverse beams in the design of *New Orleans*–class heavy cruisers, which also included welded shell plates fore and aft to reduce the hull's hydrodynamic resistance. Midship plates remained riveted in *New*

Orleans and in most combatants built during the 1930s and in World War II due to persistent concerns that welded seams could not withstand structural stresses, which materialized most heavily amidships. In carrier construction, Newport News welded 12 percent of all joints in *Ranger*, laid down in 1931, but already more than half in *Yorktown* and *Enterprise* (1934). Battleships of the *North Carolina* class and their successors were only 30 percent welded because their armor plates required special bolts (see chapter 4). Over the course of the decade, builders gradually replaced bare electrodes with more expensive coated ones to produce better ductile qualities.[39]

Merchant builders were more reluctant to introduce welding, but the technique made headway in the mid-1930s, when Sun Shipbuilding of Chester, Pennsylvania, built a pair of welded oil tankers. Shop floor practices in tanker construction differed significantly from those in naval shipbuilding. While warships were manually welded, tanker building at Sun Ship relied primarily on submerged arc welding, which could only be performed along straight lines. The technique was compatible with tanker hull designs, which featured mostly flat plates without the many curvatures that reduced hydrodynamic resistance in warships. The high speed facilitated by these curves was hardly a factor in the oil trade, where carrying capacity was considered key. Automatic welding, developed by the Linde Air Products Company under the trademark Unionmelt, featured a continuous bare electrode the arc of which was submerged in a mineral compound that conducted the electric current while protecting the weld from atmospheric nitrogen. Sun Ship, the first shipyard to apply large-scale submerged arc welding to long structural steel members, used the Unionmelt process to produce longitudinal and transverse bulkheads that subdivided the tanker *J. W. Van Dyke*'s hull into separate compartments. In the fabricating shop, beams were tack welded to plates on a large tacking table and finish welded by Unionmelt machines traveling on long tracks as they deposited the weld material. Still inside the shop, fabricated preassemblies were then welded together manually into 117-foot sections, which were hauled to the slipways for final assembly. Performed at about twenty times the speed of manual welding, submerged arc welding became the linchpin of American tanker construction in World War II and was also widely used in the construction of Liberty ships, whose designers dispensed with curved plates whenever possible to accommodate the Unionmelt process.[40]

As Sun's experience demonstrated, the development of shipyard welding capitalized on prefabrication techniques, which produced important benefits for American shipbuilding. Prefabrication involved the assembly of large hull and superstructure sections in workshops before they were hauled to the slipways for final installation on board ship. The technique was pioneered in American shipbuilding at the turn of the century by New York Ship founder Henry Morse, whose yard layout included large structural shops where sections were preassembled. Prefabrication reduced the amount of time hulls occupied the slipways, traditionally a bottleneck in busy times. Instead of building the vessel piece by piece on the slipway, workmen constructed entire bulkheads and superstructure sections in structural shops, from where they were transported on flatbed cars to the slipways, where overhead cranes lowered them for installation. Some of the most important contributions to prewar preassembly development were made by the Portsmouth Navy Yard. In 1931, it received a special Navy Department authorization to build a pair of V-class submarines with hulls that were extensively prefabricated. An observer explained, "The submarines *Porpoise* and *Pike* are being constructed in sections. A section of the boat weighing approximately twenty tons is constructed at Building 96 and after it has been riveted and welded the section is moved by crane and railroad cars and placed on the building ways in Building 115. This method of constructing a large section and moving it as one piece to the ways has proven economical and more rapid than the method which was formerly used."[41] Lloyd's chief ship surveyor observed at the end of the 1930s that "American shipyards have had large lifts [since] before welding was thought of and they are now finding these convenient for an expansion of electric welding which, in extent, is not paralleled in any other country."[42]

Advantages of prefabrication in structural shops included the ability to conduct welding in temperature-controlled environments conducive to weld uniformity. Rear Adm. Ben Moreell of the Navy Department's Bureau of Yards and Docks explained, "The successful application and general acceptance of electric welding in ship construction has made important changes in structural fabrication shop practices. This is particularly true in the naval plants where welding has replaced riveting from 45 to 65 percent in present ships and this tendency points to still greater percentages in future ships. This practice has led to the assembly of larger sections in the shop where welding can be done with

The preassembled bow of the *Essex*-class aircraft carrier *Princeton* being lowered into position on the slipway at the Philadelphia Navy Yard using the combined lifting capacity of several overhead cranes, November 9, 1944. *Commandant Fourth Naval District, "History of Naval Administration, World War II," vol. 1, Navy Department Library, Rare Book Room, Washington Navy Yard, Washington, DC*

centralized equipment and controlled temperature condition."[43] These and other techniques proliferated in American naval work prior to World War II.

Welding required substantial investments in shipyards, most of which lacked the electric power generators, distribution systems, transformers, and electrodes necessary to utilize the technique on a large scale. While this presented obvious challenges to cash-strapped private builders in the 1930s, government-owned yards obtained substantial amounts for welding equipment.[44] The navy yards at

Brooklyn, Philadelphia, Puget Sound, and Mare Island received wire upgrades to build *New Orleans*–class heavy cruisers. New power plants were built during the Public Works Administration shipbuilding program, in the course of which the Brooklyn Navy Yard doubled its annual consumption to sixteen million kilowatt hours. To build *Mahan*-class destroyers under the Public Works Administration program, Fore River installed sixteen welding machine and resistors at a cost of $72,500, a considerable investment for a yard that barely broke even for much of the decade. The resumption of battleship construction in the late 1930s required further additions. At the Brooklyn, the Navy invested $150,000 in electric cables, substations, and switching equipment in preparation for the construction of the battleship *North Carolina*. To build her sister ship *Washington*, the Philadelphia Navy Yard obtained funds for a new structural shop, and Norfolk erected a subassembly facility to construct the battleship *Alabama*.[45]

Training programs for shipyard welders were pioneered during the 1920s at the Norfolk Navy Yard under the direction of assistant shop superintendent James Owens, who "has gone far to reduce an art—an art of many obscurities and perplexities—to a science," according to Rear Adm. David Taylor, the former chief constructor of the U.S. Navy. Young metal tradesmen could enroll in the navy yard's welding school, which taught basic techniques in ten-week courses (older workers who had for years worked with pneumatic riveting guns usually lacked the steady hands necessary to bead uniform welds). "The applicant at the end of the training period must show by tests that he can work intelligently and is capable of making sound welds in flat, vertical, and overhead positions," a shop superintendent explained. "After the student has completed his course and served 3 months as a practical welder, in the Norfolk or other navy yard, . . . he will be given a preliminary welder's certificate."[46] Following a year of practical experience, a successful trainee was fully certified for shopwork, according to Navy-approved techniques. Certified welders usually worked in small teams. "On account of the need of close supervision during welding, it is recommended that only eight men be assigned to a supervisor and under no conditions more than 10 men. . . . In the Norfolk Navy Yard an electrician is assigned to take care of arc welding machines, motor generators and transformers."[47]

British builders introduced electric arc welding and prefabrication more slowly than their American counterparts, important exceptions notwithstanding. Electric arc welding was largely confined to ship repairs during the postwar decade, partly because Lloyds often rejected applications to use the new technique in merchant construction. The Admiralty, less risk-averse than the classification societies, incorporated a limited number of welded parts in its specifications for warship work and approved experimental welding in the light cruiser *Leander*, laid down at the Chatham Royal Dockyard in 1930. A year later, Cammell Laird welded and prefabricated bulkheads for the light cruiser *Achilles* in a system that was later adopted at the Devonport and Portsmouth dockyards. Welding was also extensively used during the construction of the light cruiser *Arethusa*, laid down in 1933, whose preassemblies included the superstructure, internal decks, and bottom frames. Cammell Laird's *Ark Royal* was 70 percent welded, including bulkheads, decks, about one-third of all hull plates, and the bow. A postwar review noted, "Certain firms eagerly co-operated in the development of welded ship construction, among whom may be mentioned Swan Hunter, Cammell Laird, Harland & Wolff, Denny, Smiths Dock, Stephens and Doxford."[48] "By the outbreak of war the transverse portions of the hulls, also the decks, and fore-ends of cruisers and smaller ships were largely welded and an all-welded destroyer and minesweeper had been successfully completed."[49] Generally, however, cash-strapped British builders sought to avoid welding-related investments at all cost and remained committed to riveting, which was cheaper and could be performed faster than manual welding by experienced work gangs. Shipbuilder John Batey recorded that ship repairers were more enthusiastic about welding than were builders, who were not "in any hurry to rush into this method of working."[50] The piecemeal introduction of electric arc welding in British yards, in turn, retarded the adoption of preassembly techniques. One observer reported "in the majority of shipyards to-day the transportation of structures over 10 tons is not practicable." At Cammell Laird, for example, cranes lifted nothing heavier than ten tons during the construction of *Ark Royal*, compared to the fifty-ton lifting capacity of Newport News' largest cranes.[51]

Electric arc welding had an even more checkered career in Japanese naval construction. Japan's first extensively welded warship, the 1,100-ton minelayer *Yaeyama*, laid down in 1930, was built at the Kure dockyard. Naval architects there conducted a series of welding experiments, the success of which prompted the Imperial Navy to approve the construction of larger welded vessels, notably the 10,000-ton submarine depot ship *Taigei*,[52] the keel of which was laid at the Yokosuka Navy Yard. In the course of *Taigei*'s construction, however, "frame lines in places departed as much as 80 cm from designed positions and both the bow and the stern lifted about 20 cm from the blocks," which required extensive corrections later on, the U.S. Technical Mission to Japan recorded in a post–World War II review.[53] In 1933, Kure commenced an even more ambitious project with the construction of the 11,200-ton cruiser *Mogami*, which featured an all-welded hull. When she test fired her guns during the trial trip, however, "the shock of fifteen 6-inch guns letting go at once proved too much for the welded joints," one observer reported. "They opened up, water rushed in to mix with the oil in her bunkers and she had to be towed home. Experiments with other ships of the class showed that the defect was inherent in the welded design. They simply carried too many guns for this type of hull to support against the stress of battle-firing."[54] To boot, *Mogami* and two other welded combatants sustained damage in a typhoon during the so-called Fourth Fleet Incident of 1935, which naval architects (perhaps incorrectly) blamed on welded strength members. These setbacks convinced the Imperial Navy to impose tight limits on welding in heavy combatants. The *Yamato*-class battleships laid down at Kure and Mitsubishi Nagasaki, for example, featured welded super-structures and decks to achieve weight savings, but riveting remained the pre-ferred method for strength members.[55]

German naval builders likewise encountered obstacles but remained com-mitted to the development of welded construction. Weak seams that were evi-dent in the light cruisers *Emden* and *Königsberg* also plagued their sister ship *Karlsruhe*, whose terrified crew members feared for their lives when she nearly broke in half during a hurricane. These problems did not deter naval architects at the government-owned Deutsche Werke in Kiel—"probably foremost in the study and practice of ship welding" in Germany—from using the technique in the construction of two all-welded navy oilers and the 12,000-ton pocket battle-ship *Deutschland*, whose all-welded hull attracted attention in American and British naval shipbuilding circles.[56] In submarine construction, AG Weser in Bremen combined electric arc welding with prefabrication of hull sections to build Type VII U-boats laid down in 1935. Four years later, Lloyd's ship sur-veyor observed with reference to German shipyards: "Large covered welding shops are to be found with lifting appliances up to 20 tons or more, and the general trend is towards the pre-construction of as large units as possible on the ground."[57] The widespread use of welded preassemblies enabled German builders to construct the vast submarine force that imperiled British and American shipping in World War II (see chapter 5).[58]

On the eve of the war, American and German builders were leading champions of shipyard welding and prefabrication. Shipbuilders in both countries profited from experimental welding in navy yards; but while the Germans were ambitious prime movers who entered welding in new naval construction as early as 1921 with a full-fledged combatant, the Americans acted more cautiously. After observing the failures and successes of welding in German naval shipbuilding, they adopted the technique piecemeal, finally arriving at a hybrid format of welded midship sections and riveted bows and sterns—a format that remained in place during World War II. Simultaneously, American naval builders were quick to adopt covered electrodes to improve seam reliability, in contrast to the Germans, who preferred cheaper bare electrodes that produced weaker seams but remained in use until the late 1930s. American as well as German yards combined arc welding with prefabrication, but large U.S. builders did so more extensively because they operated heavier lifting equipment than their German counterparts. Both the Royal Navy and a majority of British naval builders were convinced that the highly skilled and well-organized riveting gangs that predominated in British yards could work faster than welders. In Japan, by contrast, mishaps involving extensively welded combatants diminished enthusiasm for the new technique.[59]

MARINE ENGINEERING

Between the wars, the development of propulsion systems was influenced by strategic considerations as well as the treaty system. Under War Plan Orange, America's blueprint for a war with Japan, U.S. planners envisioned the dispatch of a fleet in the event of Japanese aggression in the Far East, but the Washington Treaty prohibited the construction of American naval bases at Guam and the Philippines, making it impossible to refuel combatants west of Hawaii. This prompted American marine engineers to develop propulsion systems for heavy combatants designed for extreme cruising ranges exceeding ten thousand miles, in contrast to the Royal Navy, which maintained refueling facilities at Singapore, and the Imperial Navy, which expected to fight near its bases and hence deprioritized endurance. American marine engineers experimented with a variety of new technologies to enhance combatant endurance and fuel efficiency along with weight. What MIT professor Rossell called "weight consciousness" proliferated as designers sought to squeeze a maximum amount of combat capability, speed, and endurance into warships whose displacement was limited under the treaty system. Their efforts included "the introduction of light weight alloys for parts such as valve wheels, ladders, grating label plates, instrument cases, etc.; the gradual substitution of weldment for castings or riveted structures in parts such as gear and turbine casings, condenser shells, bed plates, etc.; and the use of greater care in the design of machinery and fittings with a view to reducing weight."[60] First introduced in *Northampton*-class heavy cruisers, these innovations were later introduced in other types as "design practice became more dynamic and better attuned to rapid evolution," Rossell remarked. "On the whole the result was to improve greatly the quality of warships, both large and small."[61]

Most important, marine engineers developed new propulsion technology with subsystems that included boilers that generated high-temperature, high-pressure steam fed into a turbine. The latter's several thousand rotations per minute (rpm) were lowered to a few hundred rpm by reduction gear for transmission to a shaft that turned the propeller. The advantages of the new system included its smaller size, lighter weight, better fuel economy, increased power yield, and greater ruggedness compared to existing technology. The treaty system, combined with the need to cover the vast distances of the Pacific Ocean, precipitated these and other innovations in American marine engineering. Rossell noted, "Among the immediate consequences of the Washington Treaty on the design of naval machinery was the general recognition of geared turbines together with small-tube oil fired boilers as the most suitable [lightweight] type of propulsion machinery for all surface warships" that were designed to fight in distant war theaters.[62]

Marine boilers, which converted chemical energy contained in coal or oil into heat energy stored in steam, underwent significant design changes. In the late nineteenth century, the British shipbuilder Alfred Yarrow had introduced a boiler in which water was fed into tubes heated by a furnace, a technology that quickly replaced the less fuel-efficient Scotch fire-tube boiler in many applications. Marine engineers later combined the water-tube boiler with a superheater to raise steam temperatures far past the boiling point to enhance fuel efficiency. This resulted in a two-stage system in which water was first heated to the saturation point and then fed into the superheater, which used sensible heat to produce high-temperature dry steam, particularly suitable for turbines because it did not cause corrosion in blades and pipes. (In 1926, the U.S. Navy tried to include the system in *Northampton*-class heavy cruisers, whose boilers were originally designed for 450 pounds of pressure per square inch [psi], but the attempt failed as a result of shipbuilders' objections, leaving her with traditional 300 psi boilers.) In 1930, boiler tightness and ability to withstand high psi increased and their weight dropped with the introduction of welded drum construction by Babcock & Wilcox, America's largest boiler manufacturer, whose innovative design was eventually adopted as a U.S. Navy standard. Babcock & Wilcox also refined a British express boiler design featuring small tubes in order to obtain a better ratio of steam output to boiler weight, but its effectiveness was often reduced by the buildup of calcium sulfate and other boiler scale in small-diameter tubes. Chemical compounds added to feedwater in order to retard boiler scaling were tested at the Engineering Experiment Station in Annapolis and the U.S. Naval Boiler and Turbine Laboratory in Philadelphia and were eventually introduced in most American naval boilers, which were generally more reliable than their foreign counterparts.[63]

The development of boilers intersected with that of turbines, which turned the heat energy stored in boiler steam into rotations. Initially designed to drive dynamos in electric power stations, turbines were introduced into marine engineering to turn propeller shafts in *Turbinia*, the world's fastest ship, designed by Charles Parsons in 1894. The Parsons turbine was a reaction system featuring a rotor fitted with thousands of blades. The rotor, which was enclosed in a steam-tight case and fed by steam generated in a water-tube boiler, ran at high rpm to achieve its maximum efficiency. Since high rpm caused cavitation in marine propellers by producing bubbles instead of propulsion, marine engineers increased the weight and size of the Parsons turbine to slow the rotor, which had the unfortunate side effect of reducing fuel efficiency. While the Royal Navy selected Parsons turbines to power the battleship *Dreadnought* launched in 1906, the more endurance-conscious U.S. Navy initially adopted the American Curtis design for its first generation of turbine-propelled capital ships built shortly before World War I. Invented by engineer Charles Curtis, who later sold his patent to General Electric, the design incorporated impulse technology in which boiler steam was fed through nozzles that increased the steam's

Babcock & Wilcox express boiler undergoing tests at the Philadelphia Navy Yard's Naval Boiler Laboratory, 1929. The boiler featured a riveted drum, in contrast to welded construction introduced by Babcock & Wilcox in 1930.
Commandant Fourth Naval District, "History of Naval Administration, World War II," vol. 1, Navy Department Library, Rare Book Room, Washington Navy Yard, Washington, DC

velocity before it hit bucket-shaped blades fitted on a shaft, causing it to turn. In a high-pressure turbine, pressure dropped in each stage while velocity was compounded by nozzles. In addition to exploiting steam power more effectively than the Parsons design, the Curtis turbine was more compact, but nozzle deterioration in the battleship *North Dakota*'s engines convinced the U.S. Navy to switch back to Parsons turbines, which powered most American warships until the 1930s. In the meantime, the Curtis design gained acceptance in merchant construction, where it often powered cargo ships, particularly in Britain after Browns developed it into the Curtis-Brown design.[64]

Parallel efforts sought new ways to tackle the problem of turbines that ran most efficiently at rpm rates that overpowered propellers. One solution was to insert reduction gear between the turbine and the propeller shaft to decrease turbine rpm to rotations suitable for propellers. In reduction gear, a small pinion was attached to the turbine and a large-diameter wheel to the propeller

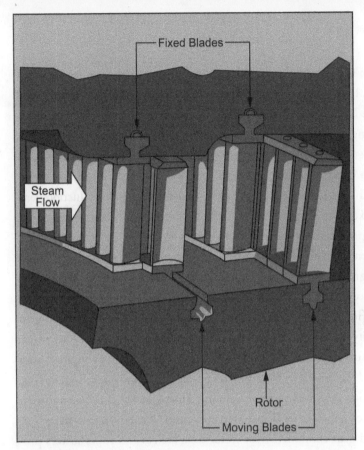

Figure 2.4.
Parsons turbine reaction blading.
Naval Machinery
Part II: Naval Turbines
(Annapolis, MD: U.S.
Naval Academy,
1946), 1–6

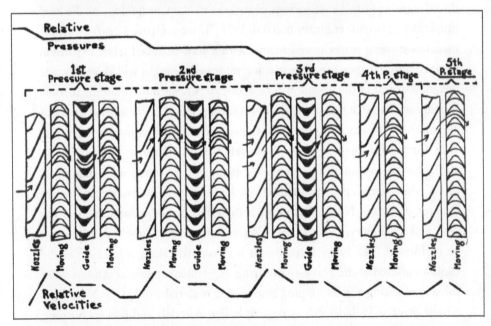

Figure 2.5. Curtis multiple-stage impulse turbine. *George J. Meyers,* Steam Turbines:
A Treatise Covering U.S. Naval Practice *(Annapolis, MD: 1917), 89*

shaft, a system first installed in the United States in the experimental navy coal ship *Neptune*, built before World War I. While early systems were equipped with single-reduction gear, later ones featured double reduction with multiple pinions, making it possible to raise turbine rpm significantly. The large amounts of power generated by marine turbines put enormous strains on pinions and wheels, which were precision engineered and manufactured. Practical experience in World War I revealed a variety of problems in double-reduction gear, particularly excessive wear in teeth, attributed by a British engineer to "Too high a tooth pressure as compared with single reduction; defective material; inferior lubrication; and faulty workmanship in regard to cutting and alignment."[65] Design problems received attention at General Electric in 1933, when marine engineer Aubrey Ross developed a "new type of 'locked train' main propulsion reduction gear which permitted building a double-reduction gear of great rigidity and light weight, and which would permit use of very much higher speed turbines than had been used before," one observer recalled after World War II.[66] Endorsed by Robinson on behalf of the Bureau of Engineering, double-reduction gear was more widely introduced in the U.S. Navy during the interwar years than in its British, Japanese, and German counterparts.[67]

Reduction gear combined with water-tube boilers and superheaters produced significant fuel cost savings compared to older technology. A Federal Shipbuilding marine engineer noted in 1921, "If we compare a geared-turbine installation using [superheated steam] with a well-designed triple expansion [reciprocating] engine installation using saturated steam, it will show that the weight and cost of the engine will be about 20 percent more than the turbine installation, and that the saving in fuel consumption of the latter will be about 30 percent."[68] In naval applications, the system confronted marine engineers with formidable challenges, Navy Secretary Curtis Wilbur pointed out in 1925. "Higher pressures and higher temperatures are constantly being advocated, which means that the metals must be subjected to stresses never before attempted" by the Navy. "Before such materials can be incorporated in the design of machinery, a vast amount of research and experimental work must be performed. The Navy Department is constantly taking advantage of the facilities offered at the Navy engineering experiment station at Annapolis in the way of testing and developing engineering materials, and at the Navy fuel-oil-test plant at Philadelphia as regards boiler materials and fuel-oil burning

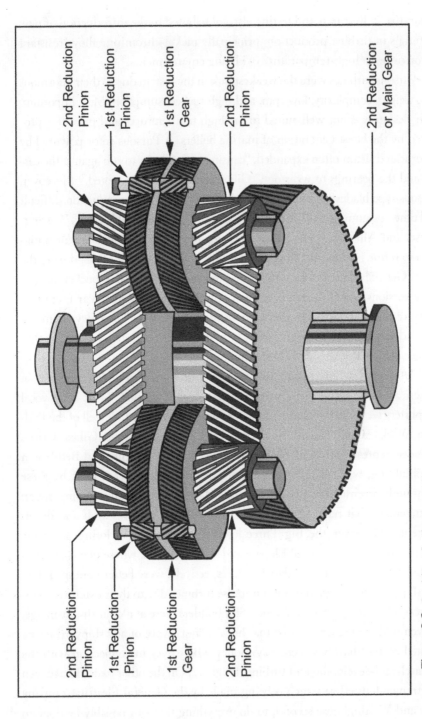

Figure 2.6. Double reduction gear.

Naval Machinery Part II: Naval Turbines
(Annapolis, MD: U.S. Naval Academy, 1946), 4-2.

apparatus."[69] Research and testing also contributed to the introduction of new materials in turbine production, principally nickel-chromium alloys resistant to corrosion in high-temperature oxidizing environments.[70]

Parsons turbines were the weakest link in the system due to their enormous size, weight, complexity, low rpm, and high fuel consumption. Most important, their design was not well-suited to the high temperatures and pressures produced by the latest generation of marine boilers. A Parsons rotor powered by superheated steam often expanded, "causing rotor blades to rub against the casing and the bearings to wear out," Gibbs, a naval architect, noted.[71] Moreover, Parsons-type blades were nonsymmetrical, rendering their production difficult and time-consuming. Fortunately for the U.S. Navy, General Electric, Westinghouse, and Allis-Chalmers financed major research and development initiatives to refine impulse turbine technology for electric power plants during the 1920s. General Electric, for example, devoted years of research to bucket designs, early versions of which had been bent out of shape in World War I–era turbines, resulting in redesigns that were nearly trouble-free. These developments enabled the Bureau of Engineering to give impulse turbine systems another chance during Roosevelt's 1933 shipbuilding program.[72]

Attempts by Bowen and Robinson to introduce Curtis-type turbines in American naval engineering stirred a great deal of conflict. Their most vocal supporters were Arthur Smith of General Electric, William Newell of the Bath Iron Works, Lynn Korndorff of Federal Shipbuilding, and Gibbs. Critics included representatives of Newport News, New York Ship, and Bethlehem Shipbuilding, who all favored reaction turbines, which were built by these firms under license from Britain's Parsons Marine Steam Turbine Company, an arrangement that relieved them of heavy investments in research and development.[73] Moreover, the Big Three loathed the prospect of losing profitable turbine contracts to General Electric and Westinghouse, whose plants at Schenectady, New York, and Philadelphia, respectively, were better equipped than the shipyards to design and build impulse turbines due to their extensive commercial work for power companies. Shipbuilders were at a clear disadvantage. Bowen told the General Board that he was "not aware of any shipyard in the United States [that] has spent any money whatsoever in connection with the research and development of turbine design. . . . On the other hand, I have seen the tremendous effort which is being made by the General Electric Company first and Westinghouse second, to do everything that can possibly be done to further the development of turbine design in the United States in order that this country may be entirely free from any necessity of resorting to English or continental design."[74]

A breakthrough occurred in 1933, when the Navy awarded two *Mahan*-class destroyers to United Shipyards of Staten Island, which recruited Gibbs & Cox as general design agent. *Mahan*-class impulse turbines were designed by General Electric and boilers by Babcock & Wilcox and Forster Wheeler. The boilers, which were rated for 400 psi and 648° Fahrenheit of total steam temperature, fed Curtis-GE turbines coupled to a double-reduction gear, a system that impressed Bowen as "the most rugged and reliable of any main drive installation ever installed in the Navy up to that time."[75] Unfortunately for its advocates, *Mahan* suffered from defective electrical systems and other problems, most of which were attributable to Gibbs & Cox's inexperience in warship design. Critics of the *Mahan* engine system complained that its design "prohibits the use of bronze for valves, fittings, etc., in the steam lines. Cast steel is the usual substitute, which gives trouble and causes construction delays due to the difficulty in obtaining good castings."[76]

Mahan's shortcomings notwithstanding, proponents of the new design persevered in their quest for high-pressure, high-temperature impulse turbines. To prevent the further use of Parsons turbines in U.S. warships, Robinson went so far as to threaten to enforce the Espionage Act, which prohibited the distribution of military secrets to foreign powers, against shipbuilders whose license contracts with Parsons obligated them to transmit performance data to the British company. In 1935, a 52,000-horsepower General Electric system that used 850° Fahrenheit steam was included in the design of *Somers*-class destroyers laid down at Federal Ship and the Bath Iron Works. Compared to the Parsons-propelled *Porter*, built at New York Ship, *Somers* achieved a 21 percent gain in cruising radius at 15 knots and a 10 percent weight saving as a direct result of her engine design. Pressure was gradually raised in subsequent systems until 1939, when the Bureau of Engineering mandated 600 psi and 850° Fahrenheit for destroyer engines.[77]

During the resumption of capital ship construction in 1937, the Navy, engine manufacturers, and shipbuilders confronted the question of whether to install similar drives in battleships, a difficult one given that the potential cost of failure was far greater in a $70 million capital ship than in a $4 million destroyer. Bowen's proposal to adopt the 600 psi/850° Fahrenheit standard for the battleships *North Carolina* and *Washington* was opposed by John Metten of New York

Ship, who warned: "this temperature should not be used for Naval work of any character. . . . The proposed installation will result in questionable reliability, and in more congested machinery compartments and more complicated operating procedure than is desirable in a capital ship."[78] Robinson told the General Board that "most of the opposition comes from the same people who [in 1926] were opposing just as strongly the use of 400 pounds of steam as compared to 300 pounds of steam [in the *Northampton* class]. These same people, and they are the shipbuilders at the Bethlehem Shipbuilding Co., Newport News Shipbuilding Co., and the New York Ship Co., opposed the use of 400 pounds as strenuously as they are now opposing 600 pounds." Echoing Bowen, Robinson attributed their attitude to a lack of experience and facilities because "They have practically no research laboratories for developing turbines so they are not in the position to go ahead and advance the art as are the people who build for shore [power] plants."[79] Shipbuilders' objections notwithstanding, the Navy selected General Electric turbines fed by Babcock & Wilcox high-pressure, high-temperature boilers for the *North Carolina* class, saving four hundred tons in weight that "could be used either to give the ship a knot and a half more speed at high powers, or to add another 14-inch gun, or to increase the armor of the ship," Bowen remarked.[80] The 600 psi/850° Fahrenheit standard remained in place in the design of battleships of the *South Dakota* and *Iowa* classes, fleet carriers of the *Essex* and *Independence* classes, cruisers of the *Alaska*, *Cleveland*, and *Baltimore* classes, and most destroyers completed in World War II. Moreover, "A very high degree of standardization and interchangeability was effected between the parts of the several 25,000 and 30,000 horsepower designs," a postwar review commented. "Lists of interchangeable parts such as turbine buckets, diaphragms, packings, bearings, oil deflectors, nozzles, etc., were compiled by the design group and the Navy which greatly facilitated servicing."[81]

The U.S. Navy's embrace of the new engine system stood in stark contrast to the Royal Navy's attitude. As early as 1927, the Admiralty approved the installation of an experimental 550 psi/750° Fahrenheit system in the destroyer *Acheron*, but her turbines suffered excessive vibrations, discrediting the high-pressure, high-temperature concept in the eyes of many British marine engineers. On the design side, Parsons faced no serious competitors in British marine turbine development, in contrast to America's more oligopolistic market structure, which included General Electric, Westinghouse, White-Forster, and Allis-Chalmers. As a result, the Royal Navy remained tethered to Parsons reaction turbines of

400 psi/700° Fahrenheit, which were more complicated to build, less reliable, more vulnerable to enemy shot due to their large size, and which consumed more fuel than their American counterparts. In 1941, a U.S. naval attaché reported from London with reference to the British, "Even in their newest ships the fuel consumption is at least 50% higher and in some cases almost 100% higher than we have in our modern designs. Due to war conditions the normal peacetime cruising radius of their ships has been reduced by as much as 50% in some classes. This latter, combined with the poor fuel economy has given their ships a comparatively short cruising radius. They are now fully alive to the mistakes they made in their pre-war designs."[82] Impressions that British combatants suffered from excessive fuel consumption and limited endurance were confirmed during the hunt for *Bismarck*, in whose final phase *King George V* had to abandon the fight and steam home running on fumes.[83]

Japanese engineers, like their British counterparts, did not push warship boiler and engine development to the limits achieved by the Americans. The Imperial Navy's Technical Department, which conducted much of the navy's technology research, developed a standard boiler named Kampon Ro-Go that featured small water tubes that exploited furnace heat more efficiently than larger tubes. Initially relying on Parsons patents, the Technical Department introduced a variety of Kampon impulse turbines and Mitsubishi Nagasaki Shipbuilding improved the Parsons design to such an extent that the Imperial Navy could gradually wean itself from British technology imports. Mitsubishi installed impulse turbines designed by the Technical Department in the destroyer *Sawakaze*, but some of their blades broke during trials. This persistent problem in Japanese marine engineering worsened with the introduction of impulse turbines, whose rotors suffered excessive vibrations when running below maximum speed.[84]

In contrast to the British and the Japanese, the Germans undertook ambitious efforts to design high-pressure, high-temperature turbine drives for warships, but the results proved troublesome. Siemens-Schuckert, Germany's leading electrical engineering firm, developed high-pressure, high-temperature boilers patented by engineer Mark Benson in 1922. Blohm & Voss, whose yard included integrated boiler works, fitted the freighter *Uckermark* with the Benson boiler, and the Reichsmarine had a similar system installed in the 2,600-ton fleet tender *Grille*, laid down at Blohm & Voss in 1934. The boiler, which was rated at 1,175 psi/878° Fahrenheit, supplied steam for a set of double-geared turbines.

Though *Grille*'s trial trip was an unmitigated disaster because boiler tubes leaked and burst, valves failed, and control instruments malfunctioned, the Reichsmarine ordered Benson boilers for seven destroyers of the *Z 1934* class built at Blohm & Voss and Germaniawerft, all of which suffered boiler problems and turbine breakdowns. AG Weser initially achieved better results with a boiler originally developed by the railroad engineer Richard Wagner, which powered the gunnery training ship *Brummer*. The navy promptly ordered 996 psi/860° Fahrenheit Wagner boilers installed in nine *Z 1934*–class destroyers built at AG Weser, Deutsche Werke Kiel, and Germaniawerft during the late 1930s. Unfortunately for the Germans, destroyers fitted with Wagner boilers likewise experienced troubles during their trial trips and service careers. The Kriegsmarine, again undeterred by obvious difficulties in design and construction, and without testing the new type thoroughly, ordered modified Wagner boilers rated at 1,250 psi/842° Fahrenheit for three *Admiral Hipper*–class heavy cruisers, whose engine performance left much to be desired. A 735 psi/950° Fahrenheit drive powered two battlecruisers of the *Scharnhorst* class, but their failure-prone turbines and boilers required extensive modifications during the war. An American postwar comparison of U.S. and German systems deemed the latter less reliable and "mediocre [in] design and manufacture," faulting them for excessive fuel consumption, poor reduction gear efficiency, and insufficient "accessibility for inspection, maintenance, and repair."[85] A postwar Royal Navy review attributed some of the problems of German marine engineering to the use of single-reduction gears: "It is obvious that while the [U.S. Navy] has achieved the gains expected from their adoption of higher steam conditions, something went seriously wrong with the German attempt. . . . Owing to [the Germans'] failure to use to use double reduction gearing, and to a somewhat unpractical outlook on the design of the machinery itself, most of the possible gains inherent in the higher conditions were squandered."[86]

The praise heaped on American boiler and turbine technology was generally well deserved. Its proponents were eager to see the new drives developed but insisted on thorough testing, unlike the Germans, who put experimental systems into serial production without awaiting trial results. After achieving ambitious technical objectives on the eve of World War II, moreover, American policymakers and marine engineers largely suspended the quest for even higher pressures and temperatures after 1939 and instead made 600 psi/850° Fahrenheit the basic performance standard for most combatants built during the war, greatly simplifying the serial production of boilers, turbines, and reduction gears. Especially in the vast Pacific War theater, their rugged and fuel-efficient turbine drives enabled American combatants to conduct long-distance operations in remote areas where repair, maintenance, and refueling facilities were scarce. More problematically, the Navy's attempt to install the new drives in all its battleships, fleet carriers, cruisers, and destroyers proved difficult in light of the limited production capacity available at the main turbine producers and a handful of reduction gear suppliers. Though additional turbine and gear plants were constructed during the war, persistent scarcity of industrial capacity forced the Navy to order simple diesel motors and even old-fashioned reciprocating engines for smaller destroyer escorts and naval auxiliaries.

CONCLUSION

Prewar naval work involved a variety of new designs and shop floor technologies, many of which were unique to warship construction. The need to design combatants with displacement not exceeding treaty-mandated tonnage caps prompted naval constructors' quest for weight savings, resulting in experiments with electric arc welding. Though some of these innovations eventually percolated into merchant work, the fact remains that they originated in naval construction. In the larger scheme of things, these findings challenge the notion that wartime weapons production relied on civilian practices.

The proliferation of electric arc welding in prewar naval work encouraged builders to introduce preassembly techniques in temperature-controlled environments. Instead of building ships according to the conventional practice of piece by piece on the slipways, they shifted a growing amount of work into fabrication shops, where shipfitters and welders assembled parts of the superstructure, bulkheads, and bottoms. To haul preassemblies from the shop floor to the slipways, yards often added cranes to their production equipment. Preassembly was more common in the United States and Germany, where welding was introduced on a large scale, than in Britain and Japan, whose yards often remained committed to riveting techniques that did not require temperature-controlled environments and could hence be performed in the open air on slipways. On the eve of World War II, many American and German yards featured cranes with larger carrying capacity than their British and Japanese counterparts, creating significant advantages in wartime construction.

3

"Superior to the Combined Strength of Our Enemies"

Naval Strategy, Shipbuilding Programs, and Navy Department Reforms, 1940–1945

In summer 1940, Congress authorized and appropriated funds for a two-ocean navy, the construction of which became the core mission of American warship builders in World War II. On the wish list of Big Navy advocates for decades, a two-ocean navy became politically feasible when the fall of France raised the specter of the United States having to confront Japan, Germany, and Italy without allies. Adm. Harold Stark, the chief of naval operations, posited, "to insure victory, we should be superior to the combined strength of our potential enemies."[1] After Pearl Harbor, the Navy asked for additional carriers, cruisers, destroyers, escort forces, and submarines that turned the United States into the world's unchallengeable sea power.

In addition to tracing the gradual evolution of naval expansion in a changing strategic context, the present chapter documents the buildup of the Navy's vast procurement apparatus. Though often derided as ineffectual by businessmen who complained loudly about "red tape," Navy administrators managed warship building quite effectively given its sheer scope and scale. This confirms historian Mark Wilson's verdict that military bureaucracies were critical to the success of industrial mobilization in providing public funds for investments in private plants, managing vast numbers of contracts, and building up complex supply chains. "Because the military and the public understood the military's core mission as fighting in combat theaters, its work on the home front was seldom fully appreciated," Wilson explains. "But the military's business divisions, together with a variety of civilian authorities, made the war economy work."[2]

ORIGINS OF THE TWO-OCEAN NAVY

The American fleet in commission in September 1939 constituted a one-ocean navy whose core mission, according to War Plan Orange, was a strategic offensive in the Pacific in the event of war with Japan. Implementation of that task became increasingly difficult with the start of the European war, when President Roosevelt instituted neutrality patrols off the Atlantic Coast, which sapped the strength of the Pacific Fleet. To bolster the Atlantic command, Roosevelt and Stark reassigned a growing number of combatants to the east, where destroyer squadrons began to escort merchantmen into the Atlantic and a Bermuda-based striking force enlisted carriers, cruisers, and destroyers to deal with German commerce raiders. By November 1941, the list of combatants withdrawn from the Pacific included three *New Mexico*–class battleships, the carrier *Yorktown*, six light cruisers, and twenty-five destroyers. Adm. James Richardson, commander in chief of the U.S. Fleet, worried that his emasculated Pacific command was becoming progressively unable to stage a Central Pacific offensive envisioned under War Plan Orange, complaining, "Every transfer of ship strength from the Pacific to the Atlantic further jeopardized the [battle force's] ability to carry through the early stages of that war plan."[3] "I know of no flag officer who wholeheartedly endorses the present ORANGE Plan," Richardson told Stark in October 1940. The "Plan had its inception primarily in the desirability of having a guiding directive for the development of the Naval Establishment to meet any international situation that might be thrust upon it," but it had over time degenerated into a transparent political ploy. "It is my belief that the impracticabilities of the ORANGE Plan, in the absence of a better one, have been periodically overlooked in order that the Department might have for budget purposes and presentation to Congress the maximum justification for the necessary enlargement of the Navy."[4] Pending a strategic review, the Pacific Fleet should be redeployed from Pearl Harbor to the less vulnerable San Diego naval base, he urged. His vocal criticism of Roosevelt's decision to keep the fleet in Hawaii eventually cost Richardson his job as fleet commander, followed by his demotion to rear admiral. Rear Adm. Richmond Turner, the Navy Department's director of war plans, who agreed that War Plan Orange was outdated, finally retired it for good in 1940. A new strategy, encapsulated in the Rainbow Five war plan, prioritized the defeat of Germany and tasked the Pacific Fleet with protection of the Malay Barrier from Malaya to the Dutch East Indies in collaboration with allied forces, but war planners were concerned that the juxtaposition of the Pacific mission with a large-scale buildup of the Atlantic Fleet again exceeded the U.S. Navy's extant capabilities.[5]

Naval shipbuilding under way at the start of the European war promised little relief from the Navy's strategic dilemma of preparing for a two-ocean war with a one-ocean navy. On September 1, 1939, American shipyards had close to 300,000 tons under construction, half of which constituted battleships scheduled for completion in 1942. By the latter year, however, Japan would have in commission a pair of *Yamato*-class battleships. Worse, by autumn 1939 Japanese shipyards had laid keels for five fleet carriers compared to only two under construction in the United States, promising to tip the balance of carrier-borne airpower decisively in Japan's favor. This scenario prompted calls for more substantial American carrier forces than what was under construction at the time. Likewise, American naval shipbuilding under way at the start of the European war did little to relieve a shortage of cruisers, another category where Japan had made significant headway prior to 1939. The U.S. Navy could claim a comfortable lead over its potential opponents in destroyers, but sheer numbers were deceptive because 81 of the 212 American destroyers in commission in 1939 dated to World War I. The 25 destroyers under construction in September 1939 were fast, well-armed, and versatile ships, leaving the high command wishing it had substantially more of their kind under construction when the crises in Europe and the Far East escalated. The prospect of U.S. entry into the war was a matter of concern to Stark, who urged Congress to authorize and provide funds for a two-ocean navy before it was too late. He argued, "Navies cannot be improvised. For the most part wars are fought and won or lost with the navies that exist at the outbreak of hostilities."[6]

Rationales for a two-ocean navy dated to the aftermath of the invasion of China in 1937, which raised the possibility of further Japanese aggression elsewhere. At the time, war planners assumed a Japanese offensive in Southeast Asia, which would prompt an American counteroffensive in the Central Pacific to recapture the Philippines and seek a decisive showdown with the Imperial Navy. The scenario hinged on the U.S. Navy's ability to concentrate most of the fleet in the Pacific, including redeployments from the East Coast via the Panama Canal, but Assistant Navy Secretary Charles Edison warned Roosevelt as early as February 1938, "If attacked on both oceans at once we are inadequately prepared. If, in addition, the canal is blocked we are crippled."[7] Senior strategists agreed. In November 1938, the Joint Planning Commission of the U.S. Army and Navy assumed for the first time a "violation of the Monroe Doctrine by one or more of the Fascist powers, and . . . a simultaneous attempt to expand Japanese influence in the Philippines," with Britain, France, and Latin America remaining neutral.[8] Planners argued that this scenario required a fleet of 40 battleships, 18 carriers, 108 cruisers, and hundreds of destroyers and submarines. Construction of a fleet this size far exceeded industrial capabilities at the time, not to mention Congress' willingness to appropriate the necessary funds.[9]

In September 1939, Stark raised the issue of naval expansion with Representative Carl Vinson (D-GA), chair of the House Committee on Naval Affairs. Convinced that a two-ocean navy was as yet politically unfeasible, Vinson proposed an authorization that would raise fleet strength by 25 percent over the then-current tonnage afloat and building. Stark's testimony before Vinson's committee stressed that the proposed increase would not produce a two-ocean navy because it was "not sufficient to defend our home waters, the Monroe Doctrine, our possessions and our trade routes against a coalition . . . of Japan, Russia, Germany and Italy. If we are attacked by the above combination, . . . something would have to be abandoned."[10] Stark's request implied the construction of roughly 2.2 million tons of combatants, more than three times the amount laid down during the entire previous decade. The $1.4 billion estimate for the 25 percent increase startled economy-minded congressmen, prompting Vinson to introduce a more modest substitute bill calling for an 11 percent increase. Passed on June 14, 1940, the act authorized the appropriation of 167,000 combatant tons and 75,000 tons of auxiliary ships for the fleet train. Appropriations followed two weeks later. Projects undertaken under the 11 percent program included important vessel classes, notably *Essex* carriers, *Baltimore* heavy cruisers, *Cleveland* light cruisers, and *Fletcher* destroyers, all of which were duplicated in subsequent shipbuilding programs.[11]

Seismic shifts in global affairs soon transformed the politics of naval expansion. In June 1940, German forces defeated France, Holland, and Belgium, leaving the army ensconced along the English Channel, the Luftwaffe poised to strike Britain, the Kriegsmarine in possession of French and Norwegian bases as staging grounds for the Battle of the Atlantic, and the Italian navy threatening Britain's Mediterranean sea lines of communication. These developments had repercussions halfway around the globe in Japan, where hardliners in the Imperial Navy calculated that the defeat of France and Holland, combined with Britain's woes at home and in the Mediterranean, left Western colonial possessions

Table 3.1. Authorizations per Two-Ocean Navy Legislation, 1940

	11 Percent Act, June 14, 1940	First Supplemental National Defense Appropriation Act, June 26, 1940	Two-Ocean Navy Act, July 19, 1940	Second Supplemental National Defense Appropriation Act, Sept. 9, 1940
Battleships		0	385,000 tons	7
Aircraft Carriers	79,500 tons	3	200,000 tons	7
Cruisers	66,500 tons	5	420,000 tons	33
Destroyers		30	250,000 tons	155
Submarines	21,000 tons	22	70,000 tons	43
Naval Auxiliaries	75,000 tons		100,000 tons	14
Appropriations				
Shipyard Plant Improvements	$35,000,000 (for navy yards only)		$150,000,000	
Armor Plant Facilities	$6,000,000			
Patrol and Escort Vessels			$50,000,000	

Public Law 757, 76th Cong., 3rd Sess., July 19, 1940; Public Law 781, 76th Cong., 3rd Sess., Sep. 9, 1940; *Annual Report of the Secretary of the Navy 1941* (Washington, DC: Government Printing Office, 1941), 27–34

in Southeast Asia largely defenseless and ripe for the picking. In Washington, some observers raised the possibility of a British collapse before the end of the year, confronting the United States with the "possibility of an Allied defeat," Stark warned.[12]

In June of that year, Stark and Capt. Charles Cooke, his offensively minded director of war plans, called for a massive increase in fleet strength that dwarfed the 11 percent program. Their proposal reflected a gloomy assessment of America's strategic prospects by the General Board in a top-secret memorandum to Stark, which assumed that the United States would face the combined might of Japan, Germany, and Italy alone. To defend the Western hemisphere and operate offensively in one ocean, the board argued, the U.S. Navy had to triple the size of its carrier force and double the number of battleships, cruisers, and destroyers. This scenario was consistent with the highly pessimistic Rainbow Four war plan, which assumed that the United States would have to fight a war without allies against German forces, which would include the surrendered British and French fleets, backed by its powerful Japanese and Italian allies. On June 18, the day after he received the General Board's report, Stark testified before Congress on behalf of a 70 percent increase in American fleet tonnage. Vinson, working hand in glove with the chief of naval operations, raised the nightmare scenario of a British surrender. In a speech supporting a two-ocean navy, he told Congress, "The axis now has at its disposal the shipyards and ammunition factories of Germany, Italy, Poland, Denmark, Norway, Holland, Belgium, France, and possibly Spain. The axis may get British shipyards."[13] Vinson shepherded the two-ocean navy bill through the House Committee on Naval Affairs, followed by a similar Senate measure sponsored by David Walsh (D-MA). Roosevelt was skeptical and told Vinson privately that the 70 percent plan—also known as the Two-Ocean Navy Act—was too large and could prove politically unpopular during the upcoming presidential campaign. After the measure had sailed through Congress without much debate, however, Roosevelt saw no alternative to signing the legislation on July 19, 1940.[14]

Vinson-Walsh, combined with the 11 percent act, authorized a true two-ocean navy whose force structure was geared toward a decisive battle pitting capital ships supported by cruisers, destroyers, and submarines against a similarly structured enemy fleet. Mahanian doctrine, which was strongly endorsed by Captain Cooke, the General Board, and the Office of the Chief of Naval Operations, served as the program's guiding principle, and the concomitant appropriations were passed by Congress in September 1940. Most important, the legislation provided for the construction of two battleships of the 58,400-ton *Iowa* class and five of the 63,000-ton *Montana* class, with 16-inch guns. The same appropriation funded the construction of 36,900-ton *Essex*-class carriers favored by Roosevelt and other proponents of naval airpower, who envisioned battles mainly fought by carriers on both sides. Most of the remaining forces were calibrated to the needs of the battle line and carrier strike forces to protect them against aircraft and submarines, with several cruisers and destroyers assigned to each capital ship (a designation extended from battleships to carriers in 1942). Moreover, Congress appropriated submarines that were designed to operate with the main force as scouts and to harass enemy surface combatants. Lastly, it funded the construction of tenders, floating repair shops, and other naval auxiliaries to provide fleet logistics support.[15]

Once implemented, these programs furnished the Navy with massive capabilities. Operations involving the new forces began in November 1943 with the

Gilberts Islands campaign, where carrier aircraft launched bombing raids on Japanese positions before amphibious craft landed U.S. Marines on the beaches. Three months later, Rear Adm. Marc Mitscher assumed tactical command of the newly formed Task Force 58, the most formidable strike force of the Pacific War, which played key roles during the invasion of the Marshall and Marianas Islands, followed by massive raids on the Imperial Navy's fleet base at Truk. During the Battle of the Philippine Sea in June 1944, Task Force 58 annihilated Japanese naval air power and four months later finished off most of the Imperial Navy's surface fleet at the Battle of Leyte Gulf. With ground forces busy securing the Philippines, the Navy proceeded in 1945 to attack Iwo Jima and Okinawa before launching carrier-borne air raids on the Japanese mainland.[16]

While the shipbuilding programs launched in 1940 produced massive capabilities for fleet action, they failed to prepare the Navy for antisubmarine warfare in the Atlantic because they did not provide for oceangoing escorts. Destroyers authorized under the two-ocean navy program were primarily earmarked for service alongside battleships and carriers, not escort duty, and $50 million for patrol and escort vessels included in the 11 percent appropriation produced only a handful of coastal forces instead of oceanic ones. The War Production Board concluded, in an implied indictment of the General Board, Stark, Cooke, and Vinson, that their shipbuilding schemes "concentrated heavily upon large combatant ships. Relatively little emphasis was placed upon small escort and antisubmarine vessels. Obviously, the history of the 1917–1918 submarine warfare had either been forgotten or disregarded."[17] Though the criticism had some merit, the fact remained that the submarine threat was more apparent than real when naval expansion got under way because the Germans were not yet engaged in all-out U-boat warfare. The heavy forces authorized in 1940 could not only serve in encounters with their Japanese counterparts (their primary mission), but also in possible confrontations with German surface raiders, which were at the time considered a more serious threat than U-boats. The belief that German surface forces constituted a serious threat was shared by the Admiralty after the pocket battleship *Graf Spee* had wreaked havoc on British shipping in 1939, followed by her half-sister *Admiral Scheer*, the heavy cruiser *Admiral Hipper*, and the battlecruisers *Scharnhorst* and *Gneisenau*. In May 1941, the Germans dispatched *Bismarck* and the heavy cruiser *Prinz Eugen* on a commerce raiding mission called Operation Rheinübung, which claimed no merchant ships but cost Britain the battleship *Hood*. Against this backdrop, proponents of the 1940 shipbuilding program had good reasons to prioritize the construction of heavy combatants to prepare for a possible clash with Germany in the Atlantic. As it turned out, however, Operation Rheinübung was Germany's last attempt to deploy heavy combatants to Atlantic commerce raiding, which henceforth relied exclusively on submarines, a development that caught the U.S. Navy flat-footed.[18]

Though the Royal Navy was better prepared to confront U-boats, its shipbuilding programs evinced weaknesses in areas where the United States developed its core strengths, notably battleships and carriers. An exclusively German threat seemed manageable to the British because the relatively small Kriegsmarine of the late 1930s had no battle line or naval air capability. Its submarine force was vulnerable to detection by sonar technology Britain had developed between the wars, leading many in the Royal Navy to believe that the submarine threat could be defused by old destroyers fitted with sonar to perform convoy duty. Though sonar turned out to be less effective than anticipated, the British developed other antisubmarine warfare capabilities, which put them ahead of the Americans and indeed everyone else, notably the highly effective *Black Swan*–class sloops for oceanic escort duty and *Flower*-class corvettes for coastal antisubmarine service. *Flower*s and the subsequent *Hunt*-class destroyer escorts were suitable for serial construction, which shifted into high gear shortly after the war started. Though the Royal Navy had significant antisubmarine capabilities on hand and in the pipeline when the Battle of the Atlantic escalated, it lacked heavily armed and fast battleships to match their Axis counterparts, again in contrast to the U.S. Navy. Construction of four 30-knot *Lion*-class battleships armed with 16-inch guns was suspended at the beginning of the war to free resources for other programs, and it never resumed. As a result, the Royal Navy lacked modern battleships equipped with the largest-caliber guns (the 28-knot *King George V* class wielded 14-inch rifles). The battlecruiser *Renown*'s 15-inch guns disabled the German battlecruiser *Gneisenau*'s fire control system during the Norwegian campaign in 1940, and 14-inch shells fired by *Prince of Wales* damaged *Bismarck*'s fuel bunkers and boilers in the Battle of the Denmark Strait of 1941, but sinking the German battleship armed with 15-inch guns a few days later required a force made up of no less than *Ark Royal*, the slow battleship *Rodney* equipped with 16-inch guns, *King George V*, three cruisers, and seven destroyers. For the next three years, the Royal Navy was worried about *Bismarck*'s sister ship *Tirpitz*, which posed a threat to Arctic convoys. Dealing with *Tirpitz* required at least two *King George V*s, according British estimates—a task that could have been more effectively accomplished by the battleship *Vanguard*, which to the Royal Navy's regret was not completed until after the war.[19]

Like the Americans, the British feared simultaneous conflicts in the Atlantic, the Mediterranean, and the Far East that required combat capabilities far in excess of what was afloat and what the shipyards could deliver. The scenario of a triple threat that worried American war planners also haunted the Imperial Chiefs of Staff, who warned the cabinet in 1937, "We cannot foresee the time when our defence forces will be strong enough to safeguard our trade, territory, and vital interests against Germany, Italy, and Japan at the same time."[20] Numerous new ships joined the fleet from 1937 to September 1939, notably *Ark Royal*, eleven light cruisers, and thirty-six destroyers, but the Royal Navy was still not prepared to meet a triple threat, which forced the Admiralty to stretch its forces wide and thin. Like the American redeployments from the Pacific to the Atlantic, Britain's buildup of its Mediterranean forces in preparation for war with Italy came at the expense of the Home Fleet, including the battleships *Barham* and *Malaya*, the carrier *Illustrious*, and several light cruisers and destroyers. Like its American counterpart, the Admiralty had difficulties placing additional contracts because "The shipyards already had a very heavy programme in hand in the autumn of 1939: by October, 825,000 tons were under construction for the Admiralty, 75,000 tons more than the total reached at the peak period of the 1914–1918 war. Besides this, one-hundred-and-seventy-six merchant ships, with a gross tonnage of 909,706, were being built," a postwar review recounted.[21] The Battle of Britain subsequently forced a reallocation of resources. In "mid-1940, when the paramount national need was considered to be more aeroplanes, labour was withdrawn from shipbuilding."[22] Builders nevertheless managed to deliver three *Illustrious*-class carriers and three *King George V*–class battleships by December 1941 and laid keels for eight light cruisers under the War Emergency Programme and the 1940 Naval Estimates, but these schemes emphasized the construction of fleet destroyers, escorts, and submarines. In an effort to implement long-standing plans to dispatch capital ships to Singapore in order to deter Japan, the Admiralty reassigned *Prince of Wales* and the battlecruiser *Repulse* from the Home Fleet to the Far East, where both were sunk shortly after the outbreak of the Pacific War. By then, the Royal Navy had also lost the carriers *Courageous*, *Glorious*, and *Ark Royal*, the battleships *Royal Oak*, *Barham*, and *Hood*, nine cruisers, and forty-three destroyers due to enemy action.[23]

Japanese naval strategy and shipbuilding programs prepared the Imperial Navy for a decisive battle but neglected the development of antisubmarine capabilities. In 1939, it still possessed a comfortable lead over its Western rivals that grew substantially with the commissioning of two *Yamato*s and a pair of *Shōkaku*-class carriers, as well as the recommissioning of four modernized *Kongo*-class battleships. The Fourth Naval Armaments Supplement Program of 1939 planned for additional capabilities, notably the carrier *Taihō* and another pair of *Yamato*s.[24] Japanese tactical planning envisioned the pummeling of the American battle line by *Yamato*s, whose 18-inch guns could engage enemy battleships while remaining outside their range, followed by a final assault by older capital ships. Simultaneously, however, the Imperial Navy made no provisions for commerce protection except four *Shimushu*-class frigates built in 1939–41 because it planned to settle scores with the United States quickly during a decisive fleet encounter. The latter failed to materialize, leaving Japan woefully unprepared to deal with American submarine attacks on merchantmen and tankers carrying raw materials from across Southeast Asia to the home islands' manufacturing and refining centers. The 1941 Rapid Naval Armaments Supplement Program finally planned for thirty *Etorofu*-class escorts, but antisubmarine training, doctrine, and tactics received little attention.[25]

America's looming two-ocean navy program, meanwhile, called into question Japan's ability to achieve a Trafalgar-type victory, which precipitated calls for preventive war. In 1941, "we have prospects of achieving victory, if we fight an early, decisive battle," Vice Admiral Kondō Nobutake of the Naval General Staff told the Imperial Headquarters–Cabinet Liaison Conference on September 14, 1940, five days after the U.S. Congress had appropriated funds for the two-ocean navy. Over the long haul, Kondo warned, the Americans were "rapidly building ships, and the gap in the ratio will become increasingly large in the future, and Japan cannot possibly overtake them, and, in that sense, if we go to war, today would be the best."[26] Navy minister Oikawa Koshirō reiterated Kondo's arguments at a Privy Council meeting on September 19. The same day, Admiral Fushimi Hiroyasu, chief of the Naval General Staff, gave his blessing for the Tripartite Pact with Germany and Italy, which was unequivocally aimed at the United States.[27]

In response to America's 1940 naval construction programs, the Imperial Navy drafted a variety of shipbuilding schemes, all of which reflected the strange mixture of excitement, overconfidence, and despair that pervaded Japanese strategic thinking in the year before Pearl Harbor. The huge Fifth Naval Armaments Supplement Program of May 1941, which called for five battleships, three carriers, and a large number of heavy cruisers and destroyers, bore an unmistakable Mahanian imprint but proved unworkable and was soon scrapped. The less ambitious Rapid Naval Armaments Supplement Program of September 1941 provided for the carrier *Unryū*, a pair of *Ibuki*-class heavy cruisers,[28] sixteen destroyers of the *Yūgumo* class[29] and ten of the *Akizuki* class,[30] and thirty-three submarines. Weeks before Pearl Harbor, the Imperial Navy requested an additional twenty-nine submarines under the Naval Armaments Supplement Program.[31]

All told, Japan proved unable to formulate an effective response to U.S. naval expansion, hardline diplomacy, and the oil embargo of July 1941, reinforcing preventive war rationales. Admiral Nagano Osami told the cabinet on July 21:

> Although at present we have prospects for victory over the United States, as time passes the probability of our success will decrease and by the latter half of next year [when the first units of the two-ocean navy program would be commissioned] we will have difficulty matching them, and thereafter things will become worse and worse; the Americans will probably prolong the issue and not settle until they finish rearming. . . . Nothing would be better than ending this without fighting. But if we decide that a clash cannot possibly be avoided, then I want you to know that we will be at a disadvantage as time passes.[32]

At the time, Vice Admiral Yamamoto Isoroku was already busy drafting the Pearl Harbor attack plan.[33]

German naval strategy and shipbuilding underwent fundamental recalibration as a result of major cutbacks in surface combatant construction and a reorientation toward submarine building in 1939. The grandiose prewar Z-Plan, which sought a large surface fleet backed by submarines to confront the Royal Navy some years in the future, became redundant with Britain's declaration of war and was canceled in September 1939. Grand Admiral Erich Raeder, the Kriegsmarine's commander in chief, decreed that only surface combatants whose construction was already well advanced—principally *Bismarck* and *Tirpitz*, the carrier *Graf Zeppelin*, and three heavy cruisers—were to be completed. While Raeder was pessimistic about Germany's chances in a naval contest with Britain (the surface navy could only hope "to die gallantly," he warned), his subordinate, Commodore Karl Dönitz and leader of the submarines, was confident that three hundred U-boats could bring Britain to its knees.[34] A construction program approved by Hitler in October 1939 that called on German shipyards to deliver twenty-nine and one-third boats a month proved difficult to implement, partly because army and air force projects absorbed manpower and materiel at the navy's expense and enjoyed higher priority ratings. Equally important, shipyard retooling for submarine construction took time during the harsh winter of 1939–40, resulting in extraordinarily low delivery rates. From September 1939 to June 1940, the navy commissioned a mere twenty units after having lost twenty-seven, leaving an aggregate force of only fifty boats, many of which were in overhauls. Deliveries increased rapidly in the closing months of 1940 and totaled 198 boats in 1941 as serial construction shifted into high gear. Combined with the establishment of naval bases in Norway and along the French Atlantic coast that greatly simplified oceanic submarine operations, these developments set the stage for the Battle of the Atlantic. Simultaneously, however, America's two-ocean navy plans greatly worried the Kriegsmarine, whose leaders viewed the United States as Germany's most dangerous enemy in the long run. Fearing that the two-ocean navy would enable the U.S. Navy to intervene decisively into the Battle of the Atlantic and seize naval bases in Greenland, Iceland, the Azores, and North Africa, Raeder told Hitler that the Naval Warfare Command wanted war with the United States in spring 1941 "in order to achieve successes during this phase of relative weakness of the USA."[35] This echoed the preventive war rationales espoused by Admiral Kondō and other Japanese leaders fearful of the strategic results of American naval construction.[36]

CONTRACT REFORMS AND FACILITY IMPROVEMENTS

On September 9, 1940, only hours after Congress had passed appropriations for the two-ocean navy, the U.S. Navy activated contracts for 199 combatants with American shipbuilders. Navy contracts from July to December 1940 alone totaled $5.5 billion, compared to $4.2 billion in contracts issued by the Army, whose per-unit cost was significantly lower than the Navy's. The swift start was partly attributable to a new system of no-bid contracts instituted as part of the 70 percent act, a major departure from peacetime routines in which the Navy had invited shipbuilders to review preliminary designs and awarded the contract to the lowest bidder in a drawn-out process. Instead of asking for competitive bids, Navy Department officials negotiated the specifics of a given contract with a preselected builder. Negotiated contracts were advantageous to shipbuilders and the Navy alike because they took into consideration extant yard expertise and specialization, explained Rear Adm. Alexander Van Keuren, chief of the Bureau of Construction & Repair:

> There are only so many building ways available in the industry at private yards and navy yards. To accomplish [the two-ocean navy programs] in the time desired we must utilize these ways and the whole capacity of the yards . . . and this result cannot be obtained with a program of so many unit contracts if competitive bids are obtained and contracts in each case are awarded to the lowest bidder. Some yards, both by experience and facilities, are better fitted for airplane carriers than others, some for submarines, and so on. Furthermore, the design staffs of certain yards are better fitted than others for certain types of work.[37]

Negotiated contracts would enable the Navy to take advantage of extant know-how by allocating specific vessel types to the best-suited yards, which in essence meant that Newport News would concentrate on the detail design and construction of carriers, Fore River on heavy cruisers, and New York Ship on light cruisers, much as they had in the prewar naval shipbuilding cartel.[38]

When Navy Department officials asked Congress for authority to award all orders on the basis of no-bid contracts, critics warned that the reform would result in unbridled profiteering. Senator Homer Bone of Washington, a feisty veteran of the Nye committee investigation that had revealed the cartel's existence, worried that no-bid contracting would undo most of the progressive reforms of the previous decade because "Every single competitive factor is absent" from negotiated contracts. "Every balance and check is absent. . . .

Here is an emergency, and you [could] elect to spend $10,000,000 more per battleship or $20,000,000 more" than the builder's actual costs, leaving the United States with enormous profits from which the government would never recover.[39] These objections faded after the fall of France, when Congress suspended competitive bidding. Given the politically sensitive nature of no-bid contracting and the vast amounts of money involved in naval shipbuilding, however, the administration and Congress instituted fairly effective controls to curb profiteering (see below). On average, private builders netted 5 percent margins, a congressional investigation revealed in 1944. Results varied significantly by firm, but none exceeded 9 percent. Though the data are not available in disaggregate form, a rough estimate indicates that construction of destroyers (the Bath Iron Works' specialty) and submarines (Electric Boat) was more profitable than heavy combatant building (New York Ship's mainstay). The federal government recaptured some profits under the Excess Profit Tax law of 1942.[40]

The naval shipbuilding industry required major upgrades to construct the two-ocean navy, particularly in existing private and government-owned yards. Responsible for building all battleships, carriers, cruisers, destroyers, and submarines during the war, these yards "constituted a nucleus of experienced management and labor which was able to assume the initial burden of the program which developed so swiftly early in the summer of 1940," a wartime congressional inquiry noted. "Had this nucleus not been available at the time it was needed, incalculable delays would inevitably have resulted."[41] Many firms, however, had neglected significant investments prior to 1939 and devoted only modest amounts

Table 3.2. Profits on Select Combatants

Company	Number of Vessels	Total Adjusted Price	Percent of After-Tax Profit to Cost
Bath Iron Works	21	$112,794,688	9
Electric Boat Company	20	$52,105,803	8
Newport News Shipbuilding & Dry Dock Company	5	$131,305,068	5
Federal Shipbuilding	38	$226,982,955	4
Bethlehem Steel Company Shipbuilding Division	29	$231,889,253	2
New York Shipbuilding Corporation	9	$219,372,527	2

Investigations of the Progress of the War Effort: Report of the House Committee on Naval Affairs, 78th Cong., 2nd Sess., 199 (1944)

to facility upgrades for naval work in 1940. Confronted with the same problem in World War I, the Navy had reimbursed private builders for facility improvements without effective program control, with the predictable result that contractors had billed the government for projects whose relevance to the war effort was questionable at best, leading to years of litigation to settle conflicting claims. To tease investments out of defense contractors, Congress permitted accelerated tax amortization of privately financed facility improvements under the Second Revenue Act of 1940, guaranteeing that projects certified as necessary for national defense reduced the contractor's tax burden and were fully depreciated in five years instead of the usual twenty. The scheme elicited only modest investments from shipbuilders, who reported $211 million for tax purposes from 1940 to 1945, compared to $383 million claimed by machinery and electrical equipment manufacturers, $518 million by aircraft and aircraft engine producers, and $814 million by iron and steel makers. Tax incentives failed to spur larger private investments in part because the National Defense Advisory Commission, whose contract specialists were well aware of the problems that had plagued facility financing in World War I, refused to rubberstamp certificates of necessity that would confirm a given project's relevance to the defense effort.[42]

Other inducement for facility investments produced similarly disappointing results. Under the Emergency Plant Facility system proffered by the National Defense Advisory Commission, private investments in plant improvements were reimbursed by the government over a sixty-month period, at the end of which the contractor could acquire the new facilities or have them removed from its premises. Like amortization, the Emergency Plant Facility scheme experienced delays because it required certificates of necessity and created tax-related accounting problems, resulting in fewer than $350 million in aggregate

Table 3.3. Facility Investments for Naval
Work under the 11 Percent Act, 1940

	Private Investments	Navy Investments
Bath Iron Works	$203,671	$1,500,000
Newport News Shipbuilding	$200,000	$6,000,000
Electric Boat	$27,000	$1,500,000
Federal Shipbuilding	$227,250	$2,000,000

Excess Profit Taxation: Joint Hearings Before the House and Senate Committees on Ways and Means, 76th Cong., 3rd Sess., 32 (1940)

investments from 1940 to 1945. Likewise, the Defense Plant Corporation (DPC), which bankrolled most defense-related facility improvements in American industry during World War II, generated little enthusiasm among naval builders. The DPC financed new plants and additions with funds provided by the Reconstruction Finance Corporation and then leased the new facilities to the contractor for a nominal fee. As under the Emergency Plant Facility scheme, the contractor could buy the improvements for an agreed-upon price after the end of the war or have them dismantled at the government's expense. The DPC provided $7 billion for facility improvements, more than one quarter of the nation's entire investment in new plants through 1945, with aircraft, aircraft engines, and parts alone accounting for $2.6 billion. The Navy netted $608 million in DPC funds, $548 million of which went into naval aircraft factories and only $59 million into shipbuilding under the auspices of the Bureau of Ships, which financed most facility improvements directly.[43]

The Navy proposed other contract reforms to render direct government investments in private plants palatable to the shipbuilders. Under existing regulations, a contractor advanced funds for facility improvements necessary to build a ship out of pocket and only after completion of the contract applied to the Treasury Department for reimbursement and relevant depreciation charges. The procedure had a variety of drawbacks for the contractor, who usually had to obtain loans to pay for upgrades. During the 1930s, U.S. Treasury officials, who lacked the technical expertise required to determine whether improvements were necessary to fulfill contracts, often refused to issue the required certificates of necessity. Under new regulations introduced in May 1940, Navy inspectors working on-site at private shipyards were empowered to approve or reject projects, and the Navy paid for necessary ones up front. Using the new procedure, the Navy financed a lion's share of facility improvements in privately owned shipyards, ordnance works, and collateral industries. Related reforms permitted fast-tracking of contract payments to the shipbuilder, who could receive up to 30 percent of a ship's price immediately after signing the contract, replacing the Navy's peacetime practice of paying the contractor piecemeal only after a project had reached certain construction milestones. As with the new facility improvement policy, the new provision for materials was intended to reduce the amount of money the contractor advanced out of its own funds.[44]

In addition to funding shipyard improvements, the Navy invested heavily in naval armor plants operated by Midvale, Bethlehem, and Carnegie-Illinois. In 1940, the nation's entire naval armor output capacity totaled only 19,000 tons annually, which was barely enough to support the construction of two battleships, let alone the eleven ones actually scheduled plus carriers and cruisers, which also required substantial amounts of armor. The Bureau of Ordnance, responsible for the production of armor as well as guns, tried to widen the bottleneck by reactivating the government-owned U.S. Naval Ordnance Plant in Charleston, West Virginia, originally built to supply armor and guns for naval construction in World War I and mothballed at the end of the war. The Navy leased parts of the massive facility to the U.S. Steel subsidiary Carnegie-Illinois in 1939, followed a year later by the rehabilitation of the entire complex at a total cost to the government of $50 million. The Bureau of Ordnance also invested heavily in armor production capacity at Carnegie-Illinois' main works at Homestead, Pennsylvania, whose operations were integrated with those of the Naval Ordnance Plant. Bethlehem Steel meanwhile invested $6 million of its own money in the reconstruction of its armor mill in Bethlehem, Pennsylvania, while the Navy provided $56.5 million. Midvale Steel of Philadelphia, the only other supplier of naval armor, invested $1.1 million into its armor production facilities in Nicetown, Pennsylvania, an amount that was dwarfed by $10 million in direct investments by the Bureau of Ordnance. Annual armor production capacity slowly rose over the course of the war, but significant shortages were evident from 1940 to 1943. The limited availability of armor until midwar contributed to the Navy's decision to prioritize the construction of carriers and light cruisers, which required less armor than battleships and large cruisers. Partly as a result, all five capital ships of the *Montana* class were canceled, only two of six *Alaska*-class large cruisers originally planned were actually completed, construction of two *Iowa*-class battleships was slowed and eventually canceled, and completion of the four remaining *Iowa*s was delayed as a result of late armor deliveries to the shipyards (see chapter 4).[45]

Navy yard expansion followed a different trajectory. As a result of investments into facility improvements since the start of the New Deal, most government-owned shipyards were better equipped to build ships under the two-ocean navy program than were private yards. The Bureau of Yards & Docks reported that a "considerable amount of work was accomplished [after

Table 3.4. Production of Heavy Armor in Gross Tons, 1939–1945

	For Battleships and Large Cruisers	For Aircraft Carriers, Heavy Cruisers, Light Cruisers, and Miscellaneous*	Total	Percentage of Armor Mill Operation
1939	7,031	165	7,196	71
1940	23,646	380	24,026	101
1941	24,748	10,830	35,578	98
1942	31,677	36,037	67,714	101
1943	30,759	46,445	77,024	65
1944	15,124	68,141	83,265	70
1945	7,192	40,804	86,752	46

*Miscellaneous armor was produced to replace battle-damaged plates, modernization of older battleships, and experimental armor.

Historical Section, Bureau of Ordnance, "Armor, Projectiles, Ammunition, Part II, Volume II," 22, Rare Book Room, Navy Department Library, Washington Navy Yard, Washington, DC

1933], partly under naval public works appropriations, but principally through allocations from National Recovery Administration, Civil Works Administration, Works Progress Administration, and Public Works Administration appropriations. Without the rehabilitation, modernization, and improvements that were accomplished in this manner, the navy yards would have been critically unprepared for the emergency."[46] Congressional appropriations for additional facility improvements under the two-ocean navy program were channeled through project orders, which were less complicated than procedures for government investments in private plants. Under well-established routines, navy yards applied to the bureaus for specific project funds, which underwent Navy Department review and, if approved, were incorporated into the Navy's budget requests presented to Congress for authorization and funding. The bureaus ordered the navy yards to proceed with projects funded by appropriations without having to apply for certificates of necessity or approval by on-site inspectors, as was the case in the private sector.[47]

NAVY DEPARTMENT ADMINISTRATIVE REFORM

The launch of the two-ocean navy program coincided with several major reorganizations of the Navy Department that enhanced its ability to manage naval expansion. Key reforms relevant to naval shipbuilding included the formation of the Bureau of Ships, the Procurement Legal Division, and the Office of Procurement & Material.

Headquartered on Constitution Avenue in Washington, DC, the Navy Department consisted of the Office of the Secretary of the Navy and his senior assistants, principally the chief of naval operations and eight bureau chiefs. Procurement involved a staggering variety of activities, an Assistant Secretary of the Navy told Congress. They included "design, development and standardization; item identification and cataloging; selection of contractors and time of contract placement; pricing; contract forms; contract appeals; patents; use of mandatory orders; renegotiation; financing; specifications; scheduling; inspection; packaging; packing and marking; contract termination; surplus property disposal; insurance; auditing; and conservation."[48]

The most important offices involved in shipbuilding were the Bureau of Ordnance, responsible for guns, armor, and ammunition; the Bureau of Yards & Docks, with jurisdiction over the navy yards; the Bureau of Construction & Repair, responsible for preliminary design and construction; and the Bureau of Engineering, in charge of boilers and engines. Until 1940, the department's shipbuilding procedures followed well-established routines. Once a contract had been signed and activated, the builder developed a ship's detail design and recruited subcontractors under the cognizance of the Bureau of Construction & Repair. Similarly, the Bureau of Engineering oversaw the construction of the propulsion system by the lead contractors for boilers and engines. The Bureau of Ordnance issued separate orders for guns, which were usually manufactured at the Washington Navy Yard, and for armor produced by Bethlehem Steel, Midvale, and Carnegie-Illinois. The shipbuilder's detail design underwent continual review by the Bureaus of Construction & Repair, Engineering, and Ordnance, which could order changes while the ship was already under construction. Navy inspectors assigned to the shipyard and the steel mills audited the construction process on site. Once the builder had delivered the ship to a navy yard, it was inspected by specialists who conducted a variety of experiments and took the ship to sea for a trial trip to ensure that its technical characteristics—speed, displacement, seaworthiness, and so on—conformed to the design. The navy yard undertook corrections before the ship was finally accepted for commissioning into the fleet.[49]

These administrative structures and routines underwent radical changes to streamline design and broaden the department's authority to manage naval expansion. Prodded by Charles Edison, Secretary of the Navy, Congress authorized the merger of the Bureaus of Construction & Repair and Engineering into the Bureau of Ships in July 1940. The initiative came in the wake of a ship-building scandal the previous year, when inspection of the newly built destroyer *Anderson* revealed poor seaworthiness. The ship was 150 tons overweight, largely because of insufficient design coordination between the Bureaus of Engineering and Construction & Repair. An internal review blamed Construction & Repair because that bureau was responsible for the overall design, but its chief pointed out that his organization had no administrative power to force Engineering to adhere to its designs. "Here was a glaring example of the lack of coordination and coordination between the Bureaus responsible for the construction of a ship," Edison later recalled.[50] A merger of the two bureaus, the most obvious solution, had run afoul on opposition from within both organizations during the interwar period because bureau chiefs sought to protect their administrative fiefdoms. In September 1939, however, Edison's persistent efforts began to bear fruit when Rear Adm. Samuel Robinson of the Bureau of Engineering integrated the design of boilers and engines with that of hulls by Construction & Repair. The initiative greatly simplified relations with shipbuilders, who no longer had to go "to the Bureau of Construction and Repair and have the buck passed to Engineering and vice versa," a Navy Department official explained. "They do not have to get on the merry-go-round at the Department and spend a week to do a half day's business as it used to be before the consolidation."[51] Under the old design system, a detail plan sent by a shipbuilder for approval "to the Bureau of Construction and Repair [would] stay there until it got approval, then go to the Bureau of Engineering and get approved there, and days and sometimes weeks would be lost before that contractor would get that plan back approved so he could proceed with the construction of the ship. Now you have one consolidated plan-approval section with [a marine engineer] on one side of the desk and a naval constructor on the other, and papers shoot back and forth in an expeditious manner."[52] Though Edison achieved the formal integration of the two organizations into the Bureau of Ships in June 1940, his attempt to include the Bureau of Ordnance in the merger evoked howls of protest from the bureau chief, Stark, and Vinson, who persuaded Roosevelt to abort this element of the Edison reforms. As a result, the design process for armor, turrets, and guns was not well integrated with that for hulls and propulsion systems, contributing to delays, which plagued ordnance design and production throughout the war. The Edison reforms nevertheless simplified the implementation of naval expansion, the launch of which coincided with the establishment of the Bureau of Ships.[53]

Subsequent initiatives fine-tuned the Navy's administrative systems under new leadership. In July 1940, Roosevelt replaced Navy Secretary Edison (who resigned to run for governor of New Jersey) with newspaper publisher Frank Knox. A midwestern Republican supporter of Roosevelt's defense policies, Knox had endeared himself to two-ocean navy proponents in 1939 when he demanded, "We must build—and as quickly as possible—a fleet in both oceans the equal of any that could be brought against us in that particular sea."[54] Though he could not claim naval expertise, Knox proved a resourceful reformer who pruned the extraordinary powers of the bureau chiefs. At the beginning of his tenure, he hired the management consulting firm Booz Allen to review and stream-line the internal organization of the Office of the Secretary of the Navy, the chief of naval operations, and the bureaus. In its detailed report on the Bureau of Ships, Booz Allen faulted the Design Branch for duplication of functions and noted that the persistence of old filing systems of Construction & Repair and Engineering created confusion, but other than that gave the new bureau high marks for professionalism and clarity in its chain of command. Much of the credit belonged to Robinson, a skilled administrator and consensus builder in a department notorious for bureaucratic infighting. Having headed the Bureau of Engineering before 1940, he had earned the respect of other bureau chiefs who were content to see one of their own appointed coordinator of shipbuild-ing to manage the merger of the Bureaus of Engineering and Construction & Repair into the Bureau of Ships.[55]

The Bureau of Ships' signature achievements under Robinson included the accelerated processing of vessel contracts and implementation of facility improve-ments. Having negotiated vessel contracts with the shipbuilders as early as July 1940, two months before Congress appropriated funds for the 70 percent fleet expansion, Robinson issued letters of intent, "that is, telling the contractor that we are going to make contracts with him," he explained.[56] "In this way we agree on the price and the conditions of the contract."[57] On September 9, hours after the president had signed the necessary appropriations into law, the Navy Depart-ment followed up with formal contracts. The Bureau of Ships used similar pro-cedures to effectuate facility improvements totaling more than $100 million at private shipyards from September 1940 to January 1941, later followed by even larger direct investments by the Navy into the industrial base. These amounts dwarfed the meager sums private builders had invested in their physical plants before the war. Fore River, for example, which had made headlines in 1939 with a privately financed, $610,000 yard development program, its largest since World War I, netted $13 million in Navy plant improvement funds in 1940 alone.[58]

The avalanche of contracts that rolled out of the Bureau of Ships in September 1940 landed on the desk of James Forrestal, a former Wall Street executive who had recently been appointed Undersecretary of the Navy. Responsible for signing the contracts on behalf of the Navy Department, he later described the procedure as follows:

> Those contracts came to me from the bureaus concerned in stacks about that high [indicating] each day. I undertook to examine those with the same scrutiny I would apply to my own business if I were conducting a similar business. After I got through the first stack, Admiral Robinson came to me and said if I wanted to go on and scrutinize each one, all right, that was one thing; but if I wanted to put through the contracts, that was another thing. That I could make my choice. So I signed them. But it became very clear to me that, if I was to discharge in a legal way the responsibilities I had, some scrutiny of those contracts had to be exercised.[59]

Under existing procedures, contracts with shipbuilders and other suppliers were drafted by bureau officials and signed by the chief in charge. The Judge Advocate General then reviewed the contract and, if it was approved, forwarded the document to the Undersecretary of the Navy for his signature, which activated the contract. These routines, which were largely based on standardized contract forms, worked reasonably well under the competitive bid system, when the Navy dealt primarily with established suppliers. Most orders for the two-ocean navy program, however, were the result of negotiated contracts, the details of which were not covered in the department's standard legal forms, which required the participation of legal experts in negotiations from the get-go, and not simply ex post facto reviews by attorneys in the Judge Advocate General's office, Forrestal argued. Shortly after taking office, he urged the recruitment of attorneys well-versed in commercial law who would actively participate in contract negotiations. After a lengthy confrontation with the Judge Advocate General, who insisted that the new organization was superfluous and potentially illegal, Forrestal established the Procurement Legal Division, directly responsible to him, placed it under the management of Herman Hensel, an experienced Wall Street lawyer, and assigned a staff attorney to each bureau. In contract negotiations with suppliers, bureau officials were henceforth responsible for negotiating technical issues, and Procurement Legal Division attorneys handled legal aspects, which further simplified procurement.[60]

Interservice coordination proved more difficult. In autumn 1940, when builders already had their hands full with 177 cargo ships, the British Shipbuilding Mission to the United States ordered 60 *Ocean*-class merchantmen from American yards, followed shortly by the U.S. Maritime Commission, which placed contracts for 200 freighters. The Navy and the Army Air Forces, responding to Roosevelt's demand for sufficient production capacity for 50,000 military aircraft a year, issued large contracts with the leading airframe and engine builders in 1940. The same year, the Army Ordnance Department placed contracts for thousands of tanks and tens of thousands of trucks. As early as April 1941, defense-related orders totaled $49 billion, with another $7 billion in the pipeline as a result of congressional appropriations for Lend-Lease. Though there was still plenty of slack in the U.S. economy as a whole—unemployment remained high at 10 percent—the growing order backlog strained the engineering sector, where defense contractors competed with manufacturers of consumer durables for plant capacity, skilled labor, and materials. These developments prompted Roosevelt in early 1941 to replace the National Defense Advisory Commission (NDAC), his principal vehicle for economic mobilization since the fall of France, with the Office of Production Management (OPM), which was tasked with collecting procurement plans from the Navy and War Departments, establishing priorities, and coordinating contract placements. Chartered as an advisory body without executive authority, the OPM proved as ineffective as the NDAC and did little to rationalize production. Combined with the Navy's failure to produce reliable materials forecasts, interservice scheduling problems became rampant. Robert Nathan of the Bureau of Research and Statistics deemed the Navy's estimates "poor guesses," particularly the raw material schedule of the Bureau of Ships, which showed "a grouping of various materials on a time basis which appears to be entirely unreasonable."[61]

In the Navy Department, these developments facilitated the formation of the Office of Procurement & Material. The bureaus, called upon to deliver consolidated quantitative data detailing the state of the two-ocean navy program and future planning, proved unable to fill these requests as a result of inadequate data-collection systems and the extreme fragmentation of procurement along bureau lines. Forrestal noted in testimony before the House Committee on Appropriations that the bureaus were largely "autonomous in their relations to the whole procurement policy of the Navy ... [without] a clear definition of policy between them as to what items, for example, the Bureau of Supplies and Accounts should procure, and what the Bureau of Ships should procure."[62] Incompatible data-collection methods made it impossible to detect procurement overlaps and duplications, leading to waste of money and resources. Lack of reliable statistics also made it difficult to establish production priorities when bottlenecks emerged. In November 1941, for example, most defense contractors reported critical shortages of machine tools, prompting Forrestal to convene a meeting with bureau heads to identify programs that could be deferred. Each bureau chief promptly claimed, without a shred of evidence, that all programs under his cognizance deserved the highest priority rating. To avoid such deadlocks, develop proper statistics, and control procurement, Forrestal established the Office of Procurement & Material in January 1942. In one of his most astute personnel decisions, Knox reassigned Robinson from his post as Bureau of Ships chief to director of the Office of Procurement & Material and had him promoted to vice admiral. Outranking "all other Navy admirals in Washington save Admiral Ernest J. King, commander in chief of the United States fleet, and Admiral Harold R. Stark, Chief of Naval Operations ... the new Navy production chief rounds out the high command triumvirate King-Stark-Robinson," the *Washington Post* reported.[63] Behind closed doors, Robinson proceeded cautiously because the bureau chiefs "never had anybody between them and the [Navy] Secretary before and I knew they would not look with any favor" on the Office of Procurement & Material, he later recounted. "So I called them all together and told them that I was going to interfere just as little as possible with their actual bureau operations."[64]

The Office of Procurement & Material streamlined procurement coordination and planning without complete centralization. Its Planning & Statistics Branch developed uniform tabulation systems for all bureaus, enabling them to record, monitor, and cross-reference the progress of each contract. The bureaus forwarded their production data to Planning & Statistics for combination into the Monthly Status Report, which listed 6,800 controlling items such as hulls, machinery, and armor, which determined the production of bolts, wire, and other subordinate items. The branch sketched a timeline for the production of each controlling item twelve to eighteen months out in its Monthly Status Report, a critical tool to synchronize production sequences across bureau lines, which allowed for maximum plant utilization. The Bureau of Ships' hull construction statistics, for example, could be cross-referenced with valve data, permitting the scheduling of valve production and delivery at the shipyard when the hull had reached the necessary state of completion. This nascent "just-in-time" delivery system enabled the Office of Procurement & Material's Production Branch to keep the War Production Board (WPB) that replaced the OPM in January 1942 apprised of the Navy's future production needs. Liaison with the new civilian mobilization agency benefited from the appointment of Frank Folsom as assistant chief in charge of the Office of Procurement & Material's Procurement Branch while he still served as head of the Procurement Policy Division at the WPB. Working closely with the Procurement Legal Division and his WPB staff, Folsom revamped Navy contracting policy and procedures for negotiated contracts that became standard throughout the bureaus.[65]

Navy negotiators drove a hard bargain with contractors as the war progressed, partly in response to revelations that builders like Newport News had accumulated enormous profits on naval work prior to Pearl Harbor. An executive order issued by Roosevelt in April 1942 along with statutory regulations empowered the Navy and other procurement authorities to audit contractor records and establish price adjustment boards in order to renegotiate contracts. Armed with data collected from builders and the Office of Procurement & Material's Price Analysis Division, Navy officials took a close look at margins, costs, and executive salaries. Newport News deemed itself particularly unlucky because it delivered the battleship *Indiana* exactly two days after renegotiation regulations took effect, which meant that the contract fell under their provisions. Like many other contractors, Newport News promptly volunteered to return $40 million in profits on $272 million in contracts to the Navy to avoid a lengthy conflict with renegotiators. Navy officials also investigated New York Ship, whose profits on the battleship *South Dakota*, five *Cleveland*-class light cruisers, and the repair ship *Vulcan* came under scrutiny despite management protestations that margins on these contracts did not exceed 3 percent. In 1944, an Office of Procurement & Material negotiator convinced New York Ship to agree to a 4.6 percent price reduction on a $55.6 million contract for a pair of

Saipan-class light carriers, saving the government $2.6 million. These developments contributed to a decline in the Navy contract price index by 15 percent from October 1942 to October 1944, a period when the wholesale commodity price index rose by 5 percent. On the corporate side, the Navy's cost-saving measures contributed to a marked decline of margins at Newport News and New York Ship.[66]

Navy officials also flexed their muscle in their intragovernmental dealings with the War Production Board. Established in January 1942 as a senior civilian coordinating organization for industrial mobilization headed by Donald Nelson of Sears Roebuck, the WPB was tasked with the mobilization of the U.S. economy to meet strategic needs formulated by the Joint Chiefs of Staff. In practice, the Navy often challenged the board's resource allocations by taking its case directly to the White House, were it could expect a sympathetic hearing. When the WPB prioritized the production of aircraft and aluminum

Chart 3.1. Newport News Shipbuilding and New York Ship
Net Profits, 1940–1945

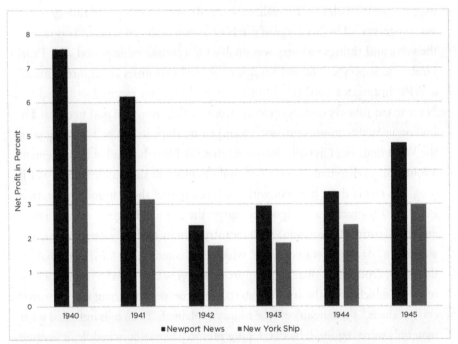

Newport News Shipbuilding and Dry Dock Company, "Financial Data 1955–1940," Annual Report 1955 (Newport News, VA: Newport News Shipbuilding and Dry Dock Company, 1955); New York Shipbuilding Corporation, Annual Reports 1940–1945 (Camden, NJ: New York Shipbuilding Corporation, 1940–1945).

and synthetic rubber at the expense of naval supplies in spring 1942, King told Roosevelt, "unless the whole priorities schedule is realigned to give assistance to those programs of greatest strategic urgency and importance, we shall continue to sacrifice the progress of naval shipbuilding in order to meet production schedules [for] tanks, planes, guns, etc., which are of no value [to] the present prospective fighting unless they can be shipped."[67] The president promptly ordered the WPB to revise its ratings in collaboration with the Navy, whose shipbuilding programs received higher priority. Nelson shortly agreed to leave contracting to the armed services without WPB oversight or input.[68]

Unencumbered by effective WPB control, the Navy, Army, Air Force, and the Maritime Commission contracted for far more material than could be delivered due to limited production capacity, aggravating interservice rivalries that were already evident before Pearl Harbor. The situation was particularly dire in machine tools, where endemic shortages made it difficult for shipyards and factories to retool their shop floors and meet production goals. Valve production for the Navy and the Air Force, for example, lagged due to the lack of machine tools until midwar, partly because "many government officials, including some in WPB, [failed to] realize the significance of valves and fittings in the war programs." The "shortage of machine tools was the most direct reason why the valve and fittings industry was unable for a considerable period after Pearl Harbor to supply valves and fittings in needed quantities at required times," a WPB historian recorded.[69] Insufficient steel supplies meanwhile forced the Navy to cut fifty-six destroyer escorts from its 1942 program and to cancel $30 million in facility improvements at four private shipyards. The following year, the WPB Statistics Division discovered that the Navy had failed to implement a Joint Chiefs directive to defer $700 million in naval shipbuilding. The WPB sought to tackle these problem with the formation of the Controlled Materials Plan (CMP), which was designed to square the production goals of the services and the Maritime Commission with industry's ability to supply steel, copper, and aluminum. At the Bureau of Ships, which implemented the CMP on behalf of the Navy, "controlled materials requirements were computed by using bills of material, which listed the critical materials and components going into approved end-products," the bureau's official history explained. "Such bills indicated what materials were required; by developing prototype erection schedule, it became possible to estimate when materials would be required for any specific end product." Estimates were submitted to the WPB, whose Requirements Committee "prepared estimates of total anticipated supply of each controlled material and determined on the basis of total supply and demand the allotment each claimant agency could have."[70] Upon receipt of allotments for a given project, the bureau revised its production plans and supplied contractors with the controlled materials. Fully implemented in July 1943, the CMP allotted to the Navy and the Maritime Commission almost a quarter of controlled steel, 18 percent of copper, and 8.4 percent of aluminum, with the remainders allocated to the Army and Air Force. In practice, however, the Navy and War Departments, the Maritime Commission, and other claimants manipulated the system by requesting more than what they forwarded to contractors, enabling them to hoard materials for emergency purposes.[71]

WARTIME SHIPBUILDING PROGRAMS

Wartime naval expansion bore the imprint of Admiral King, commander in chief of the U.S. Fleet in charge of naval operations in the Atlantic, Pacific, Asia, and coastal defense since December 1941. Succeeding Stark as chief of naval operations in March 1942, King also became senior military adviser to Navy Secretary Knox and served as a member of the Joint Chiefs of Staff. This unprecedented concentration of power was further enhanced by legislation passed in July 1942, which enabled King's staff in the chief of naval operations office to fine-tune naval expansion independent of congressional oversight. Moreover, King reduced the General Board's role in formulating shipbuilding policy, which also came under his purview. A former aviator and proponent of naval airpower since his prewar tenures as chief of the Bureau of Aeronautics and Commander Aircraft Battle Force, King sought additional carriers after Pearl Harbor at the expense of extant programs. In early 1942, he endorsed a Roosevelt plan to convert nine *Cleveland*-class light cruisers into *Independence*-class light carriers, followed in May by his directive to suspend construction of all five *Montana*-class battleships authorized under the two-ocean act in order to free up resources for the construction of additional carriers. An early believer in unrestricted submarine warfare who had unsuccessfully lobbied for a large submarine force to be included in the two-ocean navy act, he helped to convince Congress to authorize the Submarine Act of 1942, which vastly expanded submarine construction. King, who spent most of his time managing fleet operations in his capacity as commander in chief of the U.S. Fleet, left the implementation of these and other shipbuilding initiatives to Vice Adm. Frederick Horne, vice chief of naval operations.[72]

The development of adequate antisubmarine warfare (ASW) capabilities to deal with the German U-boat threat in the North Atlantic, the East Coast, and in the Gulf of Mexico remained a problem throughout King's early tenure. Britain had requested destroyer escorts to be built in American yards under Lend-Lease in August 1941, and Roosevelt quickly approved the construction of fifty units. Unfortunately, the U.S. Navy's Preliminary Design Section bickered over specifications for its own design until shortly before Pearl Harbor, leaving the United States without effective oceanic ASW capabilities when it entered the war. Instead of oceangoing destroyer escorts, the Navy had ordered 121 patrol craft that were laid down by boatyards, but few were in commission when the United States entered the war because their builders had never constructed anything according to Navy specifications. A proposal to build 250 American destroyer escorts finally received congressional authorization in January 1942, the exact time when German submarines commenced their assault on unprotected American coastal shipping during Operation Drumbeat. King, believing that "Inadequately escorted convoys are worse than none," initially refused to concentrate merchant ships into British-style convoys because the U.S. Atlantic Fleet lacked sufficient destroyers.[73]

The problem proliferated when the U.S. Maritime Commission's shipbuilding programs produced vast numbers of cargo ships, Navy Secretary Knox concluded in August 1942. "We are by no means producing enough escorts to provide sufficient convoys and it seems to me blind folly to ignore the implications of this policy. It does us little good to produce one hundred cargo ships a month if we do not produce enough escort vessels during that month to enable us to protect them when they go to sea."[74] Roosevelt, who grew increasingly frustrated with the slow progress of escort construction, told Knox, "I cannot for the life of me understand why the . . . Escort Vessels will not be delivered in volume for two years."[75] At end of 1942, he personally elevated the urgency rating of destroyer escort construction to the highest priority, causing operational mayhem in the naval shipbuilding industry. Robinson reported "almost continuous turmoil" and "great confusion" as a result of the change, and Forrestal complained about "a condition of production anarchy in plants, shipways [sic], etc."[76] Builders nevertheless managed to deliver 306 escorts in 1943, 46 more than planned. In May of that year, however, the German navy suspended submarine attacks in the North Atlantic, leaving little actual combat to be accomplished by most destroyer escorts built under the emergency program, which was cut at the end of 1943. *Buckley*-class destroyer escorts, which began to join the fleet in late 1943, performed transatlantic convoy duty, participated in the Normandy invasion, and served in the Pacific War; all told, they were responsible for sinking thirty-six German and eleven Japanese submarines.[77]

The wartime submarine program was widely considered a success. The 70 percent act of 1940 had authorized only forty-seven boats aggregating 91,000 tons, which were primarily designed to accompany the surface fleet but not to sink merchant ships. Though the United States had repeatedly denounced unrestricted submarine warfare during the interwar years, Stark and other senior officers tacitly (and perhaps illegally) endorsed the concept behind closed doors as early as November 1940, followed on December 7, 1941, by Stark's order to "execute against Japan," which signaled the beginning of submarine attacks on the Japanese merchant marine. This was easier said than done because the American submariners had not yet developed suitable tactics, were hampered by the defective Mark 14 torpedo, and lacked sufficient numbers. At King's urging, Congress passed the Submarine Act of May 1942, which authorized the construction of 200,000 tons. In 1943, the shipyards delivered fifty-six boats, followed by eighty in 1944, and thirty-two between January and August 1945. U.S. submarines sank 4.9 million gross tons of shipping, restricting Japan's ability to keep its home industries supplied with raw materials, especially crude oil from Borneo, from its far-flung maritime empire.[78]

King also pushed for the "Maximum Effort" initiative to square strategic needs with what remained of available shipbuilding capacity. Originally sketched by the Bureau of Ships on December 22, 1941, the scheme became the subject of heated controversy between the General Board, whose members sought continued battleship construction, King, who wanted more carriers, and Roosevelt, who agreed with King on carriers but also favored large numbers of small and medium-sized combatants. The matter was mostly settled in August 1942 when the president initialed plans to build additional *Essex*-class carriers and heavy and light cruisers, in addition to many smaller combatants. Roosevelt initially resisted King's efforts to include four 62,000-ton *Midway*-class carriers in the program, arguing that their construction would consume materiel and shipbuilding capacity that could be used more effectively to construct smaller carriers. Roosevelt predicted presciently "this war may well be over before the lapse of [the] three years" it would take to build these colossal ships.[79] Pressured by King, he later reluctantly approved the construction of three *Midways*, all of which were completed after the war (President Harry Truman, unaware of the controversy, had one of the carriers named *Franklin D. Roosevelt*). Few other heavy combatants ordered under the Maximum Effort Program were actually commissioned prior to VJ-day: three out of ten *Essex*-class carriers, five out of seventeen heavy cruisers, and three out of sixteen light cruisers.[80]

Roosevelt's eagerness to launch an invasion of France resulted in a landing ship program. The sheer magnitude of the scheme—Roosevelt wanted six hundred vessels to land mechanized forces in September 1942—exceeded the capacity of shipyards located on the East and West Coasts, prompting the Navy to construct new shipbuilding facilities in the Mississippi Valley. These herculean efforts notwithstanding, landing ship construction failed to provide sufficient capacity to ferry even two infantry divisions and two tank regiments across the English Channel, which contributed to the decision to postpone the invasion of France. On the other hand, 384 landing craft aggregating 58,000 tons commissioned into the U.S. Navy by the end of October 1942 sufficed for a more small-scale amphibious operation in French North Africa, which proceeded the following month, as well as amphibious operations in the Pacific. By 1944, the shipbuilders had delivered 1,088 landing ships in addition to 2,371 landing craft.[81]

British naval expansion of the global war period from December 1941 to August 1945 differed markedly from its American counterpart. Unlike the latter,

Table 3.5. Landing Ships and Landing Craft Built, July 1, 1940, to November 1, 1944

Landing Ship Dock (LSD)	15
Landing Ship Tank (LST)	823
Landing Ship Medium (LSM)	250
Landing Craft Infantry (LCI [L])	921
Landing Craft Support (LCS [L])	55
Landing Craft Tank (LCT)	1,395

Investigations of the Progress of the War Effort: Report of the House Committee on Naval Affairs, 78th Cong., 2nd Sess., 56 (1944)

which remained committed to the construction of all vessel types, British schemes focused more narrowly on light carriers, fleet destroyers, frigates, submarines, and landing craft. Constrained by the lack of shipbuilding capacity, labor, and materiel, the Future Building Committee undertook a wide-ranging reassessment of British shipbuilding in December 1942, which declared the battleship "an adjunct of the carrier," relegating it to a second-class status (no battleships were included in post-1941 shipbuilding programs).[82] Since cruisers "must be regarded as an ancillary to aircraft carriers and may sometimes be dispensed with," their construction was frequently placed on the back burner in favor of carriers.[83] A pair of 32,100-ton *Implacable*-class carriers were commissioned in 1944, but ambitious plans to build four each of the 47,000-ton *Audacious* and the 56,800-ton *Malta* classes had to be shelved (*Malta*s were canceled entirely and only two of the *Audacious*-class were completed after the war).[84] The 1942 and 1943 shipbuilding programs planned for thirteen *Colossus*-class light carriers (seven completed during the war) and four *Centaur*-class light carriers (all completed after the war). Fleet destroyers, primarily assigned to antiaircraft and antisubmarine protection of heavier fleet units and support for amphibious operations, were included in the 1942 and 1943 programs, which yielded fifty-three vessels of this type, plus another fifty-six under supplementary programs. By comparison, the U.S. Navy, which earmarked fleet destroyers for the same roles as the British but also deployed them in independent missions, commissioned 344 ships of this type from 1942 to 1945. Frigates and destroyer escorts remained essential to British commerce protection, as evidenced by the inclusion of 103 units in the 1942 and 1943 programs (many of these ships were built in Canada). Though they increasingly shared their missions with U.S.-built escort carriers, "There will always be a very large requirement for [antisubmarine] craft to deal with submarines," the Future Building Committee concluded.[85] Britain's submarine force, which had previously received little attention or funding, was slated to grow because "Submarines are the only craft which can operate in areas which our opponents can control by virtue of their shore-based aircraft and local surface craft."[86] Like many destroyers and frigates, most submarines planned for in the wartime shipbuilding programs were actually completed before the end of the war, partly because their construction consumed less time than that of carriers and cruisers. Many ships built from

1941 to 1944 joined the newly formed British Pacific Fleet, the most powerful formation assembled by the wartime Royal Navy, which did little fighting but impressed the Americans with its size, combat capabilities, and efficient organization.[87]

The Imperial Navy developed shipbuilding schemes in response to changing operational circumstances, but their implementation often bore little relation to the original plans. The Modified Circle Five Program, drafted in September 1942 after the battle of Midway had cost Japan four carriers, called for no fewer than fifteen 22,400-ton *Unryū*-class carriers and five 37,700-ton *Taihō*-class carriers, most of which were eventually canceled. American officials deemed Japan's wartime shipbuilding program "lopsided" because it "failed to achieve a balanced fleet. [Japan's] carrier forces have never been backed by a large group of fast modern battleships, and her light screening forces have become fewer and fewer."[88] The Modified Circle Five Program also included seventy-six destroyer escorts once it dawned on the Imperial Navy that increased convoy protection was necessary to counter submarine attacks. Those attacks had claimed more than half a million gross tons of shipping since the start of the war despite the torpedo problems that still bedeviled American submarines. Japanese submarine construction attracted attention and funding after some boats had achieved major successes in 1942, when they sank the carriers *Yorktown* and *Wasp*, prompting the inclusion of ninety-six large submarines in Circle Five. Designed to bolster the capability to torpedo enemy warships—Japanese submarines rarely attacked merchantmen—few of these boats were actually built and only one, *I-58*, scored a major hit when it sank the heavy cruiser *Indianapolis* after she had delivered uranium for the Hiroshima bomb to Tinian Island. The Wartime Naval Armaments Supplement Program of 1943 sought more submarines and escorts but dispensed with heavy surface combatants entirely, partly because shipyards were filled to capacity with tonnage from earlier programs and partly because Japan's labor and raw materials situation deteriorated sharply. After the onset of American strategic bombing of the home islands in November 1944, Japan launched a crash program to build midget submarines to repel a U.S. invasion of the home islands.[89]

German strategy and construction schemes of the 1942–45 period constituted the exact opposite of the U.S. Navy's approach. While the Americans sought a large variety of vessel types for a broad spectrum of combat missions, the Germans practically abandoned heavy combatant building (most of what remained of the surface fleet was redeployed to Norway to threaten Arctic convoys). The disastrous performance of the German navy at the Battle of the Barents Sea, where British destroyers chased away a pair of heavy cruisers in December 1942, prompted an irate Hitler to order all heavy warships scrapped. Although he reconsidered later, the Kriegsmarine henceforth relied almost exclusively on submarines. By January 1, 1942, shipbuilders had completed 249 boats out of 280 originally planned under a program begun two years earlier, a respectable achievement in light of the fact that army and air force projects received higher priority ratings for labor and material. Submarine construction proceeded apace in 1942 but failed to reach Admiral Dönitz's delivery benchmark of thirty boats a month. Though it became clear that the standard Type VII and Type IX boats were too slow, lacked underwater endurance, and evinced other shortcomings that rendered them vulnerable to innovative antisubmarine warfare tactics and technologies, planners failed to develop a realistic shipbuilding program that took account of the rapidly changing dynamics of the Battle of the Atlantic. Dönitz, who succeeded Raeder as navy commander in chief, finally suspended Atlantic operations in May 1943 after staggering submarine losses revealed the sheer extent of Anglo-American-Canadian superiority. Simultaneously, Dönitz, armaments minister Albert Speer, and their staffs developed the so-called Fleet Construction Program 43, which defined the parameters of German naval shipbuilding until the end of the war. Unlike its predecessors, Program 43 dispensed with all lofty planning for a postwar navy and instead focused on a new submarine type called the Type XXI that was better suited for oceanic submarine operations than its predecessors, supplemented by smaller submarines and a surface navy made up of attack craft. Approved by Hitler in June 1943, Program 43 set the stage for a vast submarine construction effort, which failed spectacularly in the closing years of the war (see chapter 5).[90]

CONCLUSION

From July 1940 to the end of the war, the size of the U.S. Navy more than tripled and the average time it took to build an aircraft carrier fell by half to reach less than sixteen months. These achievements were a "measure of good management and the strides made by the shipbuilding industry in production methods, but these could not have been achieved without superior administration of the programs by the Bureau of Ships," a postwar study concluded.[91] Critics of Navy procurement disagreed. In 1943, a congressional committee issued a searing indictment of the naval bureaucracy, disparaging "the growing number of questionnaires constantly emanating from Washington, harassing both workers and management and consuming much of their time. Many of these subjects are only remotely concerned with the construction of ships."[92]

Throughout the war, businessmen and their political allies were remarkably adept at portraying wartime procurement officials as paperwork-obsessed bureaucrats whose regulatory zeal stifled private initiative. To their critics, profit limitations and the establishment of powerful industrial mobilization agencies raised the specter of an intrusive state that was hell-bent on regulating private enterprise, not only for the duration of the war but afterward as well. In truth, the formation of organizations like the Bureau of Ships was a sensible response to internal problems in the Navy's procurement apparatus that resulted from insufficient design coordination between the Bureaus of Engineering and Construction & Repair. Moreover, the sheer scope, scale, and complexity of wartime naval expansion threatened to overwhelm the administrative capabilities of the bureau system, prompting the formation of the Office of Procurement & Material to coordinate bureau activities, institute procurement controls, renegotiate contracts to the benefit of taxpayers, and manage Navy relations with other mobilization agencies. Some of these reforms were clearly less effective than others, but the fact remains that they constituted organizational responses to real problems bedeviling Navy procurement, not a mindless expansion of government bureaucracies.

That said, the Navy's management of combatant construction was hardly beyond reproach. Most important, wartime naval construction produced a fleet that was out of sync with changing strategic realities. The two-ocean navy program of 1940, which was based on a worst-case scenario of the United States having to fight the Axis alone, remained in effect even though Britain survived the German onslaught and built a massive fleet, Japan suffered a series of devastating setbacks at Midway and Guadalcanal in 1942, and the Italian fleet surrendered in 1943. In light of these strategic developments, Roosevelt confidant James Byrnes, head of the Office of War Mobilization, demanded cutbacks, arguing that extant naval construction was "over-size and beyond our needs in the summer of 1943."[93] More fundamentally, "We must be sure that what we now are building in the shipyards is precisely what the military strategy of today—not yesterday—demands," Byrnes told the president. "The current ship program, adapted to dispose of the full fury of the submarine campaign in the Atlantic and of the entire Axis naval strength, including the Italian Navy and a large part of the French Navy, has been rendered partially obsolete by the tide of war."[94] King and his staff made token concessions, including cancellation of the *Montana* class and a reduction of destroyer escort construction, but otherwise insisted that most wartime programs for heavy combatants remain in place. In the case of *Midway*-class carriers, King even managed to persuade Roosevelt to approve their construction against his own better judgment. Heavy combatant building, in short, proved remarkably resilient to downsizing, in contrast to other programs that underwent drastic recalibration and cutbacks during the war.[95]

4

"We Can Build Anything"

Wartime Navy Yards

The implementation of wartime naval expansion fell heavily on navy yards, which launched only 14 percent of aggregate naval tonnage from 1940 to 1945 but were responsible for some of the most demanding projects in the industry. The three largest in Brooklyn, Philadelphia, and Norfolk were equipped to build battleships and carriers, while the Portsmouth Navy Yard in Maine specialized in submarines, the technical complexity of which rivaled that of larger combatants. Four smaller yards at Puget Sound, Washington; Mare Island, California; Charleston, South Carolina; and Boston were primarily responsible for destroyers. Lastly, the Navy's industrial shore establishments included four yards that did not perform new construction. At the Washington Navy Yard, the most important activity was ordnance production, while San Francisco, Long Beach, and Pearl Harbor specialized in the repair and maintenance of the Pacific Fleet. In 1944, these facilities were valued at $12 billion, comparable to the combined assets of General Motors, U.S. Steel, and American Telephone & Telegraph.[1]

A closer look at navy yard shipbuilding deepens our understanding of industrial mobilization in World War II. Many popular accounts place private enterprise at the core of narratives that emphasize entrepreneurial prowess, sometimes combined with a friendly nod at federal mobilization agencies, but more often with searing indictments of government inertia and red tape. More detached students of industrial mobilization have argued that the role of the state was confined to procurement, oversight, and resource allocation while production rested firmly in the hands of private industry, which supplied the armed forces with airframes, aircraft engines, tanks, trucks, and other military hardware. Economist Michael Carew's *Becoming the Arsenal: The American Industrial Mobilization for World War II* concludes, "The [U.S. Army's] Ordnance Department knew that it was not capable of providing the quantities of needed weapons, munitions, and supplies. Private industry would be producing 95 percent of the materiel. In like fashion the [U.S. Army] Air Corps knew it was dependent on the aircraft industry, and would need to provide that industrial sector with the means and coordination to vastly expand through 'mass production' the manufacture of the wide array of aircraft and support equipment needed for a modern air force."[2] What was true for the Army and the Air Force did not apply to the Navy, which looked back on a long tradition of building and repairing combatants in navy yards. More substantially upgraded between the wars than most private plants, shipyards owned and operated by the U.S. Navy constituted a valuable industrial resource equipped to build vastly complex weapons platforms. Rear Adm. Samuel Robinson exaggerated only slightly in 1940 when he told Congress, "We can build anything at navy yards."[3]

MANAGEMENT STRUCTURE

Navy yard shipbuilding was a decentralized endeavor under the loose oversight of the bureaus headquartered in Washington. The Bureau of Ships, which on paper exercised "management control over naval shipyards and certain other shore activities,"[4] concluded after the war that its role in "management and supervision of the work in the naval industrial establishments had been restricted, in spite of its predominant interest, and had been subject to qualifications and limitations growing out of the evolution of the field administrative organization of the Naval establishment as a whole."[5] Busy with facility development, contracting, design, and related matters, the bureau allowed local authorities to exercise wide latitude in yard organization. Navy yards shared many basic management structures, but "as a consequence of decentralized, independent organizational growth and the different responsibilities of the Navy Yards, many variations existed in particular yards," the Bureau of Ships admitted.[6] The Bureau of Yards & Docks, which under Navy regulations was charged with the "design, construction, alteration, and inspection of the public works and public utilities of the shore establishments of the Navy," maintained a greater degree of control of local navy yard affairs than the Bureau of Ships, as did the Bureau of Ordnance.[7]

Each yard was headed by a commandant, whose key aides included a captain of the yard responsible for military affairs, an industrial manager, and other functional department heads. Industrial departments, which employed 80 percent of the navy yard workforce, were usually separated into five divisions, with planning and production being the most important. The planning division, which worked in close coordination with the production division, developed timelines to schedule the delivery of subcontracted shipbuilding materials, hull erection, and the installation of machinery and ordnance. The design section of the planning division coordinated the yard's relations with outside design agents, developed blueprints for repairs and overhauls, and in some instances prepared detail designs for new construction. The core mission of the planning division was to issue job orders to the production division, which in turn consisted of shops (responsible for most mechanical work performed in production shops and foundries), hull (shell assembly), machinery (installation of turbines drives and diesel engines), and ordnance (production and installation of turrets and guns). Departments, divisions, and sections were headed by military officers with degrees in naval architecture or marine engineering who supervised civilian personnel.[8]

Though navy yard administrative structures looked coherent on paper, they contained defects that contributed to production problems. Investigations of personnel structures revealed that too many middle management positions were held by officers instead of by qualified civilians. This created problems early in the war, when the reassignment of seasoned production officers to sea duty and positions in Seabees mobile repair units deprived navy yards of some of their most experienced supervisors, who were often replaced with junior officers with little or no background in industrial management. The problem was particularly evident in the planning, personnel, and public works divisions, where almost a quarter of all officers could have been replaced with better-qualified civilians under more sensible regulations, a manpower review concluded. Personnel growth in middle management was substantial. At Boston, for example, the number of officers increased more than eightfold from 73 (1939) to 633 (1943).[9]

The Navy Department's failure to adjust its personnel policies to wartime conditions also contributed to insufficient managerial control by naval district

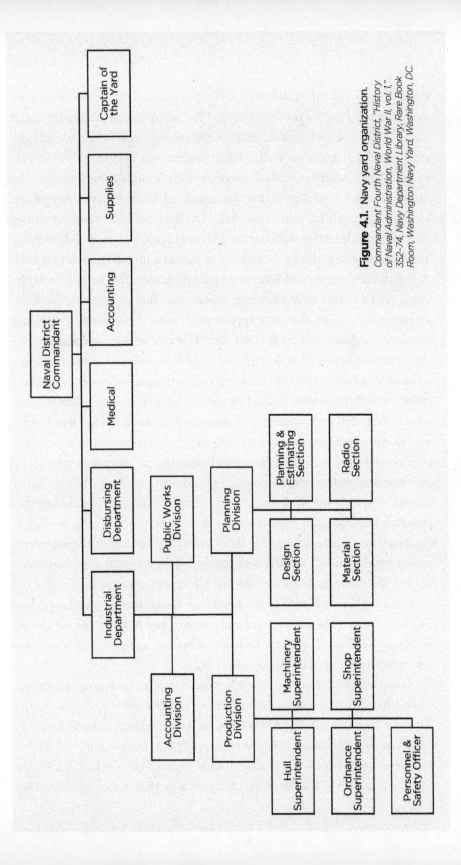

Figure 4.1. Navy yard organization.
Commandant Fourth Naval District, "History of Naval Administration, World War II, vol. 1," 352-74, Navy Department Library, Rare Book Room, Washington Navy Yard, Washington, DC.

commandants and their subordinates.[10] Commandants, flag officers who nominally headed a navy yard's military and industrial functions, usually lacked training in naval architecture, marine engineering, and industrial management. At Philadelphia, the commandant position was held from 1940 to 1942 by Rear Adm. Adolphus Watson, a veteran of the Spanish-American War who had previously served as peacetime commander of the destroyer scouting force. He was succeeded by Rear Adm. Milo Draemel, another former destroyer force commander. More frequent turnover was evident at the Brooklyn Navy Yard, which was headed by a succession of six rear admirals from 1940 to 1945. Active military service did little to prepare these men for the task of supervising yard activities in shipbuilding, repair, and other industrial areas. Navy investigators, worried that such appointments were detrimental to operating efficiency, concluded that the commandant "is not exercising, nor could he exercise, what we could call real management or supervision or control over the activities of the shipyard."[11] Shipbuilding, production planning, and repair operations in each yard were headed by an industrial manager, a nonseagoing officer designated for engineering duties only who was a trained naval architect but who often lacked "sufficient authority and responsibility to assure complete control over the yard." Managerial authority, in short, was wielded by commandants without engineering and management training while industrial managers well-versed in naval architecture and plant supervision lacked sufficient managerial clout, contributing to "a large number of faulty or illogical organizational arrangements [that have] grown up because of the absence of management control," investigators concluded. In a typical case, Brooklyn's head of the planning division developed a procurement function because the yard's supply department that was nominally responsible for purchasing had "not performed to the satisfaction . . . of this man, [so] he had to go out and set up his own activity. They were both operating, one alongside the other" in a system rubber-stamped by the commandant.[12]

Some industrial departments underwent disruptive management turnover while others profited from the long-term service of experienced officers who assured a degree of stability. At Boston, a succession of three industrial managers served between March 1942 and January 1943. At Portsmouth, by contrast, submarine construction was headed through most of the war by Capt. Henry Davis, a graduate of the Naval Academy class of 1908, who commenced his career at Brooklyn during the 1920s while working on his engineering degree in Columbia University's master's program. After serving as the Philadelphia Navy Yard's planning officer during the 1930s, Davis transferred to Portsmouth in June 1940, where he supervised that yard's construction program until 1944. Philadelphia's wartime industrial department was headed by Rear Admiral Chantry, a prominent naval architect (see chapter 2). Shortly after his arrival in Philadelphia in 1939, he appointed Capt. Theodore Schumacher, who had served under him in the Navy Department's Preliminary Design Section, as planning officer when Davis transferred to Portsmouth. Another graduate of the Naval Academy and the MIT naval architecture programs, Schumacher had taught at Annapolis during the 1920s and later supervised battleship modernizations at Boston. Following a stint in Washington, he served as naval constructor of the Battle Force and arrived at Philadelphia in 1939 to serve as design superintendent. Similarly experienced men headed industrial departments elsewhere, including industrial managers Sherman Kennedy in Brooklyn, Thomas Richey in Norfolk, and Albert Penn at Charleston.[13]

Production shops were managed by civilians who constituted the bulk of the navy yard supervisory force. Organized by trades such as pipefitting, electrical work, and so on, the shops were supervised by master mechanics who wielded considerable informal power on the shop floor. Lower-grade supervisors working under the shop master were Group IV(a) civil servants and included foremen responsible for planning shop work in accordance with production schedules and utilizing "to the best advantage of the machine facilities and skills peculiar to the various supervised workers," according to a job description. "The ability to train men for the departmental skilled jobs and supervisory jobs is essential."[14] His subordinates included quartermen, who ensured that "materials and tools are supplied to the workers as needed" and explained instructions to his subordinates. A quarterman had to be "completely familiar with the details and procedures of the trade or occupation supervised, be able to answer questions regarding practices and procedures, and be able to perform all phases of the work personally."[15] The leadingman worked directly below the quarterman and "closely supervises the workers in their assignments, correcting errors, answering questions, training the workers informally by oral instruction, often demonstrating procedures and practices by assisting in the work itself."[16]

Hierarchies were also evident among shop floor workers. Journeyman mechanics who had completed formal apprenticeships constituted Civil Service Group III employees, "skilled workers who perform independently and accept responsibility for the skilled tasks of a specific trade or occupation with but nominal supervision."[17] Job requirements were demanding. A coppersmith, for example, had to "know the procedures for developing and laying out copper forms and fittings of varying degrees of complexity," understand the "physical properties and characteristics of copper and copper alloys," be able to decipher motley blueprint symbols, and be thoroughly "familiar with ship piping systems and know shipboard locations." "The ability to judge visually bends in pipe for true radii is essential." The typical coppersmith worked "in a noisy shop in the fumes from welding, brazing, and heating operations, and in the heat from forges and heating torches; works on shipboard, usually in cramped and confined spaces."[18] A journeyman mechanic was usually assisted by a handyman classified as a Group III worker who could perform "one or more work phases of a trade, but who is not sufficiently experienced to perform all."[19] At the bottom of the shop hierarchy, helpers in Group II performed simple tasks like tack welding and chipping, followed by unskilled laborers in Group I who carried materials and tools.[20]

MANPOWER DEVELOPMENT

From 1939 to 1945, the navy yards employed on average 30 percent of the shipyard labor force. Growth rates in the private sector outpaced those of navy yards in 1942, when a large number of Maritime Commission shipyards became operational. Though private employers usually paid higher wages, workers often preferred navy yard jobs because they included benefits like pensions and annual vacations. Local labor market conditions were key determinants of navy yard manpower development. Charleston, "[l]ocated in a very thin labor market, . . . was always handicapped by the lack of experienced labor" along the South Carolina coast.[21] The Norfolk Navy Yard in Virginia's densely settled Hampton Roads area competed for shipyard labor with nearby Newport News Shipbuilding. A yard official reported in March 1943, "To fully utilize the facilities available in the navy yard requires 55,000 employees. We now have 47,000 and have remained practically static at this figure since last October."[22] Puget Sound was similarly handicapped by its close proximity to Todd-Seattle Dry Docks, Boeing, and other employers who sought skilled workers as much as the navy yard did.[23]

Chart 4.1. U.S. Shipyard Labor Force, 1939–1945

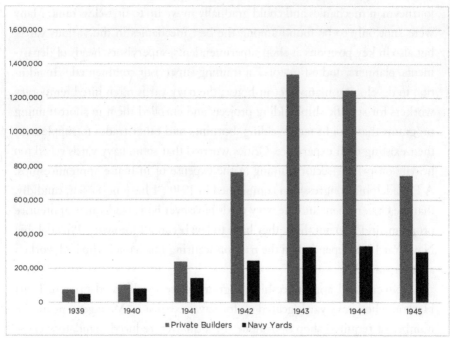

H. Gerrish Smith, "Shipyard Statistics," in The Shipbuilding Business of the United States of America, vol. 1, ed. F. G. Fassett Jr. (New York: Society of Naval Architects and Marine Engineers, 1948), 189.

During peacetime, aspiring journeyman mechanics underwent four years of craft training. To recruit apprentices, a navy yard's labor board notified the district manager of the U.S. Civil Service Commission. When Brooklyn advertised for apprentices in 1940, for example, more than 30,000 candidates applied for four hundred positions. Successful candidates, who were assigned to departments according to manpower needs, usually acquired craft training in "layout and fabrication work in the shops, field work in the dry dock, shipways and fitting-out piers, and supplementary training in the activities of related crafts."[24] Apprentices also spent six hours weekly in classrooms to learn trade theory, mechanical drawing, and blueprint reading, and occasionally attended special lectures by naval architects and marine engineers. Eighteen-year-old Howard Zinn (later a noted historian and activist) was hired as a shipfitter apprentice at Brooklyn, where he learned the trade in a "little team of the ship fitter, his apprentice—me—and then working with us and around us, a welder, a riveter, a burner, a chipper. I soon learned what all of these people did," he later recalled.[25] Upon receipt of their certificates of service, they worked as third-class journeyman mechanics and could gradually move up to first-class rank. Many were "not only to be found among the best mechanics in the various yards, but also in key positions as shop superintendents, supervisors, heads of departments, planners, and estimators," a training supervisor commented.[26] In addition to developing manpower in-house, the navy yards often hired temporary workers for specific shipbuilding projects and enrolled them in short training programs that taught tack welding, burning, and other trades to supplement their existing craft experience. Critics worried that some navy yards relied too heavily on private-sector training at the expense of in-house apprenticeships. A Philadelphia congressman complained in 1940, "I have never felt, candidly, that the Government and the navy yards have ever had an adequate apprentice program, and I do not think they have today; because I know the Philadelphia Navy Yard has depended, in the past, on securing mechanics who had worked at other yards."[27]

Conventional apprenticeship programs were recalibrated prior to Pearl Harbor, when navy yards geared up for naval expansion. Management cut the number of required shop floor hours by a quarter, reduced mandatory classroom time from six to four hours per week, eliminated the teaching of allied trade elements, and permitted full credit for overtime, all of which enabled apprentices to graduate after two years instead of the usual four. These efforts were sometimes derailed by the draft. At Philadelphia, "the apprenticeship system has been completely disrupted by the practice of drafting practically all apprentices following completion of their apprentice training," a manpower commission complained in 1944.[28] Portsmouth reported, "Just before the war the yard employed some 400 apprentices. The present number is about 80. Some 240 former apprentices are in the armed forces on military furlough."[29] Though Brooklyn experienced similar problems, its two-year apprenticeship program remained largely intact. "There are now 1,208 apprentices in training," the Industrial Survey Division noted in early 1945. "This is about four times the combined current total of Portsmouth, Boston, and Norfolk."[30]

In addition to revamping apprenticeships, navy yards adopted a variety of temporary manpower mobilization schemes. Shift and Sunday work were introduced wherever possible and daily work hours increased from eight to ten, even though the Industrial Survey Division concluded that "ten-hour shifts are considered too long and conducive to low production."[31] The quality of applicants dropped precipitously until March 1942, when the Navy Department instructed the U.S. Civil Service Commission to leave hiring to local yard labor boards for the duration of the war. Brooklyn's labor board instituted pre-employment tests, which required "the applicant to perform in a test-room or laboratory the types of duties he would perform in his trade in the shops," in contrast to the Civil Service Commission, which had declared applicants eligible for navy yard employment "solely on the basis of information they submitted on their application forms," a congressional investigation revealed.[32] Acceptance rates dropped precipitously as standards were raised. Brooklyn's labor board rejected 56 percent of more than 36,000 applicants for skilled occupations due to their failure to pass pre-employment tests from early 1942 to the end of 1944. Labor recruiters placed help-wanted advertisements in newspapers, reached out to high schools, and in one instance arranged for "a living display in a Norfolk store window where women employees of the navy yard demonstrated active production work."[33] Charleston recruited workers from as far away as Birmingham, Alabama, and Yazoo, Mississippi. "Ship fitters, ship carpenters, and machinists are hardest to secure," the U.S. Office of Education recorded. "Acute shortages are believed to exist in marine machinists, pipe fitters, and joiners."[34]

Many new hires enrolled in so-called helper-trainee programs designated for workers without formal apprenticeship training who had been employed for at least two years in any metal or woodworking trade or who had attended a vocational school. In Philadelphia's structural shop, for example, which experienced shortages of shipfitters as early as 1939, the helper-trainee program combined classroom instruction in blueprint reading and trade theory with practical shop floor training. Classroom and shop training was usually handled by quartermen, leadingmen, and journeyman mechanics who themselves attended short courses to learn instructional techniques. The quality of training programs varied by yard. At Brooklyn, "Training in all phases was found to be superior,"[35] according to the Industrial Survey Division, which recommended that Puget Sound introduce "the training procedures and pre-employment tests in effect at the Navy Yard New York."[36] Upon completion of several tests at the end of the five-month program, a helper trainee was hired as a third-rate journeyman mechanic. Helper-trainee programs produced the bulk of the navy yards' wartime workforce.[37]

Unskilled hires received instructions as "mechanic learners," a new employee category created during the war. Intended to replenish the ranks of handymen and helpers, many of whom had moved up into the ranks of third-rate journeyman mechanics, mechanic learner programs enrolled many female recruits. Philadelphia's 12,700 mechanic learners included more than 7,400 women, many of whom "were almost illiterate and had never worked under shop conditions before," according to the yard's official history (40 percent quit before their training was complete).[38] Some navy yards treated women better than others. Boston claimed to have made consistent efforts to assign female trainees "to the work that fits their individual physical and mental qualifications and in the few instances of misplacements women have been transferred to jobs more consistent with their ability to do that particular job."[39] At Norfolk the U.S. Civil Service Commission recorded, "women at present employed are trainees who work as 'on-the-job' helpers in the electrical shops for armature and coil winding; in the tool rooms; in the instrument shops as optical workers; in the paint shops; in the machine shops, where they operate lathes, drill presses, planers, and shapers; in the sheet-metal shops, where they make metal furniture; and in the welding shops. A few women are in training as plumbers."[40] While Charleston assigned most of its female hires to clerical jobs, Brooklyn's shipfitters' shop, reportedly "a bastion of masculinity if there ever was one," was portrayed as having to "take the brunt of [the] big feminine invasion" in August 1942. Five months later, the shop master promoted a mechanic learner to the position of leading woman.[41]

At its peak in 1944, Brooklyn employed more than 58,000 industrial workers, 6.8 percent of whom were women, in stark contrast to Kaiser's Portland Vancouver yard in Oregon, where women represented 30 percent of a workforce that was primarily engaged in Liberty ship construction, which did not involve the advanced shop floor skills common in naval work. At Brooklyn, women were usually relegated to unskilled jobs like tack welding after basic training in a fifty-hour course, but advanced welding instruction was largely limited to men. Women worked inside shops until June 1944, when some were admitted to the slipways, where four hundred women helped complete the carrier *Kearsarge*. Brooklyn's record contrasted with that of Philadelphia, where women represented a smaller percentage of the workforce than at any other navy yard and where supervisors "display little enthusiasm for upgrading women employees as incentive and morale booster," a manpower review commented.[42]

African Americans, who unlike women looked back on a tradition of industrial navy yard employment, often found themselves consigned to unskilled occupations. Before Pearl Harbor, blacks constituted 35 percent of Charleston's overall workforce. The Brooklyn Navy Yard was New York's largest industrial employer of African American labor in 1945, when more than 6,200 workers out of 50,000 were black. The "riveters and the chippers were usually blacks who were hired to do the toughest jobs in the Yard," Zinn recalled.[43] Though the borough of Brooklyn was considered New York's "capital of discrimination," even vocal critics conceded that navy yard hiring practices were compared favorably to private practices.[44] Discrimination remained evident in promotions, prompting some workers to file grievances with the Fair Employment Practices Commission established by Roosevelt in 1941 at the urging of civil rights leader A. Philip Randolph. Charleston outsourced craft instruction to all-white local high schools so that navy yard labor offices could cite blacks' lack of proper training as an excuse to exclude them from skilled trades in shops where "white workers would not work alongside black workers."[45] Informal discrimination was hardly unique to the Navy's southernmost shipyard. At Boston, race relations were "quite bad [and] there was a lot of resentment," according to a black worker who had been hired as a helper. Racism and craft conceit often intersected, he explained: "Many times when I went on board the ship I was asked to send the mechanic along because they didn't want to talk to a helper."[46]

Journeymen mechanics, still the backbone of navy yard workforces in most locales, were often reassigned from shops with light workloads to ones that experienced temporary labor shortages. In many trades, demand for labor oscillated during the shipbuilding process, with the mold loft shouldering a heavier-than-usual workload in the early stages, followed later by the structural shop and finally by the electrical shop, which handled a fair amount of finishing work. Overloaded shops borrowed workers from less busy ones, temporarily turning shipwrights into patternmakers, boilermakers into shipfitters, and machinists into pipefitters. Since welders were scarce in most shops, moreover, "considerable manpower [is saved] by providing mechanics of various trades with welding equipment and having them or their helpers do their own incidental tack welding," the Bureau of Ships reported.[47] In 1943, the bureau formally instructed the navy yards to enhance shop floor flexibility "through a less strict observation of trade jurisdiction customs and cognizance."[48] At Brooklyn, "Special effort is made by the borrowing shop to provide work for the borrowed units that is similar to their accustomed job to utilize them most effectively. One trade, in particular, the electrical, has received temporary assistance from outside ordnance machinists, outside machinists, plumbers, and pipefitters. The borrowed units were used to lay out, align and install cable racks, and equipment; pull in, shape and secure cable racks in racks; and stuff and pack tubes." By these means, the "Electrical Shop was able to realize a gain of 450,000 man hours from June to December 1944" alone.[49] Such transgressions across trade boundaries—usually anathema to skilled men and unions—were tolerated by navy yard workers eager for extra pay who felt reassured by management promises that the practice would cease after the war. At Philadelphia, where machinists sometimes worked as toolmakers and foundry helpers as furnacemen, workers often ignored "the strict line of trade jurisdiction and [strove] to complete any designated job within their respective shop," that yard's industrial department recorded.[50]

Brooklyn's experience illustrates some of the challenges involved in manpower development. A 1941 report revealed that yard productivity had fallen 40 percent since 1939 as the workforce had ballooned from fewer than 5,000 to 14,000. This was the result of "lack of co-ordination between crafts assigned to specific ships, poor planning of work resulting from the inexperience of the supervisors, thinly spread supervision, absence of work standards or task times, lack of understanding of yard systems, methods and routine of newly appointed supervisors, and a disposition of supervisors not to discipline employees even under circumstances warranting suspension or discharge," investigators summed up in their findings.[51] Insufficient coordination between shop trades was blamed on superintendents, who were "usually junior officers whose experience both in industry and at the Yard is limited," and on shop masters, whose responsibility was "limited to a specific job and does not extend to other jobs aboard the ship."[52] Shortages of experienced supervisors were evident in most trades, leaving many leadingmen responsible for more than one hundred shop floor workers. Supervisors were often unfamiliar with the yard's administrative systems. Workplace discipline suffered because supervisors "are willing to accept low standards for performance, attention to duty, and interest in work, and refrain from action in any but extreme cases, such as intoxication and gross insubordination."[53] Assistant Navy Secretary Ralph Bard distributed the Brooklyn report to all navy yard commandants along with instructions to read it carefully, "as these [conditions] are often common to all Yards in varying degree."[54]

Changes implemented during the war addressed some of the problems enumerated in the 1941 report. In January 1945, the Navy Department's Industrial Survey Division concluded that Brooklyn's industrial department "has been progressive and aggressive in adopting new and well conceived methods for conducting the work required of it," though not without adding that more "diligent follow through of these methods will result in greater efficiency."[55] Synchronization of crafts had improved, "but there is lacking that concentration of effort at the job on board ship to coordinate trades and to arrange the sequence of operations which is so important to obtain maximum utilization of manpower and the reduction of unnecessary stand-by time."[56] Officer-rank supervisors received far better training than they had in 1941. "The preliminary training of Ship Superintendents at New York is exceptionally well organized, and they are well indoctrinated as to the technical requirements of ship work in their jurisdiction."[57] The same was true for shop supervisors, who were hired and trained in large numbers during the war, with each leadingman now usually responsible for only a dozen workers. Familiarity with the chain of command and the yard's administrative structures remained spotty partly because the Industrial Department's organization manual had not been updated since 1939 and "is in conflict with the new navy yard regulations."[58] Worker discipline had received close attention in September 1944 with the introduction of a new shop rule system, which "appears to be working well although it is too early to judge its results."[59] New guidelines introduced strict penalties for infractions of discipline, prompting complaints that "penalties for minor offenses were excessively severe" (in March 1945 alone, the production division brought more than 3,500 charges, 80 percent of which were sustained).[60] The Navy Department's grievance procedure was so complicated that "few, if any, employees other than trained union stewards or supervisors understand its working. . . . The opinion is common among employees that nothing can be accomplished by resort to the procedure," which was likely the exact outcome desired by management.[61]

Organized labor played only a marginal role in navy yards. Unions affiliated with the American Federation of Labor's (AFL) Metal Trades Department and the Congress of Industrial Organization's (CIO) Industrial Union of Marine and Shipbuilding Workers of America (IUMSWA) maintained locals at most navy yards, but none received official recognition as collective bargaining agents. The Navy Department invited national union delegates to a labor relations conference in 1942 only as "guests and observers."[62] At Brooklyn, unofficial meetings "are held by the shop superintendent with a committee of the AFL, and occasionally with the CIO—the AFL through the Metal Trades Council claims membership of 60 per cent of mechanics in practically all shops and the CIO, 38 per cent," an investigation reported.[63] Industrial managers occasionally responded to union complaints, as Chantry did at Philadelphia when the IUMSWA Local 101 asked for faster distribution of paychecks. Officially, industrial relations were the provenance of shop committees elected by employees in each shop. These members discussed with management "questions pertaining to work, to make and receive suggestions for the improvement of physical working conditions; to promote mutual cooperation, understanding and confidence," according to a Navy Department policy instituted during the New Deal.[64] Denounced as company unions by organized labor, shop committees held regular meetings with a yard's commandant and his representatives but were barred from intervening into disciplinary actions. At Boston, the commandant stressed that "it is clearly understood that the operation of such committees will in no way interfere with the prerogatives and responsibilities of Management."[65]

PHYSICAL PLANTS AND FACILITY IMPROVEMENTS

Navy yards differed widely in terms of production facilities, the size and structure of which reflected local geography and industrial infrastructure. Charleston, situated in a small city of the same name in South Carolina, occupied 710 acres but was notorious for "an inefficient lay-out of plant and shallow-water harbor facilities which would admit no vessel larger than a 14,000-ton cruiser," a congressional investigation recorded.[66] The yard "has also been handicapped in obtaining materials and equipment due to its remoteness from large industrial areas," the Industrial Survey Division added.[67] Brooklyn, by contrast, operated in the nation's most densely settled metropolis in close proximity to

New York City's largest factories and port facilities, where the lack of inexpensive real estate resulted in overcrowding. Located on a 195-acre property that had been cobbled together haphazardly over more than century, the yard enjoyed access to the deep East River but lacked "adequate rail transportation facilities serving the yard," investigators recorded.[68] Wartime facility improvements frequently required demolition of older structures and erection of multistory production shops that had layouts less suitable for throughput than that of single-story buildings. The Philadelphia Navy Yard, which had been relocated from the crowded downtown waterfront to a 973-acre tract of land south of the city in the late nineteenth century, featured large empty lots that were suitable for wartime additions without large-scale demolitions. More problematically, Philadelphia's slipways were located perpendicular to a Delaware River section that was only 2,700 feet wide, leaving a perilously short launch path (when the battleship *New Jersey* was launched on December 7, 1942, her stern slammed into the shoals of her namesake state).[69]

Major plant improvements began as early as 1938 and continued until the end of the war at an aggregate cost of $590 million. Early projects equipped Brooklyn, Philadelphia, and Norfolk for battleship building while projects begun in 1940 and after added facilities at most yards for the construction and repair of a larger variety of vessel types. Few new slipways were added, but existing ones were fitted with new cranes, improved foundations, and welding facilities. Superdocks of 1,092 feet for construction of *Montana*-class battleships were dug out at Brooklyn, Philadelphia, and Norfolk. At Portsmouth, Boston, Charleston, Puget Sound, and Mare Island, smaller building docks were dug out and slipways constructed to accommodate destroyers, submarines, and landing ships. New warehouses and storage yards to stockpile material figured prominently in all wartime navy yards. In addition to building ships, they undertook a wide variety of related activities to enhance wartime improvements. Ship maintenance, overhauls, conversions, and repairs often required piers and graving docks that were added at all navy yards. More specialized activities that received upgrades included Boston's anchor chain forge, Philadelphia's Naval Boiler Laboratory, and materials testing laboratories at Philadelphia, Brooklyn, Norfolk, Boston, and Mare Island.[70]

A closer look at facility development at Brooklyn reveals the scale of yard improvements. During the 1930s, the yard's main shipbuilding and repair facilities included two old slipways, a structural shop, and four drydocks that dated

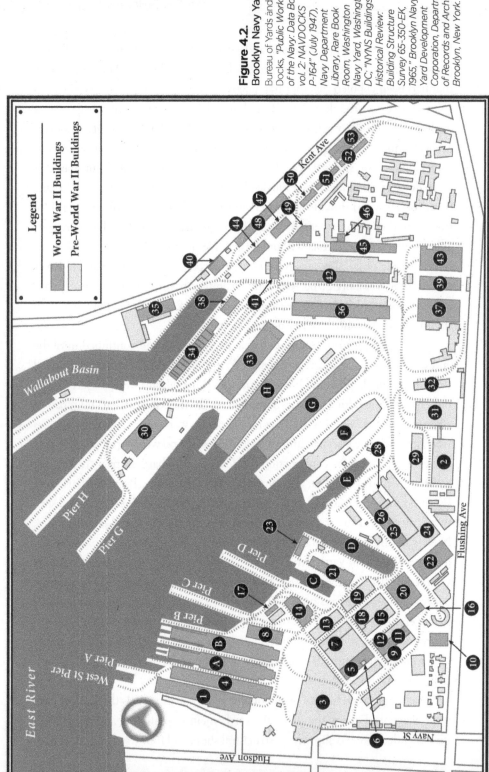

Figure 4.2.
Brooklyn Navy Yard.
Bureau of Yards and Docks, "Public Works of the Navy: Data Book. vol. 2: NAVDOCKS P-164" (July 1947), Navy Department Library, Rare Book Room, Washington Navy Yard, Washington, DC; "NYNS Buildings Historical Review: Building Structure Survey 65-350-EK, 1965," Brooklyn Navy Yard Development Corporation, Department of Records and Archives, Brooklyn, New York.

Letter	Slipways and Dry Docks	Year Built	Cost in Current Dollars
A	Building Ways No. 2	1940	2,000,000
B	Building Ways No. 1	1940	1,500,000
C	Dry Dock 1	1851	2,146,255
D	Dry Dock 4	1913	2,745,454
E	Dry Dock 2	1890	595,000
F	Dry Dock 3	1897	554,707
G	Dry Dock 5	1942	13,375,000
H	Dry Dock 6	1942	13,375,000

Number	Buildings	Year Built	Cost in Current Dollars
1	Mold loft, turret, and erection shop	1940	2,032,240
2	Supply storehouse, administration, radio and radar lab	1918	2,039,120
3	Structural shop, mold loft, and shipfitters shop	1919	3,052,552
4	Steel storage	1941	170,000
5	Pipe and copper shop	1940	430,220
6	Pipe and copper shop	1936	14,790
7	Smithery	1873	167,753
8	Subassembly shop No. 1	1942	350,000
9	Ordnance storage and sail loft	1903	159,605
10	Building trades building	1942	475,000
11	Sail and flag loft and sheet metal shop	1940	243,283
12	Ordnance storage and sail loft	1903	159,605
13	Storage	1873	195,000
14	Subassembly shop No. 2	1942	222,500
15	Pipe shop	1901	97,600
16	Locomotive house	1905 and 1945	53,628
17	Ship superintendent's building	1942	140,087
18	Electric shop	1903	16,127
19	Outside machine shop	1865	90,900
20	Central power plant	1941	2,895,700
21	Sheet metal storage	1899 and 1944	806,579
22	Ordnance machine shop, optical shop and school	1943	3,339,233
23	Turret weldment shop	1941	346,687
24	Machine and tool shop	1904	257,835
25	Machine and boiler shop	1899 and 1942	452,769
26	Machine and boiler shop	1899 and 1942	452,769
27	Supply storehouse, administration, radio and radar lab	1918	2,039,120
28	Central tool shop	1900	28,429
29	Machine shop and training school	1920	944,730
30	Production and utility building	1944	2,249,000
31	Administration office	1942	5,309,548
32	Ordnance salvage and electrical equipment shop	1899	69,100
33	Deck assembly yard	1944	2,249,000
34	Coaling plant	1942	460,500
35	Saw mill and boat shop	1942	2,280,000
36	Subassembly Shop	1944	4,790,000
37	Transportation building	1944	210,000
38	Incinerator	1942	514,800
39	Material testing laboratory	1942	3,020,000
40	Sales building	1942	212,000
41	Compressor plant	1944	545,000
42	Welding and fabricating shop	1942	2,474,496
43	Foundry	1942	1,603,000
44	Compressed gas storage	1942	115,700
45	Heavy material storehouse	1942	267,815
46	Blacksmith shop	1942	26,000
47	Paint and oil storage	1942	583,000
48	Scrap metal plant	1944	412,750
49	Metal storage	1940	58,245
50	Cement and gas storage	1942	25,000
51	Lumber storage	1941	21,000
52	Lumber storage	1941	24,000
53	Lumber storage	1942	420,000

to a period when capital ships were significantly shorter and lighter than subsequent ones. Building Ways No. 1 had to be lengthened to fit the 714-foot hull
of the battleship *North Carolina*. Her outfitting required a thirty-two-foot extension of Dry Dock No. 4, in addition to new concrete foundations to support
the 45,500-ton ship. In the structural shop, production of *North Carolina*'s prefabricated sections "requires specialized heavy tools for cutting, shaping, and
drilling and suitable crane services for handling the heavy pieces. This activity
requires considerable floor space and for efficient results should occupy a section of the shop removed from the interference of other activities and particularly from the glare of welding arcs," Rear Adm. Ben Moreell of the Bureau
of Yards & Docks explained.[71] This necessitated the construction of two new
production bays in the structural shop that together with the necessary cranes,
welding equipment, and railroad tracks cost $1.4 million. *North Carolina*'s
main gunhouses were crafted in the new $2 million turret shop that included
a mold loft and welding facilities. To the east of the turret shop, Building Ways
No. 2 underwent substantial reconstruction in 1939, when Brooklyn received
orders to build the battleship *Iowa*. To accommodate her 888-foot hull, the slipway had to be lengthened 200 feet on the land side and 100 feet into the East
River, where six thousand piles were driven into the riverbed to support the
extension. Supervised by a Bureau of Yards & Docks officer, the $2 million job
was performed by one thousand workers under the Works Progress Administration, which also provided funding for the project. After launching, *Iowa*
and later her sister ship *Missouri* were towed to pier 4 (ordnance pier), where the
main turrets were placed onto their foundations by a new hammerhead crane
featuring a lifting capacity of 350 tons that was modeled after similar structures
at Philadelphia and Norfolk.[72]

From 1941 to 1945, Brooklyn received another $71 million in plant improve-
ments, more than six times as much as had been invested during the interwar
years. The "most congested yard we have" where materials were "scattered all
over the place," Brooklyn added more than 1.5 million square feet of storage
space, most of it in multistory buildings.[73] A $5.3 million, sixteen-story build-
ing completed in 1942 housed the commandant's office, the design division, the
Office of Naval Intelligence, and vast amounts of storage space. The Material
Testing Laboratory moved into a seven-story building erected in 1942 at a cost
of $3 million. On the shipbuilding side, a new foundry featuring three produc-
tion bays was added in 1942 for $1.6 million. Other big-ticket items included

a pair of 1,092-foot superdocks completed in 1942 to accommodate 63,000-ton *Montana*-class battleships, the hulls of which were too heavy for conventional slipway launches. Though *Montanas* were never built, Brooklyn put one of the new docks to use to construct the 62,000-ton *Midway*-class carrier *Franklin D. Roosevelt*. Other plant additions included a new ordnance machine shop, a subassembly shop, and a welding and fabrication shop, all of which produced ordnance and preassemblies for *Iowa*-class battleships and carriers. Brooklyn's crowded conditions forced facility planners to develop satellite facilities, including a shipfitters shop and a welding school in Queens, New York.[74]

WARTIME WORKLOADS

Some navy yards were responsible for a broad variety of activities while others were more narrowly focused. In addition to building ships, many were responsible for repairs, overhauls, conversion of merchantmen for combat duty, and commissioning of warships built at private yards. Most East Coast navy yards concentrated on new construction, in contrast to West Coast yards, where repairs and overhauls of Pacific Fleet units took precedence over shipbuilding.

Philadelphia produced the largest amount of tonnage and handled the broadest variety of projects among the navy yards. Industrial manager Chantry commented in 1944, "I have served in many Yards most of my life, and have been in a great many private yards in a supervisory capacity, and in no Yard, public or private, have I ever encountered the diversity of work that occurs in this Yard."[75] In addition to building ships, Philadelphia recommissioned mothballed destroyers and submarines, converted merchantmen for naval service, and repaired and overhauled American, British, French, Dutch, Canadian, and Norwegian ships, some of which were built according to the metric system and required appropriate tools (notable repairs included the battleships *Resolution*, *Nelson*, and *Royal Sovereign* and the carrier *Furious* of the Royal Navy). Additionally, the navy yard was responsible for "completing, outfitting, and commissioning and making ready for sea of all vessels built privately anywhere on the Delaware River," the nation's most densely packed shipbuilding region.[76] Other activities under the cognizance of Philadelphia's commandant included the Naval Boiler Laboratory, the Naval Aircraft Factory, and the Propeller Foundry.[77]

Table 4.1. Navy Yard Construction, 1940–1945

Navy Yard	Displacement Tons
Philadelphia	274,453
Brooklyn	238,231
Boston	201,526
Norfolk	170,214
Portsmouth	160,350
Charleston	138,138
Mare Island	88,656
Puget Sound	32,216

Calculated from *Dictionary of American Naval Fighting Ships*, ed. James L. Mooney, 7 vols. (Washington, DC: Navy Department, 1959–1981)

New construction at Philadelphia initially focused on battleships, but changes in the navy's wartime shipbuilding priorities moved other activities to the fore. Prior to Pearl Harbor, the yard received orders for the *Iowa*-class battleships *New Jersey*, *Wisconsin*, and *Illinois*, but only the first two were actually completed and the last was broken up after the war 22 percent complete. In September 1940, Philadelphia also received orders to build the lead ship of the *Montana* class and its sister *Ohio*. Both were scheduled to be laid down in the yard's two new superdocks, but the Bureau of Ships suspended *Montana* construction prior to keel laying in 1942. One of the 1,092-foot superdocks originally scheduled for the *Montana* class was repurposed for six tightly sequenced projects. A batch of destroyer escorts were laid down on February 12, 1942, and floated out on July 24, 1942, followed by two batches of landing craft each in August and November 1942, respectively. After six destroyer escorts had been laid down in February 1942 and floated out in May, the superdock received the keels of two *Baltimore*-class heavy cruisers, which were towed out on August 20, 1944. Two weeks later, shipfitters laid the keel of the *Essex*-class carrier *Valley Forge*. In March 1943, the other superdock received the keel of the *Essex*-class carrier *Antietam*, which was followed in December 1944 by a pair of *Oregon*-class heavy cruisers (both of which were later cancelled and scrapped in dock).[78]

Brooklyn was responsible for a narrower range of new builds than Philadelphia, partly because it handled a heavy repair load of more than five thousand ships over the course of the war. One of Brooklyn's two superdocks, initially earmarked for new construction, was converted into a repair facility to supplement the yard's four smaller drydocks. Some of the more difficult repair jobs involved the destroyer escort *Menges*, whose aft section had been blown off by a torpedo and was replaced by the stern of her sister ship *Holder*, which had lost her forward section. Since the sheer amount of repair work arriving in the New York port overtaxed repair capabilities at the shipyard itself, the Bureau of Yards & Docks ordered the construction of a satellite facility in Bayonne, New Jersey, with a 1,092-foot dock, piers, workshops, and heavy cranes. In 1944, Bayonne received the burned-out hull of the former French passenger liner *Normandie*, which was scheduled for conversion into the troop carrier *Lafayette*, but the ship proved beyond repair and had to be scrapped. The navy yard's administrative responsibilities included coordination of landing ship transfers from inland yards to Britain, supervision of diesel engine parts production for submarines, and management of a fleet supply base, as well as inspection of repair work performed at the Todd shipyards in Brooklyn and Hoboken, New Jersey, the Bethlehem Steel yard in Weehawken, New Jersey, Brewer Dry Dock in Staten Island, the Atlantic Basin Iron Works in Brooklyn, and other repair yards in the New York area. The yard's industrial department handled the construction of four carriers, eight tank landing craft, and two *Iowa*-class battleships. Subcontracting figured prominently, according to the War Production Board, which reported that six hundred small plants "became adjuncts to the Navy Yard in the shipbuilding and ship repair programs."[79]

Boston's 843-acre navy yard was nominally three times Brooklyn's size, but the main facilities featured only a pair of graving docks and two medium-sized slipways, which accommodated nothing larger than destroyers. Repairs and overhauls were performed offsite at the South Boston Annex, which included the 1,158-foot Naval Dry Dock of World War I vintage and a 687-foot graving dock together with workshops for electrical work and pipefitting added in World War II at a cost of $26 million. In addition to twenty battleship repairs, the South Boston Annex performed twenty-three carrier overhauls and sixty-three cruiser repairs from 1941 to 1945. Repairs of British and French vessels included the battleships *Rodney* and *Richelieu* and the troop transports *Aquitania* and *Queen Mary*. Destroyers, destroyer escorts, patrol vessels, and other smaller combatants received overhauls at the Chelsea Annex, which featured a pair of new marine railways, wharves, and workshops. The navy yard itself outfitted 1,108 combatants built in the vicinity, for example the battleship *Massachusetts* and a pair of *Atlanta*-class cruisers constructed by Fore River.[80]

New construction at the Boston Navy Yard produced mostly destroyers, destroyer escorts, and landing craft. Recognized for its long-standing expertise in destroyer work, the yard received orders for eleven of the *Fletcher* class under the two-ocean navy program, later supplemented by another five of the same type. There were 175 *Fletcher*s built in ten shipyards, some of which operated half a dozen slipways (see chapter 5). At Boston, which lacked such extensive shipbuilding capacity, they were usually laid down in pairs on two slipways. The same slipways plus Dry Dock No. 5 accommodated destroyer escorts of the *Evarts* and *Buckley* classes, fifty-nine of which were delivered by Boston over the course of the war. Worker recruitment and training initially presented few problems, but the Selective Service Administration's abolishment of key deferment categories in 1942 resulted in a sudden drain of trainees as "word traveled through the yard that after the war, veterans would be allowed tremendous advantages [so that] many employees resigned to join the armed services," the yard's official history noted. Draft officials "were largely unfamiliar with quantity production plants such as Navy Yards and had only a partial conception of the problems of a new construction and repair shipyard where employees are required to be shifted from one job to another and be familiar with a comparatively wide variety of work." The loss of more than 7,000 men to military leave and another 5,800 to enlistments resulted in manpower problems that were "never entirely solved by the administrators of the Boston Navy Yard."[81]

Norfolk, better equipped with large-scale shipbuilding facilities than Boston, undertook a broader variety of projects. Originally featuring six older drydocks that served as repair facilities during the war, it added a 1,092-foot superdock modeled after similar structures at Philadelphia and Brooklyn but "was built deeper, for use in repairing and as well as building capital ships," the Bureau of Yards & Docks reported.[82] The 910-foot Building Ways No. 1 of World War I vintage received upgrades to accommodate the *South Dakota*–class battleship *Alabama* laid down in February 1940, whose three sister ships were constructed in private yards. Unlike the latter, Norfolk handled numerous other projects the completion of which frequently interfered with *Alabama*'s construction, according to the Bureau of Ships, which noted, "The rapidly increasing and violently fluctuating repair and conversion work load carried by Norfolk Navy Yard required diversion of workers from U.S.S. *Alabama* at some times and uneconomical crowding of workers at others." Moreover, "The large program of training new workers, particularly during the last year of building the U.S.S. *Alabama* [1942] when as many as 10,000 men were under training, figured heavily in the way of increasing man-hours."[83] Launching *Alabama* required time-consuming preparations because Building Ways No. 1, like its counterparts in Philadelphia, was inconveniently located on a narrow river section. As a result of these and other factors, Norfolk completed the battleship in August 1942, five months after nearby Newport News Shipbuilding had already delivered its sister ship *Indiana*. Building Ways No. 1 subsequently received the keel of the *Iowa*-class battleship *Kentucky*, which was laid down in March 1942, but her construction was suspended and the incomplete bottom structure had to be launched three months later to make room for twenty tank landing craft. Once the latter had been completed, construction of the *Essex*-class carrier *Shangri La* commenced on Building Ways No. 1 in January 1943, followed by her sister ship *Tarawa* fourteen months later. *Lake Champlain*, another carrier of the *Essex* class, was laid down in Norfolk's new superdock in March 1943. The smaller 375-foot Building Ways No. 2 was reserved for the construction of two *Gleaves*-class destroyers, ten *Buckley*-class destroyer escorts, and three *Raven*-class minesweepers, all of which were commissioned before the end of the war. From 1941 to 1945, Norfolk completed 173,000 tons of naval combatants.[84]

Portsmouth's wartime workload was in some respects unique because the yard specialized in submarines and performed little repair work that could have interfered with new construction. From summer 1940 to the end of the war, it laid down seventy-six submarines of the *Gato*, *Balao*, and *Tench* classes, whose submerged displacement exceeded 2,400 tons each (making them significantly larger than Germany's standard Mark VII submarine that displaced only 871 tons submerged). Their construction was one of the most challenging tasks in naval shipbuilding, professor of naval architecture Henry Rossell commented. "When it is considered that more than 250 miles of cable and electric wire have to be accurately threaded into this tiny hull, a faint idea may

Stern view of *South Dakota*-class battleship *Alabama* outfitting at Norfolk Navy Yard, July 3, 1942. *Photo BB 60 A/1, Box 205, RG 19, Entry LCM Construction and Launching of Ships, 1930-1955, BB-58 through BB-60, National Archives and Records Administration, College Park, MD*

be had of the intricacy of submarine construction."[85] Though the three submarine classes built at Portsmouth were similar in terms of hull size, standardization of construction proved difficult as a result of "constant design changes, additions of equipment and accomplishment of alterations," the yard's official history explained.

> Included in these changes were: the increase of hull strength, or maximum depth for submergence; addition of several types of radar; a change to direct drive with slow speed motors instead of noise-producing reduction gears; addition of considerable sonar equipment; equipment capable of withstanding the shock of depth charge; sound isolation

methods, to minimize the noise transmitted through the hull by auxiliary machinery and electrical units; and many others. This Yard has been the main design headquarters for submarines and the ships mentioned above were designed and developed at Portsmouth; thus alterations were accomplished on these ships far in advance of other submarine building activities.[86]

At the Charleston Navy Yard in South Carolina, production facilities clustered in two separate areas. "One new building ways [sic] was constructed alongside the other building ways at the northern extremity of the Yard," the Industrial Survey Division recorded. "The southerly extension consists of two building docks and shop buildings, mostly of temporary construction.... Thus the two construction activities are widely separated (1½ miles)."[87] While the so-called North Yard, which made up the original plant, laid down fourteen fleet destroyers of the *Gleaves* and *Fletcher* classes from 1940 to 1943, the South Yard built 17 *Buckley*-class destroyer escorts, 119 medium-sized LSM landing craft, and 8 larger LST tank landing ships. Shop performance differed widely. While the boiler shop master and his supervisors "maintain close surveillance on costs and on individual production," the electrical shop suffered from ineffective worker training and supervision.[88] "Urgent electrical jobs on board ships were overloaded with too many people doing too little work."[89] Low productivity was also evident in the pipe shop, where supervisors were committed to old-fashioned production methods. "Key shop personnel should be sent to visit outside yards, especially to see the pipe bending methods at New York, pipe covering at Norfolk, and modern methods for making pipe hangers at both of these yards," investigators recommended.[90] Material handling was often substandard. "Manufactured items and equipment ready for installation aboard ship were noted frequently to be carelessly dumped on pier areas and not well protected from the weather."[91] Investigators attributed some of these problems to the "character of employees obtainable in the labor markets available to the area, and the high turnover, partly due to a lack of satisfactory housing and transportation, which adversely affect men of better caliber."[92]

On the West Coast, the Mare Island Navy Yard near Vallejo, California, was primarily responsible for repairs of medium-sized combatants of the Pacific Fleet, as well as construction of destroyers, destroyer escorts, submarines, and tank landing craft. During the war, it added a fourth drydock and raised the number of slipways from two to eight. Pearl Harbor casualties that received extensive refits included the light cruiser *Helena* and the destroyers *Cassin* and *Downes*, followed in late 1942 by the heavy cruisers *San Francisco* and *Chicago*, both of which had sustained extensive damage at Guadalcanal. Having completed thirty-nine destroyer escorts in 1942–1943, Mare Island received orders for eighty-eight tank landing craft, 156-ton vessels that were assembled from sections produced under a farming-out scheme. This involved the division of the landing craft hull into fifteen sections to be constructed by eight fabricating shops in Denver, Colorado. Steel was procured from midwestern mills by Weicker Storage of Denver and distributed to the fabricating plants. Section size was limited to seventeen feet in height, ten feet in width, and fifty feet in length so each could fit onto railroad cars that had to pass through tunnels and across bridges on the 1,200-mile trip from Denver to Mare Island. Here, "all we do is weld the sections together and install machinery and equipment," a production supervisor reported. The sections "do fit and we have not had a bit of trouble" assembling them, he stressed.[93]

Puget Sound, near Bremerton, Washington, was even busier than Mare Island with Pacific Fleet repairs and rarely performed new construction. Shipbuilding "has always been a fill-in to keep the industrial manpower occupied as the load of battle damage repair would rise and fall with our fortunes or misfortunes in the Pacific," an investigator explained.[94] Featuring larger dry docks than Mare Island, Puget Sound repaired the battleships *Tennessee*, *Maryland*, *Nevada*, *California*, and *West Virginia*, all of which were damaged at Pearl Harbor, and later the *Essex*-class carriers *Wasp*, *Franklin*, and *Bunker Hill*, and the heavy cruiser *New Orleans*.

For new construction, Puget Sound added four slipways to its existing four, enabling it to lay down eight *Fletcher*-class destroyers, eight *Evarts*-class destroyer escorts, and the submarine tender *Nereus*. Wartime output totaled only 32,000 tons, the lowest construction volume among navy yards. Like its counterparts elsewhere, Puget Sound farmed out substantial amounts of work to suppliers, which produced subassemblies, valves, electrical fittings, and other items needed for new construction. Since larger firms in the area were busy with other military contracts, Puget Sound recruited smaller companies in

Heavy cruiser *New Orleans* in dry dock at Puget Sound Navy Yard prior to installation of a new bow, 1943.
Photo 44448, Box 201, RG 80-G, General Records of the Department of the Navy, General Photographs, 1913–1945, National Archives and Records Administration, College Park, MD

Seattle and Spokane, Washington. "As the work increased, and the saturation point was reached in the various localities, we moved east until we are as far as Denver," the head of the yard's farming-out board recorded. "In Denver, Montrose, and Fort Collins, Colo., we have subcontractors working under our prime contractor in Cheyenne."[95] Delivery of subcontracted items and prefabricated sections was hampered by the lack of a rail connection, so railroad cars had to be placed on barges in Seattle for shipment to Puget Sound. Transfer was often "delayed by fog, storms, tides, traffic in the congested channels, and is dependent on the availability of tugs and barges," the commandant of the 13th Naval District complained, but his repeated requests to construct a direct rail link remained unheeded by the Bureau of Yards & Docks.[96]

DESIGNING AND BUILDING *IOWA*-CLASS BATTLESHIPS

The construction of *Iowa*-class battleships was one of the most complex endeavors in the history of shipbuilding, and it was never repeated. Each vessel cost more than $130 million fully equipped, making them the most expensive weapons platforms built in World War II. Employing more manpower than any other American warship type, their design alone took two million man hours. To build one, 3,500 workers toiled for almost three million man hours in the entire range of shipyard trades from highly trained shipfitters and electricians to riveters and welders.

The *Iowa* design originated in the late 1930s, when the naval arms race escalated, prompting the U.S. Navy to order the construction of two *North Carolina*s and four *South Dakota*s. The latter, whose preliminary design was devised by then-Captain Chantry, crammed nine 16-inch guns turrets into a 35,000-displacement-ton ship with a maximum speed of 27.8 knots. The *South Dakota* design was improved in *Iowa*, whose 58,400-ton hull accommodated four turbines with an aggregate 212,000 shaft horsepower, the most powerful nonnuclear engine ever installed in an American warship, to produce maximum speeds exceeding 30 knots. Chantry, who handled the *Iowa* class during his stint as head of the Navy Department's Preliminary Design Section, devised a sloped side armor that replaced the traditional armor belt attached to the hull exterior with an internal belt installed deep inside the hull that was angled at 19 degrees to deflect plunging artillery shells. Preliminary Design forwarded the final design to the Bureau of Ships' Contract Design Branch, which worked out contract blueprints and specifications (a British visitor who observed the process commented that American contract plans were "done in much greater detail than is the case for British ships"[97]). The contract design was forwarded to the Navy Department and operational commanders for comment before Preliminary Design finalized hull blueprints and specifications showing a fine-lined, 888-foot hull with a clipper bow and a stem bulb protruding below the waterline to reduce hydrodynamic resistance.[98]

Upon completion of the preliminary design, three bureaus developed contract plans that were used to craft models and prepare rough construction estimates. The Bureau of Engineering worked on the arrangement of boilers and turbines, which closely resembled that of the *South Dakota* design. A major snafu occurred in the development of the main battery by the Bureau of Ordnance, which designed a turret the diameter of which was two feet too large for the hull, requiring a redesign for more crowded main turrets. Bureau plans were used by model makers at the Navy Department's recently opened David Taylor Model Basin in Carderock, Maryland, to build a scale model that underwent a series of tests, resulting in several modifications to the contract design. At the Brooklyn Navy Yard, ship carpenters built full-scale mockups, which were "set out in line but separated so that each could be inspected all around," a British visitor commented. "Models made on this scale are really useful and each machinery fitting and individual pipes can be shown in its correct position. The [navy yard] is very proud of these models which are prepared concurrently with the detailed drawings and are a very great help in settling all the details."[99]

Mockup of *Iowa*-class conning tower at Brooklyn Navy Yard, October 22, 1940.
Photo CP 50, BS # 49262, Box 206, RG 19, Entry LCM Construction and Launching of Ships, 1930–1955, BB-60 through BB-61, National Archives and Records Administration, College Park, MD

Orders for *Iowa* and *New Jersey*, the first two ships, were finalized in July 1939 after Congress appropriated funds for their construction. Both were assigned without competitive bidding because New York Ship, Newport News, and Fore River were in the process of laying down one *South Dakota* each and expressed no interest in additional battleships. The navy yards in Brooklyn and Philadelphia had a pair of *North Carolina*–class battleships on the stocks, but since both were scheduled for launching in 1940, there was enough room for *Iowa*s. Only days after the yards had received the formal go-ahead, Congress authorized the construction of *Missouri* and *Wisconsin*, which were assigned to Brooklyn and Philadelphia, respectively, a year later. The Two-Ocean Navy Act included yet another pair of *Iowa*s that were scheduled for later construction at the Philadelphia and Norfolk navy yards, bringing the total to six.[100]

With the contract assignments squared away, Brooklyn's design section commenced the detail design. In addition to blueprints, designers supplied specifications that listed materials to be used, production techniques, and installation methods. The *Iowa* design provided for duplicate and triplicate backup systems. "The redundancy was unbelievable," an engineer later recalled. "Something could break down [during active service], which was rare, and no one would ever know the difference."[101] Ordnance design was influenced by combat experience. According to original plans, *Iowa*s already carried a heavy secondary armament of twenty 5-inch dual-purpose guns that could perform long-range antiaircraft duty, but the original intermediate- and close-range antiaircraft batteries were eventually deemed inadequate. In 1941, the Bureau of Ordnance ordered Brooklyn's design section to replace sixteen unreliable 1.1-inch guns and twelve Browning machine guns with seventy-six 40-mm Bofors guns and sixty 20-mm Oerlikons. The switch, in addition to providing more powerful and effective antiaircraft capabilities, underlined that the "design of a combat ship is never completed," in the words of one observer. "Changes, alterations, additions keep pouring in all through the construction period and after the ship is at sea."[102] In *Iowa*s, naval architects and marine engineers proposed redesigns of hull, superstructure, propulsion, and electrical systems, most of which involved extensive discussion, revision, and bureau approval while the ships themselves already neared completion.[103]

Design flexibility, which ensured that the final product embodied the latest advances in combat technology, required close coordination between naval architects and shipbuilders. This presented particular challenges to "follow-on yards" responsible for combatants according to plans and specifications developed at "lead yards," a common practice in wartime shipbuilding. To facilitate the process during the construction of *New Jersey* and *Wisconsin*, the follow-on Philadelphia Navy Yard established a design liaison group staffed by naval architects, marine engineers, and electrical engineers who frequently visited the lead yard in Brooklyn, where *Iowa* was more advanced, "to obtain all advance information possible, either in the form of specifications, preliminary plans or completed plans. These in turn are used to advance the production work by stopping work which would be affected by changes or proceeding with a change long before completion of necessary plans," Chantry explained.[104] At a typical design conference in Brooklyn, Philadelphia representatives obtained eight preliminary plans as well as answers to more than three hundred queries about the battleship's detail design and specifications that had been submitted by Philadelphia's shop masters. Such elaborate liaison services were redundant in yards that built ships according to standardized plans that rarely changed, but they proved invaluable in battleship construction that involved a good deal of batch work and whose design changed constantly, Chantry told the Bureau of Ships. "There are many hours of paper work and design man power saved by having trained engineers at first hand to contribute the value of their knowledge and experience right on the job."[105]

Design work was intertwined with production planning, which included scheduling of materials production, processing, installation, and testing at the shipyard and subcontractors in all corners of the country. In *Iowa*-class construction, an advance planning team divided the battleship design into eleven construction groups, determined the labor and material needs for each, and developed timelines in collaboration with the production department and Brooklyn's design office. After each construction group had been broken down to the level of individual job orders, the advance planning team issued a master erection schedule with synchronized timelines for each job to ensure a tightly sequenced progression of production steps. In the engine master schedule, for example, the detail design of propeller shafts was to commence in April 1940 and be completed within seventy-five days, followed by a request for bids from subcontractors, the contract award, production of shaft sections, their delivery at the shipyard, machining, and installation, which was to be completed in early February 1942. According to the master schedule, the design, production, and installation of the main turbines and reduction gear ran parallel to that of the propeller shafts, enabling the yard to complete their installation by March 1943.[106]

Wild cards that played havoc with the master schedule included items whose production schedule remained beyond the shipyards' control, the most important being armor plate produced by steel mills under the cognizance of the Bureau of Ordnance. Steel makers reactivated their mothballed plants at a painstakingly slow rate, rendering the bureau's armor production schedule for the *Iowa* program tentative at best. The uncertain armor situation in turn created potential hazards for the master erection schedule because the "pre-established armor delivery schedule, together with the established delivery of major forgings, dominates the construction of the ship," a production manager noted.[107] Armor delays began to loom as early as 1940, when the Navy Department revised the priority rating of battleships in favor of cruisers and carriers whose completion was deemed more urgent, making it impossible to implement the battleship master erection schedule as planned. In 1941, a production officer reported that the entire "material situation has deteriorated to such an extent that the simple process of establishing desired delivery dates bears little or no relation to the dates of delivery which may be anticipated."[108]

In the structural shop meanwhile, machinists sheared, punched, and bent steel shapes. Laborers and riggers hauled plates, beams, and angles from storage areas onto the shop floor for shearing. Steel plates of up to twenty feet in length and three-eighths of an inch in thickness that made up the bulk of the battleship's shell and deck plates were shaped on a hydraulic keel bender that was adjusted by machine tool operators to conform to template contours. Since few of *Iowa*'s hull plates and frames were exactly alike, the bending equipment had to be recalibrated for each workpiece. In this respect, capital shipbuilding differed from the construction of ships in large series that dispensed with rolled plates wherever possible in order to save time. To determine the location of rivet holes, a punch operator clipped a template to a steel member, marked each hole with a prick, and punched an oval hole into the steel. The hole received its final shape only on the slipway, where steel members were precision-aligned and their overlapping holes drilled out to circular shape to ensure a tight fit.[109]

In addition to bending operations, structural shops housed production bays where shipfitters and other tradesmen erected subassemblies. Scheduling started several months before erection to facilitate an efficient layout of steel in close proximity to the appropriate tools and under shop cranes with sufficient capacity to lift the finished subassembly. Proper layout and timing according to the master erection schedule also ensured that "a complete unit of the vessel is ready for erection at the time when the vessel has reached a point at which erection of this portion can proceed piece by piece," one observer stressed. "[I]f the assembly is not ready at this time, we have lost the time advantage we attempted to gain by subassembling this portion of the vessel."[110] Major battleship subassemblies that were crafted in one of the shop's eight production bays included bottoms, tanks, bulkheads, and deckhouse sections.

The official keel laying was preceded by eight months of preparatory work on the slipway, the concrete slab of which had to be customized to accommodate the massive ship. The redesign was based on a projected launch weight of 36,000 tons, which included the hull, engines, the main belt armor, and the cradle that would carry the ship during the launch. Two thirds of the slipway was slanted seven-sixteenths of an inch per foot to the carefully calculated "declivity change point," where the slant increased to nine-sixteenth of an inch per foot down to the river to facilitate launching. On top of the slab, shipwrights installed the keel track that supported 278 oak blocks, each of which was sawed to a height of four feet nine inches to hold the hull and create working space below the large flat bottom area. On June 26, 1940, Brooklyn's shipfitters positioned *Iowa*'s first steel plates for the ceremonial keel laying a day later. Reconstruction of the slipway continued well into 1941 while hull construction was already under way, and dredging the East River at the end of the way in preparation for launching continued until mid-1942.[111]

As the keel grew forward and aft of the midship section, shipfitters and welders installed the bottom system and bulkheads. At Philadelphia, completion of *New Jersey*'s keel was delayed by production problems at the General Steel Castings Company of Eddystone, Pennsylvania, which delivered castings that proved defective after installation and had to be removed and replaced. Moreover, the Brooklyn Navy Yard reported that unexpected weld shrinkage bent the keel slightly toward starboard in *Iowa*, the construction of which was several months ahead of that of *New Jersey*. "Work was temporarily slowed while Navy Officers and engineers came from Washington to determine a way to correct the problem," a Brooklyn shipfitter later recalled. "To further complicate the problem, all of the propeller shaft holes had already been cut in the shop. All of these huge holes had to be welded closed with plating, and new shaft tunnels were then cut to house the propeller shafts. . . . Word was also sent down to Philadelphia to increase the shrinkage allowance so that the same didn't occur" in *New Jersey*.[112] Work continued apace on the triple bottom that protected engine rooms, magazines, and turret foundations from mine and torpedo explosions below the keel, with fuel tanks fitted between the outside shell and the second set of bottom plates to absorb shock waves. The bottom structures, including the lower sections of the frames, were prefabricated in the structural shop, where specially trained welders produced oil-tight tank welds, often working in cramped spaces because the plates were spaced little more than a foot apart. The feat was repeated on the ways, where shipfitters aligned the preassemblies, followed by production welders who fused the structures. Once the bottom system was in place, riggers lowered the prefabricated bulkheads into position, followed by shipfitters and welders who fastened them to the keel, bottom, and frames.[113]

The 246 separate plates that constituted each *Iowa*-class battleship's armor were produced by Midvale Steel Company of Nicetown, Pennsylvania (which was primarily responsible for side belt and deck armor), Carnegie-Illinois of Homestead, Pennsylvania (armored bulkheads), and Bethlehem Steel at Bethlehem, Pennsylvania (barbette and turret armor). The original armor schedule called for delivery of the lower belt armor to begin in October 1940, but the first plates actually arrived only a year later as a result of the Navy's decision to prioritize the completion of aircraft carriers and cruisers.[114]

Iowa-class side armor, which consisted of a ductile back and an ultrahard face that was designed to break up a projectile, was extraordinarily difficult to produce, which earned it the sobriquet "jewel steel." A typical plate of Class A armor "will weigh approximately 110 tons," the Bureau of Ordnance explained. "The treatment of this plate from design to finish machining . . . will take six to nine months."[115] The various jobs were performed by highly skilled steelworkers because "a few careless minutes [by poorly trained men] could ruin the labor of precious months."[116] Not only "the size, shape, and weight of each of the massive slabs, but even [their] metallurgical structure

Iowa-class battleship *New Jersey* under construction at the Philadelphia
Navy Yard, January 9, 1941. Note the first bulkhead installed amidships.

*Photo 20870, Box 97, RG 80-G, General Records of the Department of the Navy, General
Photographs, 1918–1945, National Archives and Records Administration, College Park, MD*

had to be determined with a precision completely out of character with the appearance of slabs so large and heavy that they required specially constructed flat-cars for transportation."[117] Midvale produced Class A armor by heating pig iron together with nickel, chrome, and other additives in a furnace and pouring the molten steel into a sand mold. The resulting ingot was forged in a 14,000-ton hydraulic press, cut into rough shape, and annealed by heating it to several hundred degrees and allowing the plate to cool slowly to eliminate forging strain. The outward-facing side of the plate was then superhardened by exposing it to carbon for two weeks, followed by reheating and reforging of the plate to near-final thickness and machining into final shape. During installation, a Class A plate was secured against the exterior hull at a 19-degree angle with specially designed armor bolts made from nickel steel. Once shipfitters had positioned an armor plate measuring thirty by ten feet, they carefully tapped sixty-six armor bolts into the backing, screwed each into a structural hull member, and secured it with a nickel steel nut. The procedure was necessary because Class A armor could not accommodate conventional through-bolts, whose heads on the face side tore off when the armor flexed sharply under the impact of a direct hit. Abutting armor plate edges were then aligned with pins and locked together with armor keys. The four-inch space that separated the armor plate face from the exterior hull had to be filled with concrete to ensure that the shock emanating from an exploding projectile was spread over as wide an area as possible and prevent shattering of the plate.[118]

Class B side armor for the *Iowa* class, which unlike Class A armor consisted of homogenous ductile steel and was designed to cause a projectile to glance off, was easier to produce and install. "Because of less complicated heat treatment class B [armor] averages six to eight weeks less [than Class A armor] and about $100 per gross ton less in cost," according to the Bureau of Ordnance.[119] After Midvale had delivered the first batch for *New Jersey*, however, problems materialized during welding, which had not been previously attempted on Class B armor. A few days after installation, weld fillets peeled off several lower belt plates, prompting an investigation that determined a significantly higher carbon content on the plates' surface than in their interior as a result of a heat-treating process applied by Midvale. The Bureau of Ships attributed this incident to the fact that the steel maker "appeared to be unaware of the increasing amount of welding this Bureau is doing" on armor plate. The incident was one of many that prompted the establishment of a committee on armor welding under the auspices of the Ferrous Metallurgical Advisory Board, which researched new electrodes, alloys, and machining techniques to improve the weldability of naval and tank armor.[120]

With the interior side belt armor in place, shipfitters, riveting gangs, and welders commenced shell plating. To prepare a plate for riveted installation, shipfitters working with riggers maneuvered the plate to its location on the frame, using the rivet holes as pilot markers, and secured the plate temporarily with bolts. Once a driller had bored the oval rivet holes to their final round shape, a holder-on working on the inside of the hull picked up a red-hot rivet with a pair of pliers and forced it into the hole. With the holder-on securing the rivet, the riveter hammered the protruding rivet end flat with a pneumatic riveting gun until it was flush with the plate. Holding-on and riveting "require strength and hard work," recalled a riveter who worked on *New Jersey*'s hull. "I had two guns. I drove the rivet with one gun and used the second gun to cut off any excess; then I would rivet it again and level it off. Work went on rapidly to keep the rivet from cooling off. . . . A red, melting-hot rivet was the best to work with. Riveters could tell from the color red of the rivet sent through by the holder-on how difficult it would be to work with. This was hard and dirty work."[121] Welded installation required different preparation by the shipfitter, who used datum lines instead of rivet holes to position the plate and temporarily secured it by a tack welder. A production welder then beaded the weld along the tapered edges in one continuous operation as a helper removed the tack welds one by one.[122]

Machinists meanwhile installed the power plant, the main components of which were built, shop tested, and disassembled for shipment to the navy yard by various subcontractors. The first to arrive were the eight main boilers manufactured by Babcock & Wilcox of New York designed to generate steam superheated to 850° Fahrenheit. Riggers lowered the huge drums onto their foundations for installation by machinists, followed by pipefitters who secured the fuel pipes between the burners and oil compartments. They also connected the steam generators to the four massive Westinghouse turbines that were installed on their foundations by machinists. Next came the four double-reduction gears, also manufactured by Westinghouse, which transmitted power from turbines running at 5,000 revolutions per minute to the propeller shafts that turned at a maximum speed of 202 revolutions. Machinists also stretched steel wires from the propeller shaft outlets aft to the reduction gear amidships to provide base lines for the propeller shaft bearings. The shafts, the longest of which measured almost 340 feet, were installed in sections but remained uncoupled from the reduction gear to avoid undue stresses on the precision-engineered transmission during launch.[123]

Launching required more than the usual preparations because *Iowa*-class battleships were the heaviest combatants ever launched from slipways. Detailed calculations were undertaken at the shipyard and at the David Taylor basin, which launched a twenty-foot model *Iowa* from scale-sized slipways to determine the most effective technique. Traditionally, a hull was transferred from its building blocks onto a pair of so-called sliding ways that ran the entire length of the ship left and right of the keel and terminated in wooden structures that supported the bow and stern. The sliding ways rested on stationary ground ways that were greased on launch day, when the last supporting timbers were sawed through and the hull slid down the ways. As a result of the model tests, Philadelphia opted for four instead of the usual two sliding ways in *New Jersey*. Two months prior to launching, ship carpenters began to replace the wooden keel blocks with collapsible sand blocks that would be opened on launch day to let their contents pour out. This allowed the hull to settle on the sliding ways, which were covered with forty-seven tons of soap and grease (careful measurements were imperative because too much lubricant could result in excessive launch speed that could harm the hull, and too little could leave the ship stuck). Ship carpenters meanwhile crafted the launch cradle, the contours of which fit snugly around *New Jersey*'s bow and stern. On December 7, 1942, the carefully choreographed movements of several hundred workers were overseen by officers and engineers in the launch control center, who communicated with the men on the slipways and on board *New Jersey* via telephone. After divers had completed their last-minute inspection of the launch path, the last shores were removed, the launch triggers were pulled at high tide, and *New Jersey* started to slide.[124] Deep inside the hull, engineers monitored the propeller shaft, which moved 0.8 inches on its bearings as the hull slid across the dropoff point.[125]

With the ship 82 percent complete, the most important item to be installed was armament. The main turret assemblies were crafted in the turret shop and transferred to the pier via barge. Riggers lifted the upper rotating assembly with a hammerhead crane, carefully positioned it over the shell deck, and slowly lowered the massive structure onto its roller paths within tolerances of less than an inch. Next came the 16-inch guns, manufactured by the Naval Gun Factory at the Washington Navy Yard from forgings supplied by Bethlehem Steel, Midvale, and Carnegie-Illinois. After the 106-ton barrels were lowered onto their girders and mounted by machinists, electricians installed the motors that trained and elevated the guns, powered the ammunition hoists, and opened and closed the breech mechanisms. Machinists and electricians also mounted and wired the gun directors (optical devices that tracked a target's range, bearing, course, and speed), an exceedingly delicate task that required a good deal of precision work. *Iowa*'s Mark 38 and Mark 37 directors, which provided fire control for the 16-inch guns and the secondary 5-inch battery, respectively, were fitted with air and fire-control radar, the installation of which was handled by specially trained electricians. Upon completion of these and other tasks, *New Jersey* was dry docked to receive her 18-foot screw propellers, which were the largest ever cast and balanced at the navy yard propeller foundry. Machinists also installed her twin rudders and connected them to the armor-protected steering gear. *New Jersey* was commissioned in May 1943, three months after *Iowa*, followed in April 1944 by *Wisconsin* at Philadelphia and *Missouri* in June 1944 at Brooklyn.[126]

Few other shipyards possessed the planning capabilities, production facilities, and shop floor skills required to build battleships, and many projects had to be abandoned as a result of labor and material shortages. Construction of *Illinois*, one of the *Iowa* class laid down at Philadelphia in December 1942, was canceled in 1945 and the incomplete hull was broken up for scrap on the slipway. The bottom structure of *Kentucky*, another *Iowa*-class battleship, lingered incomplete at the Norfolk Navy Yard until December 1944, when construction resumed. Following additional suspensions, the incomplete hull was launched in 1950, towed to Philadelphia, and scrapped nine years later. During the war, the Big Three and the navy yards in Brooklyn, Philadelphia, and Norfolk managed to deliver ten battleships after 1940, more than the combined total completed by British, German, and Japanese shipyards. Though the Royal Navy commissioned five *King George V*–class battleships during the war, it suspended the construction of *Vanguard* at Browns to save resources for smaller projects. In Germany, Blohm & Voss and the Wilhelmshaven Navy Yard delivered a pair of

Battleship *Iowa* receiving a 16-inch gun at the Brooklyn Navy Yard, autumn 1942. Note the crane's 175-ton designated carrying capacity. *Photograph 20875, Box 97, RG 80-G, General Records of the Department of the Navy, General Photographs, 1918–1945, National Archives and Records Administration, College Park, MD*

*Bismarck*s early in the war, but construction of six H-class battleships under the Z-Plan was halted before most keels had been laid, as their builders retooled for submarine construction. A similar fate befell Japan's *Yamato* class that was originally scheduled to include five units, of which only the first two were actually commissioned into the Imperial Navy (*Shinano* was completed as a carrier, the construction of 111—never named—ceased shortly after keel laying, and 797 was not laid down). The abandonment of so many projects reflected a growing realization that battleships had outlived their classic role in the line of battle à la Jutland.

NAVY YARDS IN COMPARATIVE PERSPECTIVE

American navy yards produced a far larger amount of combatant tonnage than their foreign counterparts. Britain's Royal Dockyards at Chatham, Portsmouth, and Devonport performed only a small amount of naval construction, partly because their location in southern England rendered them vulnerable to air raids. Chatham, which had the *Dido*-class light cruiser *Euryalus* under construction when the war broke out, suffered extensive damage during the Battle of Britain, when a raid killed or injured more than a hundred men. The yard completed only eleven submarines, a cruiser, and two sloops during the war. During launch preparations for the light cruiser *Sirius* in August 1940 at the Portsmouth dockyard, an air raid killed sixty-eight men and destroyed parts of the physical plant. Subsequent attacks damaged *Sirius* during outfitting, prompting her transfer to Scotts at Greenock in Scotland for completion. Other attacks (one of which damaged *Victory* of Trafalgar fame) convinced the Admiralty to curtail shipbuilding at Portsmouth, which laid down only two submarines and concentrated on repair work for the remainder of the war. Devonport, likewise subjected to heavy bombing, ceased surface combatant construction after delivering the light cruiser *Trinidad* in 1941, and it completed only a handful of T-class submarines. The air raids that derailed dockyard shipbuilding for much of the war of course had no impact on American navy yard shipbuilding (at Pearl Harbor, which did not perform new construction, the Japanese attack damaged a dry dock, the repair basin, and an electric power substation).[127]

In contrast to Britain's dockyards, Japan's navy yards at Yokosuka in Tokyo Bay, Kure near Hiroshima, Sasebo at Nagasaki, and Maizuru in Kyoto Prefecture remained the backbone of naval construction throughout the war. Like the American navy yards, they handled a broad variety of nonshipbuilding functions. Yokosuka, for example, served as headquarters of the First Naval District and included a fleet base, a major supply depot, technical schools, and a fleet communications center. The communications center transmitted Vice Admiral Yamamoto Isoroku's radio message "Climb Mount Niitaka," instructing Vice Admiral Nagumo Chuichi to proceed with the Pearl Harbor attack. In addition to designing and building ships, Yokosuka repaired combatants, produced aircraft and ordnance, operated research laboratories, and trained navy personnel. The navy yard itself was more vertically integrated than its American counterparts. Equipped with five slipways and six dry docks, it featured a "heavy forging shop with two large hydraulic presses of 900 and 1,500 tons capacity; foundries for composition castings, steel, and miscellaneous small work; electric welding apparatus; large and small furnaces; smith shops; a boiler shop . . . ; two larger machine shops with lathes up to 18 feet in diameter and gear cutting machines; turbine shop; a mold loft, and an engineering laboratory," the U.S. Office of Naval Intelligence (ONI) reported.[128] During the Doolittle raid of April 1942, a B-25 bomber dropped its payload on Yokosuka and scored a direct hit on the submarine tender *Taigei*, delaying her conversion into the light carrier *Ryūhō*, but the yard itself remained unscathed. In contrast to the British dockyards, Japanese navy yards suffered no air raid damage until the onset of U.S. strategic bombing in 1944.[129]

In the meantime, a more serious problem emerged in the form of labor short-ages, which affected Japanese naval construction even more than its American counterpart, as evinced by the slow growth of navy yard workforces. From August 1942 to November 1943, "unskilled labor increased through the use of drafted workers, schoolboys, Koreans, and prisoners, [while] the decrease in skilled workers caused serious setbacks in production," the U.S. Strategic Bombing Survey concluded after the war. Scarcity of skilled labor proliferated the following year, "with the result that newly-built ships deteriorated in qual-ity because of the simplification of building processes necessary when unskilled labor was employed."[130] The problem was confounded by steel shortages that caused disruptions in the first two years of the war, when deliveries declined from their peak in 1941. By 1944, when American builders were well-supplied with steel, Japan's "large-ship production slowed down and in many cases stopped altogether and small-ship production rose on a large scale" due to the lack of steel, the bombing survey noted. The problem was confounded by the Imperial Navy's decision late in the war to prioritize the construction of tankers to transport crude oil to home island refineries, leaving warship construction in 1944 with only one-sixth of all steel allocated to shipbuilding.[131]

Japanese navy yards achieved impressive output rates under the circum-stances. Deliveries totaled 500,000 tons from 1940 to 1945, compared to 1.3 mil-lion tons completed by American navy yards. Kure, which delivered *Yamato* in 1941, converted passenger liners into the aircraft carriers *Unyo*, *Chuyo*, and *Shinyō* after Midway in addition to laying down the 22,500-ton carriers *Kat-suragi* and *Aso* and the light cruiser *Ōyodo*. The yard also produced fifteen fleet submarines and in the final year of the war commenced several dozen midget submersibles designed to engage invasion forces, but most were still incomplete in 1945.

Chart 4.2. U.S. and Japanese Navy Yard Workforces, 1941–1945

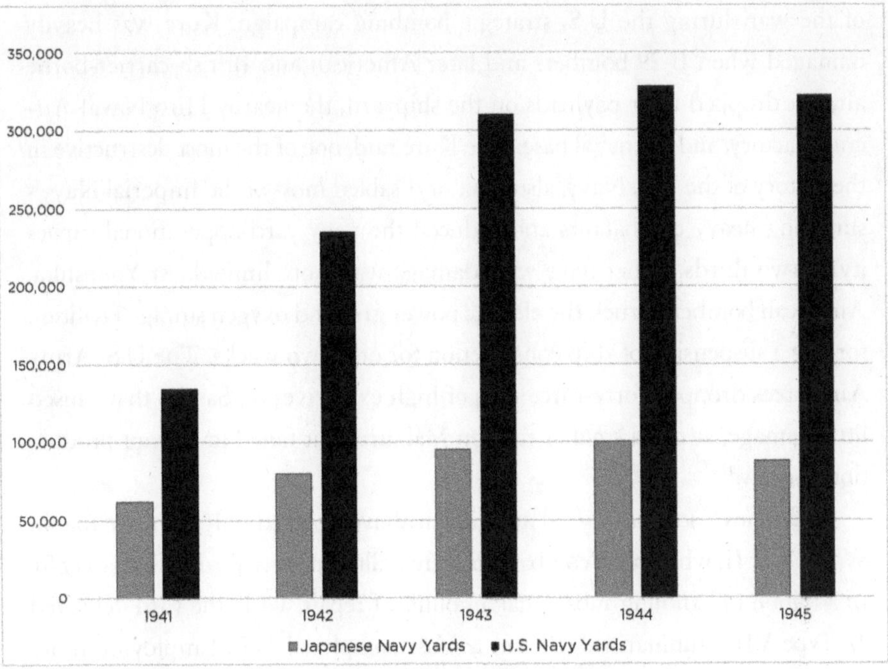

United States Strategic Bombing Survey, Japanese Naval Shipbuilding *(Washington, DC: U.S. Government Printing Office, 1946), 7;* H. Gerrish Smith, "Shipyard Statistics," in The Shipbuilding Business of the United States of America, *vol. 1, ed. F. G. Fassett Jr. (New York: Society of Naval Architects and Marine Engineers, 1948), 189.*

Yokosuka, like Kure, devoted considerable resources to aircraft carriers, notably the conversion of the submarine tenders *Shōhō* and *Ryūhō* into light carriers. By far the most challenging project involved the conversion of the *Yamato*-class battleship *Shinano* into a 72,000-ton carrier, the largest ship of its kind completed in World War II, whose size rivaled that of American *Forrestal*-class supercarriers of the 1950s. Laid down as a battleship in 1940, *Shinano* was 45 percent complete in 1942 when Yokosuka removed most interior armor, added an armored flight deck and an aircraft hangar, and completely reconfigured her superstructure, echoing the conversion of American *Cleveland*-class cruisers into *Independence*-class light carriers (see chapter 5). Commissioned at Yokosuka in November 1944, *Shinano* set course for the Kure navy yard for final outfitting and fell prey to the U.S. submarine *Archerfish*, making her the largest naval vessel ever sunk by a submarine.[132]

Japanese navy yards suffered varying degrees of damage in the final year of the war during the U.S. strategic bombing campaign. Kure was heavily damaged when B-29 bombers and later American and British carrier-borne aircraft dropped their payloads on the shipyard, the nearby Hiro Naval Aircraft Factory, and the naval base. The Kure raid, one of the most destructive in the history of the U.S. Navy, also sank or disabled most of the Imperial Navy's surviving heavy combatants and reduced the navy yard's operational capacity by two-thirds. Other navy yard damage was more limited. At Yokosuka, American bombers struck the electric power grid and oxygen storage facilities, forcing a suspension of ship construction for only two weeks. The U.S. Army Air Forces dropped forty-three tons of high explosives on Sasebo that caused little damage, as did a smaller raid on Maizuru that failed to disrupt production entirely.[133]

Germany's sole navy yard at Wilhelmshaven played only a minor role in World War II, when most combatants were built in private yards (see chapter 5). In addition to handling substantial amounts of repair work, the yard delivered 27 Type VIIC submarines (Blohm & Voss completed 173). Employing more than 20,000 workers at its peak in 1942, the yard transferred 7,500 men to submarine bases at Lorient, Saint Nazaire, and La Pallice in France to perform overhauls and train the local workforce. As the war progressed, the German navy grew increasingly wary of Wilhelmshaven because it featured an awkward layout, lacked construction bunkers, and was exposed to air raids due to its proximity to British bomber bases. The British and American air forces flew 102 missions that damaged parts of the shipyard and sank ninety ships. In May 1945, Wilhelmshaven capitulated to Canadian and Polish army units.[134]

CONCLUSION

Government-owned industrial facilities played a major role in American naval construction. Though they delivered only one-seventh of total naval tonnage commissioned in World War II, eight navy yards produced as much as twenty-five private builders of battleships, carriers, cruisers, destroyers, destroyer escorts, and submarines. Many also handled large amounts of repair work, in contrast to most private builders, who concentrated on new construction while leaving repairs to specialty firms and the navy yards (see chapter 5).

These findings challenge claims of industrial mobilization studies that assert that the role of government was confined to providing money, managing scarce resources, and performing general oversight of private enterprise. The U.S. Navy relied far more on government-owned enterprise than its British and German counterparts, contradicting narratives of American industrial mobilization in which private enterprise takes center stage in wartime production. Such interpretations are largely derived from analyses of aircraft and tank production, where the private sector indeed played a leading role, but they ignore the contribution of government-owned facilities to naval shipbuilding, a significant sector of America's wartime industrial landscape.

The evidence presented in this chapter demonstrates that shipbuilding in navy yards was closely intertwined with specialty production in private firms. Like most shipyards, they relied heavily on subcontracting with producers of armor, hull steel, turbines, and many subsystems required to build complex weapons platforms. Outsourcing was more prevalent in the United States than in Japan, where vertically integrated navy yards like Yokosuka included foundries, furnaces, and facilities to produce turbines and reduction gear. Disintegrated production formats were also a salient feature of private-sector shipbuilding, discussed in the next chapter.

5

"The Government Pays for Everything in There"

Private Builders and Contractor-Operated Yards

Established shipyards with decades-long experience in naval shipbuilding constituted the vibrant core of private-sector warship construction. Like the navy yards, they differed considerably in size and specialization. While Newport News Shipbuilding, Fore River, and New York Ship constructed mostly battleships, carriers, and cruisers, medium-sized yards like the Bath Iron Works, Electric Boat, and Federal Ship delivered destroyers and submarines. During the war, they were joined by merchant builders and engineering firms, in addition to defunct yards reactivated under government auspices. The Navy also funded the construction of wartime emergency yards, which churned out destroyer escorts and landing craft in government-owned, contractor-operated yards. All told, private and contractor-operated yards produced more than 80 percent of naval tonnage during the war. Navy funding of facility upgrades was critical to their performance. New York Ship, for example, "is practically a Government yard. The Government pays for everything in there," a congressman pointed out. "If they need extra help, extra supervisors to take care of this work and can get them, the Government pays for them."[1]

Students of industrial mobilization often emphasize the role of large corporations in American wartime production. Political economists Joe Feagin and Kelly Riddell, for example, have argued that "fulfillment of state procurement and production needs was arranged for maximum big-business input," with nearly 8 percent of $175 billion in prime defense contracts going to General Motors alone.[2] A closer look reveals that prime contractors stood atop complex production pyramids swarming with thousands of suppliers of specialty parts and subsystems. Though more than two-thirds of prime wartime contracts indeed went to one hundred corporations, only a handful were vertically integrated like

Ford's famous Willow Run aircraft factory, where even rivets were produced in-house (vertical integration is a corporate strategy that concentrates raw materials procurement, manufacture of subsystems, assembly, and sales in one organization). Recent studies of aircraft manufacture have explored alternatives involving interfirm linkages, cross-licensing, and subcontracting arrangements, which enabled core firms to assemble vast numbers of bombers and fighter planes from designs and parts supplied by specialty firms. B-29 bomber production at Boeing, Bell Aircraft, and Glenn Martin, for example, involved no fewer than 1,400 subcontractors. A case study of light cruiser construction presented later in this chapter documents similar production formats in naval work, where shipyards relied on supplier networks to produce everything from boilers and turbines to draft blowers and specialty valves. The evidence presented here strengthens the case for a reinterpretation of American industrial mobilization to include such disintegrated production formats.[3]

FACILITY IMPROVEMENTS

Naval expansion coincided with a merchant shipbuilding boom after the outbreak of war in Europe, when demand for commercial tonnage skyrocketed. The Neutrality Act of November 1939 excluded U.S. flag carriers from combat zones, but many operators circumvented the law by registering American-built merchant vessels under the Panamanian flag of convenience and selling more than one hundred to the British, many of which were replaced with new builds. The withdrawal of British tonnage from major routes meanwhile created opportunities for American carriers in the South American and Far Eastern trades, further fueling demand for cargo ships. Commercial output grew 23 percent from 1939 to 1940, and another 68 percent to reach 718,000 gross tons the following year. Beneficiaries included Newport News, Fore River, the Bath Iron Works, Federal Ship, and merchant builders, notably Sun Shipbuilding in Chester, Pennsylvania, Alabama Dry Dock in Mobile, and Bethlehem's Sparrows Point yard near Baltimore. Demand for commercial carrying capacity also spurred the establishment of new shipyards, including Ingalls of Pascagoula, Mississippi, and Seattle-Tacoma Shipbuilding in Washington State.[4]

Busy with merchant work (the Bethlehem yards alone had sixty freighters, tankers, and passenger liners under construction in spring 1940), many firms were initially wary of naval contracting because merchant work was more profitable. This changed with the passage of the Second Revenue Act of 1940, which had an across-the-board excess profit tax provision that rendered merchant shipbuilding less lucrative and prompted builders to relax their resistance to naval work. Moreover, the Navy could apply a potentially powerful new tool to force builders into naval contracting by way of yard seizures: under the Selective Service Act of 1940, the government could take possession of businesses that refused to take Navy and Army orders, leaving builders with little legal recourse.[5]

In practice, the Navy usually preferred carrots over sticks and provided generous funding for shipyard upgrades. Facility improvements had long been a bone of contention in Navy negotiations with shipyard executives, who argued that the government should finance buildings and shop floor equipment needed for naval construction but not merchant work. "The best arrangement of facilities for heavy combatant construction . . . is not ideal for building large passenger liners. Many facilities necessary for the former are not required for the latter and vice versa," John Metten of New York Ship summed up the builders' views of the matter. For example, "In the matter of crane equipment, our present capital ships require a minimum high-lift crane and transport capacity of 250 tons and preferably 300 tons; 100 tons is ample for lifts on large passenger work. Most of the large tools and other equipment for manufacturing heavy

Bethlehem Fore River outfitting dock, October 8, 1941. *From left to right*: Battleship *Massachusetts*, oil tanker *Sinclair Superflame* (Sinclair Refining Company), light cruisers *San Diego* and *San Juan*. Photograph No. 29559, RG 19, Records of the Bureau of Ships, National Archives and Records Administration, College Park, MD

turrets and for processing armor, barbettes, etc., are not adapted to merchant work."[6] Existing Navy contracting practice created financial uncertainty for private combatant builders who were unsure about the extent to which they would be compensated for yard improvements needed for naval work. Gerrish Smith of the National Council of American Shipbuilders complained in 1940: "We have some existing contracts at the present time in which . . . the builder has from one million and a half to two million dollars in each yard in new facilities without any guaranty as to what he will get [reimbursed]. And while we are told it will be equitably adjusted when we get through, that is hardly sufficient proof that you are going to get back a reasonable part of what you put into those facilities."[7] Prodded by contractors and the Navy, Congress eventually appropriated vast sums for direct Navy investments in yards engaged in new construction and repairs.[8]

Well-established warship builders claimed the lion's share of these funds. The Bethlehem yards in Fore River, San Francisco, Staten Island, and San Pedro, California, alone received $51 million for new slipways, workshops, and piers. Fore River, which had produced the bulk of Bethlehem's combatant output before the war, had four cargo ships and nine tankers under construction in 1940, in addition to two *Atlanta*-class light cruisers and the battleship *Massachusetts*. Contracts signed in July added four *Baltimore*-class heavy cruisers and four *Cleveland*-class light cruisers, but because "the yard had a large number of merchant vessels under construction at the time, the first of the new program could not be laid down before May 1941," according to the commandant of the First Naval District, where Fore River was located.[9] In September 1940, the yard received additional orders for four *Essex*-class carriers, four *Baltimore*s, and a pair of *Cleveland*s. "These new contracts were beyond the capacity of the Fore River plant at that time," the commandant wrote. The yard was therefore "awarded a plant expansion contract which increased the number of major ways from seven to ten [and] provided for [an] additional machine shop devoted entirely to turret fabrication."[10] The Navy also financed new welding facilities, X-ray equipment, boring mills, lathes, and other shop tools. Additional facilities included a new wet basin, which was serviced by a hammerhead crane that had 120 tons of lifting capacity and could accommodate a carrier or two cruisers simultaneously. Government expenditures at Fore River totaled $21 million, a substantial sum but still considerably less than the $71 million the Navy invested into the comparable Brooklyn Navy Yard.[11]

Table 5.1. Navy Investments in Private Shipyards

Shipyard	Navy Investments
Newport News Shipbuilding, VA	$21,639,832
Bethlehem Fore River, MA	$21,088,000
New York Ship, NJ	$20,264,346
Cramp Shipbuilding, PA	$20,188,517
Bethlehem San Francisco (Union Plant), CA	$18,302,900
Seattle-Tacoma Shipbuilding, WA	$14,114,132
Federal, Kearny, NJ	$9,629,347
Los Angeles Shipbuilding, San Pedro, CA	$9,043,825
Moore Drydock, Oakland, CA	$9,023,123
Tampa Shipbuilding, FL	$7,134,145
Western Pipe, San Pedro, CA	$7,055,177
Alabama Drydock, Mobile, AL	$6,412,634
Bethlehem, Staten Island, NY	$5,939,006
Bethlehem, San Pedro, CA	$5,656,565
Gulf Shipbuilding, Chickasaw, AL	$5,451,780
Marietta Manufacturing, Mt. Pleasant, WV	$4,931,642
Missouri Shipbuilding., St. Louis, MO	$4,572,213
Jeffersonville Boat, Jeffersonville, IN	$4,541,873
Ingalls Shipbuilding, Pascagoula, MS	$3,674,000
Pollock-Stockton, Stockton, CA	$3,503,485
Willamette Iron & Steel, Portland, OR	$3,300,118
Bath Iron Works, ME	$3,009,299
Bethlehem, Baltimore, ME	$2,846,952
South Portland Drydock, ME	$2,767,985
Manitowoc Shipbuilding Co., WI	$2,374,228
Charleston Shipbuilding & Drydock, SC	$1,683,086
New Jersey Shipbuilding, Perth Amboy, NJ	$1,547,829
Associated Shipbuilders, WA	$1,521,055
Lake Washington Shipyards, Houghton, WA	$1,396,491
Savannah Machinery & Foundry, GA	$1,286,178
Other (19 Shipyards)	$5,898,158
Total	$229,797,921

H. Gerrish Smith, "Shipyard Statistics," in *The Shipbuilding Business of the United States of America*, vol. 1, ed. Fredrick G. Fassett Jr. (New York: Society of Naval Architects and Marine Engineers, 1948), 164–65

Newport News was even busier with merchant work than was Fore River. Featuring seven major slipways, it had under construction the 34,000-gross-ton passenger liner *America*, ten cargo ships, and a pair of oil tankers for the U.S. Maritime Commission, plus the battleship *Indiana* and the carrier *Hornet*. By September 1940, the firm had contracted for six *Essex*-class carriers and four *Cleveland*-class light cruisers under the two-ocean navy program. To build these ships, Newport News needed a new slipway, a machine shop, and a fabrication plant, general manager John Woodward told the Navy, adding, "Our present facilities do not permit outfitting more than three large vessels at one time. . . . Therefore an additional pier with its storage and handling facilities is necessary."[12] Echoing Metten, Newport News president Homer Ferguson told Rear Adm. Samuel Robinson of the Bureau of Ships that installation of additional facilities created "a liability to the shipyard rather than an asset for the reason that the yard is at present large enough and fully equipped to handle all of their normal peace-time work; that facilities in excess of their normal requirements are subject to taxes, maintenance, etc. He felt that the cost of these facilities should be borne in their entirety by the Government on land which would be leased at nominal cost by the shipyard."[13] Robinson agreed to direct Navy financing of all facilities except the pier, whose cost was split between the government and Bethlehem. The yard also received $343,000 in new machine tools for the carrier program initiated in 1940, including grinders, slotters, and planers. Additionally, the government funded slum clearing and home construction in the overcrowded town, cementing its policy of racial segregation. In September 1940, the local supervisor of shipbuilding reported that U.S. Housing Administration "projects are under way for 352 [housing] units for white and 252 for colored persons."[14] Newport News' wartime facility improvements totaled $21.6 million, three times as much as the initial estimate.[15]

New York Ship's situation differed from Fore River's and Newport News' because the yard had no merchant work on hand in 1940 when it had under construction the battleship *South Dakota*, the seaplane tender *Curtiss*, and the navy repair ship *Vulcan*. By the end of the year, Metten had signed contracts for thirteen *Cleveland*-class light cruisers and six *Alaska*-class large cruisers, the heaviest workload among the Big Three under the naval expansion program, at an aggregate cost of $507 million. Operating only five slipways, one of which would be occupied by *South Dakota* well into 1941, New York Ship requested

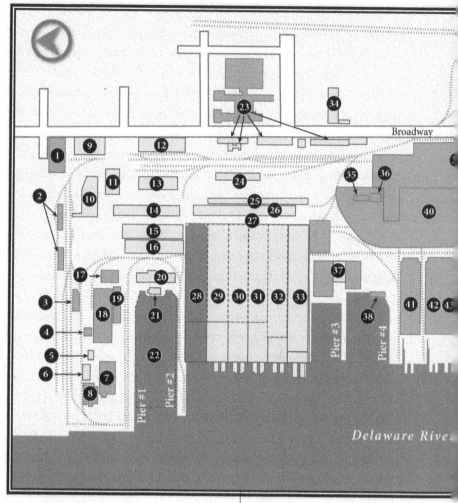

Figure 5.1. New York Ship Yard in World War II.

John F. Metten, "Shipyard Layout, Section 1: Standard Yards," in The Shipbuilding Business of the United States of America, *vol. 1, ed. Frederick G. Fassett Jr. (New York: Society of Naval Architects and Marine Engineers, 1948), foldout facing 209.*

1	Receiving Warehouse
2	Maintenance Buildings
3	Scrap Bin
4	Dry Kiln
5	Transfer Table
6	Lumber Shed
7	Copper Shop No. 1
8	Pipe and Welding Shop
9	Pattern Shop
10	Forge Shop
11	Steel Storage
12	General Warehouse
13	General Store House
14	Boiler Shop
15	Angle Shop
16	Plate Shop
17	Paint Shop
18	Outfitting Shop
19	Pipe Cover Shop

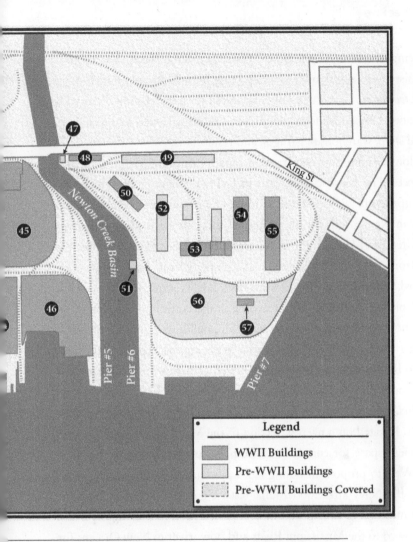

Legend

■	WWII Buildings
■	Pre-WWII Buildings
⌷	Pre-WWII Buildings Covered

Navy financing of a $9.6 million annex called the Middle Yard to accommodate five cruiser hulls simultaneously. Expecting to build seventy 6-inch main turrets for *Cleveland*s, New York Ship also asked for a turret shop fitted with overhead cranes. Other additions included an outfitting center, a copper shop, a sheet metal shop, warehouses, garages, and restaurants.[16]

Expansion of submarine construction capacity involved several interconnected projects. The Electric Boat yard in Groton, Connecticut, which featured nine slipways in 1940, invested $1 million of its own money and booked $4.6 million in Navy funds for an additional three slipways plus workshops and tools. After Pearl Harbor, the Navy provided another $13 million for the so-called Victory Yard with ten slipways on a property located half a mile from the main yard. Unfortunately for Electric Boat, facility improvements did not include new piers, resulting in overcrowding in the outfitting department. In Wisconsin, the Navy recruited Manitowoc Shipbuilding, a builder of Great Lakes ore carriers, whose president, Charles West, approached the Navy with a proposal to build warships. Manitowoc netted contracts for ten *Balao*-class submarines under the two-ocean navy program along with $2.4 million in yard improvements, later followed by contracts for more submarines and for tank landing craft. Located on a narrow section of the Manitowoc River, the yard lacked sufficient space for conventional launches perpendicular to the river, prompting West to propose installing sideways launch facilities, which was approved by the Navy after model tank tests. Upon completion, submarine hulls were transferred to Lockport, Illinois, and loaded on a floating dry dock, which was towed to the Mississippi River and downriver to New Orleans for completion elsewhere. Together with the navy yards in Portsmouth and Mare Island and Cramp Shipbuilding (see below), Electric Boat and Manitowoc made up the core of the American submarine-building industry.[17]

The Bath Iron Works, which operated five slipways, received $3 million in plant upgrades. In addition to its extant workload of four C-2 type cargo ships for the Maritime Commission, it contracted for an initial batch of twenty-three destroyers in 1940 to be completed by December 1943 at a rate of one per month. Major government-financed facilities earmarked for this endeavor included a satellite plant at Harding 3.7 miles from the shipyard, where "it was decided to provide not only a structural shop with the necessary outfit of tools and appliances, but also a storehouse and a galvanizing shop," investigators reported. "This galvanizing shop was necessary so that the time heretofore required to send materials to a distant shop (Philadelphia) could be avoided."[18] Bulkheads, longitudinals, and other preassemblies were transported from Harding to the shipyard via a rail link. Bath also received three new slipways equipped with whirler cranes, additions to a machine shop together with tools and welding equipment, and a pier extension for outfitting. The Navy financed similarly extensive plant improvements at the Bethlehem yards in Staten Island, New York, San Francisco, and San Pedro, California, and at Federal Shipbuilding in Kearney, New Jersey.[19]

In a few instances, defunct yards were resuscitated with other government funds, including $12 million in Emergency Plant Facility securities provided by the Reconstruction Finance Corporation to reopen Cramp of Philadelphia. Since its closure in 1927, the fifty-five-acre plant had been stripped of machine tools (most of which were acquired by Bath) and had fallen into disrepair. "The snows and rains had played havoc with shops and shipways, and the abandoned cranes were a pathetic sight in the eyes of the rigging crew," according to one account. "Many of the buildings were without roofs. Floors were rotted and sagging, and almost every pane of glass had been shattered."[20] Still owned by financier Averell Harriman, the defunct yard owed $7.5 million in unpaid taxes and other debts in 1940, when the property was generously valued at $4 million. Prodded by Navy Secretary Frank Knox, Harriman agreed to financial restructuring, which resulted in the formation of a new company under the auspices of Cramp Shipbuilding. During reconstruction, wrecking crews demolished six old workshops, which were replaced by a 200,000-square-foot fabrication plant for preassemblies. Six slipways received concrete foundations and were extended 120 feet into the Delaware River, a major undertaking that required $1.4 million worth of underwater work. Originally earmarked for the construction of six *Cleveland*-class light cruisers, Cramp later booked contracts for thirty-seven *Balao*-class submarines and for repair work, which was performed in a 675-foot dry dock built with $8 million in direct Navy funding.[21]

The Navy also bankrolled the construction of new shipyards with workshops and slipways that were often tailored for specific combatant types. In 1941, having belatedly recognized that the fleet lacked oceangoing escorts for convoying, the Navy launched an ambitious effort to build hundreds of destroyer escorts, whose relatively simple design made them suitable for serial construction in greenfield plants erected at Houston and Orange, Texas; Hingham, Massachusetts; and Newark, New Jersey. For landing vessels, the Navy financed the construction of other specialty yards. These government-owned, contractor-operated plants, whose combined cost exceeded $70 million, were managed by established firms.[22]

In the Midwest, Chicago Bridge & Iron netted $6.3 million in direct Navy funds to erect a "prairie shipyard" at Seneca, Illinois, for the construction of 4,080-ton tank landing ships. Chicago Bridge & Iron, which in peacetime specialized in pressurized storage tanks for oil refineries, recruited contractors to build the shipyard on a 192-acre site where "it was possible to spread the work out over a much larger area than is possible in the average shipyard with the result that much of the congestion, and consequent loss of efficiency, was avoided," hull welding superintendent Lloyd Stiles reported.[23] The completed plant featured a railroad connection, two main fabricating shops, warehouses, cranes, and slipways, in addition to automatic and manual welding equipment, shears, and bending equipment. While larger landing craft preassemblies like bottoms and main deck sections were produced on site, Chicago Iron & Bridge manufactured smaller ones at its production facilities in Chicago; Greenville, Pennsylvania; and Birmingham, Alabama, each of which "was assigned a certain portion of the ship, built the necessary jigs and specialized in the production of its particular part."[24]

Worker recruitment at Seneca was difficult because the yard was "located in a farming community with no large industrial population," the commandant of the Ninth Naval District noted. Green hands received preliminary training at newly established welding schools in nearby towns, supplemented by on-site training at the shipyard to prepare workers for Navy certification tests under the supervision of shop foremen and subforemen, most of whom had transferred to Seneca from the company's main plant in Chicago. Skilled hands were in short supply as late as May 1943, when the yard employed 6,500 workers but "needs at once 765 skilled mechanics," especially machinists, sheet metal workers, electricians, and pipe fitters.[25] Once Chicago Bridge & Iron had recruited skilled men throughout the Midwest in collaboration with the American Federation of Labor, Seneca achieved significant productivity gains

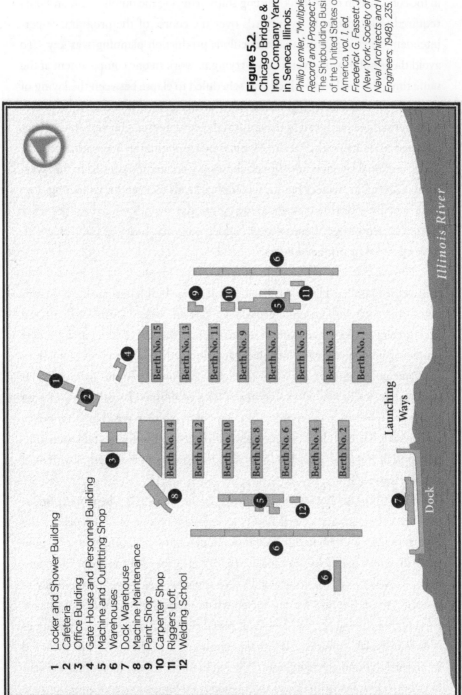

Figure 5.2.
Chicago Bridge &
Iron Company Yard
in Seneca, Illinois.

*Philip Lemler, "Multiple Yards:
Record and Prospect," in
The Shipbuilding Business
of the United States of
America, vol. 1, ed.
Frederick G. Fassett Jr.
(New York: Society of
Naval Architects and Marine
Engineers, 1948), 235.*

1 Locker and Shower Building
2 Cafeteria
3 Office Building
4 Gate House and Personnel Building
5 Machine and Outfitting Shop
6 Warehouses
7 Dock Warehouse
8 Machine Maintenance
9 Paint Shop
10 Carpenter Shop
11 Riggers Loft
12 Welding School

in the construction of 157 tank landing ships, reducing the number of man-hours required to build one by two-thirds over the course of the program. Superintendent Stiles explained that meticulous production planning was key. "To avoid the possibility of several crews trying to work in one compartment at the same time, the total time which was scheduled to elapse between the laying of the keel and commissioning was divided up into 20 work periods, and one of these periods was assigned to the crew as the definite time during which it was expected to do its work."[26] Like Manitowoc Shipbuilding, Seneca featured an unconventional layout where fifteen slipways were located parallel to the riverfront. Caterpillar tractors hauled a completed hull to a central launching way, from whence it was launched sideways into the river. Similar facilities were erected at Ambridge, Pennsylvania, and Evansville, Indiana, both of which were operated by bridge builders.[27]

The timing and sheer scale of U.S. Navy investments in private and contractor-operated plants gave American naval builders significant advantages over their foreign counterparts. In Britain, whose yards had suffered even greater neglect than American ones before the war, tooling and cranage remained inadequate well into the war, stifling the introduction of modern construction techniques. Sir Stephen Pigott of Browns told the Admiralty, "It is, of course, well known to you that our long established British yards can not utilise pre-fabrication to anything like the extent which is possible in a modern yard which has been laid out with special regard to pre-fabrication. Our limitation in lifting appliances is a most serious curtailment to the employment of pre-fabrication."[28]

The Admiralty ignored the facility problem until 1942, when an investigation headed by engineer Cecil Bentham revealed a range of deficiencies. Like Pigott, Bentham attributed the slow development of prefabrication in Britain to small cranes with a lifting capacity that rarely exceeded five tons. "The tendency now is to ask for cranes of 15 tons capacity, and there is a tendency to standardize on this size for the intermediate method of prefabricating heavy parts without going the full length of prefabricating a large area of plating as is done in North America," Bentham commented.[29] Other problems included small yard size and outdated tools. "Owing to financial stringency many works have been completely unable to spend money on necessary renovations or new plant, and this during a time when engineering practice with regard to materials, tools and machines was making great strides."[30] Crowded conditions hampered effective plant layouts because "Most of the old yards on the North East Coast and Scotland are limited in size and cannot easily expand their boundaries."[31] Many yards lacked welding equipment and in some instances even pneumatic riveting guns, which had long been standard in American yards. Generally speaking, "Most firms have succeeded in putting in a few new machines during the war period, say the last three or four years, but the effect is rather to show up how very much out of date is the remainder of the plant. The bulk of machines in some works is left from the last war or previously."[32] Bentham's recommendation to address some of the most pressing issues with public funding of facility updates led to the establishment of the Shipyard Development Committee. The latter provided funding to update naval as well as merchant yards, but the government provided only $6 million while industry invested $18 million in Britain's largest shipyard development program since World War I. The program retooled both naval and merchant yards. Most of the pneumatic riveting guns and welding tools Bentham had demanded were in place by August 1943. Select builders like Browns occasionally received discretionary Admiralty funding for twenty-five-ton cranes, but their installation was often hampered by late deliveries.[33]

In Germany, some yards were better equipped than others. At Germaniawerft in Kiel, "the cradle of the submarine in Germany" during the Great War according to the U.S. Strategic Bombing Survey, the "physical equipment . . . was allowed to become out of date and unsuitable for the modern production methods," though the yard remained a center of submarine research and design during the war.[34] The newer Deutsche Werft in Hamburg, founded in 1918, featured a "fine layout," in which "[i]ncoming raw materials flow from rail or storage in a straight line through the plate and bar shops, prefabrication area to the slipways," British investigators observed after the war.[35] AG Weser in Bremen, a large yard comparable to Newport News and Vickers Tyneside, was responsible for heavy cruisers, destroyers, and submarines. Facilities included ten slipways, three docks, and 150 buildings, "but as a result of the long period of development and growth of the yard within a confined area, the buildings were neither rationally arranged nor well spaced," the bombing survey commented after the war.[36] From 1935 to 1944, facility improvements worth $12 million, 75 percent of which was financed by the German navy directly, added a diesel engine shop, welding facilities, a foundry, cranes to lift twenty-ton pre-assemblies, living quarters for forced laborers, and a variety of machine tools. Blohm & Voss operated eight slipways and eight floating dry docks, in addition to integrated production facilities to manufacture boilers, turbines, reduction gear, propellers, and other items that American shipyards usually outsourced to subcontractors. The cost of individual projects occasionally rivaled the sums expended by the U.S. Navy on similar facilities. At Blohm & Voss, the navy invested $12.5 million in the Elbe 17 armored superdock, which was originally earmarked for battleship H construction but was later repurposed as an air raid shelter.[37]

Comparable data is unavailable for Japan, but anecdotal evidence suggests revealing trends. According to the bombing survey, Japan's "privately-owned yards did not want to increase their capital investments because of the uncertain demand before the war. During the war, improvements were undertaken, mainly in transportation and docking facilities, with little success in the latter. Several large yards rearranged shops and installed a large number of hammerhead cranes." Like in Britain, most of these changes were not completed until midwar. "Large machines such as guillotine sheers, keelbenders, and radial drills were not installed on a large scale during the war."[38] Exceptions included Mitsubishi Nagasaki, which according to U.S. Office of Naval Intelligence estimates "has facilities of great capacity, a good technical base and the necessary number of workers and engineering and technical personnel."[39] The yard featured sixty-four cranes and six covered slipways of varying sizes, the largest of which was fitted with a two-hundred-ton traveling crane (most of these facilities were damaged or destroyed in 1945, when the U.S. Army Air Forces dropped the atomic bomb on Nagasaki).[40]

MANAGERS AND WORKERS

Firms responsible for naval combatants were fairly complex organizations, and most of them were run by seasoned professionals. While upper management featured a conventional mix of functional departments, middle managers and foremen were responsible for a variety of divisions and shops found only in shipyards. Design organizations were staffed by naval architects and marine engineers, while the production and planning division "divides the ship into convenient sections and schedules the sequence of operations and material deliveries by sections and by departments in order to insure an orderly construction of the vessel with a minimum number of personnel and a minimum amount of material in storage," according to Arthur Homer of Bethlehem Shipbuilding.[41] The hull construction, machinery, and outfitting organizations were headed by superintendents and divided into two dozen shops, though variations were common.[42]

Most men who headed major firms as presidents during the war looked back on decades-long careers in the industry. Homer Ferguson, the president of Newport News who was sixty-seven years old in 1940, had graduated at the head of his class from the Naval Academy in 1892, subsequently attended Glasgow University, and spent his early career as a naval architect at the Puget Sound navy yard, the Bath Iron Works, and the Bureau of Construction & Repair before joining Newport News as superintendent in 1905. Elected president ten years later, he was instrumental in developing the yard in World War I, instituting pension plans and establishing an apprenticeship school, which became a model for other firms. Ferguson relied on a seasoned management team. John Woodward, who started his career as a draftsman at Newport News in 1914, rose through the ranks under Ferguson's tutelage and in 1936 was appointed general manager, a position he held throughout the war. William Blewett, a Cornell University graduate, likewise commenced his career as a draftsman, was appointed production manager in 1930, and remained in that position as Ferguson's right-hand man until after the war.[43]

Newport News' corporate structure changed in 1940, when members of the Huntington family sold their controlling share to a group of investors. The Huntingtons, who had owned the company since its formation in the late nineteenth century and were not required to issue annual financial statements under Securities and Exchange Commission rules, in 1940 released a prospectus which was "of great interest to buyers all over the country, [who took] steps to get a hold of that document," a banker told Congress.[44] Lured by revelations that Newport News had amassed $20 million in net profits since 1928, a consortium of sixteen investors headed by the Tri-Continental Corporation acquired all 100,000 shares of common stock in Newport News for $73 million and turned Newport News into a publicly traded company but retained Ferguson's operational management team.[45]

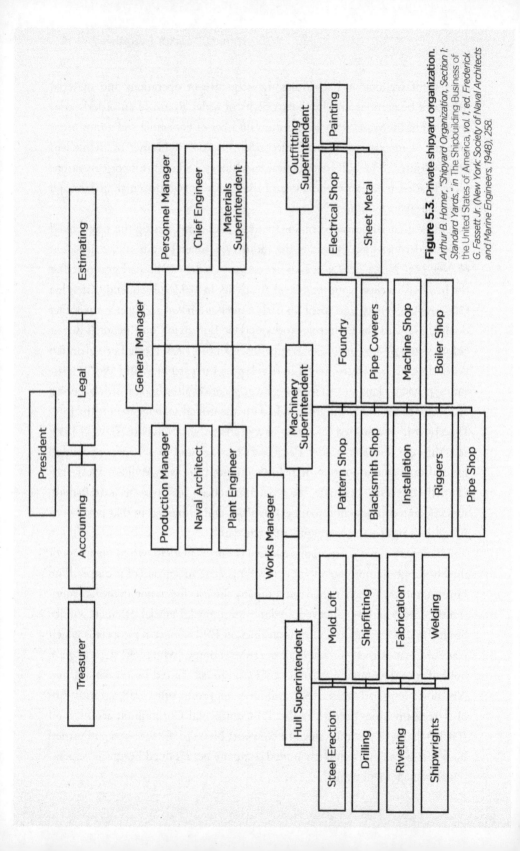

Figure 5.3. Private shipyard organization.
Arthur B. Homer, "Shipyard Organization, Section 1: Standard Yards," in The Shipbuilding Business of the United States of America, vol. 1, ed. Frederick G. Fassett Jr. (New York: Society of Naval Architects and Marine Engineers, 1948), 258.

Operational management of Bethlehem Steel's sprawling shipbuilding division was headed by Arthur Homer, an engineer who had risen through the ranks after he joined the company in 1919. Taking an active role in cargo ship construction at the Bethlehem-Fairfield yard in Baltimore, Homer left wartime naval shipbuilding in the hands of experienced local managers. Fore River was headed by William Collins, who rose from assistant hull superintendent to general manager in the 1920s and 1930s, and during the war received added responsibilities as head of the Hingham escort destroyer yard. Charles Boylan, Collins' counterpart at Bethlehem Staten Island, was a Pratt Institute graduate who had served as a machinist apprentice at the Baltimore & Ohio Railroad before commencing his career at the Staten Island yard in 1912. Appointed Staten Island's general plant manager in 1935, he also supervised operations of three Bethlehem repair yards in New York harbor. Having designed ferryboats, Boylan managed the construction of forty-seven destroyers of the *Sumner* and *Fletcher* classes in collaboration with the Gibbs & Cox naval architecture consulting firm.[46]

While Newport News and Bethlehem usually recruited senior managers from the ranks of in-house personnel, New York Ship was headed by men who had spent considerable time elsewhere. President John Metten had worked for a quarter-century at Cramp & Sons, where he rose to the position of vice president and chief engineer before the yard closed. New York Ship's board of directors brought him on board in 1933 as vice president in charge of hull and engine design and named him president a year later (see chapter 1). In addition to negotiating contracts and handling relations with the Navy Department, Metten remained involved in cruiser design during the war. In 1942, he resigned as president to concentrate on his engineering duties and handed some of his executive responsibilities to Roy Campbell, who did double duty as president and general manager. A graduate of the University of Michigan's marine engineering program, Campbell had worked as a loftsman at Newport News and was appointed superintendent of machinery of Bethlehem's Harlan plant in Wilmington, Delaware, in World War I. During his fifteen-year career with Bethlehem, he also served at the Sparrow's Point yard in Baltimore and at Fore River, where he became general superintendent. After a short stint at Babcock & Wilcox, he joined New York Ship as general manager in 1934 and became Metten's senior assistant. Metten and Campbell worked closely with the yard's two senior naval architects. Ernest Rigg, who graduated from the Royal Technical College of Scotland in 1900 with a degree in naval architecture, was apprenticed at Fairfield on the Clyde prior to taking a position as draftsman at New York Ship in 1908. Two years later, he was promoted to chief naval architect, a position he held until the early 1950s. His colleague Thomas Bossert graduated from Philadelphia's Franklin Institute and commenced a career in shipbuilding as a junior draftsman at New York Ship and then worked at Cramp & Sons until its closure, when he joined Metten's Marine Engineering Corporation. He returned to New York Ship in 1929 as assistant naval architect and played a key role in the development of the *Brooklyn*-class light cruiser design during the 1930s, the predecessor of *Cleveland*-class light cruisers and *Independence*-class carriers whose design team was headed by Bossert.[47]

Some firms were run by executives with surprisingly little shipyard management experience, which usually did not bode well for their performance. Cramp was headed from 1941 to 1943 by retired Rear Adm. William Du Bose, a distinguished naval architect who had served as chief of the Bureau of Construction & Repair. At Cramp, he was embroiled in controversies over his large salary and mismanagement of industrial relations, which led to a disastrous strike at midwar and his ouster. Du Bose's successor Henry Rossell, a professor of naval architecture at the Massachusetts Institute of Technology, was disliked by workers and shop masters for his inept handling of Cramp's delicate labor relations. General manager Ralph Weyerbacher was a retired commander whose disappointing Navy career had ended in 1937 and had been followed by a variety of unsuccessful business ventures. His most recent shipyard experience dated to 1917, when he had supervised the construction of a troop transport at the Philadelphia Navy Yard. Weyerbacher's tenure at Cramp was marred by a corruption scandal, which led to his ouster in 1943.[48]

Managerial incompetence was also evident at Los Angeles Shipbuilding & Dry Dock of San Pedro, California, which received $4.9 million in Navy plant development funds to build *Vulcan*-class repair ships, including the 16,460-ton *Ajax*. The company subsequently "wasted Five to Seven Million Dollars in the construction of the AJAX," fumed Vice Adm. Harold Bowen, at the time special assistant to the Undersecretary of the Navy, in a memorandum to his boss James Forrestal in 1943. "The AJAX and other ships have been inexcusably

delayed. There is an utter lack of cost consciousness at the yard. The organization is unsatisfactory and there are not enough key men skilled in industrial or
shipbuilding management. There are no production controls, no material controls, no budgetary controls, no progress controls."[49] An irate President Roosevelt promptly signed an executive order to have the plant seized by the Navy,
which transferred it to Todd Shipyards. That firm's executives installed a new
management team to clean up the personnel mess, conduct an inventory, sort
out finances and the organizational structure, and improve relations with the
unions, all of which enabled the yard to deliver the remaining *Vulcan*s close to
schedule. The Navy also requisitioned Brewster Aeronautical's fighter aircraft
plant in Long Island City, New York, and ordnance manufacturer York Safe
& Lock in Pennsylvania. As in the case of Los Angeles Shipbuilding, these seizures were the result of senior management's ineptitude, in contrast to the 1941
takeovers, which involved labor disputes.[50]

In most yards, middle management was the responsibility of superintendents, who reported to general managers and supervised shop foremen. Like
the more seasoned executives, these men often spent their entire careers with one
firm. At Bethlehem's San Francisco yard, which built *Fletcher*-class destroyers
and *Atlanta*-class light cruisers, the hull division was headed by Herbert Craw-
ford, who had commenced his career with Bethlehem after graduating from
high school in 1921. Harold Chanley had started working in one of Bethlehem's East Coast yards in 1916 and twenty years later moved to San Francisco,
where he was appointed superintendent of the outfitting division. His opposite
number in the engineering division was George Holmes, who had been with
the W. R. Grace Steamship Company before he was hired by Bethlehem San
Francisco in 1934. Men like Holmes supervised shop foremen, most of whom
still worked in the same plants where they had started their careers. At New
York Ship, more than 80 percent of all foremen had been employed by the
yard throughout their entire working lives, with an average tenure of more
than thirty years. Men who had joined the yard from other employers included
turret shop foreman James McCall, who had been with Cramp & Sons for many
years before he was hired by New York Ship in 1935, when it needed a turret
specialist for *Brooklyn*-class light cruisers. In 1941, his division moved into a new
building to produce turrets for the follow-on *Cleveland* class under McCall's
supervision.[51]

Like navy yards, most firms relied on core workforces of long-term employees, most of whom had undergone extensive training in their respective trades. Many had completed four-year apprenticeships run by personnel divisions in collaboration with shop foremen and rated mechanics. In some yards, apprenticeship programs expanded significantly during the war and were occasionally accelerated along the lines of navy-yard practice (see chapter 4). Newport News retained a four-year format instituted between the wars, and after Pearl Harbor it recruited a thousand high school graduates annually from small towns and rural areas in southern Virginia and North Carolina. In an average week, every Newport News apprentice received eight hours of classroom instruction in mathematics, "applied mechanics, physics, chemistry, English, industrial economics, and lecture courses by division and department heads on plant management," Ferguson explained. "The vocational training which occupies the remainder of his workweek is under the direction of a whole-time instructor and covers the full scope of the craft training, qualifying him at completion as a first-class journeyman mechanic in his trade."[52] To fill the ranks of semiskilled hull trades like welding, drilling, and caulking, Newport News trained eight thousand workers, called up-graders, whose more informal trade experience resembled that of helper-trainees in navy yards. These recruits "begin their training immediately on production work and learn to do definite things very well in 3 months—a definite single thing," Ferguson stressed. "Of course, the supervisors have to be what you might call all-around men, but you can teach men to do definite things."[53] The workforce peaked at 30,000 in 1943, including 1,200 women, only 400 of whom were shop floor workers. Newport News also employed 8,000 black men, who like their counterparts in navy yards were usually relegated to trades like riveting and caulking, which were among the dirtiest and most physically demanding in the industry (the yard's apprenticeship program excluded blacks). Wage discrimination was common at Newport News. When an African American ship painter asked for a raise, his supervisor responded that the request amounted to "too much money for a colored man."[54]

INDUSTRIAL RELATIONS

Shipyard industrial relations constituted a patchwork of local arrangements between employers and a variety of labor organizations whose fragmentation reflected broader trends in American trade unionism. Shipyard craft unions affiliated with the American Federation of Labor (AFL) were entrenched on the West Coast, particularly in Tacoma and Seattle in Washington State, Los Angeles, and San Francisco. Most of these firms handled repair work and merchant construction but little naval shipbuilding. The Industrial Union of Marine and Shipbuilding Workers of America (IUMSWA) was affiliated with the Congress of Industrial Organizations, organized workers across trade boundaries, and had strongholds at Federal Ship, Cramp, a handful of northeastern merchant and repair yards, and above all at New York Ship, where its first local had been formed in a series of violent strikes during the New Deal. Newport News, the Bath Iron Works, Electric Boat, and Fore River maintained company unions despite National Labor Relations Board (NLRB) objections. In private yards, the percentage of workers covered by collective bargaining agreements rose from 50 percent in 1940 to more than 90 percent in 1944.[55]

Attempts to establish forums for regional and national labor agreements dated to November 1940, when the National Defense Advisory Commission (a predecessor of the War Production Board) formed the Shipbuilding Stabilization Committee to sort out wage differences, which at the time contributed to high labor turnover as builders sought to lure workers from each other with better compensation. The Stabilization Committee consisted of special assistant to the Navy Secretary Joseph Powell (a former Bethlehem Shipbuilding executive), Vice Adm. Emory Land of the Maritime Commission, union representatives of the AFL Metal Trades Department, the International Association of Machinists, and the IUMSWA, together with a handful of employer representatives. The latter did not include executives of the major naval builders because Bethlehem, Newport News, the Bath Iron Works, and other employers objected to the exclusion of their company unions from the Stabilization Committee. Committee members agreed to a conditional no-strike, no-lockout pledge and the formation of zone conferences to determine standards in major shipbuilding regions. The Pacific Coast zone conference resulted in a major union victory in April 1941, when the various parties agreed on an hourly base rate of $1.12 for a first-class mechanic, which represented a significant raise for shipyard workers, in some areas by as much as 12 percent. Subsequent agreements for the Atlantic Coast and the Great Lakes likewise resulted in a $1.12 base rate, while the Gulf Coast zone conference agreed on $1.07. Employers and the Navy were happy with the no-strike pledge and with an agreement to keep base rates in place for two years instead of one demanded by the unions.[56]

In summer 1941, the IUMSWA sought a closed-shop system at Federal Ship, where it maintained one its strongest locals. Union leaders expected management to meet the demand because it wanted to avoid strikes and conflicts at a time when the Navy urged accelerated completion of combatants. In July, the National Defense Mediation Board issued a ruling that marked a major step toward a closed shop, mandating that Federal Ship fire members of Local 16 who did not pay their union dues. When shipyard president Lynn Korndorff, who was also vice president of the U.S. Steel Corporation, Federal Ship's parent company, refused to implement the decision, Local 16 called a strike in August. After rejecting the Navy's recommendation to abide by the mediation board's ruling, Korndorff upped the ante by offering to sell or lease the yard to the government. An undeterred Roosevelt shortly signed an executive order authorizing the Navy to seize the plant, which resulted in Korndorff's replacement with Bowen, though most other managers remained in place. After negotiating an end to the strike, Bowen proved an active executive who frequently consulted with superintendents, foremen, and shop floor workers. Local 16 applauded his decision to terminate Korndorff's attempts to form a company union, but was frustrated with his refusal to implement the mediation board ruling. When productivity improvements received publicity, "left-wing newspapers were gleeful because they regarded it as proof that Government management was superior to private management, and the right-wing newspapers were constantly seeking to prove that private property and private owners were being damaged," Bowen later recalled.[57] The Navy returned Federal Ship to private management in January 1942, followed by Korndorff's grudging acceptance of a National War Labor Board directive to introduce a quasi-closed-shop system, resulting in a major victory for the IUMSWA.[58]

Plant seizures were a mixed blessing for organized labor. In addition to Federal Ship, the government in 1941 took temporary control of an Air Associates aircraft plant in Bendix, New Jersey, and a North American Aviation factory in Inglewood, California, after management had refused to settle strikes. Legalized by the Selective Service Act of 1940, which empowered the president to take possession of any business that failed to comply with Army and Navy orders, these seizures signaled to business that the government would not tolerate employer intransigence in labor disputes. Expectations that plant requisitions would produce labor-friendly management were usually not met, however, and opinion polls indicated that a majority of the American public disapproved of the strikes that had triggered federal seizures in the first place, prompting some union organizers to reject government takeovers as a viable tactic.[59]

Shipyard unions occasionally scored successes in campaigns for better housing in shipbuilding hubs. In Camden, New Jersey, the U.S. Housing Corporation had invested $11 million in the construction of a 225-acre development called Yorkship for New York Ship workers in World War I, but the city suffered extreme overcrowding in World War II. "An old city with comparatively little new housing but with old homes in varying states of disrepair, Camden was suddenly flooded with defense workers who found jobs in the shipyards, Radio Corporation of America, Campbell's Soup, and other industrial plants," a union official reported. "Many workers were compelled to travel from 20 to 60 miles daily."[60] A campaign led by Local 1 of the IUMSWA resulted in the construction of six hundred housing units for union members. Newport News was less fortunate, according to the *Shipyard Worker*, the IUMSWA newspaper. "Shipyard workers are living four to six in a room; crowded in housing and buildings without adequate sanitary facilities, and packed in trailer camps in every outlying section of the city," it reported in 1941. "Some few apartments are advertised in the local papers—at exorbitant rentals—and they all state 'NO CHILDREN.' The U.S. Housing projects are inadequate and many workers are today living under the most miserable conditions."[61]

Like most labor organizations, shipyard unions presented themselves as responsible collective bargaining partners committed to the no-strike pledge issued in 1941. Prior to Pearl Harbor, the IUMSWA defended strikes as reactions to employer violations of contract agreements. In October 1941, when Local 35 of the IUMSWA called a strike at shipyard supplier American Engineering in Philadelphia, the *Shipyard Worker* reported that its members walked out because the company had refused "to meet with the Union to settle grievances or submit them to arbitration" as stipulated in a contract.[62] Such tacit endorsements of job action vanished once the United States entered the war. Union president John Green told Congress, "For us, the no-strike policy is a command to be obeyed without question," though not without adding, "we, the union officials, do not and cannot control all working conditions of management actions." In some instances, workers "have been so goaded that they have come to me and said: 'Johnny, can't we stop for just 1 day to show them they can't do this to us? We promise to make up the production when we go back.'"[63] Green refused to heed such calls and took active measures to quell wildcat strikes, most notoriously during a walkout at Cramp in 1944. The strike began after production supervisors ordered the paint department to use spray guns instead of brushes, prompting forty-two painters to refuse without a pay raise. When management fired the painters, 8,500 members of Local 42 of the IUMSWA walked out spontaneously in solidarity, triggering one of the largest strikes in wartime naval shipbuilding. The strikers accused Cramp of repeated contract violations, contempt for union representatives, and harboring expectations "that we have to take all they dish out and like it."[64] An irate Green called the walkout "inexcusable" and threatened union members who remained off the job with disciplinary action. During a contentious four-hour meeting attended by three thousand members, the president of Local 42 reluctantly defended Green's position and urged the strikers to return to work. Though his pleas were initially greeted by catcalls, a majority voted to end the strike.[65]

The IUMSWA made organizing headway in some yards but suffered grievous setbacks in others. Repeated efforts to gain employer recognition at Fore River were hampered by internal divisions between anticommunist union leaders and grassroots organizers who included left-wing radicals. Local efforts finally bore fruit in June 1945 when union elections sponsored by the NLRB resulted in an IUMSWA victory. At Newport News, by contrast, the IUMSWA failed to establish itself as a collective bargaining agent partly as a result of competition with a company union called the Peninsular Shipbuilders' Association. As early as 1939, the U.S. Supreme Court upheld an NLRB finding that the company had "dominated, given financial and other assistance to, and interfered with the administration of a labor organization of its employees."[66] After implementing cosmetic changes, Newport News recognized the company union as its collective bargaining partner without holding NLRB-sponsored elections. In 1944, the IUMSWA petitioned the NLRB to hold union elections at Newport News, but management objected that the union's proposed bargaining structure excluded timekeepers, piecework counters, and supervisors, all of whom were members of Peninsular Shipbuilders' Association. The NLRB confirmed that the IUMSWA's proposal was consistent with federal collective bargaining policy and ordered elections to be held, but Newport News appealed the decision until after the war, when the passage of the Taft-Hartley Act of 1947 inflicted a strategic defeat on American organized labor.[67]

British employers despised organized labor as much as their American counterparts did but confronted more mature trade unions, which rarely turned to the state to validate their legitimacy and collective bargaining rights. Largely unencumbered by company unions, organizations like the powerful Boilermakers Society and the Amalgamated Society of Engineers, both of which traced their roots to the midnineteenth century, were well entrenched in most yards, distributed unemployment benefits, organized worker placement, and were actively involved in craft training. In World War II, British shipyard unions opposed the employment of women and unskilled workers. They also objected to employer attempts to reassign workers from one trade to another, in contrast to American unions, which usually consented to such measures. Job action was far more common than in American naval shipbuilding even though wartime legislation outlawed strikes. In 1941, more than six thousand apprentices walked out along the Clyde to protest low wages and poor treatment by employers. When the strike continued despite wage concessions negotiated by the government, Ernest Bevin, minister of labour, a veteran trade union activist and Labour Party leader, forced the youngsters back to work with threats to have them drafted. From 1939 to 1945, British shipyard workers staged 943 stoppages that resulted in the loss of more than one million workdays. No such conflicts were evident in Germany and Japan, where trade unions had been obliterated before the war to the cheers of shipyard managers.[68]

WORKLOADS AND YARD SPECIALIZATION

In the United States, private firms were responsible for a variety of combatant types but generally enjoyed a higher degree of specialization than navy yards and foreign builders as a result of federal shipbuilding policies. As early as 1940, the Navy and the Maritime Commission agreed to separate combatant and merchant shipbuilding because their shop floor routines, skill requirements, and quality standards differed considerably. "God help any yard that has to work with the Maritime Commission and the Navy too," one observer noted. "The confusion . . . is beyond conception."[69] "Of necessity, the Navy pre-empted the services of the handful of shipyards in the country which were both experienced in the art of naval shipbuilding," a wartime congressional investigation explained. "This was necessary because of the fact that the Navy's needs covered a wide variety of complicated types of naval vessels, the success of each one of which was entirely dependent upon the skill and experience of the existing design offices and shipyards which were drafted for the task of taking the preliminary plans prepared by the Navy Department and translating them into working plans for the speedy and efficient construction of ships."[70] Capt. Howard Vickery, the Maritime Commission's vice chairman, told Congress, "we have no work at Fore River, the Bethlehem plant. The Navy has no work at Sun Shipbuilding [a tanker specialist]; the Navy has no work at [Bethlehem] Sparrow's Point."[71]

Vickery was not entirely satisfied with this arrangement because it deprived the Maritime Commission of shipbuilding expertise of yards like Newport News, where he tried to place three cargo vessels, but the Navy "[is] not permitting us to go in there," he complained.[72] The Maritime Commission still took advantage of Newport News' expertise with the establishment of North Carolina Shipbuilding, a Newport News subsidiary, which operated a greenfield yard at Wilmington, North Carolina, to build Liberty ships under the management of Roger Williams, Newport News' vice president, and other supervisory personnel reassigned from the main yard. The Navy occasionally encroached on Maritime Commission turf, for example at Seattle-Tacoma Shipbuilding, a defunct yard that had been rehabilitated with commission funds to construct cargo ships under the joint auspices of Todd Dry Dock & Construction and construction magnate Henry Kaiser. After Todd had bought Kaiser's share, the Navy recruited Seattle-Tacoma in March 1942 to build thirty-seven *Bogue*-class escort carriers for the American and British navies. Kaiser, eager to get his hands on Navy contracts, volunteered to build fifty *Casablanca*-class escort carriers at a Vancouver shipyard in Washington State but was rebuffed by the Navy Department, whose officials considered him a showboat. After Kaiser and Maritime Commission executives took the case to Roosevelt, the carrier contract went to Kaiser, to the chagrin of the Navy, which washed its hands of the project and transferred the *Casablanca* design to the Maritime Commission rather than work with Kaiser. Kaiser also designed and built *Tacoma*-class frigates under commission auspices with mixed results (see below). Such bickering notwithstanding, the separation of naval and merchant shipbuilding generally worked as planned, remained in place throughout the war, and facilitated yard specialization.[73]

To reduce interference between new construction and other yard activities, the Navy Department assigned the bulk of repair work to specialty firms. The latter usually employed the same trades as established builders but also operated dedicated facilities like dry docks and marine railways, which were less common in conventional shipyards. Moreover, ship repairers performed demanding work only occasionally handled by builders, notably reverse-engineering of damaged bows, sterns, hull sections, and superstructures the original blueprints and specifications of which were often unavailable. The Navy recruited more than seventy firms for repairs, according to Robinson, who explained in 1941, "The military importance of having these private yards available for, and familiar with, naval work is tremendous in view of the necessary numbers of vessels in service."[74] By 1942, sixty-six floating dry docks were under construction to enhance repair capacity. Contractors ranged from small waterfront shops like Dade Drydock in Miami, Florida, which operated a floating dry dock, to giants like Todd Shipyards Corporation with plants in New York State, New Jersey, Alabama, Texas, and Washington State (the Todd yard in Hoboken, New Jersey, operated six floating dry docks, the largest of which could lift 20,000 tons). Though shipbuilders occasionally performed repair work during slack times, they much preferred new construction, while firms like Newport News that systematically combined the two businesses were rare. Ships repairers, in turn, shunned new construction whenever possible. A representative of Todd Shipyards explained that "we felt that we should not go into the shipbuilding business, but continue in the one business in which we had been most successful, namely the repair business."[75] The Navy eventually convinced Todd to build the abovementioned *Bogue*-class escort carriers, in addition to forty-three destroyers of the *Sumner, Fletcher,* and *Gleaves* classes in the Seattle-Tacoma and Todd-Pacific yards near Seattle, but the firm's other yards remained dedicated to repairs. Todd's repair yards received facility upgrades and five Navy-financed floating dry docks as the Navy's aggregate annual repair volume skyrocketed from $96.7 million (1939) to $709.7 million (1943). Assignment of most contracts to repair specialists relieved builders, who could concentrate on new construction.[76]

Specialization also benefited from contract reforms instituted in 1940, which suspended competitive bidding and enabled the Bureau of Ships to assign contracts to yards that could claim long-standing expertise in the design and construction of specific vessel types (see chapter 3). For *Essex*-class carriers, the bureau selected Newport News as the lead yard because it had successfully developed the preceding *Yorktown*-class detail design. Newport News, which built nine *Essex*-class carriers, supplied blueprints, specifications, and material orders to the so-called follow-on yards, Fore River and the navy yards in Brooklyn and Philadelphia, which built another fifteen of the class. New York Ship, whose naval architects and marine engineers had developed the detail design of *Brooklyn*-class light cruisers in the 1930s, served as the lead yard for *Cleveland*-class light cruiser program of World War II (see below).

Specialization combined with naval construction experience yielded impressive results, as evidenced by the *Fletcher*-class destroyer program, which produced 175 units in one of the war's most ambitious attempts to build sophisticated combatants in large series. Unlike the preceding 2,515-ton *Benson* class, the 2,900-ton *Fletchers* were the first American destroyers whose displacement exceeded treaty limitations by a significant margin. Their large size enabled the Navy Department's Preliminary Design section to equip *Fletchers* with a main armament of five 5-inch, dual-purpose guns and ten torpedo tubes, along with ample antiaircraft and antisubmarine warfare capabilities. Their maximum design speed of thirty-seven knots and 4,800-mile endurance at fifteen knots made them well-suited for the enormous distances that had to be covered in the Pacific War theater, where most of them served. Here, they occasionally encountered their closest Japanese counterparts: the slightly larger *Yūgumo*-class armed with six 5-inch guns and eight torpedo tubes. Only nineteen of these were laid down during the war.[77]

Fletcher-class contracts went to eleven shipyards, several of which had built prewar destroyers in collaboration with Gibbs & Cox. While the overall design was handled by the Navy, Gibbs & Cox was responsible for *Fletcher* working plans. Federal Ship and the Bath Iron Works, both of which had extensive destroyer construction experience, booked more orders than other yards and completed their ships in record time, averaging 194 and 262 days from keel laying to commissioning, respectively. Both specialized in destroyers during the war (though Federal Ship also built a pair of light cruisers). At the other end of the spectrum stood the Puget Sound Navy Yard, where destroyer construction was frequently disrupted by repairs of the Pacific Fleet (see chapter 4), and newcomer Gulf Shipbuilding in Chickasaw, Alabama. Yards that performed near the average included Consolidated Shipbuilding of Orange, Texas, originally a merchant yard that was retooled for naval work with $11 million in Navy funds; Todd's Seattle-Tacoma plant, which built escort carriers in addition to destroyers; and Bethlehem San Francisco, another merchant builder with limited destroyer construction experience, which also constructed four cruisers and destroyer escorts during the war. None of these *Fletcher* builders rivaled Federal Ship and Bath in terms of volume and construction speed.[78]

A closer look at Bath's shop floor routines reveals the dynamics of specialization and serial construction. The first *Fletcher*-class destroyer was constructed according to conventional methods of building ships piece by piece on the ways in lengthy construction sequences. For example, shipfitters laid the keel and positioned plates, and then had to wait for machinists to fit boilers and turbines, pipefitters to install piping, welders to complete the hull, and electricians to stretch wires, before shipfitters could return to work on the superstructure. Serial construction began in 1941 after Bath had prodded the Bureau of Ships for additional destroyers, which would "employ [Navy-financed] facilities through at least the calendar year 1944." Like Chicago Bridge & Iron, Bath emphasized the importance of careful production planning, urging the Navy to order more destroyers in advance. "By having the orders now we could arrange for priorities and deliveries that would fit with the work in hand, and in this way we could make deliveries earlier, and at less eventual cost to the government than if the orders were delayed until the end of the present program was in sight. Not only could we, the prime contractor, fit the work in better with existing work; but a similar advantage would hold for subcontractors on whom the government is dependent for materials, particularly machinery and boilers."[79] Once Bath had received follow-on orders for *Fletcher*s, it adopted a new production system in which bulkheads, longitudinals, and superstructure sections were fabricated and welded at the new Harding plant 3.7 miles from the main plant, from where they were transported on flatbed cars to Bath. The use of preassemblies reduced the amount of time a hull sat on the slipway, traditionally a production bottleneck. Moreover, planners scheduled production so that a new *Fletcher* keel could be laid approximately every four weeks to accommodate repeat work. Shipfitters now laid the keel, raised frames, and prepared hull plates for one *Fletcher* and repeated the process on adjacent slipways without having to wait for welders, machinists, and electricians to finish their work on the first hull. Shipfitters then returned to the first slipway to install preassembled superstructure sections, which could then be fitted with radar, fire control systems, and wires by electricians who had completed their work on other hulls. In addition to saving time on the slipways, Bath's production planners worked closely with subcontractors like Babcock & Wilcox and General Electric to ensure the delivery of boilers and turbines, respectively, in a nascent just-in-time-delivery system, which reduced the amount of time subcontracted items had to be hauled in and out of warehouses. Serial construction and specialization enabled Bath to reduce the amount of time from keel laying to delivery by 57 percent from the first *Fletcher* to the last. Moreover, Bath-built *Fletcher*s cost significantly below program average and were delivered ahead of contract dates, in some instances by as much as eight months. Bath achieved similar records in the construction of twenty-nine destroyers of the *Gearing* class and twenty *Sumner*s, which had configurations that resembled *Fletcher*'s.[80]

Fletcher-class destroyers *Nicholas* and *O'Bannon* under construction at Bath Iron Works, October 1, 1940. *Photograph 410229, RG 19, Records of the Bureau of Ships, National Archives and Records Administration, College Park, MD*

Gulf Shipbuilding in Alabama failed to develop these sorts of economies. Originally built in World War I to construct cargo ships and then deactivated after the war, the yard was acquired and refurbished by Waterman Steamship in 1940 to build C-2 cargo ships for the Maritime Commission. The yard was subsequently reallocated to the Navy, which funded $5.4 million in improvements, nearly double the amount it invested in the Bath Iron Works. Worker recruitment was hampered by a lack of housing and insufficient transportation to nearby Mobile. Conversion of three C-2 attack transports proved a time-consuming endeavor, as did the construction of twenty-nine minesweepers. These programs interfered with the timely completion of seven *Fletchers* assigned to Gulf Shipbuilding, whose average of 748 days from keel laying to commissioning was the worst record among builders of the class. Construction time declined by only 15 percent from the first unit to the last.[81]

In *Balao*-class submarine construction, the lead builder Electric Boat averaged 405 days per boat from keel laying to delivery, compared to the Portsmouth

Chart 5.1. *Fletcher*-Class Destroyer Construction at Bath Iron Works: Days from Keel Laying to Commissioning, 1941–1943

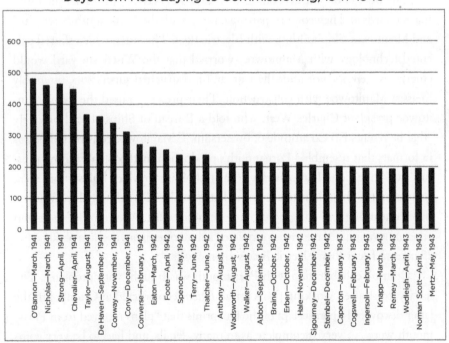

Months indicate keel-laying.

Calculated from data in Norman Friedman, U.S. Destroyers: An Illustrated Design History *(Annapolis, MD: Naval Institute Press, 2004).*

Navy Yard's average of only 214 days. The discrepancy was partly attributable to yard facilities; Portsmouth featured ample outfitting capacity while over-crowded Electric Boat lacked sufficient piers. Moreover, Electric Boat included the newly built Victory Yard, which took a while to break in and hence completed submarines at a slower pace of 425 days than the main works (386 days). Portsmouth also outproduced Electric Boat because it relied more extensively on prefabrication of subassemblies on shop floors prior to their assembly on the slipways, and because it introduced three shifts earlier in the war than did Electric Boat. Simultaneously, the navy yard coped with more design changes than the private builder, whose management objected to continuous improve-ments in submarine technology desired by the Navy. While Portsmouth gen-erally managed to incorporate changes in the design process and on the shop floor fairly smoothly, Electric Boat informed the Bureau of Ships that change orders were incompatible with speedy construction. The matter came to a head in 1943, when the bureau threatened to cut Electric Boat out of submarine design entirely unless it complied with change orders, prompting management to back down.[82]

The Bureau of Ships encouraged cooperation between the established sub-marine yards and newcomers, pairing Cramp with the Portsmouth Navy Yard and Manitowoc Shipbuilding with Electric Boat. The latter, which shared pat-ented technology with Manitowoc, worried that the Wisconsin yard would emerge as a competitor after the war, and it dispatched supervisors, ostensibly to assist Manitowoc with construction. Their presence raised the ire of Man-itowoc president Charles West, who told a Bureau of Ships official privately "that he resents EB Co attitude of ownership."[83] Manitowoc constructed *Balao*s in formats that resembled Portsmouth's production methods, fabricating pres-sure hulls in sections. It also used welding techniques in which hull sections were rotated on the shop floor to accommodate downhand welding, which was less time-consuming and dangerous than overhead work. As a result of these and other innovations, Manitowoc completed submarines in an average of 301 days, 25 percent faster than Electric Boat's main works.[84]

Cramp's collaboration with Portsmouth was fraught with problems. The navy yard drafted working plans for all *Balao*s constructed at Cramp, but the latter discovered upon receipt of the blueprints that "plans received from Ports-mouth were . . . very incomplete as to many details, and had to be very com-pletely reworked by Cramp before being satisfactory for production purposes,"

Prefabricated hull section of a *Balao*-class submarine lowered on to
the building blocks at Manitowoc Shipbuilding in Wisconsin, c. 1942.
The submarine *Pogy* receives finishing touches on the left.
P80-40-1, Wisconsin Maritime Museum Collection

management complained. The lack of design detail was partly attributable to
the fact that Portsmouth's more experienced workers did not need blueprints
detailing certain routine welding techniques, in contrast to Cramp's green hands.
Moreover, Portsmouth supplied new initial drawings for later batches of submarines that had received thorough redesigns of their main engines, electric
motors, and reduction gear. "In the practical working out of the matter, Cramp

built submarines to three different sets of plans," defeating the Navy's declared intent to "obtain full advantage of the duplication of design" in *Balao* construction. Equally troublesome, "plan information arriving from Portsmouth was universally behind schedule not only for production purposes, but also for the placing of orders for important materials," management reported.[85] To boot, the Bureau of Ships ordered 4,200 alterations to the first submarine batch and 2,400 alterations to the second. Portsmouth handled the redesign, but—busy as it was with other programs—was not the first yard to modify the actual vessels. It left that unenviable task to Cramp, which found out that some of the proposed changes were technically unfeasible. "[A]ny procedure which places a following yard in a position of becoming a 'quasi lead yard' for certain changes results in an almost unworkable situation," management lamented with some justification. Cramp exacerbated the situation by neglecting to build a full-scale wooden model to determine the feasibility of design changes, using instead the hull of *Devilfish*, the first submarine laid down at the yard in March 1942. "This may have been an unwise decision in view of the incomplete plans supplied," management admitted.[86] The yard averaged 804 days from keel laying to delivery, the worst production record in *Balao* construction.

In the larger scheme of things, Cramp's problems were attributable to a lack of specialization. Overloaded with *Cleveland*-class light cruiser construction, conversions, and repair work, the yard lacked sufficient supervisory staff and shop floor personnel necessary for submarine construction. A former Navy inspector recalled:

> The place was opened under the most adverse of conditions that you can think of. All of the competent labor had been hired by the Philadelphia Navy Yard, by New York Ship across in Camden, and by Sun [Shipbuilding of Chester, Pennsylvania] down the river a short way. It became very difficult to hire competent labor. The management in the yard was very, very lacking in know how, in discipline, and in knowledge of how to run an industrial establishment. . . . The Navy further complicated the situation by putting in one of the most complex programs you can think of: building cruisers, submarines, and handling ship conversions. . . . I was exposed daily to how not to do so many things, and it could not have been better experience for my career anywhere I wanted to go.[87]

Exceptions like Cramp notwithstanding, private American builders were generally more specialized than their British counterparts. The Admiralty took charge of merchant construction and repairs in February 1940 and established a separate organization for merchant shipbuilding; but unlike its American counterpart, it did not enforce a division between naval and merchant work by shipyard. At midwar, Cammell Laird worked simultaneously on five merchant and thirty-three naval contracts while Harland & Wolff had thirty-three merchant and forty naval orders on the books at Belfast. Though the policy enabled yards to earn cash from private owners at a time when the treasury failed to provide funds for yard improvements, the concomitant lack of specialization did not contribute to efficient plant utilization. Yards that built exclusively for the navy were often responsible for a breathtaking variety of types. Vickers Tyneside constructed the battleship *King George V*, three carriers, three light cruisers, thirteen destroyers, nine destroyer escorts, sixteen submarines, and seven tank landing ships. Repair work figured more prominently in British private shipbuilding yards than in American ones. According to a postwar review, "The peace-time practice was for repairs to Naval vessels to be carried out in the Royal dockyards, but, as soon as war broke out, their capacity was quickly overloaded," forcing the Admiralty to assign a rapidly growing amount of repair work to private yards, where it often delayed new construction.[88]

Japanese wartime shipbuilding was even less specialized, partly because the government lacked a separate procurement agency for cargo ships like the U.S. Maritime Commission. Merchant shipbuilding became the responsibility of the Imperial Navy, which piled freighter and tanker contracts on private yards already crammed with warships. Mitsubishi Nagasaki, for example, delivered more than 350,000 gross tons of merchantmen and 149,000 displacement tons of combatants during the Pacific War. Also in contrast to the United States, where specialty yards performed most repairs, private Japanese builders were responsible for overhauls, which "took up a good deal of time and space in the yards," according to the U.S. Strategic Bombing Survey. "This, plus the man-hours and materials necessary for repairs, added to the chaotic state of the yards."[89]

Most German yards focused their attention on submarines as a result of the navy's decision to suspend or cancel the construction of surface combatants early in the war (see chapter 3). What little merchant construction remained went to a handful of yards like Bremer Vulkan, which built cargo ships until midwar.

Repair work was usually handled by submarine bases in France and Norway, relieving boats of the necessity of having to return to Germany via routes controlled by the Royal Navy and the Royal Air Force Coastal Command. In new construction, the German navy relied almost exclusively on private builders with a record of combatant building before the war, notably Blohm & Voss in Hamburg, AG Weser in Bremen, Deutsche Werft in Hamburg, and Germaniawerft in Kiel. Most of these firms specialized in the construction of two submarine types, the 871-ton Type VII for the Battle of the Atlantic and the 1,152-ton Type IX for longer-range operations off the east coast of the United States. Until midwar, German production methods closely resembled their American counterparts in a system pioneered by AG Weser in the 1930s in which pressure hulls were built from eight preassemblies on site. To construct one section, shipfitters bent steel plates, fitted them around circular frames, and welded the structure to form a cylinder. Once the exterior hull had been built up on the slipway around the pressure hull, shipfitters, machinists, and electricians installed longitudinal frames, interior fittings, engines, wires, and torpedo tubes. Results were solid but hardly spectacular. Blohm & Voss, Germany's largest and most efficient builder, which delivered one Type VII a week from 1941 to 1944 (usually on Thursdays), averaged 326 days from keel laying to delivery, one-third more than the Portsmouth Navy Yard's average for much larger *Balaos*.[90]

DESIGN AND SUBCONTRACTING IN CRUISER AND CARRIER CONSTRUCTION

Naval construction relied extensively on outside suppliers while shipyards handled hull construction and outfitting. The Bureau of Ships explained, "By its very nature, shipbuilding lends itself to subcontracting. Normal practice has always been for shipyards to assemble on the site materials and equipment purchased elsewhere. Studies have indicated that as a usual thing from 40 to 50 percent of the contract price of a vessel is expended for labor and materials purchased outside the yard itself."[91] Established subcontractors who were familiar with the Navy's strict standards of quality and workmanship were joined by manufacturers of consumer durables who had to accustom themselves to the Navy's design procedures and inspection protocols. Close cooperation between subcontractors, naval architects, and marine engineers was necessary because blueprints and specifications changed continuously throughout the shipbuilding process.

These structures and dynamics were evident in the construction of *Cleveland*-class light cruisers and *Independence*-class carriers at New York Ship, Fore River, Newport News, and Cramp. Relying on New York Ship for working plans, the three follow-on yards received a large variety of components and subassemblies from specialty firms, where the complexity of production sequences often rivaled that of shipbuilding itself.

Design was centralized at the Navy's Preliminary Design Section and New York Ship. To shorten the design cycle, the Navy ordered *Cleveland*s essentially as repeats of prewar light cruisers so that many existing blueprints and specifications could be recycled with only slight modifications. As a result, the ships largely conformed to the limits of interwar naval arms treaties even though the agreements themselves had long expired. Preliminary Design conceptualized *Cleveland* as a 16,500-ton ship for a maximum speed of 33.5 knots and a range of 11,000 nautical miles. Armament included four turrets with three 6-inch guns each and six turrets with two 5-inch guns each. Their heavy batteries rendered *Cleveland*s potentially top-heavier than, for example, Britain's comparable *Swiftsure*-class cruisers with fewer turrets. Preliminary Design's attempts to tackle the problem with a wider beam failed, but a proposal by New York Ship (which had developed the detail design of the prewar *Brooklyn* class of light cruisers) to slope *Cleveland*'s side belt armor outward instead of inward to produce tumblehome improved seaworthiness. At New York Ship, seven hundred draftsmen spent a year developing blueprints for the hull, superstructure, electrical installations, turrets, and armor.[92]

Like in battleship design, changes proliferated long after the Navy had officially approved the "final" *Cleveland* working plans in February 1941. Many were the result of combat studies that suggested improved antiaircraft capabilities in *Cleveland*s, whose 1.1-inch machine guns were replaced with 40-mm Bofors guns. Further improvements in the performance of antiaircraft guns and heavy ordnance were achieved with innovative fire-control systems, some of which were mounted on masts high above the center of gravity in later *Cleveland*s. When these additions exacerbated the top-weight problem, naval architects reduced the number of aircraft catapults from two to one and replaced *Cleveland*'s armored pilot house with an unarmored one. In 1941 alone, the working plans underwent 127 major modifications, which ranged from redesigned ammunition hoists to a new stern. Additional changes materialized in 1942, when

Cruiser and aircraft carrier construction at New York Ship, March 1943. *From left to right*: The *Independence*-class aircraft carriers *Cowpens* and *Monterey* at the wet basin; aircraft carriers *Langley* and *San Jacinto*, large cruiser *Alaska*, aircraft carrier *Cabot*, and heavy cruiser *Bremerton* under the covered slipways at the center; the aircraft carrier *Bataan*, the *Cleveland*-class light cruisers *Huntington, Wilkes Barre, Atlanta,* and *Dayton* at the uncovered slipways on the right. Photograph 38414, Box 310, RG 19, Records of the Bureau of Ships, National Archives and Records Administration, College Park, MD the redesign of four *Cleveland*s as division flagships produced "very extensive plan work" for flag officer and stateroom accommodations as well as stowage for an additional motor boat.[93] Unlike Electric Boat, New York Ship diligently provided the requested blueprint revisions but complained that change orders threw monkey wrenches into *Cleveland*-class production schedules. New York Ship informed Robinson, "We have been urged repeatedly by the Secretary [of the Navy] to expedite production in every possible way and one of the factors that will affect ultimate expedited delivery of all ships is the number of changes imposed during the building period."[94] Robinson responded nonchalantly by quoting Shakespeare's *Hamlet*, telling New York Ship that "we are continually resisting the ordering of any changes. As you must recognize, however, eliminating all changes is a 'consummation devoutly to be wished' which, unfortunately, is not quite yet within our grasp."[95]

While Newport News, Fore River, and Cramp completed their *Cleveland*s as light cruisers, nine units awarded to New York Ship in 1940 underwent a radical redesign as *Independence*-class light carriers at the behest of Roosevelt, a longtime proponent of carrier aviation who grew concerned about looming shortages in 1941. Shortly after Pearl Harbor, the Navy Department authorized the conversion of a *Cleveland*-class cruiser into the light carrier *Independence*; and by June 1942, eight vessels had been added to the program. The development of working plans was handled by New York Ship, which had been privy to internal Navy Department deliberations from the outset and commenced the redesign early in 1942. To everyone's relief, it dispensed with most cruiser armor, the manufacture of which was as complicated and time-consuming as battleship armor production (see chapter 4). The carrier design featured four funnels, which were placed behind a small island superstructure. Other additions included an enclosed hangar, an elevator, an unarmored flight deck, and a catapult.[96]

Like most naval combatants, *Cleveland*s and *Independence*s were propelled by turbine systems. Turning at a maximum speed of about 3,500 revolutions per minute (rpm), their Curtis-type impulse turbine required reduction gear to produce no more than about 300 rpm to ensure optimum propeller efficiency. Gear production proved difficult because it involved a variety of precision skills and machine tools, which were in exceedingly short supply. Like armor, propulsion systems were controlling items whose arrival at the shipyard dictated the speed

of construction. "From the beginning of the wartime program it was the availability of turbines and gears which determined the production schedules of
Navy and Maritime Commission standard ships, rather than the reverse," the
War Production Board commented.[97] The Bureau of Ships admitted that facility
expansion for turbine and gear production received insufficient attention prior
to Pearl Harbor, so that "inability to obtain production of turbines and gears
resulted in compromise designs utilizing diesel propulsion of less power, and
resulted in ships with inferior speed."[98] Many destroyer escorts were in fact fitted
with diesel engines, but this was not deemed an option for the *Cleveland* class
and other large combatants. Robinson hoped to tackle the problem by reducing
the number of spare turbines and reduction gear held in reserve at the navy yards
to perform repairs to damaged propulsion systems, explaining in November
1941 that it was the Bureau of Ship's intention "to devote all energies and applicable facilities to speed up deliveries of turbines and gears to meet a current
emergency by setting back the manufacture of related shore based spares."[99]

Each *Cleveland*-class cruiser and *Independence*-class carrier was fitted with
an engine drive that delivered 100,000 horsepower via four main turbine systems. Four propeller shafts, the longest pair of which measured three hundred
feet, were held in place aft by struts and each received a bronze propeller. Production of the main components was handled by Babcock & Wilcox (boilers),
General Electric (turbines and reduction gear), Camden Forge (shafts), Birdsboro Foundry (struts), and the Cramp Brass Foundry (propellers). All five were
experienced naval contractors, maintained specialized production facilities,
and employed highly skilled labor.

Babcock & Wilcox, the nation's largest boiler manufacturer, looked back
on four decades of naval contracting experience. In addition to boilering every
American battleship built after the turn of the century, it supplied foreign customers like the Royal Navy, which had Babcock & Wilcox boilers installed in the
battleship *Dreadnought*. After World War I, it derived most of its revenue from
stationary boiler installations for commercial customers like electric power companies, but naval work remained an important side business. For the two-ocean
navy, the company initially produced naval boilers and tubes at Bayonne, New
Jersey, which also manufactured boiler tubes for the Maritime Commission,
aircraft engine bearings, and tubing for oil wells and army tanks. Though the
Bayonne plant worked in three shifts and subcontracted a sizable portion of
its workload to other tube manufacturers, it could "no longer keep abreast

of defense contracts with its present facilities," which were "twelve to fifteen months behind on . . . contract orders," Babcock & Wilcox informed Robinson in April 1941.[100] Equally important, the Bayonne plant was a hotbed of labor activism, and production was frequently disrupted by strikes. As a result, tube manufacture was shifted to an older plant in Beaver Falls, Pennsylvania, which was upgraded with $330,000 in Navy funds.[101]

Each *Cleveland* was fitted with four boilers, which produced superheated steam at pressures of six hundred pounds per square inch (psi) and a temperature of 850° Fahrenheit, the Navy's wartime standard. Babcock & Wilcox developed the design to specifications supplied by the Bureau of Engineering and later the Bureau of Ships, which reviewed the blueprints, asked for changes, and approved the "final" version. Like all naval contractors, Babcock & Wilcox exercised great care in the selection of materials, which had to be produced according to stringent technical standards detailed in the bureau's "acceptable list." Material orders for boiler plates used in drums, for example, were reviewed by an on-site navy inspector at Bayonne and forwarded to the steel mills, which produced plates in the open hearth process to 70,000 psi tensile strength in rough shapes. Tests were conducted to ensure that plates were free of defects and could be bent cold to 180 degrees, which was important because high-tensile-strength steel was prone to cracking. Upon their arrival at Bayonne, drum steel sheets were precision-cut, bent under a hydraulic press into semicircular shape, sandblasted to remove mill scale, and welded together into a cylinder shape according to Navy-approved methods Babcock & Wilcox had developed before the war. Using electrodes covered with molybdenum, welders manually cut holes for nozzles, manways, and other irregular shapes, followed by automatic welding of circumferential and longitudinal joints. Automatic welding had the advantage of maintaining a constant arc length "independent of any effort on the part of the operator, permitting him to concentrate his control only on the positioning and direction of the arc, whereas in manual welding considerable fatigue to the operator is experienced by the necessity of feeding the electrode at a uniform rate to maintain a uniformly short arc," Babcock & Wilcox's chief metallurgist explained. "[A]utomatic welding possesses a further advantage in that welding is practically continuous without starting and stopping of the arc as in the case of manual welding where relatively short lengths of electrodes are used."[102]

While Bayonne worked on drums, water tubes for *Cleveland* boilers were manufactured in Beaver Falls. Like all boiler makers, Babcock & Wilcox produced seamless tubes, which were stronger and more uniform than welded ones, the seams of which could crack under high pressure. A steel billet was heated to 2,000° Fahrenheit and placed in a piercing mill, "which rotates the billet rapidly, at the same time forcing it over a long conical tool or piercing point, the elongated but now hollow round advances over the point, and is removed from the piercing point as a tube," according to one account. "While still hot, the tube is rolled to approximate dimensions, after which it is heat treated and allowed to cool."[103] Tubes were cold drawn to tolerances of 0.1 inch by pulling a mandrel through the tube, producing a smooth inner surface to ensure even steam flow, in contrast to welded tubes, whose seams caught particles that could result in clogging. Once quality inspectors had checked the inner surface for scratches, tears, and sinks, tubes were subjected to a hydrostatic test and shipped to Bayonne for installation in the drums. The completed drums together with a superheater and an economizer were fitted into a steel case equipped with a burner that sprayed atomized fuel into a furnace lined with bricks and produced hot gas, which heated the tubes. For the *Cleveland* and *Independence* classes (which had identical engine systems), Babcock & Wilcox produced 132 boilers for new build installation plus spares.[104]

Cleveland turbines were manufactured by General Electric (GE), whose relationship with the U.S. Navy dated to the late nineteenth century. In World War II, its main works in Schenectady, New York, produced hydraulic controls for 5-inch guns, motors, main electric generators, and propulsion controls for submarines, as well as turbines for battleships, cruisers, and destroyers. Like other first-tier suppliers, GE developed its own blueprints in consultation with New York Ship, which reconciled them with the working design, forwarded them to the Bureau of Ships for approval, and distributed them to the yards involved in light cruiser construction. The Schenectady works were sufficiently equipped to design and construct turbines for the first batch of *Cleveland*s, but the sheer volume of later contracts exceeded their capacity, forcing GE to reassign cruiser gear production to a plant in Lynn, Massachusetts.[105]

Production required a good deal of precision work performed by machinists. To craft the rotor, they hand-fitted blades onto a shaft, frequently checking the outside diameter with a micrometer to ensure a tight fit against the turbine case. Upon completion of the basic structure, they assembled each turbine in the shop, balanced the blades, performed test runs, and calibrated the turbine prior to shipment to the shipyards. GE also produced double-reduction gears to transmit power from the turbine to a propeller shaft. Each included a "bull gear" featuring six hundred teeth, which were hobbed to one-ten-thousandth of an inch. Hobbing machines "that could mount an 86-ton gear blank and shape its teeth by cutters [were set up] in a special air-conditioned room where temperature and humidity were held in virtual constant," an engineer explained. "Seventeen days of continuous work was required to finish-cut the teeth on a single bull gear, not counting the many hours needed to line up the blank beforehand."[106] Rotors and cases underwent thorough testing. "This was organized through the usual General Electric Works Laboratory channels and was aided greatly by the modern techniques available in the 'magnetic particles test' to insure freedom from cracks in rotors and shells, by the rotating heat distortion tests of the rotors, and by the recently developed million-volt X-ray equipment for finding hidden defects in castings, welds, etc.," a postwar review recorded.[107]

Each turbine transmitted its rotations to a propeller shaft, which extended from the engine rooms amidships to the stern, with the longer pair measuring three hundred feet. Shafts, which consisted of eight separate sections, were forged by subcontractors and finish-machined at the shipyards. The former job went to Camden Forge, a well-established firm that had supplied forgings for locomotive engines, railroad cars, and marine applications since the turn of the century. The plant occupied a twenty-nine-acre property near the Delaware River waterfront and was equipped with horizontal and vertical furnaces, steam hammers, lathes, and planers. During the war, when it also produced rudder stocks, catapult forgings for carriers, and gun turrets along with propeller shafts for the Navy and the Maritime Commission, production capacity tripled as a result of $500,000 in company-financed investments and $2.7 million in Navy funds. Tools needed for shaft production included a $216,000 hydraulic press and a $75,000 ingot heating furnace.[108]

To manufacture shafts for *Cleveland*-class cruisers, furnacemen extracted the lower two thirds of an open-hearth ingot, which was cast into a mold, annealed, compressed into rough shape under the three-thousand-ton hydraulic press, and sawed off at the ends to produce the desired length. The forging was then forwarded to the boring mill, where a horizontal lathe adjustable to eighty feet— one of the longest in American industry—rough-turned a four-inch axial center hole to reduce the weight of the shaft. At the shipyard, the shaft sections passed through several turning lathes and were fitted with precision flanges so that the sections could be bolted together to form a long shaft. Like in rotor production, inspections occasionally revealed quality problems, as in the case of a shaft section for the lead ship of the *Cleveland* class that had an axial hole bored incorrectly, leaving a three-sixteenth-inch eccentricity toward one end of the four-inch hole. New York Ship, which was "urgently in need of this shaft in order to [maintain] our production schedule for the large lathes in our Machine Shop," requested permission to eliminate the eccentricity by boring out the hole a half-inch larger than stipulated in the specifications, presumably without compromising the forging's structural integrity.[109] The Bureau of Ships agreed to the change in order to accommodate the yard's production schedule. In light of production bottlenecks at Camden Forge and elsewhere, the bureau permitted some *Cleveland*s to be delivered with fewer spare shafts than originally planned.

Propeller shafts were held in place by struts protruding from the stern section below the waterline. The job went to Birdsboro Steel of Pennsylvania, one of the nation's oldest foundries, whose main business was mining equipment and commercial castings. This changed during the prewar naval buildup, when it began to produce struts for destroyer shafts, rudder posts for *North Carolina*–class battleships, and turret tracks for the *Iowa* class. To accommodate the Navy's need for precision castings, Birdsboro acquired a license for the Randupson process for casting steel in cement molds developed and patented in France. Used primarily for high-quality work, the Randupson process produced true-to-pattern castings by replacing sand used in conventional foundry work with concrete made from silica and Portland cement. The Navy Department, duly impressed with the results, provided Birdsboro with $8 million for wartime plant improvements, including a new finishing shop, cranes, annealing furnaces, and molding machines (the Navy figure was dwarfed by a $30 million Army investment, which enabled Birdsboro to produce cast armor for tanks).[110]

For the *Cleveland* class, foundrymen built wood struts and placed them in the Randupson cement mixture. The wood was removed once the cement hardened, leaving a clean mold with sharp contours, which received the steel pour. After the metal had cooled, foundrymen removed the mold, machined and bored the strut, and x-rayed the casting. Inspections revealed that several struts contained hot tears, which resulted from shrinkage stresses when the cast cooled (the same problem bedeviled destroyer struts Birdsboro produced for the Bath Iron Works around this time). Given the shipyards' tight production schedule, the Bureau of Ships recommended repairing the struts instead of casting new ones, a procedure that was applied to several defective casts Birdsboro delivered to the *Cleveland* builders.[111]

Lastly, each cruiser propulsion system included eight screw propellers (including four spares) manufactured by the Cramp Brass Foundry of Philadelphia. Originally a division of Cramp & Sons, the foundry had survived the shipyard's demise in 1927, was acquired by the Baldwin Locomotive Works three years later, and remained one of the nation's leading bronze and brass specialists during the Depression, producing gears for marine hoisting equipment and drawbridges in addition to propellers for merchantmen and combatants. The foundry expanded significantly after 1940 to enhance production capacity for Navy and Maritime Commission work.[112]

Each *Cleveland*-class propeller measured eleven feet ten inches in diameter, weighed 6.3 tons, and was made from solid manganese bronze, which could be cast and machined thinner than steel to save weight and reduce resistance as the propeller blade cut through the water. Specifically calibrated for *Cleveland*'s 100,000 horsepower engines and the contours of her underwater body, the propeller design featured four curved blades protruding from a streamlined hub. The blades, which were essentially hydrofoils to transform engine torque into propulsive thrust to move the ship, were raked backwards to achieve an efficient flow of water through the propeller to generate a twelve-foot pitch (the theoretical distance the propeller traveled in one revolution). Like all Navy propeller designs, *Cleveland* wheels underwent rigorous testing at the David Taylor Model Basin in Carderock, Maryland, which resulted in detail changes. Upon approval of the design by the Bureau of Ships, New York Ship forwarded the plans and specifications to Cramp Brass, whose foundrymen crafted a brick mold and poured the castings. "The metal is poured from gigantic furnaces into great ladles, from which it passes into the mold," an engineering journal described the process. "All eyes are on the foreman—the calmest, steadiest man of the lot. An unhurried nod: a wave of the hand. Brawny arms grasp the handwheel. Slowly the ladles tilt and then golden liquid metal falls from the lips of the ladles into the running boxes, from which it travels into the great mould in the depth beneath the workers' feet." Once the casting had cooled and a rigger lifted it from the pit, "highly skilled men working with pneumatic chisels . . . take [the casting skin] off in strips in the midst of an all-enveloping boom of noise as the enormous bronze casting reverberates like some gigantic organ under the rapid blows of the expertly handled chisels."[113] The casting was then placed on a cutting machine, which sliced off the riser and cut a tapered hole so the propeller could eventually be inserted into the shaft. The casting was then placed on a planer, which moved forward and backward across the blades' surfaces to effect true pitch. Riggers placed the propeller on a precision-leveled table, where machinists using a graduated ruler marked out blade thickness according to blueprints and remedied uneven surfaces. In the final step, a grinder fitted with abrasive disks removed small imperfections, and the shavings were removed with an emery cloth. Though the quality of the final product depended to a significant extent on precision designs, craft experience remained key because "shop practices in producing propellers is largely empirical," a production supervisor explained.[114]

Some *Cleveland* suppliers outsourced parts of the production process to second-tier subcontractors. American Engineering of Philadelphia, founded in the nineteenth century to produce auxiliary equipment for steamships, supplied windlasses for all *Cleveland*s, as well as capstans and steering gear for many other combatants. Its overcrowded plant, staffed by more than 1,800 workers as early as 1941, was located on a site with little room for additions, prompting the firm to farm out welding and gear cutting to second-tier suppliers in the vicinity. While American Engineering encountered few problems, other manufacturers of *Cleveland* parts complained that second-tier firms lacked sufficient know-how and equipment. Atwood & Morrill of Salem, Massachusetts, which produced specialized bleeder valves, told the Bureau of Ships, "we have been sub-letting certain types of equipment to approximately twenty or twenty-two plants in and around the Boston area. The type of work which they have been able to take, however, is only that which does not need to be precision work."[115] Unwilling to finance the necessary plant improvements at its own works, Atwood & Morrill applied for and received $200,000 in government funds for factory additions and tools to perform valve engineering in-house.[116]

Valve production was one of the tightest bottlenecks in naval and merchant shipbuilding, largely because designs were unstandardized (valve makers produced more than four thousand distinct types during the war). *Cleveland* builders procured valves from eight different suppliers, each of which produced a range of specialty designs. Grove Regulator of Oakland, California, for example, manufactured four basic types of pressure valves, including a patented one developed specifically for naval applications. The Bureau of Ships reported that "Grove makes the finest and most expensive pressure reducers in the country today. ... There are many places in Navy vessels where only the Grove regulator is acceptable," which was unfortunate given its exorbitant price.[117] Deliveries to the shipyards suffered delays because production required highly specialized equipment, making it impossible to offload more than 20 percent of Grove's subcontracts to second-tier firms. Similar problems plagued valve production at other key subcontractors, notably Schutte & Koerting of Philadelphia and Manning Maxwell & Moore of Bridgeport, Connecticut.[118]

Though many suppliers of the *Cleveland* program maintained up-to-date production equipment and good relations with second-tier firms, some were past their prime and treated their subcontractors poorly. Examples include B. F. Sturtevant of Hyde Park, Massachusetts, a specialty manufacturer of ventilating fans. Its most important product was a draft blower, which was designed to force air into boiler furnaces to increase oil combustion, a patented technology Sturtevant had developed since the late nineteenth century to improve the fuel economy of marine engines. Unfortunately for shipbuilders and the Navy, management of this critical sole-source supplier was "ultra-conservative" and profits were "removed and not enough plowed back into plant and equipment," a Navy investigator complained. Its plant and equipment were "old, outdated, not in good repair." A handful of machine tools represented the only wartime investment, and plant management was "exactly what would be expected in a business" run by stingy owners.[119] Relations with second-tier firms were strained because the company "browbeats [them] when they make mistakes. Complaints are made that [Sturtevant] 'rides' the subcontractor until it becomes unbearable."[120] The Navy Department considered seizing the plant, but in the end assumed only limited responsibility for material procurement.[121]

Conditions were even worse at Howarth Pivoted Bearings in Philadelphia, which produced patented engine thrust bearings for *Cleveland*s, one of only two companies in the entire country to specialize in this line of business. "There is no substitute for such equipment," according to Bowen, who was dispatched by Forrestal in June 1943 to seize the troubled plant.[122] A financial review determined that Howarth was technically insolvent, even though the

Navy had advanced funds for operating expenditures. Inadequate shop methods were evident everywhere; most machine tools were thirty years old, poorly maintained, and could not "produce the close tolerances required"; responsible suppliers refused to deal with Howarth on account of its "very unsatisfactory credit position"; inventory control was nonexistent; and "Twenty-four line shaft bearings for Navy cruisers were fabricated and machined incorrectly, along with approximately 400 thrust bearing shoes."[123] To make matters worse, the IUMSWA Local 35's contract with Howarth was set to expire shortly after the seizure, but Bowen refused to negotiate a new one, prompting the national union to accuse him of an "unprecedented violation of collective bargaining rights."[124] After temporarily ousting the old owner, Bowen appointed Westinghouse as managing agent to reorganize and retool the plant, institute proper shop floor practices, and establish cost accounting systems, with the result that shipments increased by 300 percent within a year.[125]

PREFABRICATION, MODULAR CONSTRUCTION, AND THE BATTLE OF THE ATLANTIC

In contrast to batch-constructed combatants and submarines for fleet duty, American and British escorts and German submarines were built in serial formats. While American and British yards used prefabrication techniques, however, the Germans introduced a modular system at midwar that marked a radical departure from conventional shipbuilding.

To hunt submarines, the U.S. Navy ordered 1,005 destroyer escorts, 563 of which were completed in six classes (*Evarts, Buckley, Cannon, Edsall, Rudderrow,* and *Butler*). Though designers sought a uniform hull, circumstances beyond their control forced changes from one class to the next. The *Evarts* class featured General Motors tandem diesels, but a lack of sufficient engine production capacity prompted a switch to turboelectric drives in the *Buckley* class, and the hull had to be lengthened from 300 to 306 feet to accommodate the bulkier propulsion system. The longer hull was retained in subsequent classes, but propulsion switched back to diesels in *Cannon*s when production bottlenecks widened, and later to geared turbines in *Edsall*s. Strategic changes resulted in other design changes in 1943, when the German submarine threat diminished and demand for fast attack transports for amphibious operations proliferated, prompting the addition of larger superstructures in destroyer escorts to accommodate troops. Design freezes, which were a staple of Fordist production systems, were as unfeasible in destroyer escort construction as in most other areas of naval shipbuilding, which is why their builders preferred the phrase "multiple construction" over "mass production."

The *Buckley* design produced the largest number of destroyer escorts with 154 units completed. Preliminary designs for these 1,620-ton vessels were supplied by the Bureau of Ships to Fore River, which handled the detail design for all shipyards tasked with *Buckley*-class construction. The largest number of *Buckley*s was assigned to Bethlehem Hingham, a government-owned yard constructed with $34 million in Navy funds and supervised by managers from nearby Fore River. Featuring sixteen ways, a sheet metal shop, a fabrication and assembly building, and more than a hundred cranes, Hingham's layout was more conducive to serial construction than that of established yards, which had grown piecemeal over the decades, *Fortune* magazine explained. The yard "has large enough spaces to maneuver prefabricated sections; the spaces are in the right geometrical relation to one another; and they are served by smoothly continuous trailer ways and crane reaches. Work marches in a remarkably straight line to each way from its prefabricating hinterland in the yards and on to the assembly floor."[126] Hingham's "basic organizational setup . . . is identical to that at the [Fore River] Yard," Bethlehem reported.[127] Worker morale and productivity initially left a good deal to be desired. "An unseasoned yard, peppered with recently isolationist Boston-area Irishmen building protection for convoys toward Britain, [Hingham] needed all the incentives to efficiency and patriotism it could muster," *Fortune* commented.[128] Once the workforce was broken in, Hingham built *Buckley*s faster than any other yard except Fore River, and construction time fell by more than two-thirds from the first *Buckley* to the last. Hulls were built from sections, which were "wheeled onto the slipway and welded up by teams of women welders, the skin, the frames, and the keel welded together, and the system was that every ship was one week ahead of the next slipway; every week, maybe it was Monday, one ship was launched without fail," a British visitor later recalled. Subcontractors delivered components and subsystems. "Every day the railway came into Bethlehem-Hingham shipyard; you might see a train load of funnels coming in, a train load of engines, a train load of rudders, a train load of propellers, all coming from all over the states."[129]

Table 5.2. *Buckley*-Class Builders

Builder	Number of Ships	Average Construction Time from Keel Laying to Delivery in Days
Bethlehem-Hingham, Massachusetts	64	155
Consolidated, Orange, Texas	18	191
Defoe Shipbuilding Company, Bay City, Michigan	13	195
Bethlehem, San Francisco	12	236
Philadelphia Navy Yard	10	281
Charleston Navy Yard, South Carolina	15	210
Norfolk Navy Yard, Virginia	10	152
Bethlehem Fore River, Quincy, Massachusetts	9	87
Dravo Corporation, Pittsburgh	3	207

Bruce H. Franklin, *The* Buckley-*Class Destroyer Escorts* (Annapolis, MD: Naval Institute Press, 1999), 176–84

While *Buckley*s were built to Navy standards of material quality and workmanship, patrol frigates of the *Tacoma* class were constructed according to less demanding commercial standards under Maritime Commission supervision. Simplified construction, it was argued, would enable cargo shipbuilders unfamiliar with naval requirements to build combatants without having to retool their shop floors with equipment calibrated for naval work. Basic *Tacoma* specifications were developed in 1942 by Gibbs & Cox, which modified the British *River*-class frigate design to suit American shipbuilding methods by replacing riveting with welding in many specifications. The detail design, which was handled by Kaiser Cargo in Oakland, California, called for a 2,400-ton, 301-foot welded hull propelled by simple reciprocating engines to be produced by general engineering firms. Kaiser's Richmond Yard No. 4 near San Francisco, the *Tacoma*-class lead yard, was tasked with purchasing material for all other builders and with expediting its delivery.[130]

Implementation of the program proved difficult. Blueprints had to be redrafted because Kaiser's naval architects were accustomed to designing prefabricated sections weighing up to fifty tons, which could be lifted by cranes in Kaiser's West Coast yards but not in midwestern ones, where most shipyard cranes could lift only ten tons. Delivery of *Tacoma*s built in Great Lakes yards suffered delays in winter, when the Sault Ste. Marie canal connecting Lake Superior and Lake Huron was frozen, forcing builders to deliver them via the Mississippi River. Other problems plagued Walsh-Kaiser of Providence, Rhode Island, which built more frigates than any other yard but proved unable to achieve the sorts of productivity improvements evident at Hingham and the Bath Iron Works (Walsh-Kaiser's keel-laying-to-delivery time actually increased sharply halfway through the program). The last builder to join the other eight in April 1943, Walsh-Kaiser relied on a subcontractor network that was centered near the California and midwestern yards, with the result that many components and subsystems for frigates built in Providence had to be hauled across the continent via an increasingly overburdened rail system. The Maritime Commission meanwhile "failed to supply boilers, engines, pipe and pipe fittings, and other accessories so that hull after hull had to be launched in various stages of completion with little or no outfitting," investigators reported.[131] Walsh-Kaiser's construction rates also suffered because increasingly diverse projects began to interfere with one another. Already far behind in the delivery of six Liberty ships, it signed contracts for twenty-one *Tacoma*s in February 1943, followed two months later by an order for thirty-two *Artemis*-class combat cargo vessels and another six Libertys, leaving the yard overburdened with three vastly different shipbuilding projects in a pattern that resembled Cramp's. Quality problems, including substandard welds, were endemic throughout the program, particularly in *Tacoma*s built by Kaiser Richmond No. 4. The latter delivered the lead ship of the class in November 1943, but repair crews spent the next ten months fixing technical problems before the ship departed for the Pacific, long after the Battle of the Atlantic for which the frigates had been designed had subsided. The episode reinforced the U.S. Navy's loathing of Kaiser and warship construction in merchant yards. In 1945, it transferred nineteen *Tacoma*s to the USSR as part of Project Hula to equip the Soviet navy for offensive operations against Japan.[132]

Britain's Admiralty likewise relied on merchant yards to construct naval escorts according to commercial standards. In 1939, it recruited Smiths Dock, a builder without naval experience, to redesign a whale catcher as a corvette, laying groundwork for the construction of 267 *Flower*-class vessels. Having issued contracts for the succeeding 151-unit *River*-class frigates designed by Smiths Dock for simplified construction in merchant yards, the Admiralty experimented

Tacoma-class patrol frigate *Davenport* outfitting at Leathem D. Smith Shipbuilding in Sturgeon, Wisconsin, January 12, 1944. Ice buildup frequently delayed the delivery of Great Lakes–built *Tacomas* during winter months. *Photo CR 50, MCc 8824, MC 1993, Box 511, RG 19, Entry LCM, Construction and Launching of Ships, 1930–1955, PF-53 through PF-102, National Archives and Records Administration, College Park, MD*

Table 5.3. *Tacoma*-Class Builders

Builder	Number of Ships	Average Construction Time from Keel Laying to Delivery in Days
Walsh-Kaiser, Providence, Rhode Island	21	245
Consolidated Shipbuilding, Wilmington, California	18	182
Kaiser Richmond # 4, California	12	226
Walter Butler Shipbuilders, Superior, Wisconsin	12	377
Globe Shipbuilding, Superior, Wisconsin	8	440
Leathem Smith Shipbuilding Company, Sturgeon, Wisconsin	8	451
American Shipbuilding, Cleveland, Ohio	7	400
American Shipbuilding, Lorain, Ohio	6	465
Froemming Bros., Milwaukee, Wisconsin	4	338

Dictionary of American Naval Fighting Ships, ed. James L. Mooney, 7 vols. (Washington, DC: Navy Department, 1959–1981) with new designs for *Loch*-class frigates (all of which were named after Scottish lakes). Seeking to recruit structural engineering firms to construct prefabricated sections that would be shipped to yards for final assembly, Sir Stanley Goodall, director of naval construction, ordered *Loch*s to be designed according to commercial standards, which were to be developed by shipbuilders in collaboration with the merchant classification societies and structural engineers. The shipbuilders initially resisted the project because they "don't want bridge builders in the job," Goodall complained. "I got depressed; it looks as though the builders [*sic*] steady opposition to pre fab is gaining ground."[133] Some shipbuilders eventually gave in and participated in the design, which called for 2,250-ton ship (almost exactly the size of *Tacoma*s) powered by reciprocating engines for a maximum speed of twenty knots.[134]

The *Loch* design dispensed as much as possible with curved shapes, the production of which required bending equipment unavailable in structural engineering works. Unlike Kaiser Cargo, *Loch* designers factored in shop floor conditions from the outset, developing a 307-foot hull that fit into most merchant builders' slipways. Also in contrast to Kaiser Cargo, "In arranging the division of the structure into units for prefabrication it was necessary to limit the weight to 2 ½ tons to suit the crane capacity at shipbuilding yards," the Admiralty's assistant director of naval construction recorded. "About 80 per cent of the hull structure is prefabricated, and welded or riveted connections were adopted for manufacture of the units as best suited to the resources of the structural engineers employed." More than a hundred nonmarine firms produced 1,360 prefabricated sections for each *Loch* from straight plates and beams, which gave the frigates a box-like appearance. The Admiralty's warship construction superintendent established a drafting office in Glasgow, which turned designs only trained shipbuilders could understand into blueprints for nonspecialists. To further facilitate prefabrication of sections outside the shipyards, the Admiralty planned to freeze the design for two years, in contrast to conventional naval construction practice in Britain, where design changes after keel laying were as common as in the United States.[135]

In practice, the *Loch* program produced mixed results. As a result of rigorous inspections at the structural engineering works, "parts for prefabricated frigates [are] coming together beautifully," Goodall observed in response to shipbuilders who had predicted that sections would not fit.[136] Browns completed the first frigate, named *Loch Fada*, in 307 days. The controller of the Royal Navy had predicted a longer construction cycle, telling Goodall that the ship "must be built as a prototype and this may mean [*Loch Fada* is] more slowly built."[137] Expectations that subsequent *Loch*s could be completed faster were not met, however. Two yards averaged better than Browns, but nine constructed frigates that were completed by August 1945 at considerably higher averages. The overall average of 370 days from keel laying to delivery of *Loch*s was close to the *Tacoma*-class average of 347 days, but the latter program was hardly a model of construction efficiency. The disappointing record of *Loch*-class construction was primarily attributable to the fact that British escorts received low priority ratings to free up labor and materiel for landing craft construction, which shifted into high gear in late 1943 in preparation for the Normandy invasion and when the Battle of the Atlantic subsided. Long keel-laying-to-delivery averages were also the result of a questionable Admiralty decision to centralize outfitting at Dalmuir near Glasgow and Hendon Dock in Sunderland, both of which were progressively unable to complete the large number of hulls delivered by the shipyards as the program unfolded. A postwar review concluded that frigate construction using prefabricated sections "was not pressed on for sufficiently long a period for [a] definite conclusion to be reached about it."[138]

Table 5.4. *Loch*-Class Builders

Builder	Number of Ships	Average Construction Time from Keel Laying to Delivery in Days
Burntisland	3	277
Charles Hill	4	289
Browns	1	307
Caledon	3	354
Barclay Curle	1	356
Henry Robb	4	367
Harland & Wolff	8	385
Blyth Dry Dock	2	397
Smiths Dock	2	397
Hall Russell	1	406
Swan Hunter	3	440
Alisa	1	469

Calculated from data in Patrick Boniface, Loch *Class Frigates* (Lodge Hill, UK: Maritime Press, 2013), 244–47

Germany undertook a vastly more ambitious attempt to build submarines in modular formats. By midwar, the outdated Type VII submarine was overwhelmed by British, Canadian, and American antisubmarine warfare technology and tactics. In May 1943 alone, the Kriegsmarine lost forty-three U-boats to enemy escorts and aircraft, prompting Grand Admiral Karl Dönitz to suspend submarine operations in the Atlantic. In shipbuilding, "Black May" forced the Germans to seek a new departure with the more advanced Type XXI developed by Glückauf Engineering, the principal submarine design office of the Ministry of Armament and War Production. Unlike its predecessors, which were essentially submersible torpedo launch platforms that could dive for a few hours to attack enemy ships and evade the hunters at slow speeds, the Type XXI was the world's first true submarine, with large batteries that enabled it to cruise underwater for extended periods and recharge them by running diesel engines in combination with a snorkel. Capable of underwater speeds of about fifteen knots, the boat was far more likely to escape convoy escorts than the 7.6-knot Type VII, and it boasted a range of 11,100 nautical miles, almost double that of older types. Informed that serial construction using conventional shipbuilding techniques could only begin in March 1945, Dönitz turned to armaments minister Albert Speer, who tasked automotive engineer Otto Merker with the development of a modular system designed to produce the first Type XXIs a year earlier.[139]

Merker proposed to divide submarine construction into three phases. In the first, steel fabricators like MAN Werk Gustavsburg and Dortmunder Union (some of which used concentration camp labor) produced hollow sections by bending steel plates around frames. Once implemented, phase one employed more than half of all German steel fabrication plants, which forwarded sections to fifteen shipyards like Bremer Vulkan and Deutsche Werke Hamburg, where engines, pipes, electrical systems, and other fittings were installed to form modules in the second phase. Third, the modules went to Blohm & Voss, AG Weser, and Schichau-Werke Danzig for final assembly into complete submarines. Merker's plan to manufacture complex preassemblies and modules in dispersed locations was the single most ambitious serial production scheme in World War II naval work, far beyond the parameters of sectional construction methods employed by the Americans and the British.[140]

Modular construction failed spectacularly. Rudolf Blohm, a veteran ship-builder and owner of Blohm & Voss, pointed out that many blueprints developed by Glückauf "had to be changed because they were either not practical or entirely useless: for example, the steering mechanism was a total failure and the first boats completed by the ship assembling yards could not be steered."[141] Standardization proved impossible because the navy asked for more than a hundred major design changes, with the result that "Each boat is different, because measurement deviations were so great that in the parts to be connected that each pipe had to be fitted separately," Blohm complained. "The real mass production of Type XXI was never started and the devices for it were never even designed."[142] Subcontractors suffered chronic shortages of alloy steel, nuts, and bolts. Phase one steel fabricators lacked the precision tools and shop floor skills required to work within the 2-millimeter tolerances that were necessary to ensure proper fit during final assembly (some sections were 32 millimeters off). Welds "showed deficiencies which endangered the safety of the boat and many deficient welds had to be eliminated and done over."[143] Procurement planning for subcontracted items like steering mechanisms, snorkel lifting devices, valves, and pipes started far too late, making it impossible for phase two producers to deliver complete modules to final assembly yards, which had to construct many items in-house. Blohm also complained that phase two yards frequently failed to pressure-test pipes, fittings, and valves, and often delivered incomplete modules to final assembly yards. (Merker responded to such criticism by accusing Blohm, a Nazi stalwart, of defeatism and sabotage of the German war effort.)[144]

In the end, the three final assembly yards spent an average of 120 days fixing production mistakes, three weeks longer than it took them to assemble the boats. Perhaps surprisingly, given German industry's reputation for precision engineering, its steel fabricators proved far less capable of producing satisfactory sections than their counterparts in the United States and Britain, where shipbuilders rarely complained about faulty preassemblies for destroyer escorts, frigates, and landing craft. Contradicting another bit of conventional wisdom, procurement and production planning in Germany was far less organized than in the United States, and there was chaos throughout the program. In the end, only two of the one hundred Type XXI submarines completed by 1945 were deployed to the Atlantic, and neither scored a hit. The most fortunate side effect of this colossal waste of resources was that it prevented Germany from resuming the Battle of the Atlantic late in the war.[145]

CONCLUSION

Private firms delivered the bulk of the fleet that fought in World War II, but their achievements would have been impossible without massive government assistance. Though shipyards that had survived the interwar years constituted major industrial assets, many had suffered underinvestment into physical plant and shop floor equipment that had to be rectified before builders could begin to construct the two-ocean navy. The federal government responded with a variety of initiatives from tax incentives to direct Navy investments, all of which vastly enhanced the private sector's ability to construct technologically advanced combatants. Recipients of government largesse included not only shipbuilding firms, but also subcontractors responsible for the manufacture of specialty parts in disintegrated batch production formats.

Private builders' ability to deliver vast amounts of combatant tonnage also benefited from yard specialization urged by federal authorities. Differentiation was largely the handiwork of seasoned professionals in the Navy Department and the U.S. Maritime Commission who were familiar with each yard's core strength in particular designs as a result of prewar experience. Targeted exploitation of niche specialties in American naval shipbuilding stood in marked contrast to British and Japanese practices, where even basic differentiation between merchant and naval construction by yard was less common than in the United States. At the other end of the spectrum, German shipyards largely abandoned the construction of surface combatants and merchant vessels to focus on submarines, but Merker's attempts to push specialization beyond the limits of what was technically feasible produced disappointing results.

The evidence presented in this chapter adds important nuances to our understanding of the American war economy. In contrast to studies that focus almost exclusively on the role of large-scale corporations, the account presented here calls attention to disintegrated production formats in which shipyards relied extensively on subcontractors and suppliers of subsystems. These formats were hardly unique to naval shipbuilding. In military aircraft production, for example, General Motors' Eastern Aircraft Division relied on no fewer than three thousand suppliers of specialty parts, while other core firms outsourced the production of entire cockpits and fuselage sections. Subcontracting mobilized a large variety of firms, which played a more important role in wartime production than what they receive credit for in conventional narratives of American industrial mobilization.[146]

Conclusion

Warship Building, Batch Production, and the U.S. Industrial Economy

On September 2, 1945, a fleet of more than two hundred vessels swayed at anchor in Tokyo Bay, where their crews witnessed Japan's surrender. Most were American combatants, landing ships, and transports, supplemented by a handful of British, Australian, and New Zealand warships. Shortly before 9:00 a.m., stone-faced representatives of the Japanese government stepped on board the battleship *Missouri*, commissioned at the Brooklyn Navy Yard in 1944, on whose forward deck they signed the surrender documents. The Imperial Navy's battered *Nagato*, a battleship launched at Hiroshima's Kure Navy Yard in 1919 that had served as Vice Admiral Yamamoto Isoroku's flagship during the Pearl Harbor attack, anchored a few hundred yards off *Missouri*'s port side.

The U.S. naval forces assembled in Tokyo Bay that day were a graphic illustration of America's shipbuilding capabilities. Except five battleships of World War I vintage, most had been launched since 1922, and the bulk had been commissioned after Pearl Harbor. The latter included light fleet carrier *Bataan* (built by New York Ship), the heavy cruiser *Quincy* (Fore River), the light cruiser *Oakland* (Bethlehem San Francisco), the destroyer *Caperton* (Bath Iron Works), the destroyer escort *Kendall C. Campbell* (Federal Ship), and *Archerfish* (Portsmouth Navy Yard), the submarine that had sunk the giant aircraft carrier *Shinano* in 1944.

Yamamoto, who had witnessed America's economic might during his tour of duty as Japan's naval attaché in Washington during the early 1920s, had warned Japanese warmongers before Pearl Harbor, "Anyone who has seen the factories in Detroit and the oil fields in Texas knows that Japan lacks the national power for a naval race with America."[1] Like many observers of the U.S. industrial landscape, Yamamoto neglected to mention America's shipyards, whose products not

227

only overwhelmed the Imperial Navy but also played a major role in the Battle of the Atlantic and the amphibious landings in the Pacific, the Mediterranean, and Normandy. Their production formats and shop floor practices had little in common with Detroit's vaunted assembly lines that so impressed Yamamoto and eventually historians of industrial mobilization.

Documenting the industrial underpinnings of American sea power, the preceding chapters have investigated key features of naval shipbuilding before and during World War II. Heavy combatants like battleships, fleet carriers, and cruisers were usually built in small batches, in the most extreme case battleships of the *Iowa* class, only four of which were actually completed. Destroyers, destroyer escorts, and submarines were constructed in larger numbers, but design freezes were rare. Even tank landing ships, more than eight hundred of which had been delivered by 1944, were built with slight variations within each class. An economist writing after the war related the following telling anecdote: The Navy had persuaded a contractor to construct tank landing ships "on the strength of the argument that it would be able to build fifty ships all alike. When the fiftieth ship was delivered, the company sent to the Navy Department pictures of the first and fiftieth ship, mounted in one frame, with the title 'Fifty ships, all alike!' The ships looked alike, yes, but the recipient of the picture understood the full meaning of the company's sarcasm."[2]

Batch formats involved a high degree of production flexibility in workshops and on slipways to accommodate design changes and combatants of various types. Most shipyards featured general-purpose facilities and shop floor equipment suitable for a range of projects. At the Brooklyn Navy Yard, superdocks were initially earmarked for the construction of *Montana*-class battleships, but when those were canceled, the docks were repurposed for *Midway*-class carrier building and for combatant overhauls. Slipway cranes at the Philadelphia Navy Yard, each of which was designed to lift fifty tons, could be combined to hoist preassemblies weighing several times as much. On shop floors, jack clamps could be recalibrated to correct weld distortions in plates of varying sizes. In some instances, shipbuilders installed more specialized equipment needed to build combatants, for example turret shops and armor-processing equipment, which was not necessary to construct merchantmen, but flexible specialization was evident in most yards.

Like many batch-production industries, naval shipbuilding relied heavily on skilled and well-trained labor. "The labor force in a yard building combatant ships tends to be . . . of a higher order of skill" compared to workforces involved in Liberty ship construction, the Harvard team noted. "One requirement, for instance, is for skilled electricians who can install the extraordinarily complex electronic devices; assembling, testing, and installing the fire-control apparatus of the guns likewise develops special skills of a high order."[3] Though repeat work was evident in some trades, closer investigation reveals important nuances. Welding, for example, involved fairly routinized tasks performed by workers who often beaded seams measured in hundreds of feet per day. But, in contrast to production welders in Kaiser shipyards who usually received a few weeks of training so they could bead simple seams according to commercial standards, Navy welders often underwent training in advanced techniques. Moreover, while welders in Kaiser yards usually worked with automated equipment to produce straight welds that did not require advanced skills, Navy welders often beaded curved seams using hand-held electrodes and sometimes performed overhead welding, a dangerous task that required special training.

Lastly, naval construction involved far-flung subcontracting networks. Eschewing vertical integration, warship builders relied on suppliers to produce armor, guns, turbines, boilers, and many other specialty items and subsystems. In some instances, suppliers clustered near the shipyards in regional agglomerations, for example in Pennsylvania, where Bethlehem, Midvale, Camden Forge, Cramp Brass Foundry, and the Babcock & Wilcox boiler tube works in Beaver Falls manufactured armor and subsystems for New York Ship, the Philadelphia Navy Yard, and Cramp Shipbuilding. This regional concentration reflected long-term developments that dated to the late nineteenth century, when the Delaware Valley had emerged as America's shipbuilding hub. This exemplified historian Philip Scranton's notion that "Batch production can be prosecuted most effectively in spaces with densely concentrated specialist firms, each of which may intersect with others in fairly complex productive sequences."[4] By World War II, the network extended across the country, with East Coast naval builders relying on specialty suppliers located as far away as California. The Bureau of Ships commented that in "the subcontracting process, practically every State of the Union contributes a share."[5]

Batch formats, flexible specialization, extensive use of skilled labor, and subcontracting were common among naval builders in the United States, Britain, Japan, and Germany, but comparisons reveal that American warship building enjoyed a multitude of advantages over its foreign counterparts. First, the prewar naval construction cartel enabled the Big Three to survive the doldrums along the lines of Britain's comparable Warshipbuilders' Committee; but unlike the latter it also fostered yard specialization, which enabled the Big Three to develop type-specific design and construction know-how that served them well during the war. Second, suspicions that private builders reaped exorbitant profits from naval work, which were reinforced by the Nye committee revelations, prompted the federal government to invest in navy yard shipbuilding capacity on a scale unparalleled in the American private sector and overseas except in Japan, creating design and construction capabilities suitable for some of the most complex naval shipbuilding jobs. Third, the prewar U.S. Navy encouraged builders to experiment with new shop floor methods to a far greater extent than the British and Japanese navies, whose builders were more reluctant to embrace electric arc welding and prefabrication as a result of technical problems they experienced early on. Fourth, American naval work was better organized than comparable British, Japanese, and German endeavors, thanks largely to the Navy and the Maritime Commission's insistence that wartime merchant construction be allocated to cargo ship specialists and greenfield yards, overhauls be performed by repair yards, and new construction of heavy combatants be handled by yards with long-standing experience in the field. In contrast to Germany's even more specialized submarine construction efforts, the Americans avoided radical departures from established shipbuilding practice during the war, thus sparing them the problems that doomed the Type XXI program. Lastly, U.S. builders received far larger amounts of government investments into facilities than their foreign counterparts, a development that was in the final analysis attributable to America's enormous wealth and ability to raise money for the war effort. The sheer scale of the wartime programs, combined with enormous government investments in facilities, enabled American builders to conduct naval construction on a scale unparalleled anywhere in the world.

In macroeconomic contexts, naval shipbuilding was in many respects a unique industry whose structures and dynamics had little in common with those of other U.S. economic sectors during the period discussed here. More dependent on government contracting than other manufacturers of capital goods, it featured a mix of private firms and state-owned enterprises that was rare in America's capitalist economic landscape. Its business cycles were unrelated to general trends because naval work expanded and contracted in response to changes in national security policy, not conventional market mechanisms of commercial supply and demand. The latter were evident in merchant construction, but it too evinced important differences from other sectors of the interwar economy. In contrast to industries like automobiles, consumer nondurables, and services, the 1920s never roared in shipbuilding because the carrying trades were oversupplied with commercial tonnage built in vast amounts during the Great War and after. The industry did not feel the immediate effects of the recession of 1920 and 1921 because ships take longer to build than bicycles, but it contracted in 1922 at the exact time when the rest of the economy entered the boom period of the 1920s. The Washington Naval Treaty ratified later that year dealt a further blow to shipyards equipped for naval work and contributed to the closure of some firms at mid-decade, predating the collapse of the U.S. economy by several years. Merchant marine legislation passed in 1928 reinvigorated the industry short-term, but its effects dissipated in the early 1930s, when shipbuilding began to suffer along with the rest of the U.S. economy.

Its historically close relationship with the American state rendered shipbuilding a prime candidate for proto-Keynesian policies during the early New Deal, when it was resuscitated by a hefty injection of government money, in contrast to most other sectors. The industry remained insulated from macroeconomic trends like the Roosevelt recession of 1937, which stunted U.S. economic growth but had negligible consequences for builders who thrived on naval rearmament and merchant construction for the U.S. Maritime Commission, formed in 1936. Most of the economy recovered from the Depression in 1940, but demand trajectories diverged by industry. Warship builders initially sought to meet the Navy's needs for ships that were designed to confront the threat of enemy surface combatants in the Pacific and the Atlantic, later to deal with the German submarine menace, and finally to prepare for amphibious landings. The production of tanks, artillery, and trucks, by contrast, was initially tethered to British and French orders, later to Lend-Lease, and above all to the U.S. Army's strategic and tactical needs in the Southwest Pacific, the

Mediterranean, and later Western Europe, while military aircraft producers equipped the U.S. Army Air Forces and to a lesser extent the Royal Air Force for the bomber offensives against Germany and Japan.

Though its political economy and business cycles differed in many respects from those of other sectors, naval shipbuilding exhibited characteristics that were more common than many historians of American industry would concede. Its batch formats and extensive use of skilled labor were core elements of cutting-edge production systems before and during World War II, not quaint leftovers of nineteenth-century artisanal practices that collected dust in remote corners of the American industrial economy. Naval shipbuilding shared these features with other engineering industries, most importantly military aircraft production. For too long, our understanding of this vital sector has been distorted by mistaken beliefs that Henry Ford's famous bomber plant at Willow Run, Michigan, was as paradigmatic of the wartime aircraft industry as the Kaiser yards were of World War II shipbuilding. Willow Run, the world's largest factory, where workers trained in a narrow range of tasks built B-24 Liberator bombers in assembly-line formats borrowed from the automobile industry, was an "isolated, and, in many ways, failed experiment," historian Robert Ferguson has argued. "Mass production as explanation allowed scholars to regard the aircraft industry, including its technology, organization, and politics as reiterations of master narratives" of Fordism reigning supreme in American industrial mobilization. "In this respect, historians have shared Henry Ford's contempt for nuance."[6]

Investigations of wartime aircraft manufacture have uncovered production systems that had more in common with naval construction than with bomber manufacture at Willow Run. Jonathan Zeitlin has shown that batch production was widespread because the U.S. armed forces froze designs only temporarily to allow contractors to complete 1,500 planes at a time before specifications changed for the next batch.[7] Ferguson's work on wartime collaboration between Grumman and General Motors' Eastern Aircraft Division has demonstrated that GM was far more willing than Ford to "abandon specialized machine tools and opt for a certain amount of hand work and ad hoc tooling," which were common at Grumman and other established aircraft manufacturers.[8] "Grumman's strengths lay in its workforce and its traditions of practice, honed to such a degree that even as a large company, it still operated as though it was a small, familial, batch-production operation" during the war, Ferguson concludes. "GM brought its administrative experience to the job, enabling it to transform aircraft production into a continent-wide endeavor in a matter of months."[9]

The evidence presented in this book supports the case for a revisionist interpretation of American industrial mobilization to include batch formats, but it also adds important caveats. Scranton has observed, "Batch and custom efforts intersected with bulk manufacturing at virtually every step in the creation of the nation's transportation, power, and communications systems."[10] This verdict holds true for naval shipbuilding, where welders and riveters toiled hand in hand with shipfitters, machinists, and other highly skilled workers. Warship building relied on a broad spectrum of shop floor practices that reflected the enormous diversity of the American industrial economy, where standardization and batch formats, skilled and semiskilled labor, as well as private business and the state converged to forge the instruments of U.S. naval, military, and economic dominance in the twentieth century.

NOTES

Introduction: The Workshop of American Sea Power

1. Homer L. Ferguson, "Newport News Shipbuilding and Dry Dock Company," in *Historical Transactions*, ed. Society of Naval Architects and Marine Engineers (New York: Society of Naval Architects and Marine Engineers, 1943), 221.

2. The short list of book-length scholarly studies of the twentieth-century U.S. naval shipbuilding industry includes Frederick M. Black, *Charlestown Navy Yard, 1890–1973*, vol. 1 (Boston: Boston National Historical Park, National Park Service, U.S. Department of the Interior, 1988); Jeffrey M. Dorwart, *The Phila-delphia Navy Yard from the Birth of the U.S. Navy to the Nuclear Age* (Philadelphia: University of Pennsylvania Press, 2001); Edward J. Marolda, *The Washington Navy Yard: An Illustrated History* (Washington, DC: Naval Historical Center, 1999); Rodney K. Watterson, *32 in '44: Building the Portsmouth Submarine Fleet in World War II* (Annapolis, MD: Naval Institute Press, 2011); and Gary E. Weir, *Forged in War: The Naval-Industrial Complex and American Submarine Construction, 1940–1961* (Washington, DC: Naval Historical Center, 1993).

3. Bureau of Ships, "An Administrative History of the Bureau of Ships during World War II, vol. 2," 167, n.d., Navy Department Library, Rare Book Room, Washington Navy Yard, Washington, DC.

4. Richard J. Overy, *Why the Allies Won* (New York: Norton, 1995), 180–244; G. R. Simonson "The Demand for Aircraft and the Aircraft Industry, 1907–1958," *Journal of Economic History* 20 (Sep. 1960): 361–82.

5. See for example Philip Scranton, *Proprietary Capitalism: The Textile Manufac-ture at Philadelphia, 1800–1885* (Philadelphia: Temple University Press, 1987); Philip Scranton, *Endless Novelty: Specialty Production and American Industrial-ization, 1865–1925* (Princeton, NJ: Princeton University Press, 1997); Robert G. Ferguson, "One Thousand Planes a Day: Ford, Grumman, General Motors and the Arsenal of Democracy," *History and Technology* 21 (June 2005): 149–75.

6. Harvard Graduate School of Business Administration, *The Use and Disposition of Ships and Shipyards at the End of World War II: A Report Prepared for the United States Navy Department and the United States Marine Commission* (Washington, DC: Government Printing Office, 1945), 161.

7. *To Expedite Naval Shipbuilding: Hearings on H.R. 9822 Before the House Committee on Naval Affairs,* 76th Cong., 3rd Sess., 3203 (1940) (statement of Rear Adm. Samuel M. Robinson, chief of the Bureau of Engineering).

8. "Improving Power Endurance of Naval Warships," *Bureau of Ships Journal* 6 (Apr. 1958): 11.

Chapter 1. "A Highly Specialized Art"

1. Richard J. Overy, *Why the Allies Won* (New York: Norton, 1995), 192.

2. *Merchant Marine: Hearings before the House Committee on the Merchant Marine and Fisheries,* 70th Cong., 1st Sess., 259 (1928) (statement of Homer L. Ferguson, president, Newport News Shipbuilding & Dry Dock Company).

3. John G. B. Hutchins, "History and Development of the Shipbuilding Industry in the United States," in *The Shipbuilding Business of the United States of America,* vol. 1, ed. Frederick G. Fassett Jr. (New York: Society of Naval Architects and Marine Engineers, 1948), 52–55; William J. Williams, *The Wilson Administration and the Shipbuilding Crisis of 1917: Steel Ships and Wooden Steamers* (Lewiston, NY: Edwin Mellen, 1992); for an excellent overview of long-term technological trends, see William H. Thiesen, *Industrializing American Shipbuilding: The Transformation of Ship Design and Construction, 1820–1920* (Gainesville: University Press of Florida, 2006).

4. Hutchins, "History and Development," 53; *The Use and Disposition of Ships and Shipyards at the End of World War II: A Report Prepared for the United States Navy Department and the United States Maritime Commission by the Graduate School of Business Administration Harvard University* (Washington, DC: Government Printing Office, 1945), 168; Norman Friedman, *U.S. Destroyers: An Illustrated Design History* (Annapolis, MD: Naval Institute Press, 2004), 42–46; Kenneth Warren, *Steel, Ships and Men: Cammell Laird, 1824–1993* (Liverpool, UK: Liverpool University Press, 2011), 188–89.

5. Thomas Buckley, "The Icarus Factor: The American Pursuit of Myth in Naval Arms Control, 1921–36," *Diplomacy and Statecraft* 4 (1993): 124–37; John Jordan, *Warships after Washington: The Development of Five Major Fleets 1922–1930* (Barnsley, UK: Seaforth Publishing, 2011).

6. Buckley, "The Icarus Factor," 137–42; John R. Wilson, "The Quaker and the Sword: Herbert Hoover's Relations with the Military," *Military Affairs* 38

(Apr. 1974): 42–44; Emily O. Goldman, *Sunken Treaties: Naval Arms Control Between the Wars* (University Park: Pennsylvania State University Press, 1994), 8–17; Norman Friedman, "Naval Strategy and Force Structure," in *At the Crossroads Between Peace and War: The London Naval Conference in 1930*, ed. John Maurer and Christopher Bell (Annapolis, MD: Naval Institute Press, 2014), 201–28; Robert C. Stern, *The Battleship Holiday: The Naval Treaties and Capital Ship Design* (Barnsley, UK: Pen & Sword, 2017).

7. Sun Shipbuilding, "Summary of Profit or Loss on Hulls, Year 1923," Series 1, Corporate Records and Financial Information, Box 2, Sun Company Corporate Records, 1890–1984, Hagley Museum and Library, Wilmington, DE; "Sun Shipbuilding Company Announced as Successful Bidder for New West Coast Express Passenger Ship Costing $1,027,000," *Marine Engineering* 27 (Apr. 1922): 27; on general developments, see H. Gerrish Smith, "Shipyard Statistics," in *The Shipbuilding Business of the United States of America*, vol. 1, ed. Frederick G. Fassett Jr. (New York: Society of Naval Architects and Marine Engineers, 1948), 155–60.

8. "Exhibit No. 4412: Bethlehem Steel Company. Answers to Questions Submitted by Mr. D. Y. Wemple, Investigator for the U.S. Senate Special Committee Investigating the Munitions Industry," *Munitions Industry, Part 35: Exhibits on Wartime and Post-War Financing. Hearings Before the Special Senate Committee Investigating the Munitions Industry*, 74th Cong., 2nd Sess. (1936), 12,131–34; Joe H. Camp, "Birch Rod to Arsenal: A Study of the Naval Ordnance Plant at South Charleston, West Virginia, and the Search for a Government Industrial Policy" (PhD diss., West Virginia University, 2002); on the Naval Gun Factory, see Secretary of the Navy, *Annual Report Fiscal Year 1929* (Washington, DC: Government Printing Office, 1929), 286; and Edward J. Marolda, *The Washington Navy Yard: An Illustrated History* (Washington, DC: Naval Historical Center, 1999), 59.

9. *Navy Department Appropriation Bill for 1929: Hearings Before Subcommittee of the House Committee on Appropriations*, 70th Cong., 1st Sess., 822–23 (1928) (statement of Rear Adm. J. D. Beuret, chief of the Bureau of Construction and Repair); see also Thomas Heinrich, *Ships for the Seven Seas: Philadelphia Shipbuilding in the Age of Industrial Capitalism* (Baltimore, MD: Johns Hopkins University Press, 1997), 206–13.

10. "Proposal: Merger of N.Y. Ship & Newport News, July 30, 1932," reprinted in *Munitions Industry, Part 19: Naval Shipbuilding: New York Shipbuilding Corporation. Hearings Before the Special Senate Committee Investigating the Munitions Industry*, 74th Cong., 1st Sess., 5,232 (1935).

11. Bardo to Board of Directors of New York Shipbuilding Corporation, Oct. 18, 1934, reprinted in *Munitions Industry, Part 19*, 5,258.

12. *The Use and Disposition of Ships and Shipyards*, 174; William L. Tazewell, *Newport News Shipbuilding: The First Century* (Newport News, VA: Mariners' Museum, 1986), 105.

13. Wakeman to Lewis, Mar. 4, 1927, reprinted in *Munitions Industry, Part 21: Naval Shipbuilding: Bethlehem Shipbuilding Corporation. Hearings Before the Special Senate Committee Investigating the Munitions Industry*, 74th Cong., 1st Sess., 6,106 (1935).

14. Daniel D. Strohmeier, "A History of Bethlehem Steel Company's Shipbuilding and Ship Repairing Activities," *Naval Engineers Journal* 75 (May 1963): 266–69; *The Use and Disposition of Ships and Shipyards*, 172–73; Daniel M. Wilson, *Three Hundred Years of Quincy, 1625–1925: Historical Retrospect of Mount Wollaston, Braintree, and Quincy* (Boston: Wright & Brown, 1926), 267–70.

15. "The Trade Outlook: Shipbuilding," 3, CP 110, CAB 24/179; "Report on Assistance to Shipbuilding," CP 532, CAB 24/169, both in National Archives of the United Kingdom, Kew; Joint Committee of the Shipbuilding Employers' Federation and Shipyard Trade Unions, *Report of Joint Inquiry into Foreign Competition and Conditions in the Shipbuilding Industry* (London: Whitehead Morris, 1926); C. Kielhorn, "Die ersten schnellen Motorfrachtschiffe für den Liniendienst um die Erde Teil I," *Werft—Reederei—Hafen* 8 (Feb. 1927): 58–61; Lewis Johnman and Hugh Murphy, *British Shipbuilding and the State Since 1918: A Political Economy of Decline* (Ithaca, NY: Regatta Press, 2002), 24; Michael S. Moss, *Shipbuilders to the World: 125 Years of Harland and Wolff, Belfast 1861–1986* (Belfast, UK: Blackstaff Press, 1986), 267; Nick Robins, *Wartime Standard Ships* (Barnsley, UK: Seaforth Publishing, 2017), 23–32; Warren, *Steel, Ships and Men*, 190–96, 210–17; on Clyde shipyard closures, see Dan P. McWiggins, "Sunrise in the East, Sunset in the West: How the Korean and British Shipbuilding Industries Changed Places in the 20th Century" (PhD diss., University of Texas at Austin, 2013), 61.

16. John D. Scott, *Vickers: A History* (London: Weidenfeld & Nicolson, 1963), 152–66; Ian Buxton and Ian Johnston, *The Battleship Builders: Constructing and Arming British Capital Ships* (Barnsley, UK: Seaforth Publishing, 2013), 64; Joseph F. Clarke, *Building Ships on the North East Coast: A Labour of Love, Risk, and Pain, Part 2: C 1914-C 1980* (Whitley Bay, UK: Bewick Press, 1997), 221–22.

17. On Yarrow's foreign destroyer and boiler contracts, see "Meeting of the Board of Directors," July 28, 1931, UGD 266/1/3, Glasgow University Archive

Services, UK; see also "Yarrow and Co.," (London) *Times*, Dec. 15, 1928; "Yarrow and Co.," (London) *Times*, Dec. 30, 1932; on Yarrow and Thornycroft's prototype work, see David K. Brown, *Atlantic Escorts: Ships, Weapons & Tactics in World War II* (Barnsley, UK: Seaforth Publishing, 2007), 51–54; on White, see David L. Williams and Richard P. de Kerbrech, *J. Samuel White & Co. Shipbuilders* (Stround, UK: History Press, 2012), 83–84.

18. Quoted in Gilbert A. H. Gordon, *British Seapower and Procurement Between the Wars* (Annapolis, MD: Naval Institute Press, 1988), 76.

19. Quoted in Gordon, *British Seapower*, 76; see also Christopher W. Miller, *Planning and Profits: British Naval Armaments Manufacture and the Military-Industrial Complex, 1918–1941* (Liverpool, UK: Liverpool University Press, 2018), 27–42; John R. Hume and Michael S. Moss, *Beardmore: The History of a Scottish Industrial Giant* (London: Heinemann, 1979), 174.

20. Buxton and Johnston, *Battleship Builders*, 292.

21. "Report for the Board Meeting in London on Friday, 29th August 1930," 6, Upper Clyde Shipbuilders, Clydebank Division: Reports to Board and Committee, UCS 1/2/1, Glasgow University Archive Services, UK.

22. Hird to Bell, May 29, 1930, Upper Clyde Shipbuilders, Clydebank Division: Reports to Board and Committee, UCS 1/2/1, Glasgow University Archive Services, UK (quote); Anthony Slaven, "A Shipyard in Depression: John Browns of Clydebank," *Business History* 19 (July 1977): 192–200; Ian Johnston, *Ships for All Nations: John Brown & Company Clydebank, 1847–1971* (Annapolis, MD: Naval Institute Press, 2015), 174–95.

23. Swan, Hunter, & Wigham Richardson Ltd., Shareholder Minute Book No. 1, DS.SWH1/2, Tyne & Wear Archives, Newcastle upon Tyne, UK; Ian Buxton, *Swan Hunter Built Warships* (Cornwall, UK: Maritime Books, 2007), 3–4; Buxton and Johnston, *Battleship Builders*, 89–92; Clarke, *Building Ships on the North East Coast*, 227–33.

24. "The Fate of the Former Imperial German Naval Yards," *Shipbuilder* 24 (Jan. 1921), 33–34; Dirk J. Peters, "Deutsche Werften in der Zwischenkriegszeit (1918–1939): Teil 1," *Deutsches Schiffahrtsarchiv* 28 (2005): 95–134; Marc Fisser, "Die deutsche Seeschiffahrt am Ende des Ersten Weltkrieges und in der Weimarer Republik," *Deutsches Schiffahrtsarchiv* 13 (1990): 111–42; Peter Doepgen, *Die Washingtoner Konferenz, das Deutsche Reich und die Marine: Deutsche Marinepolitik 1921 bis 1935* (Bremen, Germany: Hauschild, 2005), 124–42; on the Blohm & Voss shipyard, see Olaf Mertelsmann, *Zwischen Krieg, Revolution und Inflation: Die Werft Blohm & Voss 1914–1923* (Munich, Germany: C. H. Beck, 2003), and the informative discussion in "Reviews of Olaf Mertelsmann,

Zwischen Krieg, Revolution und Inflation: Die Werft Blohm & Voss 1914–1923 with a Response by Olaf Mertelsmann," *International Journal of Maritime History* 16 (Dec. 2004): 265–308.

25. Jesse E. Saugstad, *Shipping and Shipbuilding Subsidies: A Study of State Aid to the Shipping and Shipbuilding Industries in Various Countries of the World* (Washington, DC: Department of Commerce, 1932), 185–86; Reinhart Schmelzkopf, *Die deutsche Handelsschifffahrt 1919–1939*, vol. 1: *Chronik und Wertung der Ereignisse in Schifffahrt und Schiffbau* (Oldenburg, Germany: Stalling, 1974), 74–77; Dieter Pfliegensdörfer and Jörg Wollenberg, "Die Werftenkrise der zwanziger Jahre: Ein Lehrstück für heute," in *"Stell dir vor, die Werften gehören uns": Krise des Schiffbaus oder Krise der Politik?* ed. Heiner Heseler and Hans Jürgen Kröger (Hamburg, Germany: VSA, 1983), 167–71; Peter Kuckuk and Hartmut Pophanken, "Die AG 'Weser' 1933 bis 1945: Handels- und Kriegsschiffbau im Dritten Reich," in *Bremer Großwerften im Dritten Reich*, ed. Peter Kuckuk (Bremen, Germany: Edition Temmen, 1993), 11–15.

26. Office of Chief of Naval Intelligence, Intelligence Report, Serial 75-44, December 26, 1944, 1–2, Box 1175, RG (hereafter "RG") 38, Intelligence Division, Confidential Reports of Naval Attaches 1940–1946, National Archives at College Park, College Park, MD (hereafter "NACP").

27. "Japan. Navy Estimates. 1927–28. Portion Dealing with Fleet and New Construction," May 12, 1927, T 161/648/2, National Archives of the United Kingdom, Kew; Mitsubishi Economic Research Bureau, *Japanese Trade and Industry: Present and Future* (London: Macmillan, 1936), 300–302; Frank P. Purvis, "Japan's Contribution to Naval Architecture," *Transactions of the Institution of Naval Architects* 67 (1925): 27–40; Mark R. Peattie, "Japanese Naval Construction, 1919–1941," in *Technology and Naval Combat in the Twentieth Century and Beyond*, ed. Phillips P. O'Brien (London: Frank Cass, 2007): 93–95.

28. Mitsubishi Zōsen Kabushiki Kaisha, *Naval Vessels 1887–1945: Mitsubishi Zosen Built* (Tokyo: Nippon Kobo, 1956), 16–17, 38–43; Mitsubishi Zōsen Kabushiki Kaisha, *Nihon no shosen 1887–1958/ Brief Shipbuilding History of the Company* (Tokyo: Mitsubishi Zōsen Kabushiki Kaisha, 1960), 9–10, 180–87; Takao Shiba, "Succeeding Against Odds, Courting Collapse: How Mitsubishi Shipbuilding and Kawasaki Dockyard Managed the Post-WWI Slump," *Japanese Yearbook on Business History* 2 (1986): 100–118; Fukasaku Yukiko, *Technology and Industrial Growth in Pre-War Japan: The Mitsubishi-Nagasaki Shipyard 1884–1934* (London: Routledge, 1992), 124–35.

29. Saugstad, *Shipping and Shipbuilding Subsidies*; Anthony J. Watts, *Japanese Warships of World War II* (New York: Doubleday, 1967), 25–37; Takao, "Succeeding against Odds."

30. *Munitions Industry, Part 21*, 5,831–42 (statement of S. W. Wakeman, Bethlehem Shipbuilding Corporation); *Sundry Legislation Affecting the Naval Establishment 1930–1931: Hearings Before the House Committee on Naval Affairs*, 71st Cong., 3rd Sess., 3630 (1930) (statement of Watson B. Miller, National Rehabilitation Committee, American Legion).

31. *Munitions Industry, Part 20: Naval Shipbuilding: Newport News Shipbuilding and Dry Dock Company. Hearings Before the Special Senate Committee Investigating the Munitions Industry*, 74th Cong., 1st Sess., 5,459–66 (1935) (statement of Homer L. Ferguson, president of the Newport News Shipbuilding and Dry Dock Company); Norman Friedman, *U.S. Aircraft Carriers: An Illustrated Design History* (Annapolis, MD: Naval Institute Press, 1983), 69–77.

32. Gary E. Weir, *Forged in War: The Naval-Industrial Complex and American Submarine Construction, 1940–1961* (Washington, DC: Naval Historical Center, 1993), 18; Ralph L. Snow, *Bath Iron Works: The First Hundred Years* (Bath, ME: Maine Maritime Museum, 1987), 209–12.

33. The key players were Armstrong-Whitworth, Beardmore, Cammell-Laird, Browns, Fairfield, Hawthorn-Leslie, Palmers, Scott, Stephen, Swan Hunter, Thornycroft, Vickers, White, and Yarrow. Harland & Wolff joined the group later; see Miller, *Planning and Profits*, 47–76; the following discussion is based on Miller's valuable study.

34. "Memorandum Submitted by Sir Charles Craven Relating to Arrangements Between British Firms Engaged in Warship Building," reprinted in *Minutes of Evidence taken before the Royal Commission on the Private Manufacture of and Trading in Arms* (London: His Majesty's Stationery Office, 1936), 436 (quote); see also Paul Ingram and Arik Lifschitz, "Kinship in the Shadow of the Corporation: The Interbuilder Network in Clyde River Shipbuilding, 1711–1990," *American Sociological Review* 71 (Apr. 2006): 339.

35. Jeffrey M. Dorwart, *The Philadelphia Navy Yard from the Birth of the U.S. Navy to the Nuclear Age* (Philadelphia: University of Pennsylvania Press, 2001), 146–57; Frederick M. Black, *Charlestown Navy Yard, 1890–1973*, vol. 1 (Boston: Boston National Historical Park, National Park Service, U.S. Department of the Interior, 1988), 406–21; on battleship modernizations, see Bureau of Construction and Repair, *Annual Report of the Bureau of Construction and Repair for Fiscal Year Ended June 30, 1925* (Washington, DC: Government

Printing Office, 1925), 8–9. Post–World War I policy differed from that of the 1960s, when the Brooklyn Navy Yard was closed and the San Francisco and Mare Island navy yards merged at the initiative of Robert McNamara, who sought to implement cost savings during his tenure as secretary of defense; Julius Duscha, *Arms, Money, and Politics* (New York: Ives Washburn, 1965), 108; the Portsmouth Navy Yard, which had originally been included in McNamara's list, escaped closure and also survived the post–Cold War Base Realignment and Closure initiative, which phased out the navy yards at Philadelphia, Charleston, and Mare Island.

36. *To Authorize the Construction of Certain Naval Vessels: Hearings on H.R. 11526 Before the Senate Committee on Naval Affairs*, 70th Cong., 1st Sess., 94, 99 (1928) (statement of Representative Frederick W. Dallinger).

37. Bardo to Palen, Apr. 4, 1928, reprinted in *Munitions Industry, Part 21*, 5,626.

38. *Hearings on H.R. 11526*, 109.

39. *Hearings on H.R. 11526*, 124–25.

40. *To Authorize the Construction of Certain Naval Vessels for Replacement and Additions, and for Other Purposes (H.R. 6661 and H.R. 8230): Hearings Before the House Committee on Naval Affairs*, 71st Cong., 3rd Sess., 639 (1931); Secretary of the Navy, *Annual Report Fiscal Year 1931* (Washington, DC: Government Printing Office, 1931), 54; *Investigation of the Progress of the War Effort*, vol. 5: *Gibbs & Cox: Hearings Before the House Committee on Naval Affairs*, 78th Cong., 2nd Sess., 3,948 (1944) (Statement of Rear Adm. E. L. Cochrane, chief of the Bureau of Ships).

41. Bardo to Hoover, Mar. 10, 1932, reprinted in "Shipbuilder Urges Replacement Program," *Marine Engineering* 37 (Apr. 1932): 141.

42. *Sundry Legislation Affecting the Naval Establishment 1931–1932*, 636 (1932) (Statement of Rear Adm. George H. Rock, chief constructor, U.S. Navy) (quote); see also "Shipbuilding Declines During 1932 in United States Shipyards," *Marine Engineering* 38 (Jan. 1933): 310–11; *The Use and Disposition of Ships and Shipyards*, 174.

43. Anthony Slaven, "Self-Liquidation: The National Shipbuilders Security Ltd and British Shipbuilding in the 1930s," in *Charted and Uncharted Waters: Proceedings of a Conference on the Study of British Maritime History*, ed. Sarah Palmer and Glyndwr Williams (London: Queen Mary College, 1983), 132 (quote).

44. On net profits and losses in American shipbuilding, see U.S. Department of Commerce, *Statistical Abstract of the United States* (Washington, DC: Government Printing Office, 1933–39); on Fairfield, see Directors' Meeting, Nov. 13,

1935, Minute Book No. 6, UCS2/1/6, Mitchell Library Special Collections, Glasgow UK; and Buxton and Johnston, *Battleship Builders*, 79–82; on German developments, see Schmelzkopf, *Die deutsche Handelsschifffahrt 1919–1939*, vol. 1, 149–53.

45. Anton Kinch, *Charge It to the Navy* (Milwaukee, WI: A. Kinch, 1945), 6 (quote); see also "Enters Equipment Field," *Marine Review* 61 (Nov. 1931): 63.

46. Paolo E. Colletta, *American Secretaries of the Navy*, vol. 2 (Annapolis, MD: Naval Institute Press, 1980), 657 (quote).

47. Leigh, "Memorandum for the Secretary of the Navy," Mar. 8, 1934, and Bastedo, "Memorandum for the President," June 2, 1936, both in Folder Navy, 1933–Sep. 1936, Navy Dept., Series 4: Departmental Correspondence, Franklin D. Roosevelt, Papers as President: The President's Secretary's File (PSF), 1933–1945, Franklin D. Roosevelt Presidential Library & Museum, Hyde Park, New York (hereafter FDRL); on Roosevelt's role in facilitating the delivery of Argentinian battleships, see "Dispute over Warship," *New York Times*, Feb. 18, 1915, 9; Thomas C. Hone, "The Evolution of the U.S. Fleet, 1933–1941: How the President Mattered," in *FDR and the U.S. Navy*, ed. Edward J. Marolda (New·York: St. Martin's Press, 1998), 78–80; on Swanson, see Allison Saville, "Claude Augustus Swanson," in *American Secretaries of the Navy*, vol 2: *1913–1972*, ed. Paolo E. Coletta (Annapolis, MD: Naval Institute Press, 1980): 655–67.

48. Land to Swanson, Mar. 17, 1933, quoted in John C. Walter, "The Navy Department and the Campaign for Expanded Appropriations, 1933–1938," (PhD thesis, University of Maine, 1972), 65.

49. Darrow, "Navy Building Urgent," Apr. 30, 1933, Folder Dept. of the Navy Mar.–May 1933, Official File 18, FDRL.

50. James F. Cook, *Carl Vinson: Patriarch of the Armed Forces* (Macon, GA: Mercer University Press, 2004), 82 (quote); *Munitions Industry, Part 21*, 5,700–5,702; National Emergency Council, *Report to the President of the United States from the Acting Executive Director of the National Emergency Council* (Washington, DC: Government Printing Office, 1935), 123.

51. Bureau of Yards & Docks, "Projects to be Undertaken Under the National Industrial Recovery Act of 1933," June 19, 1933, Folder Dept. of the Navy Jan.–June 1940, Official File 18, FDRL; "Navy Department Awards Ship Contracts of $130,000,000 to Private Yards—Allocation of Ships to Navy Yards," *Marine Engineering* 38 (Sep. 1933): 6; Public Works Administration, *Letter from the Administrator of Public Works Transmitting Pursuant to Senate Resolution No. 190 a Report of the Business of the Federal Emergency Administrator of*

Public Works for the Period Ending February 15, 1934 (Washington, DC: Government Printing Office, 1934), 56–60; *Senate Document No. 40. Letter from the Secretary of the Treasury. Statement Relative to Funds under the N.R.A.*, 74th Cong. 1st Sess., 92 (1935).

52. U.S. Senate, Special Committee Investigating the Munitions Industry, *Munitions Industry, Preliminary Report of the Special Committee on Investigation of the Munitions Industry*, 74th Cong., 1st Sess., 52–53 (1935).

53. "Cord into Ships," *Time*, Aug. 14, 1933, 41.

54. Henry Roosevelt to FDR, Aug. 22, 1934, Folder Dept. of the Navy Aug.–Oct., 1934, Official File 18, FDRL; *Munitions Industry, Part 18*, 4,576–81 (statement of John F. Metten, president of the New York Shipbuilding Corporation).

55. "Agreement between John F. Metten and William Cramp and Sons Ship and Engine Building Company, 1927," John Farrell Metten Material, Box 1, Folder 1, Hagley Museum and Library, Wilmington, DE; U.S. Senate, Special Committee Investigating the Munitions Industry, *Part 18*, 4,561–81; *Munitions Industry, Part 36: Report on Government Manufacture of Munitions. Hearings Before the Special Senate Committee Investigating the Munitions Industry*, 74th Cong., 2nd Sess., 12,070 (1936).

56. Bossert to FDR, undated [June 1937], Folder Dept. of the Navy, Misc. Naval Building, 1937–1938, FDRL.

57. *The Use and Disposition of Ships and Shipyards*, 173.

58. "Report of Visit of Subcommittee of House Naval Affairs Committee Bath Iron Works Corporation, Bath, Me.," June 26, 1941, Box 182, Entry A1 1266-I, Bureau of Ships General Correspondence, 1940–1945, RG 19, NACP; *Munitions Industry, Part 23: Naval Shipbuilding: Federal Shipbuilding and Dry Dock Co.; Bath Iron Works Corp.; Sun Shipbuilding and Dry Dock Co., United Dry Docks, Inc.: Hearings Before the Special Senate Committee Investigating the Munitions Industry*, 74th Cong., 1st Sess., 6,658–71 (1935) (statement of Lynn H. Korndorff, president of Federal Shipbuilding and Dry Dock Company); Snow, *Bath Iron Works*, 217–78.

59. *Munitions Industry, Part 1: Electric Boat Co. Hearings Before the Special Senate Committee Investigating the Munitions Industry*, 73rd Cong., 267–71 (1934) (statement of Lawrence Y. Spears, president of Electric Boat Company); *The Use and Disposition of Ships and Shipyards*, 173.

60. *Munitions Industry, Part 23*, 6,916–18 (statement of Clinton Bardo, former president of New York Shipbuilding Corporation).

61. Office of Chief of Naval Intelligence, Intelligence Report, Serial 75-44, 2.

62. *Japan's Shipping and Shipbuilding Position, 1928–36: OIR Report No. 4712, June 25, 1948* (Washington, DC: Department of State, Division of Research for Far East, 1948), 6–7; "Replacement Shipbuilding in Japan," *Far Eastern Review* 30 (Aug. 1934): 379–82; Goldman, *Sunken Treaties*, 178; Mark E. Stille, *The Imperial Japanese Navy in the Pacific War* (Oxford, UK: Osprey Publishing, 2014), 92–95; Andreas Meyhoff, *Blohm & Voss im "Dritten Reich": Eine Hamburger Großwerft zwischen Geschäft und Politik* (Hamburg, Germany: Christians, 2001), 75–76.

63. "Ships on the Ways: Newport News and the Huntington Dynasty," *Fortune* 14 (Nov. 1936): 178.

64. U.S. Maritime Commission, *Report to Congress for the Period Ended October 25, 1939* (Washington, DC: Government Printing Office, 1940), 1; "Maritime Commission Shipbuilding at Navy Yards," n.d. [1937], Folder Charles Edison, Navy Dept., Series 4: Departmental Correspondence, Franklin D. Roosevelt, Papers as President: The President's Secretary's File (PSF), 1933–1945, FDRL; Frederic C. Lane, *Ships for Victory: A History of Shipbuilding under the U.S. Maritime Commission in World War II* (Baltimore, MD: Johns Hopkins University Press, 1951), 10–21.

65. *Merchant Marine Act of 1936*, 74th Cong., 1st Sess., June 29, 1936.

66. Manley R. Irwin, *Silent Strategists: Harding, Denby, and the U.S. Navy's Trans-Pacific Offensive, World War II* (Lanham, MD: University Press of America, 2013), 118; on Navy plans to convert passenger liners into aircraft and seaplane carriers, see Friedman, *U.S. Aircraft Carriers*, 127.

67. David C. Evans and Mark R. Peattie, *Kaigun: Strategy, Tactics, and Technology in the Imperial Japanese Navy, 1887–1941* (Annapolis, MD: Naval Institute Press, 1997), 206–12.

68. Quoted in Douglas Ford, "U.S. Naval Intelligence and the Imperial Japanese Fleet During the Washington Treaty Era, c. 1922–36," *Mariner's Mirror* 93 (Aug. 2007): 281.

69. Waldo Heinrichs, "The Role of the U.S. Navy," in *Pearl Harbor as History: Japanese-American Relations 1931–1941*, ed. Dorothy Borg and Shumpei Okamoto (New York: Columbia University Press, 1973), 208 (quote); on the First Naval Armament Replenishment Plan, see U.S. Army Far East Command, *Outline of Naval Armament and Preparations for War, Part I* (Washington, DC: Department of the Army, Office of the Chief of Military History, 1952), 11–13; on War Plan Orange, see John M. Barrett, "An Analysis of the Causal Factors Behind the United States Navy's Warship-Building Programs from 1933 to

1941" (master's thesis, U.S. Army Command and General Staff College, 2005), 35; on U.S. naval intelligence, see Justin Z. Pyke, "Blinded by the Rising Sun? American Intelligence Assessments of Japanese Air and Naval Power, 1920–1941" (master's thesis, University of Calgary, 2016), 77–78.

70. "Presidential Statement Issued upon Signing the Vinson Navy Bill," Mar. 27, 1934, *Public Papers and Addresses of Franklin D. Roosevelt. 1934*, vol. 3: *The Advance of Recovery and Reform* (New York: Macmillan, 1938), 172.

71. Robert Dallek, *Franklin D. Roosevelt and American Foreign Policy, 1932–1945* (New York: Oxford University Press, 1995), 76 (quote).

72. Sadao Asada, *From Mahan to Pearl Harbor: The Imperial Japanese Navy and the United States* (Annapolis, MD: Naval Institute Press, 2006), 198–206; U.S. Army Far East Command, *Outline of Naval Armament*, 59–60.

73. Quoted in Malcolm Muir, "Rearming in a Vacuum: United States Navy Intelligence and the Japanese Capital Ship Threat, 1936–1945," *Journal of Military History* 54 (Oct. 1990): 476.

74. "Japanese Disputes Leahy on Building," *New York Times*, Feb. 4, 1938, 3.

75. *Establish the Composition of the United States Navy: Hearings Before the House Committee on Naval Affairs*, 75th Cong., 3rd Sess., 1,972 (1938) (statement of Adm. William D. Leahy, chief of naval operations).

76. Muir, "Rearming in a Vacuum"; on naval intelligence, see John Prados, *Combined Fleet Decoded: The Secret History of American Intelligence and the Japanese Navy in World War II* (Annapolis, MD: Naval Institute Press, 1995); and Ford, "U.S. Naval Intelligence and the Imperial Japanese Fleet," 281–306.

77. Bossert to FDR, undated [June 1937], Folder Dept. of the Navy, Misc. Naval Building, 1937–38, FDRL.

78. FDR to Bossert, June 23, 193: Folder Dept. of the Navy, Misc. Naval Building, 1937–38, FDRL.

79. "Editorial," *Marine Engineering* (July 1937): 356.

80. "Pleads for Shipyards," *New York Times*, July 29, 1937, 9 (quote); see also Donald W. Mitchell, "What Our Warships Cost," *The Nation*, Sep. 23, 1939, 320–22.

81. Moore to Roosevelt, Oct. 11, 1937, Folder Dept. of the Navy, Misc. Naval Building, 1937–1938, FDRL.

82. New York Shipbuilding Corporation, *Annual Report for the Year Ending December 31, 1938* (Camden, NJ: New York Shipbuilding Corporation, 1939), 1.

83. "Newport News Low Bidder on All Alternate Designs for Two Matson Cargo Ships," *Marine Engineering* (July 1936): 419; "$17,500,000 Firm Bid Submitted

by Newport News, Lowest Bidder on United States Lines Cabin Ship," *Marine Engineering* (Oct. 1937): 553; "Four Shipbuilders Submit Tenders on Panama Railroad Steamship Passenger Vessels," *Marine Engineering* (May 1937): 289; "Bethlehem and Sun Ship Submit Low Bids for Building Export Ships," *Marine Engineering* (June 1938): 294; "New York Shipbuilding Corporation Gets $23,000,000 Naval Contract," *Marine Engineering* (Nov. 1938): 540; *Navy Department Appropriation Bill for 1939: Hearings Before the Subcommittee of House Committee on Appropriations*, 75th Cong., 3rd Sess., 786 (1937) (statement of Charles Edison, Assistant Secretary of the Navy); Griffith Borgeson, *Errett Lobban: His Empire, His Motorcars: Auburn, Cord, Duesenberg* (Princeton, NJ: Automobile Quarterly, 1984), 216.

84. Quoted in Borgeson, *Errett Lobban*, 205.

85. "United States Asiatic Fleet, Situation in the Pacific: Studies Prepared Under Direction of Admiral Yarnell," Nov. 26, 1937, Box 70, Subject File 1900–1947, General Records of the Department of the Navy, RG 80, National Archives, Washington, DC.

86. Quoted in John E. Moon, *Confines of Concept: American Strategy in World War II*, vol. 2 (New York: Garland, 1988), 871.

87. John V. Haight Jr., "Franklin D. Roosevelt and a Naval Quarantine of Japan," *Pacific Historical Review* 40 (May 1971): 207.

88. *Establish the Composition of the United States Navy*, 1942 (statement of Adm. William D. Leahy, chief of naval operations); see also U.S. Naval Attaché Tokyo, "Third Replenishment Program," Jan. 22, 1937, Folder Departmental Correspondence, Estimates of Potential Military Strength, Documents G. Naval Attaché Tokyo, vol. I, Jan. 18, 1937, to June 9, 1938, Navy, Franklin D. Roosevelt, Papers as President: The President's Secretary's File, 1933–1945, FDRL; Cooke, "Memorandum for the Secretary," Oct. 30, 1939, Box 70, Subject File 1900–1947, General Records of the Department of the Navy, RG 80, National Archives, Washington, DC; Evans and Peattie, *Kaigun*, 318–19, 385; Stephen W. Roskill, *Naval Policy Between the Wars*, vol. 2: *The Period of Reluctant Rearmament 1930–1939* (Annapolis, MD: Naval Institute Press, 1976), 325–26; Wilhelm Deist, "Die Aufrüstung der Wehrmacht," in *Das Deutsche Reich und der Zweite Weltkrieg*, vol. 1: *Ursachen und Voraussetzungen der deutschen Kriegspolitik* (Stuttgart, Germany: Deutsche Verlags-Anstalt, 1979), 450.

89. "The President Recommends Increased Armaments for Defense," Jan. 28, 1938, *Public Papers and Addresses of Franklin D. Roosevelt. 1938: The Continuing Struggle for Liberalism* (New York: Macmillan, 1941), 69.

90. Quoted in Muir, "Rearming in a Vacuum," 477; see also *Second Deficiency Appropriation Bill for 1938: Hearings Before the Subcommittee of the House Committee on Appropriations,* 75th Cong., 3rd Sess., 481–511 (1938) (statement of Rear Adm. William D. Leahy, chief of naval operations).

91. Quoted in Walter, "The Navy Department," 303.

92. Quoted in Walter, "The Navy Department," 303.

93. Bureau of Construction and Repair, Bureau of Engineering, and Bureau of Ordnance to Secretary of the Navy, July 14, 1938, Box 63, General Board Subject File 1900–1947, GB 420-2, 1937–1938 to GB 420-2, 1941–1942, General Records of the Department of the Navy, RG 80, National Archives and Records Administration Washington, DC; "Newport News and Bethlehem Yards Awarded Contracts for a Battleship," *Marine Engineering* 43 (Dec. 1938): 588; "New York Shipbuilding Corporation Awarded Contract for a Battleship," *Marine Engineering* 44 (Jan. 1939): 28.

94. Defrees, Memorandum for the Assistant Secretary of the Navy, Feb. 2, 1938, Box 63, General Board Subject File 1900–1947, GB 420-2, 1937–1938 to GB 420-2, 1941–1942, General Records of the Department of the Navy, RG 80, National Archives and Records Administration Washington, DC; "Bethlehem Ship," *Fortune* 16 (Sep. 1937): 82–83; "Ships on the Ways: Newport News and the Huntington Dynasty," *Fortune* 14 (Nov. 1936): 70.

95. Mitsubishi Zōsen Kabushiki Kaisha, *Naval Vessels 1887–1945,* ii; Ambrose Greenway, *Cargo Liners: An Illustrated History* (Barnsley, UK: Seaforth Publishing, 2011), 74–75; Thomas G. Mahnken, *Uncovering Ways of War: U.S. Intelligence and Foreign Military Innovation, 1918–1941* (Ithaca, NY: Cornell University Press, 2002), 68–69.

96. The treaty was the result of British concerns that Hitler would unilaterally annul the Versailles limits, prompting the Ramsay MacDonald government to seek a negotiated agreement on future warship building that allowed Germany to build its surface fleet up to 35 percent of British tonnage and permitted parity in submarines. Joseph Maiolo, *The Royal Navy and Nazi Germany, 1933–39: A Study in Appeasement and the Origins of the Second World War* (London: Macmillan Press, 1998), 429–30.

97. Deutsche Schiff- und Maschinenbau Aktiengesellschaft in Bremen, "Bericht des Vorstandes," May 1938, WA 65/40.1938, Geschäftsberichte Krupp-Konzern, Historisches Archiv Krupp, Essen, Germany; Bremer Vulkan, *Schiffbau und Maschinenfabrik*; "Werft Ausbau," Apr. 1939, 7, 2121/1–1207, Bremer Vulkan, Akten und Geschäftsbücher, Bremen State Archives, Germany; Peter Kuckuk

and Hartmut Pophanken, "Die A.G. 'Weser' 1933 bis 1945: Handels-und Kriegsschiffbau im Dritten Reich," in *Bremer Großwerften im Dritten Reich*, ed. Peter Kuckuk (Bremen, Germany: Edition Temmen, 1993), 46–68; Meyhoff, *Blohm & Voss*, 119–53; Adam Tooze, *The Wages of Destruction: The Making and Breaking of the Nazi Economy* (New York: Penguin, 2007), 72–73; Schmelzkopf, *Die deutsche Handelsschifffahrt*, vol. 1, 219–23.

98. Quoted in Eric Grove, "A War Fleet Built for Peace: British Naval Rearmament in the 1930s and the Dilemma of Deterrence versus Defence," *Naval War College Review* 44 (1991): 84.

99. Maiolo, *The Royal Navy and Nazi Germany*, 111–32.

100. "Naval New Construction Programmes and Their Execution. 1935–1945. Unpublished Narrative Used in the Compilation of British War Production: Final Draft," n.d., 5, CAB 102/527, National Archives of the United Kingdom, Kew.

101. Admiralty Statement of the First Lord of the Admiralty Explanatory of the Navy Estimates 1937, Feb. 1937, ADM 116/3596, National Archives of the UK, Kew; on British rearmament, see J. P. D. Dunbabin, "British Rearmament in the 1930s: A Chronology and Review," *Historical Journal* 18 (Sep. 1975): 587–609; Andrew Boyd, *The Royal Navy in Eastern Waters: Linchpin of Victory* (Barnsley, UK: Seaforth Publishing, 2017), 20–115; on Swan Hunter, see Board of Directors Meeting May 4, 1937, and June 29, 1937, Swan, Hunter, & Wigham Richardson Ltd. Directors' Minute Book No. 6, DS.SWH/1/4/6, Tyne and Wear Archives, Newcastle upon Tyne, UK; on Vickers and Royal Dockyards, see Scott, *Vickers*, 218–19; on Fairfield, see Directors' Report and Statement of Accounts, Nov. 16, 1936, Minute Book No. 6, UCS2/1/6, Mitchell Library Special Collections, Glasgow; on Cammell Laird, see Gordon, *British Seapower*, 187; Hugh Peebles, *Warshipbuilding on the Clyde: Naval Orders and the Prosperity of the Clyde Shipbuilding Industry, 1889–1939* (Edinburgh, UK: John Donald, 2000), 139; on Royal Dockyards, see William Ashworth, *Contracts and Finance* (London: Her Majesty's Stationery Office, 1953), 255.

102. "Shipbuilding Companies' Earnings," *Fairplay*, Jan. 12, 1939, 85.

103. On Fairfield, see Directors' Report and Statement of Accounts, Nov. 16, 1936, Minute Book No. 6, UCS2/1/6, Mitchell Library Special Collections, Glasgow, UK; Peebles, *Warshipbuilding on the Clyde*, 143–45; on profitability of the three *King George V*–class battleships, see Buxton and Johnston, *Battleship Builders*, 243.

104. Boyd, *The Royal Navy in Eastern Waters*, 10.

105. FDR to Gehrman, Apr. 10, 1940, Folder Dept. of the Navy, Misc. Naval Building, 1940, FDRL.

106. Irving B. Holley Jr., *Buying Aircraft: Materiél Procurement for the Army Air Forces* (Washington, DC: U.S. Army Center for Military History, 1964).

Chapter 2. "An Unending Effort to Satisfy the Needs for High Speed and Great Strength"

1. Gregory Hooks and Gregory McLauchlan, "The Institutional Foundation of Warmaking: Three Eras of U.S. Warmaking, 1939–1989," *Theory and Society* 21 (Dec. 1992): 770.

2. Harvard Graduate School of Business Administration, *The Use and Disposition of Ships and Shipyards at the End of World War II* (Washington, DC: Government Printing Office, 1945), 160–61.

3. J. H. King, "Marine Boilers for Higher Pressures and Temperatures and their Contribution to Greater Economy," *Journal of the American Society for Naval Engineers* 40 (1928): 238.

4. George H. Rock, "Education of Naval Constructors and Naval Architects," *Transactions of the Society of Naval Architects and Marine Engineers* 40 (1932): 199.

5. Rock, "Education of Naval Constructors," 197–99; Bureau of Construction and Repair, *History of the Construction Corps of the United States Navy* (Washington, DC: Government Printing Office, 1937), 41–42.

6. "Personal," *Marine Engineering and Shipping Review* 44 (Oct. 1939): 495; Entry, "Chantry, Allan J., Jr. (1883–1959)," in Alastair Wilson and Joseph F. Callo, *Who's Who in Naval History: From 1550 to the Present* (London: Routledge, 2004), 62.

7. Harold G. Bowen, *Ships, Machinery, and Mossbacks: The Autobiography of a Naval Engineer* (Princeton, NJ: Princeton University Press, 1954), 37.

8. Bowen, *Ships, Machinery, and Mossbacks*, 38.

9. Bowen, *Ships, Machinery, and Mossbacks*, 182.

10. Ivan Amato, *Pushing the Horizon: Seventy-Five Years of High Stakes Science and Technology at the Naval Research Laboratory* (Washington, DC: Naval Research Laboratory, 2001), 157–59.

11. "Reminiscences of Samuel Murray Robinson: Oral History, 1963," 2, Naval History Project, Oral History Research Office, 1964, Special Collections, Columbia University Library, New York.

12. "Reminiscences of Samuel Murray Robinson," 14.

13. "Reminiscences of Samuel Murray Robinson," 15.

14. "Reminiscences of Samuel Murray Robinson," 18.

15. "Robinson, Samuel Murray," *Cyclopædia of American Biography vol. G, 1943–1946* (New York: James White & Co., 1946), 293–94; Amato, *Pushing the Horizon*, 72–76.

16. David K. Brown, *A Century of Naval Construction: The History of the Royal Corps of Naval Constructors, 1883–1983* (London: Conway, 1983), 11–13; Fukasaku Yukiko, *Technology and Industrial Growth in Pre-War Japan: The Mitsubishi-Nagasaki Shipyard 1884–1934* (London: Routledge, 1992), 109–11; Frank P. Purvis, "Japan's Contribution to Naval Architecture," *Transactions of the Royal Institution of Naval Architects* 67 (1925): 31. The author is indebted to Professor Eike Lehmann for information on German naval constructor training between the wars; see also Schiffbautechnische Gesellschaft, *75 Jahre Schiffbautechnische Gesellschaft 1899–1974* (Hamburg, Germany: Schiffbautechnische Gesellschaft, 1974).

17. Lawrence B. Chapman, "University Education in Ship Construction and Marine Transportation," *Transactions of the Society of Naval Architects and Marine Engineers* 28 (1920): 1 (quote); see also "Shipping Men Honor Professor L. B. Chapman," *Pacific Marine Review/The Log* 47 (July 1952): 24.

18. On Webb, see Federal Writers' Project, *New York Learns: A Guide to the Educational Facilities of the Metropolis* (New York: Barrows & Co., 1939), 148.

19. *Investigation of the Progress of the War Effort*, vol. 5: *Gibbs & Cox, Incorporated: Hearings Before the House Committee on Naval Affairs*, 78th Cong., 1st Sess., 3,944–49 (1944) (statement of Rear Adm. E. L. Cochrane, chief of the Bureau of Ships); Bureau of Construction & Repair and Bureau of Engineering to Secretary of the Navy, Aug. 1937, reprinted in *Navy Department Appropriation Bill for 1939: Hearings Before the Subcommittee of House Committee on Appropriations*, 75th Cong., 3rd Sess., 545–46 (1937); Steven Ujifusa, *A Man and His Ship: America's Greatest Naval Architect and His Quest to Build the S.S. United States* (New York: Simon & Schuster, 2012), 142.

20. Alexander M. Charlton, "From General Board to Trial Board: The Evolution of a Man-of-War," *Journal of the American Society for Naval Engineers* 42 (1930): 46.

21. Bowen, *Ships, Machinery, and Mossbacks*, 69 (quote); never one to miss an opportunity to chide shipbuilders for their conservatism, Bowen added, "New York Ship's Mr. J. F. Metten fought this innovation, almost to the point of losing a contract, although $50,000 was included in the contract for the cost of the model." Bowen, *Ships, Machinery, and Mossbacks*, 69; on the model basin, see Rodney Carlisle, *Where the Fleet Begins: A History of the David Taylor Research Center* (Washington, DC: Naval Historical Center, 1998), 11–130.

22. Memo No. 3: Notes on Talk with Cdr. Kniskern, Dec. 12, 1942, Report on W. Forbes' Visit to U.S.A., ADM 281/106, National Archives of the United Kingdom, Kew.

23. Charlton, "From General Board to Trial Board," 61.

24. Bowen, *Ships, Machinery, and Mossbacks*, 69.

25. Van Keuren and Robinson, "Organization. Part I. Assignment of Consolidated Duties to Divisions and Offices," Oct. 5, 1939, Box 17, Commandant's Files, Headquarters Third Naval District, Record Group 181, National Archives and Records Administration, Northeast Region, New York; U.S. Department of the Navy, *U.S. Navy Regulations 1920* (Washington, DC: Government Printing Office, 1920), 138–39; Historical Section, Bureau of Ships, "An Administrative History of the Bureau of Ships During World War II," vol. 1, n.d., 52–58, Rare Book Room, Navy Department Library, Washington Navy Yard, Washington, DC; George C. Manning and T. L. Schumacher, *Principles of Naval Architecture and Warship Construction* (Annapolis, MD: Naval Institute Press, 1924), 128–33; John T. Kuehn, *Agents of Innovation: The General Board and the Design of the Fleet that Defeated the Japanese Navy* (Annapolis, MD: Naval Institute Press, 2008), 8–22; John T. Kuehn, *America's First General Staff: A Short History of the Rise and Fall of the General Board of the Navy, 1900–1950* (Annapolis, MD: Naval Institute Press, 2017), 1–8; Scott T. Price, "A Study of the General Board of the U.S. Navy, 1929–1933" (master's thesis, University of Nebraska, 1989), 109.

26. Charles François, "Notes on Some Researches and Tendencies of Contemporary Naval Construction," *Transactions of the Royal Institution of Naval Architects* 73 (1931): 269.

27. Henry E. Rossell, *Riveting and Arc Welding in Ship Construction* (New York: Simmons Boardman Publishing, 1934), 82.

28. "American Engineers Plan Cargo Ship Without Rivets," *Marine Engineering* 25 (Aug. 1920): 701 (quote); see also P. Schoenmaker and G. DeRooy, "More Modern Methods and Steels in Welded Ship Construction," *Welding Journal* 18 (May 1939): 275; David Arnott, "Welding in Shipbuilding," *Journal of the American Society for Naval Engineers* 53 (Jan. 1941): 211–27.

29. Rossell, *Riveting and Arc Welding*, 82–84; L. W. Schuster, "The Effect of Contamination by Nitrogen on the Structure of Electric Welds," *Journal of the American Society for Naval Engineers* 43 (Feb. 1931): 140–47; "Navy to X-Ray Vital Parts of Fleet," *Marine Engineering* 44 (Jan. 1939): 22; A. Karsten, "Die röntgenographische Feinstruktur-Untersuchung und ihr Wert für die Schiffbautechnik," *Schiffbau, Schiffahrt und Hafenbau* 37 (June 1936): 204–6.

30. W. O. Schrader, "Progress of Electric Welding in Shipbuilding," *Marine Engineering* (Sep. 1936): 500–506; J. Lyell Wilson, "Ship Welding," *Marine Engineering* (Nov. 1936): 634–36; B. A. Russell, "Welding as Viewed by the Shipbuilder," *Marine Engineering* 44 (July 1939): 316–20; William H. Thiesen, *Industrializing American Shipbuilding: The Transformation of Ship Design and Construction, 1820–1920* (Gainesville: University Press of Florida, 2006), 185.

31. "The Germanischer Lloyd Regulations for Electric Welding," *Marine Engineer and Motorship Builder* 55 (1932): 116–17; Dirk J. Peters, "Deutsche Werften in der Zwischenkriegszeit (1918–1939). Teil 2: Symptome der Krise, Stilllegungen Schließungen, Fusionen und Innovationen (1924–1934)," *Deutsches Schiffahrtsarchiv* 32 (2009): 177–78; Herrmann Lottmann, Paul Küchler, and Herrmann Burkhardt, "'Heute weiß ich, daß der Versuch scheitern mußte': Drei Originalberichte aus den Anfängen der Lichtbogenschweißtechnik in der deutschen Kriegsmarine und der Handelsschiffahrt," *Schiff und Zeit* 13 (1981): 45–47; see also Bruce A. Watson, *Atlantic Convoys and Nazi Raiders: The Deadly Voyage of HMS Jervis Bay* (Westport, CT: Praeger, 2006), 21.

32. Bureau of Construction and Repair, *C. and R. Bulletin No. 1: All-Welded Garbage Lighter, YG16: A Discussion of the Electric Welding Process of Ship Construction* (Washington, DC: Government Printing Office, 1931), 1.

33. Galen H. Moore, "Welded Machinery Foundations for Ships," *Journal of the American Welding Society* 10 (1932): 38.

34. Russell, "Welding as Viewed by the Shipbuilder," 318; see also Arnott, "Welding in Shipbuilding," 216.

35. "Pity the Welder," *Marine Engineering* (Mar. 1939): 124.

36. Homer N. Wallin and Henry A. Schade, "The Design and Construction of an Arc Welded Naval Auxiliary Vessel," in *Designing for Arc Welding: Second Lincoln Arc Welding Prize Competition Papers*, ed. A. F. Davis (Cleveland, OH: Lincoln Electric Company, 1933): 149–94; F. J. Cleary, "The Material Laboratory, U.S. Navy Yard, New York," *Journal of the American Society of Naval Engineers* 43 (1930): 75; W. P. Roop, "Features of Practice Affecting Design," *Transactions of the Society of Naval Architects and Marine Engineers* 44 (1936): 335–37; James B. Hunter, "Some Effects of Welding on Ship Construction," *Transactions of the Society of Naval Architects and Marine Engineers* 45 (1937): 9–12; Russell, "Welding as Viewed by the Shipbuilder," 317–18; *Navy Department Appropriation Bill for 1939*, 432 (1937) (statement of Rear Adm. William G. Du Bose, chief of the Bureau of Construction and Repair).

37. "Marine Welding Advanced," U.S. Naval Institute *Proceedings* 57 (Aug. 1931): 1,108.

38. Moore, "Welded Machinery Foundations for Ships," 38.

39. "Report of the Chief of the Bureau of Construction and Repair," U.S. Secretary of the Navy, *Annual Report of the Secretary of the Navy for Fiscal Year 1932* (Washington, DC: Government Printing Office, 1933), 256–57; George C. Manning, *Principles of Warship Construction and Damage Control* (Annapolis, MD: Naval Institute Press, 1935), 184–85; Bela Ronay, "The Fundamentals of Electric Arc Welding," *Journal of the American Society of Naval Engineers* 46 (1934): 21–30; Norman L. Mochel, "Ten Years of Welding Development," *Journal of the American Society of Naval Engineers* 48 (1936): 455–75.

40. "Arc-Welded Tanker J. W. Van Dyke," *Marine Engineering* 43 (1938): 166–71; Lester M. Goldsmith, "The High-Pressure, High-Temperature Turbo-Electric Tanker J.W. Van Dyke," *Marine Engineering* 43 (1938): 548–58, 570.

41. Quoted in Rodney K. Watterson, *32 in '44: Building the Portsmouth Submarine Fleet in World War II* (Annapolis, MD: Naval Institute Press, 2011), 77.

42. James Montgomerie, "Shipbuilding Practice Abroad," *Transactions of the North-East Coast Institution of Engineers and Shipbuilders* 54 (1938): 168; on Morse, see Thiesen, *Industrializing American Shipbuilding*, 192–96.

43. *Second Deficiency Appropriation Bill for 1938: Hearings Before the Subcommittee of the House Committee on Appropriations*, 75th Cong., 3rd Sess., 529 (1938) (statement of Rear Adm. Ben Moreell, chief of the Bureau of Yards and Docks).

44. U.S. manufacturers generally made only "modest investments in instrumentation" during the 1930s; Alexander J. Field, "Technological Change and U.S. Productivity Growth in the Interwar Years," *Journal of Economic History* 66 (Mar. 2006): 216.

45. *Munitions Industry, Part 21: Naval Shipbuilding: Bethlehem Shipbuilding Corporation. Hearings Before the Special Senate Committee Investigating the Munitions Industry*, 74th Cong., 1st Sess., 6,154 (1935).

46. James W. Owens, *Fundamentals of Welding Gas, Arc and Thermit: A Textbook for Governmental Engineering Departments, Colleges, Technical Schools, Etc.* (Cleveland, OH: Penton, 1923), 516.

47. Owens, *Fundamentals of Welding*, 504, 506–7.

48. Bolster, "Execution of the Naval New Construction Programmes, 1939–1945," 158, CAB 102/524, National Archives of the United Kingdom, Kew.

49. Errington, "Execution of Naval New Construction Programme 1936–1939," 37, CAB 102/533, National Archives of the United Kingdom, Kew.

50. Quoted in Joseph F. Clarke, *Building Ships on the North East Coast: A Labour of Love, Risk, and Pain, Part 2: C 1914-C 1980* (Whitley Bay, UK: Bewick Press, 1997), 260.

51. Quoted in Clarke, *Building Ships on the North East Coast*, 261; see also William Bennett, "Recent Developments in Special Quality Steels for Shipbuilding," *Transactions of the Society of Naval Architects and Marine Engineers* 39 (1931): 75 and 79; Lewis Johnman and Hugh Murphy, "Welding and the British Shipbuilding Industry: A Major Constraint?" in *The Royal Navy, 1930–2000: Innovation and Defence*, ed. Richard Harding (London: Frank Cass, 2005), 97–98; Ian Buxton and Ian Johnston, *The Battleship Builders: Constructing and Arming British Capital Ships* (Barnsley, UK: Seaforth Publishing, 2013), 111–12, 146–47, 226, 239; David K. Brown, "Early Welding for the Royal Navy," *Journal of Naval Engineering* 34 (Dec. 1992): 220–22; *Two Hundred & Fifty Years of Shipbuilding by the Scotts at Greenock* (Greenock, UK: n.p., 1961), 117.

52. Later converted into a light fleet carrier and renamed *Ryūhō*.

53. U.S. Technical Mission to Japan, *Report No. S-81(N): Welding in Japanese Naval Construction* (San Francisco: U.S. Technical Mission to Japan, 1946), 7.

54. Fletcher Pratt, *Sea Power and Today's War* (New York: Harrison-Hilton Books, 1939), 176–77.

55. Janusz Skulski, *Battleships Yamato and Musashi* (London: Bloomsbury, 2017), 12; Technical Mission to Japan, *Report No. S-81*.

56. Hans H. Diergarten, "German Ship Builders Use Arc Welding Extensively," *Metal Progress* 22 (July 1932): 60 (quote).

57. Montgomerie, "Shipbuilding Practice Abroad," 168.

58. Kurt Arendt and Heinrich Oelfken, "Die Baumethoden der deutschen U-Boote 1935–1945," in *100 Jahre Verbands- und Zeitgeschehen*, ed. Verband der Deutschen Schiffbauindustrie e. V. (Hamburg, Germany: Storck, 1984), 66–72; originally written in 1947 by Arendt, AG Weser's former director of construction, the report was edited by Oelsken in 1948. On shipyard welding at the Wilhelmshaven Navy Yard, see Paul Küchler, "Die Lichtbogenschwei-ßung im Schiffbau," *Schiffbau, Schifffahrt und Hafenbau* 34 (Jan. 1933): 8–10.

59. On the introduction of covered electrodes in naval construction, see *Annual Report of the Secretary of the Navy for the Fiscal Year 1931* (Washington, DC: Government Printing Office, 1931), 43; *Annual Report of the Secretary of the Navy for the Fiscal Year 1940* (Washington, DC: Government Printing Office, 1940), 26.

60. Henry E. Rossell, "Types of Naval Ships," in *Society of Naval Architects and Marine Engineers, Historical Transactions 1893–1943* (New York: Society of Naval Architects and Marine Engineers, 1945), 310.

61. Rossell, "Types of Naval Ships," 310.

62. Rossell, "Types of Naval Ships," 310 (quote); Carl L. Lamb, "The Effect of Disarmament and Treaty Limits Upon Naval Engineering," *Journal of the American Society for Naval Engineers* 42 (1930): 641–50; John Jordan, *Warships after Washington: The Development of the Five Major Fleets, 1922–1930* (Annapolis, MD: Naval Institute Press, 2015).

63. R. C. Brierly, "The Development of B. & W. Boilers for Naval Vessels: Test of Four Boilers at the Fuel Oil Testing Plant," *Journal of the American Society for Naval Engineers* 41 (1929): 634–55; E. R. Fish, "The Characteristics of Modern Boilers," *Journal of the American Society for Naval Engineers* 40 (1928): 108; "Boiler Tube Failure—Metallographic Examination," *Bulletin of Engineering Information* 13 (May 1924): 26–27; *Naval Machinery Part IV: Marine and Naval Boilers* (Annapolis, MD: Naval Institute Press, 1935), 53.

64. Edgar C. Smith, *A Short History of Naval and Marine Engineering* (1938; repr. Cambridge, UK: Cambridge University Press, 2013), 271–87; John W. M. Sothern, *The Marine Steam Turbine: A Practical Description of the Parsons and Curtis Marine Steam Turbines as Presently Constructed, Fitted, and Run* (Fourth Edition) (London: Crosby Lockwood, 1916), 231–35; William M. McBride, *Technological Change and the United States Navy, 1865–1945* (Baltimore, MD: Johns Hopkins University Press, 2000), 95.

65. R. J. Walker and S. S. Cook, "Mechanical Gears, of Double Reduction, for Merchant Ships," *Transactions of the Institution of Naval Architects* 63 (1921): 69.

66. Glenn B. Warren, *Development of Steam Turbines for Main Propulsion of High-Powered Combatant Ships* (New York: Society of Naval Architects and Marine Engineers, 1946), 2.

67. "Reminiscences of Samuel Murray Robinson," 17; see also John E. Burkhart, "The Present Trend in Marine Engineering in the United States of America," *Journal of the American Society for Naval Engineers* 50 (1938): 434.

68. "William W. Smith, Comment on E. H. Rigg, 'Design and Construction of Passenger Steamers,'" *Transactions of the Society of Naval Architects and Marine Engineers* 29 (1921): 295; see also James C. Hodge, "Marine Boiler Drums of Fusion Welded Construction," *Journal of the American Society for Naval Engineers* 45 (1933): 149–64; Smith, *A Short History of Naval and Marine Engineering*, 288–302. Alternatives to mechanical reduction gear included the turboelectric drive in which the turbine was coupled to a generator that fed electric motors connected to propeller shafts; installed in the battlecruisers-turned–aircraft carriers of the *Lexington* class, the technology was abandoned by the U.S. Navy

during the interwar years. William M. McBride, "Strategic Determinism in Technology Selection: The Electric Battleship and U.S. Naval-Industrial Relations," *Technology and Culture* 33 (Apr. 1992): 248–77.

69. *Annual Reports of the Navy Department for Fiscal Year 1925* (Washington, DC: Government Printing Office, 1926), 35.

70. *Annual Reports of the Navy Department for Fiscal Year 1925*, 35.

71. Quoted in Ujifusa, *A Man and His Ship*, 144.

72. Robert Warriner, "Reduction Gear for Ship Propulsion," *Transactions of the Society of Naval Architects and Marine Engineers* 29 (1921): 13–21; on General Electric's bucket research and development, see Warren, *Development of Steam Turbines*, 20–21.

73. From 1927 to 1934, Newport News paid more than $82,000 in royalties to Parsons; *Munitions Industry, Part 20: Naval Shipbuilding: Newport News Shipbuilding and Dry Dock Company. Hearings Before the Special Senate Committee Investigating the Munitions Industry*, 74th Cong., 1st Sess., 5,644 (1935).

74. Bureau of Ships, "An Administrative History of the Bureau of Ships During World War II," vol. 1, n.d., 27, Rare Book Room, Navy Department Library, Washington Navy Yard, Washington, DC (quote); see also Norman Friedman *U.S. Destroyers: An Illustrated Design History* (Annapolis, MD: Naval Institute Press, 2004), 88.

75. Bowen, *Ships, Machinery, and Mossbacks*, 62.

76. Charles P. Wetherbee, "High Pressure and Superheat Aboard Ship," *Transactions of the Society of Naval Architects and Marine Engineers* 43 (1935): 225.

77. John F. Sonnett, "Report for the Under Secretary on Gibbs & Cox, Inc.," 1944, 22–36, Box 156, General Records of the Department of the Navy, Records of Secretary of the Navy James Forrestal, 1940–1947, Commercial Plants File, 1940–1945, Record Group 80, National Archives at College Park, College Park, MD; William M. McBride, "Powering the U.S. Fleet: Propulsion Machinery Design and American Engineering Culture, 1890–1945," in *New Interpretations in Naval History: Selected Papers from the Seventeenth Naval History Symposium Held at the United States Naval Academy, 10–11 Sep. 2009*, ed. Marcus O. Jones (Newport, RI: Naval War College Press, 2016), 60–61.

78. John Metten to Battleship Advisory Board, Apr. 28, 1938, reprinted in Bowen, *Ships, Machinery, and Mossbacks*, 369–70 (quote).

79. Quoted in McBride, "Powering the U.S. Fleet," 61.

80. *Second Deficiency Appropriation Bill for 1938: Hearings Before the Subcommittee of the House Committee on Appropriations,* 75th Cong., 1st Sess., 1937, 489 (quote);

see also Bowen, "Statement to the General Board," 1938, reprinted in Historical Section, Bureau of Ships, "An Administrative History of the Bureau of Ships During World War II," vol. 1, 131, Rare Book Room, Navy Department Library, Washington Navy Yard, Washington, DC.

81. Warren, *Development of Steam Turbines*, 15.

82. Bowen, *Ships, Machinery, and Mossbacks*, 114.

83. Historian David Brown confirms the Americans' verdict: "The biggest failing in British ships lay in their machinery. . . . [The Royal Navy] entered the war with machinery which was much heavier, more bulky, less reliable and far less (25%) economical than that used in the" U.S. Navy; David K. Brown, *The Design and Construction of British Warships 1939–1945: The Official Record*, vol. 1: *Major Surface Vessels* (Annapolis, MD: Naval Institute Press, 1996), 11.

84. U.S. Technical Mission to Japan, *Report No. S-01-2: Characteristics of Japanese Naval Vessels, Article 2: Surface Warship Machinery Design* (San Francisco: U.S. Technical Mission to Japan, 1945), 7–14; Fukasaku, *Technology and Industrial Growth in Pre-War Japan*, 165–79; Matsumoto Miwao, "The 'Structural Disaster' of the Science-Technology-Society Interface From a Comparative Perspective with a Prewar Accident," in *Reflections on the Fukushima Daiichi Nuclear Accident: Toward Social-Scientific Literacy and Engineering Resilience*, ed. Joonhong Ahn, Cathryn Carson, et al. (Cham, Switzerland: Springer, 2015), 194–207.

85. Henry Schade, "German Wartime Technical Developments," *Transactions of the Society of Naval Architects and Marine Engineers* 54 (1946): 94–95 (quotes).

86. R. G. Raper, "Main Machinery: How Do We Stand?" *Papers on Engineering Subjects* 7 (Sep. 1946): 68 and 75 (quote). I am indebted to Capt. William O'Neill for calling attention to this source and for making it available; see also Andreas Meyhoff, *Blohm & Voss im "Dritten Reich": Eine Hamburger Großwerft zwischen Geschäft und Politik* (Hamburg, Germany: Christians, 2001), 126–28; Peter Kuckuk, *Die Ostasienschnelldampfer Scharnhorst, Potsdam und Gneisenau des Norddeutschen Lloyd: Ein Beitrag zur Schiffbau- und Schiffahrtsgeschichte des Dritten Reiches* (Bremen, Germany: Hauschild, 2005), 61–62; Gerhard Koop and Klaus-Peter Schmolke, *German Destroyers of World War II: Warships of the Kriegsmarine* (Barnsley, UK: Seaforth Publishing, 2003), 41–44; Peter Kuckuk and Hartmut Pophanken, "Die AG 'Weser' 1933 bis 1945: Handels- und Kriegsschiffbau im Dritten Reich," in *Bremer Großwerften im Dritten Reich*, ed. Peter Kuckuk (Bremen, Germany: Edition Temmen, 1993), 56–58; Jak M. Showell, *Hitler's Navy: A Reference Guide to the Kriegsmarine 1935–1945* (Annapolis, MD: Naval Institute Press, 2009), 121.

Chapter 3. "Superior to the Combined Strength of Our Enemies"

1. "Our Proposed Navy Considers Chance of Allies' Defeat," *New York Times*, Jan. 12, 1940, 2.

2. Mark R. Wilson, *Destructive Creation: American Business and the Winning of World War II* (Philadelphia: University of Pennsylvania Press, 2016), 90–91.

3. James O. Richardson, *On the Treadmill to Pearl Harbor: The Memoirs of Admiral James O. Richardson* (Washington, DC: Government Printing Office, 1973), 403.

4. Commander in Chief Pacific Fleet to Chief of Naval Operations, Oct. 22, 1940, reprinted in *Pearl Harbor Attack: Hearings before the Joint Committee on the Investigation of the Pearl Harbor Attack, Part 33: Proceedings of Navy Court of Inquiry*, 79th Cong., 1st Sess., 1,192 (1946).

5. "U.S. Pacific Fleet Operating Plan Rainbow Five (Navy Plan O-1, Rainbow Five)," reprinted in *Pearl Harbor Attack: Hearings before the Joint Committee on the Investigation of the Pearl Harbor Attack, Part 17: Joint Committee Exhibits Nos. 111 Through 128*, 79th Cong., 2nd Sess., 2,571–87 (1946); Stark, "Memorandum for the President," Feb. 5, 1940, Box 59, Navy Dept., Series 4: Departmental Correspondence, Franklin D. Roosevelt, Papers as President: The President's Secretary's File (PSF), 1933–1945, Franklin D. Roosevelt Presidential Library & Museum, Hyde Park, New York (hereafter FDRL); Waldo Heinrichs, *Threshold of War: Franklin D. Roosevelt and American Entry into World War II* (New York: Oxford University Press, 1990), 38–44; Norman Friedman, *U.S. Destroyers: An Illustrated Design History* (Annapolis, MD: Naval Institute Press, 2004), 165–66.

6. Stark quoted in Richard Snow, *A Measureless Peril: America in the Fight for the Atlantic, the Longest Battle of World War II* (New York: Scribner, 2010); Chairman of the General Board to Secretary of the Navy, Aug. 31, 1939, Folder Navy, Jan.–Sep. 1939, Navy Dept., Series 4: Departmental Correspondence, Franklin D. Roosevelt, Papers as President: The President's Secretary's File (PSF), 1933–1945, FDRL. This so-called "Are We Ready?" memorandum included a long list of deficiencies that led the General Board to believe that the U.S. Navy was unprepared for a serious emergency that "requires immediate mobilization of the entire Naval Establishment with the prospect of conducting a major naval war." See also Historical Section, Bureau of Ships, "An Administrative History of the Bureau of Ships During World War II," vol. 2, 4–5, Rare Book Room, Navy Department Library, Washington Navy Yard, Washington, DC; *Annual Report of the Secretary of the Navy 1939* (Washington, DC: Government Printing Office, 1939), 3–4; on Japanese naval strategy and tactics, see

Stephen Pelz, *Race to Pearl Harbor: The Failure of the Second London Naval Conference and the Onset of World War II* (Cambridge, MA: Harvard University Press, 1975), 35–39.

7. Edison, "Memorandum for the President," Feb. 23, 1938, Folder Charles Edison, Navy Dept., Series 4: Departmental Correspondence, Franklin D. Roosevelt, Papers as President: The President's Secretary's File (PSF), 1933–1945, FDRL.

8. "Study of J[oint] Action in Event of Violation of Monroe Doctrine by Fascist Powers," Nov. 12, 1938, quoted in Maurice Matloff and Edwin M. Snell, *Strategic Planning for Coalition-Warfare, 1941–1942* (Washington, DC: Government Printing Office, 1980), 5.

9. Joel R. Davidson, *The Unsinkable Fleet: The Politics of U.S. Navy Expansion in World War II* (Annapolis, MD: Naval Institute Press, 1996), 14.

10. "Our Proposed Navy Considers Chance of Allies' Defeat," 2.

11. Callaghan, "Memorandum for the President," Nov. 3, 1939, Folder Navy, Oct.–Dec. 1939, Navy Dept., Series 4: Departmental Correspondence, Franklin D. Roosevelt, Papers as President: The President's Secretary's File (PSF), 1933–1945, FDRL; Stark, "Increase of the Navy—Special 25% Increase of Authorization," Nov. 3, 1939, Box 63, Subject File 1900–1947, General Board, General Records of the Department of the Navy, Record Group 80, National Archives Building, Washington, DC; Public Law No. 629, 76th Cong., 3rd Sess., To Establish the Composition of the United States Navy, June 14, 1940; Elmer A. Lewis, *Laws Relating to National Defense Enacted During the Seventy-Eighth Congress* (Washington, DC: Government Printing Office, 1945), 128; B. Mitchell Simpson, *Admiral Harold R. Stark: Architect of Victory, 1939–1945* (Columbia, SC: University of South Carolina Press, 1989), 16–38; Stephen S. Roberts, "U.S. Navy Building Programs During World War II," *Warship International* 18 (1981): 223–27.

12. "Our Proposed Navy Considers Chance of Allies' Defeat," 1. Though these fears were exaggerated, a Japanese attack on British possessions in the Far East would likely have shaken the British Empire to the core, much as it did when that attack finally came in December 1941; David Edgerton, *Britain's War Machine: Weapons, Resources, and Experts in the Second World War* (New York: Oxford University Press, 2011), 76–78.

13. *Congressional Record*, 76th Cong., 3rd Sess., June 22, 1940, 9,065.

14. Stark, "Memorandum for the President," June 18, 1940, Folder May–June 1940, Navy Dept., Series 4: Departmental Correspondence, Franklin D. Roosevelt,

Papers as President: The President's Secretary's File (PSF), 1933–1945, FDRL; Davidson, *The Unsinkable Fleet*, 19–21; Robert W. Love, "The U.S. Navy and Operation *Roll of Drums*," in *To Die Gallantly: The Battle of the Atlantic*, ed. Timothy J. Runyan and Jan M. Copes (Boulder, CO: Westview Press, 1994), 99; John Major, "The Navy Plans for War," in *In Peace and War: Interpretations of American Naval History, 1775–1978* (Westport, CT: Greenwood Press, 1984), 250–51; James E. Cook, *Carl Vinson: Patriarch of the Armed Forces* (Macon, GA: Mercer University Press, 2004), 150–51.

15. U.S. War Production Board, *Shipbuilding Activities of the National Defense Advisory Commission and Office of Production Management, July 1940 to December 1941* (Washington, DC: War Production Board, 1945), 5–9; Vincent P. O'Hara, *The U.S. Navy Against the Axis: Surface Combat 1941–1945* (Annapolis, MD: Naval Institute Press, 2007), 2–3; Donald A. Yerxa, *Admirals and Empire: The United States Navy and the Caribbean, 1898–1945* (Columbia, SC: University of South Carolina Press, 1991), 119; David C. Evans and Mark R. Peattie, *Kaigun: Strategy, Tactics, and Technology in the Imperial Japanese Navy, 1887–1941* (Annapolis, MD: Naval Institute Press, 1997), 319; Dave McComb, *U.S. Destroyers 1934–45: Pre-war Classes* (Oxford, UK: Osprey Publishing, 2010), 21.

16. For a concise summary, see George W. Baer, *One Hundred Years of American Sea Power: The U.S. Navy, 1890–1990* (Stanford, CA: Stanford University Press, 1996), 181–272.

17. War Production Board, Policy Analysis and Records Branch, Office of the Executive Secretary, *The Naval and Maritime Shipbuilding Programs, May 1940 to June 1944* (Washington, DC: War Production Board, 1944), 2 (quote); see also Knudsen to Robinson, Dec. 2, 1940, and Frank Knox, "Memorandum for the President," Dec. 28, 1940, both in Folder Nov.–Dec. 1940, Navy Dept., Series 4: Departmental Correspondence, Franklin D. Roosevelt, Papers as President: The President's Secretary's File (PSF), 1933–1945, FDRL.

18. Norman Polmar and Edward Whitman, *Hunters and Killers Vol. 1: Anti-Submarine Warfare from 1776 to 1943* (Annapolis, MD: Naval Institute Press, 2015), 149–50. American fears that the Germans could dispatch *Bismarck*'s sister ship *Tirpitz* on a repeat of Operation Rheinübung were voiced by Adm. Ernest King at the Arcadia conference in early 1942, one of the rare occasions when the anglophobic chief of naval operations agreed with First Sea Lord Admiral Sir Dudley Pound; Clay Blair, *Hitler's U-boat War: The Hunters, 1939–1942* (New York: Random House, 1996), 445; on British concerns about German surface raiders, see Andrew Lambert, "Seapower 1939–1940: Churchill and the Strategic Origins of the Battle of the Atlantic," in *Seapower: Theory*

and Practice, ed. Geoffrey Till (Ilford, UK: Frank Cass, 1994), 92; on the potential use of *Iowa*-class battleships against German commerce raiders, see Malcolm Muir, "The Capital Ship Program in the United States Navy, 1934–1945" (PhD diss., Ohio State University, 1976), 149–50.

19. Polmar and Whitman, *Hunters and Killers Vol. 1*, 99–101; Stephen W. Roskill, *The War at Sea, 1939–1945*, vol. 1: *The Defensive* (London: Her Majesty's Stationery Office, 1954), 588–89; James P. Levy, *The Royal Navy's Home Fleet in World War II* (New York: Palgrave Macmillan, 2003), xv; Peter Elliott, *Allied Escort Ships of World War II: A Complete Survey* (Annapolis, MD: Naval Institute Press, 1977), 136–40, 171–99; Norman Friedman, *British Destroyers and Frigates: The Second World War and After* (Barnsley, UK: Seaforth Publishing, 2006), 67–82. I share the revisionist conclusion that the Royal Navy was strategically, tactically, and technologically far better prepared to meet the German submarine threat than Roskill and others have given it credit for. George Franklin, *Britain's Anti-Submarine Capability, 1919–1939* (London: Frank Cass, 2003).

20. Quoted in Paul M. Kennedy, "The Tradition of Appeasement in British Foreign Policy 1865–1939," *British Journal of International Studies* 2 (Oct. 1976): 212.

21. "Naval New Construction Programmes and Their Execution. 1935–1945. Unpublished Narrative Used in the Compilation of British War Production: Final Draft," n.d., 123, CAB 102/527, National Archives of the United Kingdom, Kew.

22. "Naval New Construction Programmes and Their Execution. 1935–1945," 2.

23. George Moore, *Building for Victory: The Warship Building Programmes of the Royal Navy 1939–1945* (Gravesend, UK: World Ship Society, 2002), 22–61; Vincent P. O'Hara, *Struggle for the Middle Sea: The Great Navies at War in the Mediterranean Theater, 1940–1945* (Annapolis, MD: Naval Institute Press, 2009); Andrew Gordon, "The Admiralty and Imperial Overstretch, 1902–1941," in *Seapower: Theory and Practice*, ed. Geoffrey Till (Ilford, UK: Frank Cass, 1994), 70–83; numbers of British warships lost derived from Stephen W. Roskill, *The War at Sea, 1939–1945*, vol. 3, Part II: *The Offensive* (London: Her Majesty's Stationery Office, 1961), 439–41.

24. One *Yamato*-class battleship was completed in 1944 as the fleet carrier *Shinano* and the second, known only as Warship 111, was suspended in December 1941 and broken up on the stocks at the Kure Navy Yard. Evans and Peattie, *Kaigun*, 319.

25. Atsushi Oi, "Why Japan's Anti-Submarine Warfare Failed," U.S. Naval Institute *Proceedings* 78 (June 1952): 587–90; Mark E. Stille, *Imperial Japanese Navy Antisubmarine Escorts 1941–45* (Oxford, UK: Osprey Publishing, 2017), 46–47;

William H. Garzke, *Battleships: Axis and Neutral Battleships in World War II* (Annapolis, MD: Naval Institute Press, 1985), 85–115.

26. Quoted in Pelz, *Race to Pearl Harbor*, 218.

27. Asada Sadao, *From Mahan to Pearl Harbor: The Imperial Japanese Navy and the United States* (Annapolis, MD: Naval Institute Press, 2006), 223–24; Michael A. Barnhardt, *Japan Prepares for Total War: The Search for Economic Security, 1919–1941* (Ithaca, NY: Cornell University Press, 1987), 214; Heinrichs, *Threshold of War*, 183; Hans Lengerer and Tomoko Rehm-Takahara, "Japanese 'Kaibokan' Escorts, Part I," *Warship* 30 (Apr. 1984): 124–34; and Hans Lengerer and Tomoko Rehm-Takahara, "Japanese 'Kaibokan' Escorts, Part II," *Warship* 31 (July 1984): 171–84.

28. *Ibuki* was converted into an aircraft carrier and her sister ship "No. 301" was broken up on the stocks in 1942.

29. Eight of the sixteen were actually built.

30. Six of the ten were actually built.

31. Office of the Chief of Naval Operations, Division of Naval Intelligence, Serial 47–43: "Japanese Navy Shipbuilding Program," Jan. 10, 1943, Box 1216, RG 38 Intelligence Division, Confidential Reports of Naval Attaches 1940–1946, Record Group 19, National Archives at College Park, College Park, MD (hereafter "NACP").

32. Quoted in Pelz, *Race to Pearl Harbor*, 223.

33. Evans and Peattie, *Kaigun*, 359–60.

34. Michael Salewski, *Die deutsche Seekriegsleitung 1935–1945*. Band 1: *1935–1941* (Frankfurt, Germany: Bernard & Graefe, 1970), 91.

35. Quoted in Holger H. Herwig, *Politics of Frustration: The United States in German Naval Planning, 1889–1941* (Boston: Little, Brown, 1976), 221.

36. Eberhard Rössler, *Geschichte des deutschen Ubootbaus* (Munich, Germany: J. F. Lehmann, 1975), 187–88; Blair, *Hitler's U-boat War*, 102; Bernd Stegemann, "Die erste Phase der Seekriegsführung bis zum Frühjahr 1940," and Bernd Stegemann, "Die zweite Phase der Seekriegsführung bis zum Frühjahr 1941," in *Das Deutsche Reich und der Zweite Weltkrieg*, vol. 2: *Die Errichtung der Hegemonie auf dem europäischen Kontinent*, ed. Klaus A. Maier et al. (Stuttgart, Germany: Deutsche Verlags-Anstalt, 1979), 182–85, 345–50.

37. *To Establish the Composition of the United States Navy, to Authorize the Construction of Certain Naval Vessels, and for Other Purposes: Hearings Before the House Committee on Naval Affairs on H.R. 7665 and H.R. 8026*, 76th Cong., 3rd Sess., 1,943 (1940) (statement of Rear Adm. Alexander H. Van Keuren, chief of the Bureau of Construction and Repair).

38. Bartholomew H. Sparrow, *From the Outside In: World War II and the American State* (Princeton, NJ: Princeton University Press, 1996), 167–68.

39. *To Expedite Naval Shipbuilding: Hearings Before the Senate Committee on Naval Affairs on H.R. 9822 to Expedite Naval Shipbuilding, and For Other Purposes*, 76th Cong., 3rd Sess., 19 (1940) (statement of Capt. C. W. Fisher, Construction Corps, director of shore establishments).

40. Compton, "Memorandum for the President," July 3, 1940, Folder Dept. of the Navy July–Aug. 1940, Official File 18, FDRL; New York Shipbuilding Corporation, Memorandum, Feb. 12, 1941, Box 797, Bureau of Ships General Correspondence 1940–1945, NACP; U.S. National Defense Advisory Commission, *National Defense Program Contracts and Expenditures (Exclusive of Contracts Not Made Public)* (Washington, DC: Office of Government Reports, 1940); *Investigations of the Progress of the War Effort. Report of the House Committee on Naval Affairs*, 78th Cong., 2nd Sess., 197 (1944); *Investigation of the Progress of the War Effort: Hearings Before the House Committee on Naval Affairs. Renegotiation of War Contracts*, 78th Cong., 1st Sess., 724 (1943) (statement of Roger Williams, executive vice president of Newport News Shipbuilding); see also Robert H. Connery, *The Navy and Industrial Mobilization in World War II* (Princeton, NJ: Princeton University Press, 1951), 115–24, 202. For profit data in naval aircraft production, see Sparrow, *From the Outside In*, 183, which documents that profits fell at Grumman and Consolidated Aircraft.

41. *Investigations of the Progress of the War Effort* (1944), 75.

42. *Amortization of Defense Facilities* (Chicago: Machinery and Allied Products Institute, 1952), 29.

43. Historical Section, Bureau of Ships, "An Administrative History of the Bureau of Ships During World War II," vol. 1, 132, Rare Book Room, Navy Department Library, Washington Navy Yard, Washington, DC; Julius A. Furer, *Administration of the Navy Department in World War II* (Washington, DC: Government Printing Office, 1959), 245; Gerald White, *Billions for Defense: Government Financing by the Defense Plant Corporation During World War II* (Tuscaloosa: University of Alabama Press, 1980), 57–58, 70–71, 78, 136; U.S. Surplus Property Administration, *Report of the Surplus Property Administration to the Congress, January 31, 1946* (Washington, DC: Government Printing Office, 1946), 6; Sparrow, *From the Outside In*, 192.

44. *To Expedite Naval Shipbuilding: Hearings Before the Senate Committee on Naval Affairs on H.R. 9822 to Expedite Naval Shipbuilding* (1940), 7–10; Simpson, *Admiral Harold R. Stark*, 16–38.

45. Historical Section, Bureau of Ordnance, "Armor, Projectiles, Ammunition, Part II, Volume II," 11–21, Rare Book Room, Navy Department Library, Washington Navy Yard, Washington, DC; Buford Rowland and William B. Boyd, *The U.S. Navy Bureau of Ordnance in World War II* (Washington, DC: Bureau of Ordnance, 1953), 42–44.

46. Bureau of Yards and Docks, *Building the Navy's Bases in World War II: History of the Bureau of Yards and Docks and the Civil Engineer Corps, 1940–1946*, vol. 1 (Washington, DC: Government Printing Office, 1947), 169.

47. Woodson to Chief of Bureau of Ships, Oct. 3, 1940, Box 810, Entry A1 1266-J, Bureau of Ships General Correspondence 1940–1945, Record Group 19, NACP.

48. Quoted in Sparrow, *From the Outside In*, 165.

49. *Reorganization of the Navy Department and Transfer of the Construction Corps to the Line: Hearings Before the Senate Committee on Naval Affairs on S. 4026 (H.R. 9266) and S. 9450 (H.R. 9450)*, 76th Cong., 3rd Sess., 7–9 (1940) (statement of Lewis Compton, Assistant Secretary of the Navy).

50. Bureau of Ships, "An Administrative History of the Bureau of Ships During World War II," vol. 1, 31.

51. *Hearings on S. 4026 (H.R. 9266) and S. 9450*, 14.

52. *Hearings on S. 4026 (H.R. 9266) and S. 9450*, 14.

53. Smith, "Memorandum to the President," Apr. 3, 1940, and FDR, "Memorandum for the Acting Secretary of the Navy," June 24, 1940, both in Folder Dept. of the Navy June–July 1940, Official File 18, FDRL; Bureau of Ships, "An Administrative History of the Bureau of Ships During World War II," vol. 1, 37–41; *Reorganization of the Navy Department and Transfer of the Construction Corps to the Line*, 7–9; Rowland and Boyd, *U.S. Navy Bureau of Ordnance*, 34–36.

54. *Nomination of William Franklin Knox: Hearings Before the Senate Committee on Naval Affairs*, 76th Cong., 3rd Sess., 4 (1940) (statement of William F. Knox).

55. Booz, Fry, Allen, and Hamilton, "The Organization of the Bureau of Ships, Aug. 1, 1941," reprinted in Bureau of Ships, "An Administrative History of the Bureau of Ships During World War II," vol. 1, 48–75; Charles Edison, "Memorandum for the President," n.d. [June 1940], Folder May–June 1940, Navy Dept., Series 4: Departmental Correspondence, Franklin D. Roosevelt, Papers as President: The President's Secretary's File (PSF), 1933–1945, FDRL; Entry, "Robinson, Samuel Murray," *Cyclopædia of American Biography vol. G, 1943–1946* (New York: James White & Co., 1946), 293–94; on Knox, see

George H. Lobdell, "Frank Knox," in *American Secretaries of the Navy*, vol 2: *1913–1972*, ed. Paolo E. Coletta (Annapolis, MD: Naval Institute Press, 1980), 677–727; Gary E. Weir, *Building American Submarines, 1914–1940* (Washington, DC: Naval Historical Center, 1991), 109; Paul A. C. Koistinen, *Arsenal of World War II: The Political Economy of World War II, 1940–1945* (Lawrence: University Press of Kansas, 2004), 107–8.

56. *Sundry Legislation Affecting the Naval Establishment 1941. Hearings Before the House Committee on Naval Affairs*, 77th Cong., 1st Sess., 25 (1941) (statement of Rear Adm. Samuel M. Robinson, chief of the Bureau of Ships).

57. *Third Supplemental National Defense Appropriation Bill for 1942*, Part 2: *Hearings Before the Subcommittee of the House Committee on Appropriation on Military and Naval Establishments and Lend-Lease*, 77th Cong., 1st Sess. 4 (1941) (statement of Rear Adm. Samuel M. Robinson, chief of the Bureau of Ships).

58. Bethlehem Steel Company, Shipbuilding Division, Fore River Yard, "Special Shipbuilding Facilities Required for 11% Program," Oct. 25, 1940, Box 195, Entry 1266, Bureau of Ships General Correspondence 1940–1945, Record Group 19, NACP; *Additional Shipbuilding and Ordnance Manufacturing Facilities for the United States Navy, and for Other Purposes: Hearings on H.R. 1437 Before the House Committee on Naval Affairs*, 77th Cong., 1st Sess., 26 (1941) (statement of Rear Adm. Samuel M. Robinson, chief of the Bureau of Ships); "$3,861,053,312 for Naval Construction: Navy Department Places Contracts for Two-Hundred Combatant Ships," *Marine Engineering* 46 (Oct. 1940): 110–12.

59. *Navy Department Appropriation Bill for 1943: Hearings Before the Subcommittee of the House Committee on Appropriations*, 77th Cong., 2nd Sess., 61 (1942) (statement of James V. Forrestal, Undersecretary of the Navy).

60. Connery, *The Navy and the Industrial Mobilization*, 64–72; Sparrow, *From the Outside In*, 168, 174.

61. Nathan, Memorandum, Aug. 11, 1941, quoted in Charles H. Coleman, *Shipbuilding Activities of the National Defense Advisory Commission and Office of Production Management, July 1940 to December 1941* (Washington, DC: War Production Board, 1946), 80 (quote); Frederic C. Lane, *Ships for Victory: A History of Shipbuilding under the U.S. Maritime Commission in World War II* (Baltimore, MD: Johns Hopkins University Press, 1951), 42–43; Irving B. Holley Jr., *Buying Aircraft: Matériel Procurement for the Army Air Forces* (Washington, DC: U.S. Army Center for Military History, 1964), 229–73; Charles K. Hyde, *Arsenal of Democracy: The American Automobile Industry in World War II*

(Detroit, MI: Wayne State University Press, 2013), 20; Alan L. Gropman, *Mobilizing U.S. Industry in World War II: Myth and Reality* (Washington, DC: National Defense University, 2001), 35–36.

62. *Supplemental Navy Department Appropriation Bill for 1943: Hearings Before the Subcommittee of the House Committee on Appropriations*, 78th Cong., 1st Sess., 48 (1943) (statement of James V. Forrestal, Undersecretary of the Navy).

63. "Vice Admiral Robinson, Navy's New Production Boss, Already Holds Shipbuilding Record, Aims for Another," *Washington Post*, Feb. 8, 1942, B5.

64. "Reminiscences of Samuel Murray Robinson: Oral History, 1963," 28, Naval History Project, Oral History Research Office, 1964, Special Collections, Columbia University Library, New York (quote); see also FDR to Robinson, Jan. 31, 1942, Folder Dept. of the Navy Jan.–Feb. 1942, Official File 18, FDRL; Harold G. Vatter, *The U.S. Economy in World War II* (New York: Columbia University Press, 1985), 11–12, 36–37; Sparrow, *From the Outside In*, 175–76.

65. *Investigation of the Naval Defense Program: Supplemental Report. House Report No. 2371: Supplemental Report By the House Committee on Naval Affairs*, 77th Cong., 2nd Sess., 4–5 (1942); *Investigation of the National Defense Program: Hearings Before the Special Senate Committee Investigating the National Defense Program, Part 25: Reconversion. Disposal of Surplus Property*, 78th Cong., 2nd Sess., 11,124–25 (1944) (statement of Rear Adm. J. M. Irish, assistant chief of naval operations); Furer, *Administration of the Navy Department*, 838–46.

66. On Newport News, see *Investigation of the Progress of the War Effort: Hearings Before the House Committee on Naval Affairs. Renegotiation of War Contracts*, vol. 2, 78th Cong., 1st Sess., 715–16 (1943) (statement of Roger Williams, executive vice president of Newport News Shipbuilding); on New York Ship, see *Investigation of the Progress of the War Effort: Hearings Before the House Committee on Naval Affairs. Renegotiation of War Contracts*, 78th Cong., 1st Sess., 557–81 (1943) (statement of John F. Metten, chairman of the board, New York Shipbuilding Corporation); and Wilson, *Destructive Creation*, 169–70; on Navy contract price index, see Office of Procurement & Material, Price Analysis Division, "Pricing in Navy Procurement," reprinted in *1945 Extension of Termination Date of Renegotiation Act: Hearings for the House Ways and Means Committee*, 79th Cong. 1st Sess., 77–79 (1945).

67. King, Memorandum to the President, Mar. 26, 1942, quoted in Civilian Production Administration, Bureau of Demobilization, Special Study No. 26, *Shipbuilding Policies of the War Production Board, January 1942–November 1945* (Washington, DC: Civilian Production Administration, 1947), 21.

68. Davidson, *The Unsinkable Fleet*, 44. The U.S. Navy's noncooperation with the WPB resembled the procurement policies of the Imperial Navy, which placed orders directly with contractors without consulting the Munitions Administration, throwing a monkey wrench into strategic economic planning in wartime Japan. Richard Rice, "Economic Mobilization in Wartime Japan: Business, Bureaucracy, and Military in Conflict," *Journal of Asian Studies* 38 (Aug. 1979): 705.

69. *Shipbuilding Policies of the War Production Board*, 74. Production also lagged due to the lack of standardization: suppliers produced 4,000 different valves and 38,000 types of steel fittings.

70. Historical Section, Bureau of Ships, "An Administrative History of the Bureau of Ships During World War II," vol. 2, 217–18.

71. Civilian Production Administration, *Shipbuilding Policies of the War Production Board*, 14, 59, 67; Paul A. C. Koistinen, "Mobilizing the World War II Economy: Labor and the Industrial-Military Alliance," *Pacific Historical Review* 42 (Nov. 1973): 443–78; Koistinen, *Arsenal of World War II*, 320–26. For an informative reassessment of the CMP, see Wilson, *Destructive Creation*, 143–44.

72. FDR, "Executive Order: Reorganization of the Navy Department and the Naval Service Affecting the Office of the Chief of Naval Operations and the Commander in Chief, United States Fleet," Mar. 12, 1942, Folder Dept. of the Navy Mar.–Apr. 1942, Official File 18, FDRL; *Investigations of the Progress of the War Effort* (1944), 52; Davidson, *Unsinkable Fleet*, 33–36; Norman Friedman, *U.S. Aircraft Carriers: An Illustrated Design History* (Annapolis, MD: Naval Institute Press, 1983), 189–90; Ernest King and Walter M. Whitehill, *Fleet Admiral King: A Naval Record* (New York: Norton, 1952), 491–92.

73. Nathan Miller, "The American Navy, 1922–1945," in *Navies and Global Defense: Theories and Strategies*, ed. Keith Nelson and Elizabeth J. Errington (Westport, CT: Praeger, 1995), 155 (quote). The tactical considerations behind King's thinking were spelled out by Forrestal, who told undersecretary of war Robert Patterson in March 1942, "It is inadvisable to form vessels into large convoys until effective protection can be furnished, since this would give enemy submarines the opportunity to attack large formations instead of single ships with consequent increase rather than decrease in losses." Quoted in Jeffrey G. Barlow, "Roosevelt and King: The War in the Atlantic and European Theaters," in *FDR and the U.S. Navy*, ed. Edward J. Marolda (New York: St. Martin's Press, 1998), 182. Additionally, King effectively wanted to use convoys as bait to lure out and sink U-boats, whereas the British—who initially shared this view—came to understand that what really mattered was the "safe and timely arrival of the convoy." Marc Milner, "Anglo-American

Naval Co-operation in the Second World War, 1939–1945," in *Maritime Strategy and the Balance of Power: Britain and America in the Twentieth Century*, ed. John B. Hattendorf and Robert S. Jordan (New York: St. Martin's Press, 1989), 250.

74. Jeffrey G. Barlow, "The Views of Stimson and Knox on Atlantic Strategy and Planning," in *To Die Gallantly*, ed. Runyan and Copes, 34.

75. FDR to Knox, July 27, 1942, Folder Dept. of the Navy July–Aug. 1942, Official File 18, FDRL.

76. Quoted in Wilson, *Destructive Creation*, 154–55.

77. Dam to Roosevelt, June 2, 1941, Folder Jan.–June 1941, Navy Dept., Series 4: Departmental Correspondence, Franklin D. Roosevelt, Papers as President: The President's Secretary's File (PSF), 1933–1945, FDRL; U.S. Department of the Navy, Office of the Chief of Naval Operations, *Combatant Shipbuilding 11/42 to 7/1/46* (Washington, DC: Department of the Navy, 1946), 1093; War Production Board, Policy Analysis and Records Branch, Office of the Executive Secretary, *The Naval and Maritime Shipbuilding Programs, May 1940 to June 1944* (Washington, DC: War Production Board, 1944), 9; Bruce H. Franklin, *The Buckley-Class Destroyer Escorts* (Annapolis, MD: Naval Institute Press, 1999); Elliott, *Allied Escort Ships of World War II*, 451–77; Ken Brown, *U-Boat Assault on America: Why the U.S. Was Unprepared for War in the Atlantic* (Annapolis, MD: Naval Institute Press, 2017); Office of the Chief of Naval Operations, *Combatant Shipbuilding*, 1,093; Joel I. Holwitt, *"Execute against Japan": The U.S. Decision to Conduct Unrestricted Submarine Warfare* (College Station: Texas A&M University Press, 2009)

78. Holwitt, *"Execute against Japan"*; Theodore Roscoe, *United States Submarine Operations in World War II* (Annapolis, MD: Naval Institute Press, 1949), 252–60, 491.

79. Davidson, *Unsinkable Fleet*, 34 (quote).

80. *Investigations of the Progress of the War Effort* (1944), 51; Friedman, *U.S. Aircraft Carriers*, 201–4; Roberts, "U.S. Navy Building Programs," 233–34.

81. Norman Friedman, *U.S. Amphibious Ships and Craft: An Illustrated Design History* (Annapolis, MD: Naval Institute Press, 2002), 219–20; Matloff and Snell, *Strategic Planning for Coalition Warfare*, 192–94; Duncan S. Ballantine, *U.S. Naval Logistics in the Second World War* (rprt., Newport, RI: Naval War College Press, 1998), 56–57.

82. "Record of a Meeting of the Sea Lords held in the Upper War Room, Admiralty House, at 1530 on the 15th December, 1942, to discuss New Construction Problems," ADM 1/12515, National Archives of the United Kingdom,

Kew; Rear Admiral Sir Arthur Lumley, the Sea Lord responsible for naval aviation, had argued the same point a year earlier; see George Moore, *Building for Victory: The Warship Building Programmes of the Royal Navy 1939–1945* (Gravesend, UK: World Ship Society, 2002), 62.

83. "Record of a Meeting of the Sea Lords held in the Upper War Room, Admiralty House, at 1530 on the 15th December, 1942, to discuss New Construction Problems," ADM 1/12515, National Archives of the UK.

84. "Record of a Meeting of the Sea Lords."

85. "Record of a Meeting of the Sea Lords."

86. "Record of a Meeting of the Sea Lords."

87. Jon Robb-Webb, "Light Two Lanterns, the British Are Coming by the Sea: Royal Navy Participation in the Pacific 1944–1945," in *British Naval Strategies East of Suez, 1900–2000: Influences and Actions*, ed. Greg Kennedy (London: Routledge, 2003), 128–53.

88. U.S. Navy, Pacific Fleet and Pacific Ocean Areas, *Japanese Naval Shipbuilding: "Know Your Enemy!" CinCPac-CinCPOA Bulletin 142-45* (Washington, DC, 1945), 2.

89. U.S. Army, Military History Section Headquarters, Army Forces Far East, *Outline of Naval Armament and Preparations for War. Japanese Monograph No. 172* (Washington, DC: Office of the Chief of Military History, Department of the Army, n.d.).

90. Guntram Schulze-Wegener, *Die deutsche Kriegsmarine-Rüstung 1942–1945* (Hamburg, Germany: Mittler, 1997).

91. Furer, *Administration of the Navy Department in World War II*, 261.

92. *Report of Subcommittee of Committee on Naval Affairs on Private Shipbuilding Companies on the Pacific Coast*, 77th Cong., 2nd Sess., 21.

93. Quoted in Davidson, *Unsinkable Fleet*, 101.

94. Byrnes to FDR, Sep. 6, 1943, Folder Dept. of the Navy June–Sep. 1943, Official File 18, FDRL.

95. Davidson, *Unsinkable Fleet*, 101–18; on wartime cancellations of Army and Air Force contracts, see Wilson, *Destructive Creation*, 147–59.

Chapter 4. "We Can Build Anything"

1. Bartholomew H. Sparrow, *From the Outside In: World War II and the American State* (Princeton, NJ: Princeton University Press, 1996), 162.

2. Michael Carew, *Becoming the Arsenal: The American Industrial Mobilization for World War II, 1938–1942* (Lanham, MD: University Press of America, 2010),

158–59; for a critique of heroic entrepreneurship tales, see Mark R. Wilson, *Destructive Creation: American Business and the Winning of World War II* (Philadelphia: University of Pennsylvania Press, 2016).

3. *To Establish the Composition of the United States Navy, to Authorize the Construction of Certain Naval Vessels, and for Other Purposes: Hearings Before the House Committee on Naval Affairs*, 76th Cong., 3rd Sess., 1,892 (1940) (statement of Rear Adm. Samuel M. Robinson, coordinator of shipbuilding).

4. Julius A. Furer, *Administration of the Navy Department in World War II* (Washington, DC: Government Printing Office, 1959), 18.

5. Bureau of Ships, "An Administrative History of the Bureau of Ships During World War II," n.d., vol. 1, 135, 137, Navy Department Library, Rare Book Room, Washington Navy Yard, Washington, DC.

6. Bureau of Ships, "Administrative History," vol. 1, 137.

7. *Sundry Legislation Affecting the Naval Establishment, No. 89: Manpower Utilization in the Navy Yard, New York: A Report of the Johnson Subcommittee of the House Committee on Naval Affairs*, 79th Cong., 1st Sess., 880 (1945) (quote); "Industrial Survey Division Report No. 5: Industrial Activities New York Navy Yard," Jan. 6, 1945, 4, Box 810, Entry A1 1266-J, Bureau of Ships General Correspondence 1940–1945, Record Group (hereafter "RG") 19, National Archives at College Park, College Park, MD (hereafter "NACP").

8. Bureau of Ships, "Administrative History," vol. 1, 135–44; Commandant Fourth Naval District, "History of Naval Administration, World War II, vol. 1," 352–74, Navy Department Library, Rare Book Room, Washington Navy Yard, Washington, DC; Cochrane to Secretary of the Navy, May 25, 1945, Box 834, Entry A1 1266-J, Bureau of Ships General Correspondence 1940–1945, RG 19, NACP; Charles W. Fisher, "Industrial Organization of Navy Yards," U.S. Naval Institute *Proceedings* 48 (May 1922): 761–87; *Sundry Legislation Affecting the Naval Establishment, No. 89: Manpower Utilization in the Navy Yard, New York*, 876–80.

9. "Final Report of the Navy Manpower Survey Board to the Secretary of the Navy," June 28, 1944, 17, Box 1, PC-31, Entry 261, RG 80, General Records of the Department of the Navy, NACP; Frederick Black, *Charlestown Navy Yard, 1890–1973* (Boston: Boston National Historical Park, National Park Service, U.S. Department of the Interior, 1988), 511–12; on Brooklyn management shortages, see Kennedy to Personnel Officer, Bureau of Ships, Dec. 7, 1942, Enclosure A, Entry A1 1266-J, Bureau of Ships General Correspondence 1940–1945, RG 19, NACP.

10. Naval district commanders and navy yard commanders were usually one and the same person; see U.S. Department of the Navy, *Administrative Reference Service Report No. 7A: Principal Officials and Officers, Navy Department and United States Fleet, September 1, 1939–June 1, 1945* (Washington, DC: Office of Records Administration, Administrative Office, Navy Department, 1945), 5–7.

11. *Investigation of the National Defense Program: Reorganization of Navy Yards: Executive Session. Hearings Before the Special Senate Committee Investigating the National Defense Program*, 79th Cong., 1st Sess., 8 (1945) (statement of Cdr. Richard M. Paget, management engineer, Navy Department).

12. *Investigation of the National Defense Program: Reorganization of Navy Yards*, 10 (quote); "Admiral Watson Will Retire," (Philadelphia) *Navy Yard Beacon*, Aug. 28, 1942: 1; Black, *Charlestown Navy Yard*, 514.

13. Stanley Owen Davis, letter to the editor, *Saugeen Times*, July 21, 2015; "T. L. Schumacher," *Transactions of the Society of Naval Architects and Marine Engineers* 60 (1952): 655; "Capt. Enright Goes to Boston," (Philadelphia) *Navy Yard Beacon*, Oct. 9, 1942, 1, 6; "Thomas B. Richey," *Transactions of the Society of Naval Architects and Marine Engineers* 57 (1949): 596; Black, *Charlestown Navy Yard*, 505–14.

14. "Foreman" in War Production Board, Shipbuilding Stabilization Branch, "Preliminary Study: Job Descriptions for the Ship and Boat Building and Repair Industry," April 1943, Box 6, Series 2, Subseries 6, Industrial Union of Marine and Shipbuilding Workers of America Archives, University of Maryland Libraries' Archival Collections, College Park, MD (hereafter "Job Descriptions").

15. "Quarterman, Leaderman, Sub-Foreman," in "Job Descriptions."

16. "Leadingman, Leader, Leaderman, Work Leader," in "Job Descriptions"; see also *Seniority Rights for Employees at Government Navy Yards, Arsenals, Etc.: Hearings Before the Senate Committee on Naval Affairs*, 79th Cong., 1st Sess., 84–85 (1945) (statement of Dolphus E. Henry, machinist, Norfolk Navy Yard).

17. "Mechanic Journeyman," in "Job Descriptions."

18. "Coppersmith," in "Job Descriptions."

19. "Handyman," in "Job Descriptions."

20. Black, *Charlestown Navy Yard*, 541.

21. *Investigation of the Progress of the War Effort. Policies and Practices Relating to Civil Employment in the Navy Department: Report of the House Committee on Naval Affairs*, 79th Cong., 2nd Sess., 8 (1947) (quote); see also Penn to Vinson, Mar. 18, 1941, 4, Box 885, Entry A1 1266-J, Bureau of Ships General Correspondence 1940–1945, RG 19, NACP.

22. *Investigation of Congested Areas, Part 1: Hampton Roads, Virginia, Area: Hearings Before a Subcommittee of the House Committee on Naval Affairs*, 78th Cong., 1st Sess., 80 (1943) (statement of Captain Hooker, Norfolk Navy Yard).

23. *Investigation of Congested Areas, Part 6: Puget Sound, Washington, Area: Hearings Before a Subcommittee of the House Committee on Naval Affairs*, 78th Cong., 1st Sess., 1,301–11 (1943) (statement of Rear Adm. C. S. Gillette, industrial manager, Puget Sound Navy Yard).

24. L. Q. Moss, "Navy Yard Apprentice Training," *Marine Engineering* 40 (Oct. 1935): 377.

25. Howard Zinn, Brooklyn Navy Yard Oral History Collection, Dec. 8, 2008, 2.

26. Moss, "Navy Yard Apprentice Training," 376.

27. *To Establish the Composition of the United States Navy, to Authorize the Construction of Certain Naval Vessels, and for Other Purposes: Hearings on H.R. 10100 Before the House Committee on Naval Affairs*, 76th Cong., 3rd Sess., 3,590–91, (1940) (statement of Rep. Michael J. Bradley) (quote); Apprentice/Apprentice Boy, Box 6, Series 2.6, Research Department, Industrial Union of Marine and Shipbuilding Workers of America Archives, Special Collections, University of Maryland Libraries, College Park, MD; Morris Silverman, "Lt. Comdr. Gokey Instructs Future Shipbuilders," *The* [Philadelphia Navy Yard] *Apprentice* 7 (Mar. 1937): 2; "Shipfitter School Starts 29th Year," [New York Navy Yard] *Shipworker*, Dec. 17, 1941, 4; "Skilled Labor Shortage Seen at Navy Yard," *Brooklyn Eagle*, Dec. 14, 1938, 2; Kenneth M. Swezey, "Boys Build Battleships in Navy Yard Apprentice Schools," *Popular Science Monthly*, Mar. 1937, 56–57, 124.

28. Navy Manpower Survey Group "A," Fourth Naval District, "Industrial Department: Discussion and Comments by Divisions, Activities, or Subjects for Military and Civilian Personnel," Jan. 17, 1944 to Feb. 2, 1944 (quote), Box 1, Manpower Survey Group, RG 181, National Archives and Records Administration–Mid-Atlantic Region (Philadelphia); Wade to All Shop Masters and Section Heads, Aug. 13, 1941, Box 41, Records of the U.S. Naval Districts and Shore Establishments, Philadelphia Naval Shipyard, Central Subject Files, Industrial Manager, 1920–1957, A 3-2 (1941) to A 3-2 (1942), Entry 447, RG 181, NARA-Mid-Atlantic Region (Phila.) (hereafter "Central Subject Files, Entry 447, RG 181, NARA-Mid-Atlantic Region [Phila.]"); Henry E. Rossell, *The Training of Shipyard Personnel* (New York: Society of Naval Architects and Marine Engineers, 1941), 6.

29. Quoted in Rodney K. Watterson, *32 in '44: Building the Portsmouth Submarine Fleet in World War II* (Annapolis, MD: Naval Institute Press, 2011), 72.

30. "Industrial Survey Division Report No. 5," 13.

31. "Industrial Survey Division Report No. 5," 12.

32. *Sundry Legislation Affecting the Naval Establishment, No. 89: Manpower Utilization in the Navy Yard, New York*, 901.

33. *Investigation of Congested Areas, Part 1: Hampton Roads*, 81 (quote); "Hiring in Skilled Trades Is Streamlined by New Test Given Before Employment," [New York Navy Yard] *Shipworker*, Sep. 15, 1942, 4.

34. "Labor Requirements for the Shipbuilding Industry," *Service Bulletin on Defense Training in Vocational Schools* 8 (Feb. 1941): 5 (quote); *Sundry Legislation Affecting the Naval Establishment, No. 89: Manpower Utilization in the Navy Yard, New York*, 901; Fritz P. Hamer, *Charleston Reborn: A Southern City, its Navy Yard and World War II* (Charleston, SC: History Press, 2005), 55.

35. *Sundry Legislation Affecting the Naval Establishment, No. 89: Manpower Utilization in the Navy Yard, New York*, 903.

36. "Industrial Survey Division Report No. 12: Industrial Activities Puget Sound Navy Yard, Bremerton, Washington," May 29, 1945, 15, Box 898, Entry A1 1266-J, Bureau of Ships General Correspondence 1940–1945, RG 19, NACP.

37. Commandant Fourth Naval District, "History of Naval Administration, World War II, vol. 1," 618–20, Navy Department Library, Rare Book Room, Washington Navy Yard, Washington, DC; Enright, "Memorandum of Conference," Mar. 23, 1939, and Enright, "Industrial Department Memorandum: Helper Trainees," Oct. 30, 1941, both in Box 41, Central Subject Files, Entry 447, RG 181, NARA-Mid-Atlantic Region (Phila.); Wade to All Shop Masters, May 12, 1942, Box 42, Central Subject Files, Entry 447, RG 181, NARA-Mid-Atlantic Region (Phila.); Henry Tatowicz, Oral History interview conducted by Benjamin Filene, July 29, 1987, 3–4, Brooklyn Navy Yard Oral Histories, 1995.005.010, Brooklyn Historical Society, Brooklyn; Jack Grossman, Oral History interview conducted by Sady Sullivan, May 4, 2010, 1–2, 2010.003.031, Brooklyn Historical Society, Brooklyn.

38. Commandant Fourth Naval District, "History of Naval Administration, World War II, vol. 1," 621–22, Navy Department Library, Rare Book Room, Washington Navy Yard, Washington, DC.

39. "History of the Boston Navy Yard (Industrial Department), Chapter III: Manpower and Industrial Relations," Commandant of First Naval District, "History of Naval Administration, World War II, vol. 8, 21–22," Navy Department Library, Rare Book Room, Washington Navy Yard, Washington, DC.

40. Lucille F. McMillin, *The Second Year: A Study of Women's Participation in War Activities of the Federal Government* (Washington, DC: U.S. Government Printing Office, 1943), 40.

41. "Over 600 Women Due Here as Machinists," [New York Navy Yard] *Shipworker*, Aug. 27, 1942, 2.

42. Rood to Senior Member of Navy Manpower Survey Board, Apr. 14, 1943, Manpower Survey Group, Box 1 (quote), RG 181, NARA-Mid-Atlantic Region (Phila.); Wade to Masters of Shops 17, 31, 53, and 81, Dec. 2, 1941, Box 41, Central Subject Files, Entry 447, RG 181, NARA-Mid-Atlantic Region (Phila.); Schumacher, "Planning Division Memorandum 4/42," Dec. 16, 1942; Chenoweth to All Shop Masters, Feb. 24, 1942, both in Box 42, Central Subject Files, Entry 447, RG 181, NARA-Mid-Atlantic Region (Phila.); "Leading-woman Named," [New York Navy Yard] *Shipworker*, Nov. 23, 1942, 1; "Uncle Sam and His Nieces," [Philadelphia] *Navy Yard Beacon*, July 3, 1942, 5; Arnold Sparr, "Looking for Rosie: Women Defense Workers in the Brooklyn Navy Yard, 1942–1946," *New York History* 81 (2000): 319–31.

43. Howard Zinn, *Oral History*, 2.

44. Carla Dubose-Simons, "The 'Silent Arrival': The Second Wave of the Great Migration and Its Effects on Black New York, 1940–1950," (PhD diss., City University of New York, 2013), 54.

45. Hamer, *Charleston Reborn*, 53 (quote).

46. Black, *Charlestown Navy Yard*, 574 (quote); see also R. Scott Baker, *Paradoxes of Desegregation: African American Struggles for Educational Equity in Charleston, South Carolina, 1926–1972* (Charleston: University of South Carolina Press, 2006), 36.

47. "Practices at Various Navy Yards and U.S. Naval Drydocks in Effect to Reduce Stand-By Time and to Effect Better Utilization of Available Manpower," n.d., Box 43, Central Subject Files, Entry 447, RG 181, NARA-Mid-Atlantic Region (Phila.).

48. Bureau of Ships, Oct. 21, 1943, quoted in [New York Navy Yard] Production Officer to Commandant, May 11, 1945, Box 810, Entry A1 1266-J, RG 19, Bureau of Ships General Correspondence 1940–1945, NACP.

49. [New York Navy Yard] Production Officer to Commandant, May 11, 1945, 17-1, Entry A1 1266-J, RG 19, Bureau of Ships General Correspondence 1940–1945, NACP.

50. Wade to Production Officer, Nov. 17, 1943, Box 43, Central Subject Files, Entry 447, RG 181, NARA-Mid-Atlantic Region (Phila.).

51. Industrial Relations Counselors, "Report on Industrial Relations in the New York Navy Yard," Apr. 11, 1941, 26, Box 33, Entry A1 1266-J, Bureau of Ships General Correspondence 1940–1945, RG 19, NACP, 2.

52. Industrial Relations Counselors, "Report on Industrial Relations in the New York Navy Yard," 9.

53. Industrial Relations Counselors, "Report on Industrial Relations in the New York Navy Yard," 32.

54. Bard to Navy Yard Commandants, May 1, 1941, Box 33, Entry A1 1266-J, Bureau of Ships General Correspondence 1940–1945, RG 19, NACP.

55. "Industrial Survey Division Report No. 5," 1.

56. "Industrial Survey Division Report No. 5," 5.

57. "Industrial Survey Division Report No. 5," 5.

58. "Industrial Survey Division Report No. 5," 4.

59. "Industrial Survey Division Report No. 5," 13.

60. *Sundry Legislation Affecting the Naval Establishment, No. 89: Manpower Utilization in the Navy Yard, New York*, 909.

61. *Sundry Legislation Affecting the Naval Establishment, No. 89: Manpower Utilization in the Navy Yard, New York*, 905.

62. Bard to Commandants, Oct. 27, 1942, Box 42, Central Subject Files, Entry 447, RG 181, NARA-Mid-Atlantic Region (Phila.).

63. Industrial Relations Counselors, "Report on Industrial Relations in the New York Navy Yard."

64. Assistant Secretary of the Navy to All Navy Yards and Stations, Mar. 16, 1935, quoted in Black, *Charlestown Navy Yard*, 461.

65. Commandant's Order No. 193, Aug. 31, 1943, quoted in Black, *Charlestown Navy Yard*, 580; on Chantry, see "Loc. 101 Proposals Studied on Accrued Leave Pay Bill," *Shipyard Worker*, Apr. 7, 1944, 2; on IUMSWA opposition to shop committees, see "Local 101 Offers 7-Point Program for More Manpower in Navy Yard," *Shipyard Worker*, Jan. 28, 1944, 8.

66. *Investigations of the Progress of the War Effort: Policies and Practices Relating to Civil Employment in the Navy Department*, 8.

67. "Industrial Survey Division Report No. 7: Industrial Activities U.S. Navy Yard Charleston, S.C.," Feb. 1, 1945, 3, Box 855, Entry A1 1266-J, Bureau of Ships General Correspondence 1940–1945, RG 19, NACP.

68. *Sundry Legislation Affecting the Naval Establishment, No. 89: Manpower Utilization in the Navy Yard, New York*, 876.

69. Howard to Commandant Fourth Naval District, Feb. 15, 1943, Box 330, Entry A1 1266-B, Bureau of Ships General Correspondence 1940–1945, RG 19, NACP; Jeffrey M. Dorwart, *The Philadelphia Navy Yard from the Birth of the U.S. Navy to the Nuclear Age* (Philadelphia: University of Pennsylvania Press, 2001), 167.

70. Bureau of Yards and Docks, "Public Works of the Navy: Data Book, Vol. 2: NAVDOCKS P-164," (July 1947), Navy Department Library, Rare Book Room, Washington Navy Yard, Washington, DC; *Navy Department Appropriation Bill for 1942: Hearings Before the Subcommittee of the House Committee on Appropriations*, 77th Cong., 1st Sess., 263 (1941) (statement of Rear Adm. Samuel M. Robinson, chief of the Bureau of Ships); Bureau of Yards and Docks, *Building the Navy's Bases in World War II: History of the Bureau of Yards and Docks and the Civil Engineer Corps, 1940–1946*, vol. 1 (Washington, DC: Government Printing Office, 1947), 169–200.

71. *Second Deficiency Appropriation Bill for 1938: Hearings Before the Subcommittee of the House Committee on Appropriations*, 75th Cong., 3rd Sess., 539 (1938) (statement of Rear Adm. Ben Moreell, chief of the Bureau of Yards and Docks).

72. "NYNS Buildings Historical Review: Building Structure Survey 65-350-EK, 1965," Brooklyn Navy Yard Development Corporation, Department of Records and Archives, Brooklyn, New York; Thaddeus V. Tuleja, "A Short History of the New York Navy Yard," (1959), Navy Department Library, Rare Book Room, Washington Navy Yard, Washington, DC; "Ready to Begin 'Iowa,'" U.S. Naval Institute *Proceedings* 66, no. 7 (July 1940): 1033; "Millions Voted for Big Navy," *Brooklyn Eagle*, June 7, 1938, 2; "Big Job for Navy Yard," *Brooklyn Eagle*, June 5, 1939, 10.

73. *Navy Department Appropriation Bill for 1940: Hearings Before the Subcommittee of the House Committee on Appropriations*, 76th Cong., 1st Sess., 171 (1941) (Statement of Rear Adm. Ben Moreell, chief of the Bureau of Yards and Docks).

74. *Sundry Legislation Affecting the Naval Establishment: Hearings Before the House Committee on Naval Affairs*, 77th Cong., 1st Sess., 675 (1941); "Industrial Survey Division Report No. 5," 7; "NYNS Buildings Historical Review: Building Structure Survey 65-350-EK, 1965," Brooklyn Navy Yard Development Corporation, Department of Records and Archives, Brooklyn, New York; Bureau of Yards and Docks, *Building the Navy's Bases*, 178–83.

75. Minutes of Meeting Jan. 19, 1944, 2, Survey of the Industrial Department Philadelphia Navy Yard, Manpower Survey Board, 1944, Box 1, Entry 447 D,

Records of the U.S. Naval Districts and Shore Establishments, Central Subject Files, Industrial Manager, 1920–1957, A 3-2 (1941) to A 3-2 (1942), RG 181, NARA-Mid-Atlantic Region (Phila.).

76. Minutes of Meeting Jan. 19, 1944, 2, Survey of the Industrial Department Philadelphia Navy Yard, Manpower Survey Board, 1944, Box 1, Entry 447 D, Record Group 181, Records of the U.S. Naval Districts and Shore Establishments, Philadelphia Naval Shipyard, National Archives and Records Administration, Philadelphia Branch.

77. Commandant Fourth Naval District, "History of Naval Administration, World War II, vol. 1," 9–19, Navy Department Library, Rare Book Room, Washington Navy Yard, Washington, DC; Dorwart, *The Philadelphia Navy Yard*, 166–90.

78. Seiller, New Construction Ways Schedule, July 23, 1943, Box 42, Central Subject Files, Entry 447, RG 181, NARA-Mid-Atlantic Region (Phila.); Commandant Fourth Naval District, "History of Naval Administration, World War II, vol. 1," 552, Navy Department Library, Rare Book Room, Washington Navy Yard, Washington, DC; Bureau of Yards and Docks, "Public Works of the Navy: Data Book, Vol. 2," 67–106.

79. Quoted in Sparrow, *From the Outside In*, 197–98; Field Production Officer to Commandant, May 7, 1945, Box 810, Entry A1 1266-J, Bureau of Ships General Correspondence 1940–1945, RG 19, NACP; Commandant of Navy Yard, New York, to Undersecretary of the Navy, Nov. 6, 1943, reprinted in *Problems of American Small Business*, Part 30: *Navy Yard Subcontracting and the Type C Contract: Hearings Before the Special Senate Committee to Study and Survey Problems of Small Business Enterprises,* 78th Cong., 1st Sess., 4,152–53 (1943); Commandant Third Naval District, "History of Naval Administration, World War II, vol. 5, Appendix C," 1–32, Navy Department Library, Rare Book Room, Washington Navy Yard, Washington, DC; Minutes of Conference, Aug. 24, 1942, Box 41, Central Subject Files, Entry 447, RG 181, NARA-Mid-Atlantic Region (Phila.).

80. Commandant First Naval District, "History of Naval Administration, World War II, vol. 8," Chapter I, 4–24, Chapter II, "Recapitulation of Repairs," "Vessels Outfitted at Navy Yard, Boston, Mass., from 1 Jan. 1939–15 Aug. 1945," Navy Department Library, Rare Book Room, Washington Navy Yard, Washington, DC; Black, *Charlestown Navy Yard*, 626–32.

81. Commandant First Naval District, "History of Naval Administration, World War II, vol. 8," Part II, Chapter I, Section 1, 3.

82. Bureau of Yards and Docks, *Building the Navy's Bases*, 191.

83. Bureau of Ships, Memorandum, Apr. 17, 1943, reprinted in *Investigation of the National Defense Program: Reorganization of Navy Yards: Additional Report of the Special Senate Committee Investigating the National Defense Program, Report No. 10, Part 16*, 78th Cong., 2nd Sess., 329 (1944).

84. Commandant to Chief of Bureau of Yards & Docks, Sep. 5, 1942; Roose to Powell, Mar. 25, 1942, both in Box 881, Entry A1 1266-J, Bureau of Ships General Correspondence 1940–1945, RG 19, NACP; Bureau of Yards and Docks, "Public Works of the Navy: Data Book, Vol. 2," 294–302.

85. Henry E. Rossell, "What Cramp Shipbuilding Company Is Doing for the War Effort: Remarks to the City Business Club of Philadelphia," Aug. 9, 1943, 2–3, Speeches Ledger, J. Welles Henderson Archives and Library Cramp Collection, Independence Seaport Museum Library, Philadelphia.

86. Commandant First Naval District, "History of Naval Administration, World War II, vol. 8," Chapter III, 5–6.

87. "Industrial Survey Division Report No. 7," 3.

88. "Industrial Survey Division Report No. 7," 8

89. "Industrial Survey Division Report No. 7," 9.

90. "Industrial Survey Division Report No. 7," 9.

91. "Industrial Survey Division Report No. 7," 9.

92. "Industrial Survey Division Report No. 7," 10 (quote); see also Navy Yard Development Association Charleston, S.C., *Navy Day*, Oct. 7, 1939, 17–25; Hamer, *Charleston Reborn*, 37–91.

93. *Problems of American Small Business, Part 30*, 4,050 (quote); "Memo No. 10: Notes on Visit to Mare Island Navy Yard," ADM 281/106, National Archives of the United Kingdom, Kew; Arnold S. Lott, *A Long Line of Ships: Mare Island's Century of Naval Activity in California* (Annapolis, MD: Naval Institute Press, 1954), 209–21.

94. *Problems of American Small Business, Part 30*, 4,034–36 (statement of Capt. John A. Kennedy, Office of the Chief of Naval Operations).

95. *Problems of American Small Business, Part 30*, 4063 (statement of Lt. Cdr. J. Clyde Smith, secretary of the Farming Out Program, Puget Sound Navy Yard).

96. Commandant 13th Naval District to Chief of Bureau of Yards & Docks, Mar. 31, 1942 (quote); see also "Industrial Survey Division Report No. 12" and Commandant 13th Naval District to Chief of Bureau of Ships, Jan. 31, 1942, both in Box 898, Entry A1 1266-J, Bureau of Ships General Correspondence 1940–1945, RG 19, NACP.

97. "Memo No. 3: Notes on Talk with Cdr. Kniskern," Dec. 18, 1942, ADM 281/106, National Archives of the United Kingdom, Kew.

98. "I Cruised on the Iowa," *Popular Science Monthly*, Jan. 1945, 81–82; Norman Friedman, *U.S. Battleships: An Illustrated Design History* (Annapolis, MD: Naval Institute Press, 1985), 281–326; Robert F. Sumrall, *Iowa Class Battleships: Their Design, Weapons and Equipment* (Annapolis, MD: Naval Institute Press, 1988), 23–31. See also Rodney P. Carlisle, *Where the Fleet Begins: A History of the David Taylor Research Center, 1898–1998* (Washington, DC: Naval Historical Center, 1998), 131–57.

99. "Memo No. 11: Notes on Visit to Battleship 'Iowa,'" 1, ADM 281/106, National Archives of the United Kingdom, Kew (quote); Sumrall, *Iowa Class Battleships*, 32–34; Friedman, *U.S. Battleships*, 311–12.

100. *Navy Department Appropriation Bill for 1941: Hearings Before the Subcommittee of the House Committee on Appropriations,* 76th Cong., 3rd Sess., 657–59 (1941) (Statement of Rear Adm. Samuel M. Robinson, chief of the Bureau of Ships).

101. Gordon Calhoun, "Design and Construction of USS Wisconsin," *Daybook* 6 (Summer 2000): 14.

102. Bureau of Ships, "Administrative History," vol. 1, 538.

103. Matthewson to Chief of Bureau of Ships, Jan. 28, 1942; Reuse to Chief of Bureau of Ships, Feb. 10, 1942; Kennedy to Bureau of Ships, Mar. 12, 1942; Watson to Chief of Bureau of Ships, Mar. 31, 1942; Reuse to Chief of Bureau of Ships, Apr. 6, 1942, all in Box 328, Entry A1 1266-J, Bureau of Ships General Correspondence 1940–1945, RG 19, NACP; Friedman, *U.S. Battleships*, 322–23.

104. Chantry to Bureau of Ships, n.d. (1945), Box 834, Entry A1 1266-J, Bureau of Ships General Correspondence 1940–1945, RG 19, NACP.

105. Chantry to Bureau of Ships, n.d. (1945) (quote); Machinery and Hull Superintendents to New Construction Ship Superintendents, Dec. 19, 1941, Box 41, Central Subject Files, Entry 447, RG 181, NARA-Mid-Atlantic Region (Phila.); Sanville, "Report of Liaison Service to Navy Yard, New York," Jan. 7, 1944, Box 42, Central Subject Files, Entry 447, RG 181, NARA-Mid-Atlantic Region (Phila.).

106. Abraham Solov, "Scheduling the Work of the Drafting Room: The Application of Scheduling in the Design Section of the Brooklyn Navy Yard," *Journal of the American Society of Naval Engineers* 57 (Aug. 1945): 317–23.

107. Enright, "Memorandum: New Construction—Material Progress and Scheduling For," Dec. 8, 1941, Box 40, Central Subject Files, Entry 447, RG 181, NARA-Mid-Atlantic Region (Phila.).

108. Enright, "Memorandum: New Construction—Material Progress and Scheduling For," Dec. 8, 1941, Box 40, Central Subject Files, Entry 447, RG 181, NARA-Mid-Atlantic Region (Phila.).

109. *Shipfitting Practice: A Manual of Instruction for Pre-Employment and Supplementary Training* (Harrisburg, PA: Department of Public Instruction, 1942), 20, 129–34.

110. H. F. Garyantes, *Handbook for Shipwrights* (New York: McGraw-Hill, 1944), 163.

111. Chantry to Chief of Bureau of Construction & Repair, Dec. 8, 1939; Chantry to Chief of Bureau of Construction & Repair, Jan. 17, 1940, Box 41, RG 181, NARA-Mid-Atlantic Region (Phila.).

112. "Building the Iowa Class Battleships," *Jerseyman* 6 (Oct. 2007): 9.

113. Dunning, Memorandum for File, Dec. 27, 1941, Box 41, RG 181, NARA-Mid-Atlantic Region (Phila.); Haeberle to Chief of Bureau of Construction and Repair, May 1, 1940, Box 331, Entry A1 1266-J, Bureau of Ships General Correspondence 1940–1945, RG 19, NACP; New York Navy Yard, "Flat, Vertical Keel and Riders Plate Betw. Frs 82–131," Aug. 2, 1939, Reel 5482-9, Bureau of Ships Records of the Shipbuilding Division, RG 19, NACP; Sumrall, *Iowa Class Battleships*, 132.

114. Sumrall, *Iowa Class Battleships*, 170.

115. Historical Section, Bureau of Ordnance, "Armor, Projectiles, Ammunition, Part II, Volume II," 3, Rare Book Room, Navy Department Library, Washington Navy Yard, Washington, DC.

116. Buford Rowland and William B. Boyd, *The U.S. Navy Bureau of Ordnance in World War II* (Washington, DC: Bureau of Ordnance, 1953), 37.

117. Rowland and Boyd, *The U.S. Navy Bureau of Ordnance*, 37.

118. *Naval Ordnance: A Text-Book Prepared for the Use of the Midshipmen of the United States Naval Academy* (Annapolis, MD: Naval Institute Press, 1921), 471–77; Sumrall, *Iowa Class Battleships*, 126.

119. Bureau of Ordnance, "Armor, Projectiles, Ammunition, Part II, Volume II," 3.

120. Chief of Bureau of Ships to Chief of Bureau of Ordnance, Dec. 12, 1941 (quote); Penn to Naval Inspector of Ordnance Nicetown, Apr. 17, 1940; Chantry to Bureau of Ships, Aug. 15, 1941, Bureau of Ships to Commandant Philadelphia, Aug. 27, 1941, Box 336, RG 19, NAB; Zornig to Commandant Philadelphia Navy Yard, Nov. 21, 1942; Randall to Commandant Philadelphia Navy Yard,

May 13, 1943, Central Subject Files, Entry 447, RG 181, NARA-Mid-Atlantic Region (Phila.); *Welding of Armor in World War II* (Watertown, MA: Watertown Arsenal, 1946); Sumrall, *Iowa Class Battleships*, 123–32. The author is indebted to Nathan Okun for detailed information on armor production and installation methods.

121. "Riveter John Boyle," *Jerseyman* 2 (May 2003): 3.

122. *Shipfitting Practice*, 130–34.

123. "USS New Jersey BB-62: Machinery Erection Schedule," n.d., and Gildner, "Minutes of Conference," June 12, 1940, Box 42, Central Subject Files, Entry 447, RG 181, NARA-Mid-Atlantic Region (Phila.).

124. Howard to Phila. Navy Yard Commandant, Feb. 15, 1943, Box 330, RG 19, NACP.

125. Seiller to Director of David Taylor Model Basin, Sep. 4, 1942; Saunders to Phila. Navy Yard Commandant, Sep. 12, 1942; "Launching Report USS New Jersey," Apr. 23, 1943, all in Box 330, RG 19, NACP; Allan J. Chantry, "Launching of USS 'New Jersey' and USS 'Wisconsin,'" *Transactions of the Society of Naval Architects and Marine Engineers* 52 (1944): 391–438.

126. *Authorizing Major Alterations to Certain Naval Vessels and Additional Shipbuilding Facilities and Equipment for the Navy: Hearings Before the Senate Committee on Naval Affairs on H.R. 1053 (S. 355) and H.R. 1437 (S. 356)*, 77th Cong., 1st Sess., 18 (1941) (statement of Rear Adm. W. R. Furlong, chief of the Bureau of Ordnance).

127. On Portsmouth bombing raid, see U.S. Naval Attaché London, Intelligence Report, Serial 1043, May 23, 1941, Box 415, RG 38 Intelligence Division, Confidential Reports of Naval Attaches 1940–1946, NACP; see also Alan C. Mitchell, "Requiem for a Royal Dockyard," *Marine Engineers Review* (Apr. 1984): 20; Philip MacDougall, *The Chatham Dockyard Story* (Rochester, UK: Rochester Press, 1981), 148–52.

128. Office of the Chief of Naval Operations, Division of Naval Intelligence, Op-16-FE 37–44, "Yokosuka Naval Base," September 1944, 13, Box 417, RG 38, Intelligence Division, Confidential Reports of Naval Attaches 1940–1946, NACP.

129. Office of the Chief of Naval Operations, "Yokosuka Naval Base," 16.

130. U.S. Strategic Bombing Survey, *Japanese Naval Shipbuilding* (Washington, DC: U.S. Government Printing Office, 1946), 10–11.

131. U.S. Strategic Bombing Survey, *Japanese Naval Shipbuilding*, 11 (quote); Takashi Nishiyama, *Engineering War and Peace in Modern Japan, 1868–1964* (Baltimore, MD: Johns Hopkins University Press, 2014), 127; Tom Tompkins,

Yokosuka: Base for an Empire (Novato, CA: Presidio, 1981), 38–45; on steel allocations, see Mark D. Roehrs, *World War II in the Pacific* (Armonk, NY: M. E. Sharpe, 2004), 160–61.

132. Geoffrey Bennett, *Naval Battles of World War II* (Barnsley, UK: Pen & Sword, 2003), 46–49; Mark Stille, *Imperial Japanese Navy Destroyers 1919–45: Asashio to Tachibana* (Oxford: Osprey Publishing, 2013).

133. U.S. Strategic Bombing Survey, *Japanese Naval Shipbuilding*, 13; Office of Chief of Naval Intelligence, Op-16-FE 70-45, Sasebo Naval Base, July 1945, Box 417, RG 38, Intelligence Division, Confidential Reports of Naval Attachés 1940–1946, NACP.

134. Eberhard Rössler, *Die deutschen Uboote und ihre Werften: Eine Bilddokumentation* über *den deutschen Ubootbau von 1935 bis heute* (Munich, Germany: Bernhard & Graefe, 1990), 229–32; Gerhard Koop, Kurt Galle, Fritz Klein, *Von der Kaiserlichen Werft zum Marinearsenal: Wilhelmshaven als Zentrum der Marinetechnik seit 1870* (Munich, Germany: Bernard & Graefe, 1982), 67–68.

Chapter 5. "The Government Pays for Everything in There"

1. *Investigation of the Progress of the War Effort: Hearings Before the House Committee on Naval Affairs: Renegotiation of War Contracts*, 78th Cong., 1st Sess., 574 (1943).

2. Joe R. Feagin and Kelly Riddell, "The State, Capitalism, and World War II: The U.S. Case," *Armed Forces and Society* 17 (Oct. 1990): 74 (quote); on General Motors, see Fred R. Kaen, "World War II Prime Defence Contractors: Were They Favoured?" *Business History* 53 (Dec. 2011): 1,072.

3. On the B-29, see Jacob Vandermeulen, *Building the B-29* (Washington, DC: Smithsonian Museum Press, 1995). The notion that industrial mobilization privileged large corporations that reaped exorbitant profits was challenged after the war by James Fesler, the War Production Board's official historian, who pointed out that critics of economic concentration "failed to distinguish between prime contracts and subcontracts. The concentration revealed [in wartime investigations] pertained only to prime contracts; it pointed to no very clear conclusion regarding the extent of subcontracting, which was the logical method for bringing many small shops into the defense program." James L. Fesler, *Industrial Mobilization for War: A History of the War Production Board*, vol. 1 (Washington, DC: Civilian Production Administration, 1947), 147. Recent research finds no evidence of above-average financial performance of prime defense contractors; see Kaen, "World War II Prime Defence Contractors," 1,044–73.

4. A. J. Grassnick, "New Ingalls Shipyard," *Marine Engineering* 45 (Jan. 1940): 38–53; Sea Fox and Frederick Lykes, "Turbine-Drive C-3 Cargo Ships," *Marine Engineering* 45 (May 1940): 54–61; Charles S. Mann, "New Seattle-Tacoma Shipyard," *Marine Engineering* 46 (Mar. 1941): 54–64; René De La Pedraja, *The Rise and Decline of U.S. Merchant Shipping in the Twentieth Century* (New York: Twayne Publishers, 1992), 133–35; H. Gerrish Smith, "Shipyard Statistics," in *The Shipbuilding Business of the United States of America*, vol. 1, ed. Frederick G. Fassett Jr. (New York: Society of Naval Architects and Marine Engineers, 1948), 70; Charles H. Coleman, *Shipbuilding Activities of the National Defense Advisory Commission and Office of Production Management, July 1940 to December 1941* (Washington, DC: War Production Board, 1946), 91–102.

5. Quoted in Mark R. Wilson, *Destructive Creation: American Business and the Winning of World War II* (Philadelphia: University of Pennsylvania Press, 2016), 195.

6. John F. Metten, "Shipyard Layout, Section 1. Standard Yards," in *The Shipbuilding Business of the United States of America*, vol. 1, ed. Frederick G. Fassett Jr. (New York: Society of Naval Architects and Marine Engineers, 1948), 202.

7. *To Expedite Naval Shipbuilding: Hearings Before the Senate Committee on Naval Affairs on H.R. 9822 to Expedite Naval Shipbuilding, and For Other Purposes*, 76th Cong., 3rd Sess., 3,218 (1940) (statement of H. Gerrish Smith, National Council of American Shipbuilders).

8. "Statement Indicating the Plant Expansion and Facility Additions Which Have Been Financed by Private Capital Upon the Solicitation of the Navy Department," reprinted in *Excess Profits Taxation, 1940: Joint Hearings of the Senate Committee on Finance and the House Committee on Ways and Means*, 76th Cong., 3rd Sess., 31–32 (1940).

9. "History of the Boston Navy Yard (Industrial Department), Chapter III: Manpower and Industrial Relations," 2, Commandant of First Naval District, History of Naval Administration, World War II, vol. 8, Navy Department Library, Rare Book Room, Washington Navy Yard, Washington, DC.

10. "History of the Boston Navy Yard," 2.

11. Homer to Secretary of the Navy, June 25, 1940, and enclosure dated June 20, 1940; Collins to Supervisor of Shipbuilding, Sep. 10, 1940; Simmers to Supervisor of Shipbuilding, Sep. 20, 1940; Watson to Supervisor of Shipbuilding, Oct. 31, 1940, and enclosure dated Oct. 25, 1940, all in Box 195, Entry A1 1266-L, RG (hereafter "RG") 19, Bureau of Ships General Correspondence 1940–1945, National Archives at College Park, College Park, MD (hereafter "NACP"); Metten, "Shipyard Layout, Section 1," 203.

12. Woodward to Rawlings, June 26, 1940, Box 792, Entry A1 1266-L, RG 19, Bureau of Ships General Correspondence 1940–1945, NACP.

13. "Minutes of a Conference held June 10, 1940," Box 792, Entry A1 1266-L, RG 19, Bureau of Ships General Correspondence 1940–1945, NACP.

14. Supervisor of Shipbuilding to Secretary of the Navy, Sep. 18, 1940, Box 792, Entry A1 1266-L, RG 19, Bureau of Ships General Correspondence 1940–1945, NACP.

15. Woodward to Supervisor of Shipbuilding, Aug. 12, 1940; Cox to Bureau of Ships, Oct. 22, 1940; Bureau of Ships to Supervisor of Shipbuilding, Mar. 13, 1941 and Enclosure A, all in Box 792; Entry A1 1266-L, RG 19, Bureau of Ships General Correspondence 1940–1945, NACP; U.S. Office of Naval Intelligence, Fifth Naval District, "Investigation Report," Sep. 5, 1941, Box 796, all boxes in Entry A1 1266-L, RG 19, Bureau of Ships General Correspondence 1940–1945, NACP; Dravo Corporation, *Submerged Shipways: An Account of Pioneer Engineering and Construction of Two Horizontal Shipways of Unique Design at Newport News, Virginia, 1940–1942* (Pittsburgh, PA: Dravo Corporation, 1945); John F. Metten, "Shipyard Layout, Section 1," 203–7.

16. "Supplemental Contract for Acquisition and Installation of Special Additional Plant Equipment and Facilities Required to Expedite the National Defense Program," Sep. 1, 1940; Robinson, Minutes of a Meeting with the New York Shipbuilding Company, June 11, 1940; Metten to Contract Division, June 25, 1940, all in Box 797, Entry A1 1266-L, RG 19, Bureau of Ships General Correspondence 1940–1945, NACP; Wood to New York Shipbuilding Corp., Mar. 2, 1942, and Exhibit 1, Box 798, all boxes in Entry A1 1266-L, RG 19, Bureau of Ships General Correspondence 1940–1945, NACP; on contract totals, see *The Revenue Bill of 1941. Report 673*, Part 3: *Individual Views to Accompany H.R. 5417* (Robert LaFollette), 77th Cong., 1st Sess., 17 (1941); see also Metten, "Shipyard Layout, Section 1," 207–10.

17. Colvin, "Minutes of Conference, Dec. 31, 1941," Box 42, and Forrestal to Electric Boat, Jan. 29, 1942, both in Entry A1 1266-L, RG 19, Bureau of Ships General Correspondence 1940–1945, NACP; Gary E. Weir, *Forged in War: The Naval-Industrial Complex and American Submarine Construction, 1940–1961* (Washington, DC: Naval Historical Center, 1993), 19–34; John D. Alden, *The Fleet Submarine in the U.S. Navy: A Design and Construction History* (Annapolis, MD: Naval Institute Press, 1979), 81.

18. "Report of Visit of Subcommittee of House Naval Affairs Committee, Bath Iron Works Corporation, Bath, Me," June 26, 1941, 2, Box 182, Entry A1 1266-L, RG 19, Bureau of Ships General Correspondence 1940–1945, NACP.

19. Kiernan to Bureau of Ships, Feb. 6, 1941, Box 181; Kiernan to Bureau of Ships, Jan. 1, 1942, Box 182; Corman to Rawlings, July 27, 1942, Box 183; Irish to Chief of Bureau of Ships, Nov. 18, 1941, Box 203; "Supplemental Contract for the Acquisition and Installation of Special Additional Plant Equipment and Facilities Required to Expedite the National Defense Program," Sep. 9, 1940, Box 452; all boxes in Entry A1 1266-L, RG 19, Bureau of Ships General Correspondence 1940–1945, NACP.

20. William G. Du Bose, "Cramp—From Windjammer to Steel and Steam," n.d., 2, Speeches Ledger, Cramp Collection, J. Welles Henderson Archives and Library, Independence Seaport Museum Philadelphia.

21. *Cramp Shipbuilding Company, Philadelphia, Pennsylvania, 1940–1944* (Philadelphia: Cramp Shipbuilding Company, 1944); Supervisor of Shipbuilding Philadelphia to Bureau of Ships, Dec. 11, 1940, Box 332, Entry A1 1266-L, Bureau of Ships General Correspondence 1940–1945, RG 19, NACP; "Cramp Drydock," *Cramp Ways* 2 (July 1945): 6–8; for additional details, see Thomas Heinrich, "Jack of All Trades: Cramp Shipbuilding, Mixed Production, and the Limits of Flexible Specialization in American Warship Construction, 1940–1945," *Enterprise and Society* 11 (June 2010): 275–315.

22. Joel Davidson, *The Unsinkable Fleet: The Politics of the U.S. Navy Expansion in World War II* (Annapolis, MD: Naval Institute Press, 1996), 59.

23. L. C. Stiles, "Welding of LST's at Seneca, Ill.," *Journal of the American Welding Society* 24 (Nov. 1945): 1,053.

24. Stiles, "Welding of LST's," 1,058.

25. Lofquist to Assistant Secretary of the Navy, Jan. 26, 1943, Box 287, Entry A1 1266-L, RG 19, Bureau of Ships General Correspondence 1940–1945, NACP.

26. Stiles, "Welding of LST's," 1,055.

27. Woodson to Chief of the Bureau of Supplies and Accounts, July 6, 1942; Vosburgh to Chief of the Bureau of Ships, Mar. 30, 1942, Box 287; Pillsbury, Memorandum of Calls Made to A.F. of L. Headquarters in Washington on Skilled Workers for Seneca, Jan. 21, 1943, Box 288; Chicago Bridge & Iron Co., "Zoning Plan: Police and Fire Protection for Seneca Shipyard," Dec. 18, 1942, Box 291, all boxes in Entry A1 1266-L, RG 19, Bureau of Ships General Correspondence 1940–1945, NACP; Pillsbury to Forrestal, Apr. 14, 1944, Box 154, Commercial Plants File, Records of Secretary of the Navy James Forrestal, 1940–1947, Entry 261, RG 80, General Records of the Department of the Navy, NACP.

28. Pigott to Goodall, Sep. 18, 1942, Upper Clyde Shipbuilders, Clydebank Division, Admiralty Letter Book, Sep. 5, 1942, to Dec. 4, 1942, UCS 1/15/1, Glasgow University Archive Services, UK.

29. Bentham, "Report to Machine Tool Controller on the Equipment of Shipyards and Marine Engine Works," Sep. 20, 1942, 6, BT 28/319, National Archives of the United Kingdom, Kew.

30. Bentham, "Report to Machine Tool Controller," 2.

31. Bentham, "Report to Machine Tool Controller," 4.

32. Bentham, "Report to Machine Tool Controller," 9.

33. Pigott to Mathias, Dec. 15, 1942, Upper Clyde Shipbuilders, Clydebank Division, Admiralty Letter Book, Dec. 5, 1942, to Feb. 7, 1943, 1942, UCS 1/15/2, Glasgow University Archive Services, UK; Correlli Barnett, *The Audit of War: The Illusion and Reality of Britain as a Great Nation* (London: Papermac, 1987), 118–19; Brian Newman, *Materials Handling in British Shipbuilding, 1850–1945* (Glasgow, UK: Centre for Business History in Scotland, 1996).

34. U.S. Strategic Bombing Survey, Munitions Division, *Friedrich Krupp Germaniawerft Kiel* (Washington, DC: U.S. Strategic Bombing Survey Munitions Division, 1947), 1.

35. British Intelligence Objectives Sub-Committee, Shipbuilding, *Notes on Visits to Blohm und Voss, Deutsche Werft, Germania Werft and Deschimag* (London: His Majesty's Stationery Office, 1947).

36. U.S. Strategic Bombing Survey, Munitions Division, *Deutsche Schiff und Maschinenbau Bremen, Germany* (Washington, DC: US Strategic Bombing Survey Munitions Division, 1947), 6.

37. Oberfinanzdirektion Bremen, "Bericht über die bei der Firma Aktien-Gesellschaft 'Weser' Bremen getroffenen Feststellungen wegen Forderungen und Verbindlichkeiten des Deutschen Reiches," Apr. 6, 1962, 4, 42/4-10; Deschimag to Elsner, July 26, 1944, 4, 42/4/-3, Bremen State Archives, Germany; on Blohm & Voss, see British Intelligence Objectives Sub-Committee, *Shipbuilding: Notes on Visits to Blohm und Voss, Deutsche Werft, Germania Werft and Deschimag* (London: His Majesty's Stationery Office, 1947), 5–9; Andreas Meyhoff, *Blohm & Voss im "Dritten Reich": Eine Hamburger Großwerft zwischen Geschäft und Politik* (Hamburg: Christians, 2001), 178–87.

38. U.S. Strategic Bombing Survey, *Japanese Naval Shipbuilding* (Washington, DC: U.S. Government Printing Office, 1946), 12–13.

39. Office of the Chief of Naval Operations, Division of Naval Intelligence, Serial 76-44, "Japan—Principal Data on Shipbuilding Industry," Dec. 26, 1944, Box

1175, RG 38 Intelligence Division, Confidential Reports of Naval Attaches 1940–1946, NACP.

40. Office of the Chief of Naval Operations, Division of Naval Intelligence, Op-16-FE 35-45, "Mitsubishi Shipyard at Nagasaki," April 1945, Box 1176, RG 38, Confidential Reports of Naval Attaches 1940–1946, NACP.

41. Arthur B. Homer, "Shipyard Organization, Section 1: Standard Yards," in *The Shipbuilding Business of the United States of America*, vol. 1, ed. Frederick G. Fassett Jr. (New York: Society of Naval Architects and Marine Engineers, 1948), 258.

42. Homer, "Shipyard Organization," 258–60; William B. Ferguson, *Shipbuilding Cost and Production Methods* (New York: Cornell Maritime Press, 1944), 9–20.

43. U.S. Office of Naval Intelligence, Fifth Naval District, "Investigation Report: Newport News Shipbuilding and Dry Dock Company, Newport News, Virginia," July 1, 1941, 1–2, Box 796, Entry A1 1266-L, RG 19, Bureau of Ships General Correspondence 1940–1945, NACP; Newport News Shipbuilding and Dry Dock Company, *The Apprentice School* (Newport News, VA: Newport News Shipbuilding and Dry Dock Company, 1935); Oswald L. Harvey, *Report on Apprenticeship System of Newport News Shipbuilding and Dry Dock Company, Newport News, Va.* (Washington, DC: Federal Committee on Apprenticeship, Division of Labor Standards, U.S. Department of Labor, 1940); Cernida W. Adams, *Collis Porter Huntington*, vol. 2 (Newport News, VA: Mariners' Museum, 1954), 635–41; William L. Tazewell, *Newport News Shipbuilding: The First Century* (Newport News, VA: Mariners' Museum, 1986), 203.

44. *Proposed Amendments to the Securities Act of 1933 and to the Securities Exchange Act of 1934: Hearings Before the House Committee on Interstate and Foreign Commerce*, 77th Cong., 1st Sess., 197 (1941) (statement of R. McLean Stewart, chairman, Securities Acts Committee, Investment Bankers Association of America).

45. "Trust Group Buys Shipbuilding Unit," *New York Times*, May 8, 1940, 38; Kenneth Maxy, "End of a Dynasty: Wall St. Buys Newport News," *Shipyard Worker*, Aug. 16, 1940, 5; Robert T. Swaine, *The Cravath Firm and Its Predecessors, 1819–1948*, vol. 2: *The Cravath Firm Since 1906* (New York: Ad Press, 1948), 629.

46. "Arthur Homer," *New York Times*, June 19, 1972, 36; *Maryland in World War II: Industry and Agriculture* (Baltimore, MD: Maryland Historical Society, 1951), 373–74; "William H. Collins," *Transactions of the Society of Naval Architects and Marine Engineers* 56 (1948): 578–80; "Charles N. Boylan," *Transactions of the Society of Naval Architects and Marine Engineers* 64 (1956): 642.

47. Federal Bureau of Investigation, Newark Field Office, "New York Shipbuilding Corporation, Camden, New Jersey," Nov. 12, 1940, 7–8, Box 801, Entry A1 1266-L, RG 19, Bureau of Ships General Correspondence 1940–1945, NACP; "Agreement between John F. Metten and William Cramp and Sons Ship and Engine Building Company, 1927," John Farrell Metten Material, Box 1, Folder 1, Hagley Museum and Library, Wilmington, DE; "New Officers of New York Ship," *Marine Engineering* 39 (December 1934): 474–75; "T. H. Bossert," *Marine Engineering* 40 (Feb. 1940): 75; "Ernest H. Rigg," in William S. Myers, *Prominent Families of New Jersey*, vol. 2 (New York: Lewis, 1945), 1,094; "Ernest H. Rigg," *Transactions of the Society of Naval Architects and Marine Engineers* 64 (1956): 648.

48. Heinrich, "Jack of All Trades," 282.

49. Bowen, Memorandum for the Under Secretary, Oct. 18, Box 157, Entry 261, Commercial Plants File, Records of Secretary of the Navy James Forrestal, 1940–1947, RG 80, General Records of the Department of the Navy, NACP.

50. Bowen to Forrestal, Mar. 21, 1944, Box 157, Entry 261, Commercial Plants File, Records of Secretary of the Navy James Forrestal, 1940–1947, RG 80, General Records of the Department of the Navy, NACP; on Brewster and York Safe & Lock, see Wilson, *Destructive Creation*, 211–12.

51. U.S. Office of Naval Intelligence, Twelfth Naval District, "Investigation Report: Bethlehem San Francisco," May 5, 1942, 27–28, Box 224; New York Ship foreman data calculated from Federal Bureau of Investigation, "Survey of the New York Shipbuilding Corporation," Dec. 11, 1940, 3–5, Box 801, both boxes in Entry A1 1266-L, RG 19, Bureau of Ships General Correspondence 1940–1945, NACP.

52. *Investigation of the National Defense Program*, Part 17: *Hearings Before the Special Senate Committee Investigating the National Defense Program: Farm Machinery and Equipment, Concrete Barges, Army Commissions and Military Activities of Motion Picture Personnel, Pipe Line Transportation, Absenteeism in the Defense Industry*, 78th Cong., 1st Sess., 6,975 (1943) (statement of Homer L. Ferguson, chairman of the board and president, Newport News Shipbuilding & Dry Dock Company).

53. *Investigation of the National Defense Program*, Part 17, 6,977.

54. Quoted in James T. Sparrow, *Warfare State: World War II Americans and the Age of Big Government* (New York: Oxford University Press, 2011), 179; *Investigation of the National Defense Program*, Part 17, 6,977–78; on similar training programs at New York Ship, see Campbell to Supervisor of Shipbuilding

Camden, Nov. 18, 1942, Box 800, Entry A1 1266-L, RG 19, Bureau of Ships General Correspondence 1940–1945, NACP; and *National Defense Migration, Part 14: Hearings Before the Select House Committee Investigating National Defense Migration: Trenton Hearings*, 77th Cong., 1st Sess., 5,705–14 (1941) (statement of H. E. Parker, industrial relations manager, New York Shipbuilding Corporation).

55. *Production in Shipbuilding Plants*, Part 1: *Executive Hearings Before the House Committee on the Merchant Marine and Fisheries*, 78th Cong., 1st Sess., 3 and 120 (1943) (statements of John P. Frey, president, Metal Trades Department, American Federation of Labor, and of John Green, president, Industrial Union of Marine and Shipbuilding Workers of America) 120; *Conditions of Government Contracts: Hearings Before Subcommittee No. 1 of the House Committee on the Judiciary*, 76th Cong., 3rd Sess., 75–77 (1940) (statement of John Green, president, Industrial Union of Marine and Shipbuilding Workers of America); Edward M. Marsh, *Wartime Employment, Production, and Conditions of Work in Shipyards* (Washington, DC: Government Printing Office, 1945), 52; David Palmer, *Organizing the Shipyards: Union Strategy in Three Northeast Ports, 1933–1945* (Ithaca, NY: Cornell University Press, 1998), 184–88.

56. Joseph W. Powell, "Labor in Shipbuilding," in *The Shipbuilding Business of the United States of America*, vol. 1, ed. Frederick G. Fassett Jr. (New York: Society of Naval Architects and Marine Engineers, 1948), 285–87; Frederic C. Lane, *Ships for Victory: A History of Shipbuilding under the U.S. Maritime Commission in World War II* (Baltimore, MD: Johns Hopkins University Press, 1951), 268–87.

57. Harold G. Bowen, *Ships, Machinery, and Mossbacks: The Autobiography of a Naval Engineer* (Princeton, NJ: Princeton University Press, 1954), 217.

58. Bowen, *Ships, Machinery, and Mossbacks*, 207–23; David F. Winkler, "The Construction of USS Atlanta and the Navy Seizure of Federal Shipbuilding," *Northern Mariner* 24 (Apr. 2014): 135–52.

59. Wilson, *Destructive Creation*, 194–208.

60. R. J. Thomas, *Housing for Defense* (Detroit: United Auto Workers, 1942), 28.

61. "Newport News Men Are Getting Wise to PSA," *Shipyard Worker*, June 27, 1941, 4.

62. "Local 35 Strike Holds Firm at American Eng'g," *Shipyard Worker*, Oct. 10, 1941, 1 (quote).

63. *Investigation of the National Defense Program*, Part 17, 7,349.

64. General Membership of Local 42 to General Executive Board, Jan. 6, 1944, Box 90, Series 5, Local 42 General Correspondence, Industrial Union of

Marine and Shipbuilding Workers of America Archives, University of Maryland Archives, College Park, MD.

65. Baugh to Schaffer, Dec. 30, 1943; John Green, "Statement on Cramp Situation," Jan. 7, 1944; both in Box 90, Series 5, Local 42 Box 90, Series 5, Local 42, General Correspondence, Industrial Union of Marine and Shipbuilding Workers of America Archives, University of Maryland Archives, College Park, MD; Herbert Moyer to Chief of Bureau of Ships, Dec. 20, 1943, Box 341, Entry A1 1266-L, Bureau of Ships General Correspondence 1940–1945, RG 19, NACP.

66. *NLRB v. Newport News Shipbuilding & Dry Dock Co.*, 308 U.S. 241 (1939).

67. On Fore River, see Palmer, *Organizing the Shipyards*, 180–231; on Newport News, see "In the Matter of Newport News Shipbuilding and Dry Dock Company and Industrial Union of Marine and Shipbuilding Workers of America—CIO," Aug. 4, 1944, *Decisions and Orders of the National Labor Relations Board*, vol. 57 (Washington, DC: Government Printing Office, 1945), 1,053–61; *National Labor Relations Act and Proposed Amendments*, Part 21: *Hearings Before the Senate Committee on Education and Labor*, 76th Cong., 1st Sess., 4,018–26 (1939) (statement of Phillip H. Van Gelder, secretary-treasurer, Industrial Union of Marine and Shipbuilding Workers of America) for a summary of prewar developments.

68. Lewis Johnman and Hugh Murphy, *British Shipbuilding and the State Since 1918* (Ithaca, NY: Regatta Press, 2002), 60–93; Joseph F. Clarke, *Building Ships on the North East Coast: A Labour of Love, Risk, and Pain*, Part 2: *C 1914–C 1980* (Whitley Bay, UK: Bewick Press, 1997), 334–37.

69. *Walsh-Kaiser Co.: Hearings Before the Subcommittee on Production in Shipbuilding Plants of the House Committee on the Merchant Marine and Fisheries*, 78th Cong., 2nd Sess., 20 (1944) (statement of Representative Joseph J. O'Brien, New York).

70. *Investigations of the Progress of the War Effort: Report of the House Committee on Naval Affairs*, 78th Cong., 2nd Sess., 51 (1944).

71. *First Supplemental National Defense Appropriation Bill for 1942: Hearings Before the Subcommittee of the House Committee on Appropriations*, 77th Cong., 1st Sess., 465 (1941) (statement of Capt. Howard L. Vickery, member, U.S. Maritime Commission Member).

72. *First Supplemental National Defense Appropriation Bill for 1942*, 465.

73. Tazewell, *Newport News Shipbuilding*, 181–86; Lane, *Ships for Victory*, 149, 613–14.

74. *Navy Department Appropriation Bill for 1942: Hearings Before the Subcommittee of the House Committee on Appropriations*, 77th Cong., 1st Sess., 241 (1941) (statement of Rear Adm. Samuel M. Robinson, chief of the Bureau of Ships).

75. *Investigation of the National Defense Program, Part 5: Hearings Before the Special Senate Committee Investigating the National Defense Program: Emergency Shipbuilding Program*, 77th Cong., 1st Sess., 1,568 (1941) (statement of James E. Barnes, Washington representative, Todd Shipbuilding Corporation and Affiliates).

76. *Establishing an Office of Budget and Reports in the Navy Department, and for Other Purposes (H.R. 3782): Hearings Before the House Committee on Naval Affairs*, 77th Cong., 1st Sess. 1,671–76 (1941) (statement of Samuel M. Robinson, chief of the Bureau of Ships); *Investigation of the Naval Defense Program: Supplemental Report. House Report No. 2371: Supplemental Report By the House Committee on Naval Affairs*, 77th Cong., 2nd Sess., 13 (1942); Smith, "Shipyard Statistics," 165–78; C. Bradford Mitchell, *Every Kind of Shipwork: A History of Todd Shipyards Corporation, 1916–1981* (New York: Todd Shipyards Corporation, 1981), 118–64.

77. Norman Friedman, *U.S. Destroyers: An Illustrated Design History* (Annapolis, MD: Naval Institute Press, 2004), 111–23; Mark E. Stille, *USN Destroyer vs IJN Destroyer: The Pacific 1943* (Oxford, UK: Osprey Publishing, 2012), 67–70.

78. Calculated from data in Friedman, *U.S. Destroyers*, 456–73.

79. Sewell to Robinson, May 28, 1941, Box 181, Entry A1 1266-L, RG 19, Bureau of Ships General Correspondence 1940–1945, NACP.

80. Robinson, "Minutes of Meeting Held June 12, 1940"; Kiernan to Bath Iron Works Corporation, July 15, 1940; Kiernan to Bath Iron Works Corporation, Dec. 5, 1940, both in Box 181, "Report of Visit of Subcommittee of House Naval Affairs Committee Bath Iron Works Corporation, Bath, Me," June 26, 1941, Box 182; General Accounting Office, "In re: Bath Iron Works Corporation," May 27, 1944, Box 184, all boxes in Entry A1 1266-L, RG 19, Bureau of Ships General Correspondence 1940–1945, NACP; *Investigation of the Progress of the War Effort: Report of the House Committee on Naval Affairs*, 78th Cong., 2nd Sess., 189–90, 201 (1944); Ralph L. Snow, *Bath Iron Works: The First Hundred Years* (Bath, ME: Maine Maritime Museum, 1987), 315–64.

81. "Chickasaw Shipyards Sold to Gulf Shipbuilding Corp.," *Marine Progress* 9 (1938): 50; *National Defense Migration, Part 32: Hearings Before the Select House Committee Investigating National Defense Migration: Huntsville Hearings*, 77th Cong., 2nd Sess., 12,113–18 (1942) (statement of Harry Hill, vice president, Gulf Shipbuilding & Dry Dock Company).

82. Alden, *The Fleet Submarine in the U.S. Navy*, 78–79.

83. Quoted in Weir, *Forged in War*, 26.

84. Alden, *The Fleet Submarine in the U.S. Navy*, 81.

85. Bureau of Ships quoted in Weir, *Forged in War*, 28

86. "Narrative Notes On Cramp Shipbuilding Company—Part I: Basic Narrative 1940–1943," 4, Cramp Collection, J. Welles Henderson Archives and Library, Independence Seaport Museum Library, Philadelphia.

87. James Bethea quoted in Weir, *Forged in War*, 30–31; see also Heinrich, "Jack of All Trades."

88. "Naval New Construction Programmes and Their Execution. 1935–1945. Unpublished Narrative Used in the Compilation of British War Production: Final Draft," n.d., 124, CAB 102/527; "'B' Firms: Merchant Shipbuilding Programme," n.d., ADM 116/4991, both in National Archives of the United Kingdom, Kew.

89. U.S. Strategic Bombing Survey, *Japanese Naval Shipbuilding* (Washington, DC: Government Printing Office, 1946), 4 (quote); see also Mitsubishi Zōsen Kabushiki Kaisha, *Nihon no shosen 1887–1958/Brief Shipbuilding History of the Company* (Tokyo: Mitsubishi Zōsen Kabushiki Kaisha, 1960), 10–11; Mark P. Parillo, *The Japanese Merchant Marine in World War II* (Annapolis, MD: Naval Institute Press, 1993), 154–62.

90. James Montgomerie, "Shipbuilding Practice Abroad," *Transactions of the North-East Coast Institution of Engineers and Shipbuilders* 54 (1938): 168; Kurt Arendt and Heinrich Oelfken, "Die Baumethoden der deutschen U-Boote 1935-1945," in *100 Jahre Verbands- und Zeitgeschehen*, ed. Verband der Deutschen Schiffbauindustrie e. V. (Hamburg, Germany: Storck, 1984), 66–72; Eberhard Rössler, *Geschichte des deutschen Ubootbaus* (Munich, Germany: J. F. Lehmanns, 1975), 207–13.

91. Chief of the Bureau of Ships to Chief of Office of Procurement & Material, Oct. 12, 1942, reprinted in *Problems of Small Business Enterprises*, Part 10: *Smaller Concerns in War Production I: Hearings Before the Special Subcommittee to Study and Survey the Problems of Small Business Enterprises*, 76th Cong., 2nd Sess., 1,228 (1942).

92. Crisp to Superintending Constructor Newport News, May 1, 1940; Wood to Supervisor of Shipbuilding Camden, Aug. 28, 1940, Box 424; New York Shipbuilding Corporation, Memorandum, Feb. 12, 1941, Box 797, both boxes in Entry A1 1266-L, RG 19, Bureau of Ships General Correspondence 1940–1945, NACP; *Investigation of the Progress of the War Effort*, vol. 5: *Gibbs & Cox:*

Hearings Before the House Committee on Naval Affairs, 78th Cong., 2nd Sess., 3,942–44 (1944) (statement of Rear Adm. E. L. Cochrane, chief of the Bureau of Ships).

93. Howard to Bureau of Ships, Jan. 17, 1941 (quote); see also Bureau of Ships to Supervisor of Shipbuilding Camden, Aug. 16, 1940, both in Box 427; Bureau of Construction and Repair to Supervisor of Shipbuilding Camden, Apr. 10, 1940; "Minutes of Meeting Held on 9 April 1941," Box 424; "Contract #437— USS 'Independence' (CV22)—ex-CL59: List of applicable changes authorized while still a 'CL' (light cruiser)," Dec. 1, 1942, Box 1234; Ellis to Supervisor of Shipbuilding Camden, Apr. 15, 1941, Box 459; Enclosure A of Bossert to Supervisor of Shipbuilding Camden, Aug. 25, 1942, Box 414; Bossert to Supervisor of Shipbuilding Camden, Nov. 18, 1940, Box 427; all boxes in Entry A1 1266-L, Bureau of Ships General Correspondence 1940–1945, RG 19, NACP.

94. Metten to Supervisor of Shipbuilding Camden, June 9, 1941, Box 450, Entry A1 1266-L, Bureau of Ships General Correspondence 1940–1945, RG 19, NACP.

95. Robinson to Metten, June 24, 1941, Box 450 (quote); see also Robinson to Supervisor of Shipbuilding Camden, June 25, 1941, Box 424, Entry A1 1266-L, RG 19, Bureau of Ships General Correspondence 1940–1945, NACP.

96. Metten to Bureau of Ships, Dec. 14, 1942; Broderick to Supervisor of Shipbuilding Camden, Dec. 22, 1942; Tooke to Supervisor of Shipbuilding Camden, Jan. 9, 1943; Bossert to Bureau of Ships, Sep. 18 1943, all in Box 1234; Bossert to Supervisor of Shipbuilding Camden, Mar. 7, 1942; Bossert to Supervisor of Shipbuilding Camden, Box 1235, Entry A1 1266-L, Bureau of Ships General Correspondence 1940–1945, RG 19, NACP; Norman Friedman, *U.S. Aircraft Carriers: In Illustrated Design History* (Annapolis, MD: Naval Institute Press, 1983), 159–91.

97. Civilian Production Administration, Bureau of Demobilization, *Special Study No. 26: Shipbuilding Policies of the War Production Board, January 1942– November 1945* (Washington, DC: Civilian Production Administration, 1947), 61.

98. Bureau of Ships, "An Administrative History of the Bureau of Ships during World War II, vol. 2," 182, n.d., Navy Department Library, Rare Book Room, Washington Navy Yard.

99. Robinson to All Supervisors of Shipbuilding, Nov. 17, 1941, reprinted in Bureau of Ships, "Administrative History of the Bureau of Ships, vol. 2," 83.

100. Robinson to Secretary of the Navy, May 7, 1941, Box 169, Entry A1 1266-L, Bureau of Ships General Correspondence 1940–1945, RG 19, NACP.

101. Kranzfelder to Head of Design Bureau of Ships, Jan. 3, 1941; "Memorandum of Conference Held in the Bureau of Ships," Apr. 18, 1941, both in Box 169, Entry A1 1266-L, RG 19, Bureau of Ships General Correspondence 1940–1945, NACP.

102. James C. Hodge, "The Welding of Pressure Vessels," *Journal of the American Society for Naval Engineers* 48 (1936): 511 (quote); see also W. A. Brooks, "The Building and Inspection of a Boiler," *Journal of the American Society for Naval Engineers* 43 (1931): 43–53.

103. "Chapter 6: Construction Details of Two-Drum and Three-Drum Express Boilers," in *Naval Machinery 1946 Part I* (Annapolis, MD: U.S. Naval Academy, 1946), I-6-3.

104. "Construction Details of Two-Drum and Three-Drum Express Boilers," I-6-3.

105. Bossert to Supervisor of Shipbuilding Camden, Aug. 29, 1940, Box 424; Metten to Supervisor of Shipbuilding Camden, Sep. 19, 1941, Box 450; Butler to Inspector of Naval Material, Lynn, Mass., July 25, 1942, Box 452, Entry A1 1266-L, RG 19, Bureau of Ships General Correspondence 1940–1945, NACP; John A. Miller, *Men and Volts at War: The Story of General Electric in World War II* (New York: Bantam Books, 1948), 9–14.

106. David O. Woodbury, *Battlefronts of Industry: Westinghouse in World War II* (New York: Wiley, 1948), 59–60.

107. Glenn B. Warren, *Development of Steam Turbines for Main Propulsion of High-Powered Combatant Ships* (New York: Society of Naval Architects and Marine Engineers, 1946), 34 (quote); Hanson to Bureau of Ships, June 3, 1941, and Ruling to Inspector of Machinery, Schenectady, July 15, 1941, both in Box 450, Entry A1 1266-L, RG 19, Bureau of Ships General Correspondence 1940–1945, NACP; A. A. Ross, "Gears for U.S. Defense and Trade," *Marine Engineering* 44 (Dec. 1940): 62–67; E. K. Henley, "Propulsion Machinery in the Process of Construction," *Marine Engineering* 48 (Sep. 1942): 214–18; Miller, *Men and Volts at War*, 9–14.

108. W. R. Furlong to Camden Forge, Nov. 5, 1940; W. R. Furlong to Camden Forge, Nov. 20, 1940; Walter S. Cox to Bureau of Ordnance, Oct. 3, 1941; Walter S. Cox to Bureau of Ships, Sep. 29, 1942, Box 264, Entry A1 1266-L, RG 19, Bureau of Ships General Correspondence 1940–1945, NACP; "Camden Forge Company: AD 482-09," Dec. 4, 1947, Box 6, Series 2, Subseries 6, Industrial Union of Marine and Shipbuilding Workers of America Archives, University of Maryland Archives, College Park, MD; R. Michel, "Factor of Safety and Working Stresses of Marine Propulsion Shafting," *Journal of the American Society for Naval Engineers* 54 (Feb. 1942): 50–57.

109. Mills to Supervisor of Shipbuilding Camden, Nov. 5, 1940, Box 459, Entry A1 1266-L, RG 19, Bureau of Ships General Correspondence 1940–1945, NACP.

110. G. Clymer Brooke, *Birdsboro: Company with a Past Built to Last* (New York: Newcomen Society, 1959), 17–18.

111. Hiemke, Memorandum of Phone Conservation, Apr. 29, 1941; Miller to Bureau of Ships, Oct. 15, 1941; Miller to Bureau of Ships, Feb. 4, 1942, Box 458; Miller to Bureau of Ships, Oct. 21, 1942; Miller to Bureau of Ships, Feb. 17, 1943, Box 459; see also Cannon to Bureau of Ships, Nov. 13, 1940; Colvin, Minutes of Conference, Dec. 16, 1941; Bale, Memorandum, Mar. 28, 1942, Box 228; Heppenstall to Bureau of Ships, Dec. 7, 1945, Box 230, all boxes in Entry A1 1266-L, RG 19, Bureau of Ships General Correspondence 1940–1945, NACP.

112. Nelson to Smith, Sep. 13, 1941; Mills to Supervisor of Shipbuilding Camden, Apr. 15, 1941, and enclosure "Specification CL-5," all in Box 459, Entry A1 1266-L, Bureau of Ships General Correspondence 1940–1945, RG 19, NACP; "Baldwin Acquires Cramp-Morris Properties," *Marine Engineering* 36 (1931): 303.

113. "Birth of a Propeller," *Marine Engineering* 64 (Mar. 1940): 61.

114. L. M. Atkins, "The Manufacture of Marine Propellers," *Journal of the American Society for Naval Engineers* 47 (May 1935): 229 (quote); see also Wood to New York Shipbuilding Corporation, Feb. 18, 1942; McBride to Chief of the Bureau of Ships, Mar. 25, 1942; Wood to New York Shipbuilding Corporation, June 15, 1942, all in Box 459, Entry A1 1266-L, Bureau of Ships General Correspondence 1940–1945, RG 19, NACP; E. A. Stevens Jr., "The Hull and its Screw Propeller," *Journal of the American Society for Naval Engineers* 54 (Aug. 1942): 372–406.

115. "Memorandum of Conference Held in Bureau of Ships," Feb. 24, 1941, 2, Box 165, Entry A1 1266-L, RG 19, Bureau of Ships General Correspondence 1940–1945, NACP.

116. On American Engineering, see U.S. Office of Naval Intelligence, "Investigation Report: American Engineering Company, Philadelphia, Pennsylvania, July 17, 1941," 1–9, Box 131, Entry A1 1266-L, RG 19, Bureau of Ships General Correspondence 1940–1945, NACP; Bennett to Stewart, Jan. 24, 1944, Box 131, Entry A1 1266-L, 19, Bureau of Ships General Correspondence 1940–1945, NACP; On Atwood & Morrill, see "Contract NOd 2796, March 12, 1941," U.S. Navy Shipbuilding Contracts Vol. 12, Navy Department Library, Rare Book Room, Washington Navy Yard, Washington, DC.

117. Small to Lynge, Mar. 22, 1942, Box 549, Entry A1 1266-L, RG 19, Bureau of Ships General Correspondence 1940–1945, NACP.

118. On Grove, see Wolpman to Bureau of Ships, Mar. 1, 1942; "Negotiations for the Expansion of Plant Facilities," Apr. 18, 1942; Stewart to Bureau of Ships, July 3, 1943, both in Box 549, Entry A1 1266-L, RG 19, Bureau of Ships General Correspondence 1940–1945, NACP; "Grove," *Journal of the American Society of Naval Engineers* 54 (Feb. 1942): 68. On Schutte & Koerting, see Teller to Bureau of Supplies and Accounts, Mar. 31, 1941, Box 424; Hamner to Schutte & Koerting, Apr. 9, 1942; Schutte & Koerting to Hamner, Apr. 14, 1942, Box 924, Entry A1 1266-L, RG 19, Bureau of Ships General Correspondence 1940–1945, NACP. On Manning, Maxwell, and Moore, see Merrill to Rawlings, Oct. 26, 1942; Kane, "Memorandum," Jan. 8, 1943, Box 707, Bureau of Ships General Correspondence 1940–1945, RG 19, NACP; see also Bureau of Ships, "Administrative History, vol. 2," 182.

119. Clark to Brand, June 24, 1943, Box 970, Bureau of Ships General Correspondence 1940–1945, RG 19, NACP.

120. Downward to Colvin, Mar. 2, 1942, Box 970, Bureau of Ships General Correspondence 1940–1945, RG 19, NACP.

121. "Memorandum of Conference Held in Bureau of Ships," Apr. 1, 1941; Collins to Supervisor of Shipbuilding Quincy, June 12, 1941; Colvin, "Minutes of Conference," Jan. 12, 1942; Hyland to Sturtevant, Mar. 13, 1943, Box 970, Entry A1 1266-L, RG 19, Bureau of Ships General Correspondence 1940–1945, NACP; Hyland to Inspector of Naval Material Pittsburgh, July 15, 1941, Box 450, Bureau of Ships General Correspondence 1940–1945, RG 19, NACP; B. F. Sturtevant, *Mechanical Draft: A Practical Treatise* (Catalogue No. 98) (Chicago, 1898), 279–81.

122. Bowen, *Ships, Machinery, and Mossbacks*, 236.

123. Bowen, *Ships, Machinery, and Mossbacks*, 237.

124. Quoted in Bowen, *Ships, Machinery, and Mossbacks*, 239.

125. *Shipyard Worker*, May 22, 1942, 8; "Memorandum of Conference," Apr. 19, 1940, Entry A1 1266-C, RG 19, Bureau of Ships General Correspondence 1940–1945, NACP.

126. "Bethlehem Ship," *Fortune* 32 (Aug. 1945): 222.

127. Pratt to Navy Cost Inspector, June 22, 1945, Box 194, Entry A1 1266-L, RG 19, Bureau of Ships General Correspondence 1940–1945, NACP; see also National Labor Relations Board, "In the Matter of Bethlehem-Hingham Shipyard, Inc. and Bethlehem-Hingham Shipyard Independent Union," *Decisions and Orders of the National Labor Relations Board*, vol. 60 (Washington, DC: Government Printing Office, 1945), 1,075–79.

128. "Bethlehem Ship," 222.

129. Quoted in Bruce H. Franklin, *The Buckley-Class Destroyer Escorts* (Annapolis, MD: Naval Institute Press, 1999), 19.

130. David H. Hendrickson, *The Patrol Frigate Story: The Tacoma-Class Frigates in World War II and the Korean War 1943–1953* (Jacksonville, FL: Fortis, 2011).

131. *Walsh-Kaiser Co.: Hearings*, 307–8 (Report on Survey: Walsh-Kaiser Shipyard, Providence, RI, Nov. 22, 1943).

132. Richard A. Russell, *Project Hula: Secret Soviet-American Cooperation in the War against Japan* (Washington, DC: Naval Historical Center, 1997), 22–24.

133. Quoted in David K. Brown, *Nelson to Vanguard: Warship Design and Development 1923–1945* (Barnsley, UK: Seaforth Publishing, 2000), 131.

134. Clarke, *Building Ships on the North East Coast*, 325–26; Patrick Boniface, *Loch Class Frigates* (Lodge Hill, UK: Maritime Press, 2013), 1–6.

135. A. W. Watson, "Corvettes and Frigates," *Transactions of the Institution of Naval Architects* 89 (1947): 165–85; David K. Brown, *The Design and Construction of British Warships 1939–1945: The Official Record*, vol. 2: *Submarines, Escorts and Coastal Forces* (Annapolis, MD: Naval Institute Press, 1996), 55–60.

136. Quoted in David K. Brown, *Atlantic Escorts: Ships, Weapons, and Tactics In World War II* (Barnsley, UK: Seaforth Publishing, 2007), 123.

137. Quoted in Brown, *Nelson to Vanguard*, 131.

138. "Naval New Construction Programmes," 248.

139. For a concise overview, see Adam Tooze, *The Wages of Destruction: The Making and Breaking of the Nazi Economy* (New York: Penguin, 2008), 612–18.

140. Rössler, *Geschichte des deutschen Ubootbaus*, 302–8.

141. Blohm, Memorandum for Gauleiter of Hamburg, Sep. 4, 1944, reprinted as Exhibit E (English translation) in U.S. Strategic Bombing Survey, Munitions Division, *Blohm & Voss Shipyards, Hamburg, Germany* (Washington, DC: U.S. Strategic Bombing Survey, 1947), E-1.

142. Blohm, Memorandum for Gauleiter of Hamburg, E-3.

143. Blohm, Memorandum for Gauleiter of Hamburg, E-4.

144. Arendt and Oelfken, "Baumethoden der deutschen U-Boote," 78–85.

145. Henry Schade, "German Wartime Technical Developments," *Transactions of the Society of Naval Architects and Marine Engineers* 54 (1946): 84–90; U.S. Strategic Bombing Survey, Submarine Branch, *German Submarine Industry Report* (Washington, DC: Government Printing Office, 1947).

146. Charles K. Hyde, *Arsenal of Democracy: The American Automobile Industry in World War II* (Detroit, MI: Wayne State University Press, 2013), 106.

Conclusion: Warship Building, Batch Production, and the U.S. Industrial Economy

1. Quoted in Gregory D. Sumner, *Detroit in World War II* (Charleston, SC: History Press, 2015), 16.

2. James Culliton, "Economics and Shipbuilding," *The Shipbuilding Business of the United States of America*, vol. 1, ed. Frederick G. Fassett Jr. (New York: Society of Naval Architects and Marine Engineers, 1948), 5.

3. *The Use and Disposition of Ships and Shipyards at the End of World War II: A Report Prepared for the United States Navy Department and the United States Maritime Commission by the Graduate School of Business Administration Harvard University* (Washington, DC: Government Printing Office, 1945), 161.

4. Philip Scranton, "Diversity in Diversity: Flexible Production and American Industrialization, 1880–1930," *Business History Review* 65 (Spring 1991): 35.

5. Chief of the Bureau of Ships to Chief of Office of Procurement & Material, Oct. 12, 1942, reprinted in *Problems of Small Business Enterprises*, Part 10: *Smaller Concerns in War Production I: Hearings Before the Special Subcommittee to Study and Survey the Problems of Small Business Enterprises*, 76th Cong., 2nd Sess., 1,228 (1942).

6. Robert G. Ferguson, "One Thousand Planes a Day: Ford, Grumman, General Motors and the Arsenal of Democracy," *History and Technology* 21 (June 2005): 150.

7. Jonathan Zeitlin, "Flexibility and Mass Production at War: Aircraft Manufacture in Britain, the United States, and Germany, 1939–1945," *Technology and Culture* 36 (Jan. 1995): 59.

8. Ferguson, "One Thousand Planes a Day," 166 (quote); on tooling, see Cristiano A. Ristuccia and Adam Tooze's important study "Machine Tools and Mass Production in the Armaments Boom: Germany and the United States, 1929–44," *Economic History Review* 66 (2013): 953–74.

9. Ferguson, "One Thousand Planes a Day," 168.

10. Scranton, "Diversity in Diversity," 32.

BIBLIOGRAPHY

Primary Sources
Archival Collections

Bremen State Archives, Bremen, Germany

Brooklyn Historical Society, Brooklyn, NY

Brooklyn Navy Yard Development Corporation, Brooklyn, NY

Camden County Historical Society of New Jersey, Camden, NJ

Columbia University Archives, New York, NY

Franklin D. Roosevelt Presidential Library and Museum, Hyde Park, NY

Hagley Museum & Library, Wilmington, DE

Hamburg State Archives, Hamburg, Germany

Historical Society of Pennsylvania, Philadelphia, PA

J. Welles Henderson Archives and Library, Independence Seaport Museum, Philadelphia, PA

Krupp Historical Archive, Essen, Germany

Mitchell Library Special Collections, Glasgow, UK

National Archives of the United Kingdom, Kew

National Archives of the United States, College Park, MD

National Archives of the United States, Mid-Atlantic Region, Philadelphia, PA

National Archives of the United States, Northeast Region, New York, NY

National Archives of the United States, Washington, DC

Navy Department Library, Washington Navy Yard, Washington, DC

Tyne & Wear Archives in Newcastle Upon Tyne, UK

University of Glasgow Archives, Glasgow, UK

University of Maryland Libraries' Archival Collections, College Park, MD

Wirral Archives, Birkenhead, UK

Public Documents

British Intelligence Objectives Sub-Committee. *Shipbuilding: Notes on Visits to Blohm und Voss, Deutsche Werft, Germania Werft and Deschimag*. London: His Majesty's Stationery Office, 1947.

Bureau of Construction and Repair. *Annual Report of the Bureau of Construction and Repair for Fiscal Year Ended June 30, 1925*. Washington, DC: Government Printing Office, 1925.

————. *C. and R. Bulletin No. 1: All-Welded Garbage Lighter, YG16: A Discussion of the Electric Welding Process of Ship Construction*. Washington, DC: Government Printing Office, 1931.

————. *History of the Construction Corps of the United States Navy*. Washington, DC: Government Printing Office, 1937.

Bureau of Yards and Docks. *Building the Navy's Bases in World War II: History of the Bureau of Yards and Docks and the Civil Engineer Corps, 1940–1946*. Vol. 1. Washington, DC: Government Printing Office, 1947.

Civilian Production Administration, Bureau of Demobilization, Special Study No. 26. *Shipbuilding Policies of the War Production Board, January 1942–November 1945*. Washington, DC: Civilian Production Administration, 1947.

Coleman, Charles H. *Shipbuilding Activities of the National Defense Advisory Commission and Office of Production Management, July 1940 to December 1941*. Washington, DC: War Production Board, 1946.

Decisions and Orders of the National Labor Relations Board. Vol. 57. Washington, DC: Government Printing Office, 1945.

Fesler, James L. *Industrial Mobilization for War: A History of the War Productions Board*. Vol. 1. Washington, DC: Civilian Production Administration, 1947.

Furer, Julius A. *Administration of the Navy Department in World War II*. Washington, DC: Government Printing Office, 1959.

Harvey, Oswald L. *Report on Apprenticeship System of Newport News Shipbuilding and Dry Dock Company, Newport News, Va.* Washington, DC: Federal Committee on Apprenticeship, Division of Labor Standards, U.S. Department of Labor, 1940.

Japan's Shipping and Shipbuilding Position, 1928–36: OIR Report No. 4712, June 25, 1948. Washington, DC: Department of State, Division of Research for Far East, 1948.

Lewis, Elmer A. *Laws Relating to National Defense Enacted During the Seventy-Eighth Congress*. Washington, DC: Government Printing Office, 1945.

Marsh, Edward M. *Wartime Employment, Production, and Conditions of Work in Shipyards.* Washington, DC: Government Printing Office, 1945.

Merchant Marine Act of 1936. 74th Cong., 1st Sess., June 29, 1936.

Minutes of Evidence Taken before the Royal Commission on the Private Manufacture of and Trading in Arms. London: His Majesty's Stationery Office, 1936.

National Emergency Council. *Report to the President of the United States from the Acting Executive Director of the National Emergency Council.* Washington, DC: Government Printing Office, 1935.

National Labor Relations Board. *Decisions and Orders of the National Labor Relations Board.* Vol. 60. Washington, DC: Government Printing Office, 1945.

Public Works Administration. *Letter from the Administrator of Public Works Transmitting Pursuant to Senate Resolution No. 190 a Report of the Business of the Federal Emergency Administrator of Public Works for the Period Ending February 15, 1934.* Washington, DC: Government Printing Office, 1934.

Rowland, Buford, and William B. Boyd. *The U.S. Navy Bureau of Ordnance in World War II.* Washington, DC: Bureau of Ordnance, 1953.

Saugstad, Jesse E. *Shipping and Shipbuilding Subsidies: A Study of State Aid to the Shipping and Shipbuilding Industries in Various Countries of the World.* Washington, DC: Department of Commerce, 1932.

U.S. Army, Military History Section Headquarters, Army Forces Far East. *Outline of Naval Armament and Preparations for War. Japanese Monograph No. 172.* Washington, DC: Office of the Chief of Military History, Department of the Army, n.d.

U.S. Army Far East Command. *Outline of Naval Armament and Preparations for War, Part I.* Washington, DC: Department of the Army, Office of the Chief of Military History, 1952.

U.S. Department of Commerce. *Statistical Abstract of the United States.* Washington, DC: Government Printing Office, 1933–39.

U.S. Department of the Navy. *Administrative Reference Service Report No. 7A: Principal Officials and Officers, Navy Department and United States Fleet, September 1, 1939–June 1, 1945.* Washington, DC: Office of Records Administration, Administrative Office, Navy Department, 1945.

———. *Officers of the Navy and Marine Corps on Active Duty in the District of Columbia.* Washington, DC: Government Printing Office, 1938.

———. *U.S. Navy Regulations 1920.* Washington, DC: Government Printing Office, 1920.

U.S. Department of the Navy, Office of the Chief of Naval Operations. *Combatant Shipbuilding 11/42 to 7/1/46*. Washington, DC: U.S. Department of the Navy, 1946.

U.S. Maritime Commission. *Report to Congress for the Period Ended October 25, 1939*. Washington, DC: Government Printing Office, 1940.

U.S. National Defense Advisory Commission. *National Defense Program Contracts and Expenditures (Exclusive of Contracts Not Made Public)*. Washington, DC: Office of Government Reports, 1940.

U.S. Navy, Pacific Fleet and Pacific Ocean Areas. *Japanese Naval Shipbuilding: "Know Your Enemy!" CinCPac-CinCPOA Bulletin 142-45*. Washington, DC, 1945.

U.S. Secretary of the Navy. *Annual Reports Fiscal Years 1922–1945*. Washington, DC: Government Printing Office, 1923–1946.

U.S. Strategic Bombing Survey. *Japanese Naval Shipbuilding*. Washington, DC: Government Printing Office, 1946.

U.S. Strategic Bombing Survey, Munitions Division. *Blohm & Voss Shipyards, Hamburg, Germany*. Washington, DC: U.S. Strategic Bombing Survey, 1947.

———. *Deutsche Schiff und Maschinenbau Bremen, Germany*. Washington, DC: US Strategic Bombing Survey Munitions Division, 1947.

———. *Friedrich Krupp Germaniawerft Kiel*. Washington, DC: U.S. Strategic Bombing Survey Munitions Division, 1947.

U.S. Strategic Bombing Survey, Submarine Branch. *German Submarine Industry Report*. Washington, DC: Government Printing Office, 1947.

U.S. Surplus Property Administration. *Report of the Surplus Property Administration to the Congress, January 31, 1946*. Washington, DC: Government Printing Office, 1946.

U.S. Technical Mission to Japan. *Report No. S-01-2: Characteristics of Japanese Naval Vessels, Article 2: Surface Warship Machinery Design*. San Francisco: U.S. Technical Mission to Japan, 1945.

———. *Report No. S-81(N): Welding in Japanese Naval Construction*. San Francisco: U.S. Technical Mission to Japan, 1946.

U.S. War Production Board. *An Introduction to Shipbuilding, Prepared and Made Available by Shipbuilding Division, Bethlehem Steel Company*. Washington, DC: Government Printing Office, 1942.

———. *Shipbuilding Activities of the National Defense Advisory Commission and Office of Production Management, July 1940 to December 1941*. Washington, DC: War Production Board, 1945.

U.S. War Production Board, Policy Analysis and Records Branch, Office of the Executive Secretary. *The Naval and Maritime Shipbuilding Programs, May 1940 to June 1944.* Washington, DC: War Production Board, 1944.

The Use and Disposition of Ships and Shipyards at the End of World War II: A Report Prepared for the United States Navy Department and the United States Maritime Commission by the Graduate School of Business Administration Harvard University. Washington, DC: Government Printing Office, 1946.

Congressional Hearings, Debates, and Reports

1945 Extension of Termination Date of Renegotiation Act: Hearings for the House Ways and Means Committee. 79th Cong. 1st Sess. (1945).

Additional Shipbuilding and Ordnance Manufacturing Facilities for the United States Navy, and for Other Purposes: Hearings on H.R. 1437 Before the House Committee on Naval Affairs. 77th Cong., 1st Sess. (1941).

Authorizing Major Alterations to Certain Naval Vessels and Additional Shipbuilding Facilities and Equipment for the Navy: Hearings Before the Senate Committee on Naval Affairs on H.R. 1053 (S. 355) and H.R. 1437 (S. 356). 77th Cong., 1st Sess. (1941).

Conditions of Government Contracts: Hearings Before Subcommittee No. 1 of the House Committee on the Judiciary. 76th Cong., 3rd Sess. (1940).

Congressional Record. 76th Cong., 3rd Sess. (June 22, 1940).

Establish the Composition of the United States Navy: Hearings Before the House Committee on Naval Affairs. 75th Cong., 3rd Sess. (1938).

Establishing an Office of Budget and Reports in the Navy Department, and for Other Purposes (H.R. 3782): Hearings Before the House Committee on Naval Affairs. 77th Cong., 1st Sess. (1941).

Excess Profits Taxation, 1940: Joint Hearings of the Senate Committee on Finance and the House Committee on Ways and Means. 76th Cong., 3rd Sess. (1940).

First Supplemental National Defense Appropriation Bill for 1942: Hearings Before the Subcommittee of the House Committee on Appropriations. 77th Cong., 1st Sess. (1941).

Investigation of Congested Areas, Part 1: Hampton Roads, Virginia, Area: Hearings Before a Subcommittee of the House Committee on Naval Affairs. 78th Cong., 1st Sess. (1943).

Investigation of Congested Areas, Part 6: Puget Sound, Washington, Area: Hearings Before a Subcommittee of the House Committee on Naval Affairs. 78th Cong., 1st Sess. (1943).

Investigation of the National Defense Program: Hearings Before the Special Senate Committee Investigating the National Defense Program, Part 25: Reconversion. Disposal of Surplus Property. 78th Cong., 2nd Sess. (1944).

Investigation of the National Defense Program, Part 5: Hearings Before the Special Sen-ate Committee Investigating the National Defense Program: Emergency Shipbuilding Program. 77th Cong., 1st Sess. (1941).

Investigation of the National Defense Program, Part 17: Hearings Before the Special Senate Committee Investigating the National Defense Program: Farm Machinery and Equipment, Concrete Barges, Army Commissions and Military Activities of Motion Picture Personnel, Pipe Line Transportation, Absenteeism in the Defense Industry. 78th Cong., 1st Sess. (1943).

Investigation of the National Defense Program: Reorganization of Navy Yards: Addi-tional Report of the Special Senate Committee Investigating the National Defense Program, Report No. 10, Part 16. 78th Cong., 2nd Sess. (1944).

Investigation of the National Defense Program: Reorganization of Navy Yards: Executive Session. Hearings Before the Special Senate Committee Investigating the National Defense Program. 79th Cong., 1st Sess. (1945).

Investigation of the Naval Defense Program: Supplemental Report. House Report No. 2371: Supplemental Report By the House Committee on Naval Affairs. 77th Cong., 2nd Sess. (1942).

Investigation of the Progress of the War Effort: Hearings Before the House Committee on Naval Affairs. Renegotiation of War Contracts. 78th Cong., 1st Sess. (1943).

Investigation of the Progress of the War Effort: Policies and Practices Relating to Civil Employment in the Navy Department: Report of the House Committee on Naval Affairs. 79th Cong., 2nd Sess., 8 (1947).

Investigations of the Progress of the War Effort: Report of the House Committee on Naval Affairs. 78th Cong., 2nd Sess. (1944).

Investigation of the Progress of the War Effort, Vol. 5: Gibbs & Cox: Hearings Before the House Committee on Naval Affairs. 78th Cong., 2nd Sess. (1944).

Merchant Marine: Hearings before the House Committee on the Merchant Marine and Fisheries. 70th Cong., 1st Sess. (1928).

Munitions Industry, Part 1: Electric Boat Co. Hearings Before the Special Senate Com-mittee Investigating the Munitions Industry. 73rd Cong. (1934).

Munitions Industry, Part 18: Naval Shipbuilding: New York Shipbuilding Corporation. Hearings Before the Special Senate Committee Investigating the Munitions Industry. 74th Cong., 1st Sess. (1935).

Munitions Industry, Part 19: Naval Shipbuilding: New York Shipbuilding Corporation. Hearings Before the Special Senate Committee Investigating the Munitions Industry. 74th Cong., 1st Sess. (1935).

Munitions Industry, Part 20: Naval Shipbuilding: Newport News Shipbuilding and Dry Dock Company. Hearings Before the Special Senate Committee Investigating the Munitions Industry. 74th Cong., 1st Sess. (1935).

Munitions Industry, Part 21: Naval Shipbuilding: Bethlehem Shipbuilding Corporation. Hearings Before the Special Senate Committee Investigating the Munitions Industry. 74th Cong., 1st Sess. (1935).

Munitions Industry. Part 23: Naval Shipbuilding: Federal Shipbuilding and Dry Dock Co.; Bath Iron Works Corp.; Sun Shipbuilding and Dry Dock Co., United Dry Docks, Inc.: Hearings Before the Special Senate Committee Investigating the Munitions Industry, 74th Cong., 1st Sess. (1935).

Munitions Industry, Part 24: Limitation of War Profits and Naval Shipbuilding: Hearings Before the Special Senate Committee Investigating the Munitions Industry. 74th Cong., 1st Sess. (1935).

Munitions Industry, Part 35: Exhibits on Wartime and Post-War Financing. Hearings Before the Special Senate Committee Investigating the Munitions Industry. 74th Cong., 2nd Sess. (1936).

Munitions Industry, Part 36: Report on Government Manufacture of Munitions. Hearings Before the Special Senate Committee Investigating the Munitions Industry. 74th Cong., 2nd Sess. (1936).

Munitions Industry, Preliminary Report of the Special Committee on Investigation of the Munitions Industry. 74th Cong., 1st Sess. (1935).

National Defense Migration, Part 14: Hearings Before the Select House Committee Investigating National Defense Migration: Trenton Hearings. 77th Cong., 1st Sess. (1941).

National Defense Migration, Part 32: Hearings Before the Select House Committee Investigating National Defense Migration: Huntsville Hearings, 77th Cong., 2nd Sess. (1942).

National Labor Relations Act and Proposed Amendments, Part 21: Hearings Before the Senate Committee on Education and Labor. 76th Cong., 1st Sess. (1939).

Navy Department Appropriation Bill for 1929: Hearings Before Subcommittee of House Committee on Appropriations. 70th Cong., 1st Sess. (1928).

Navy Department Appropriation Bill for 1939: Hearings Before the Subcommittee of House Committee on Appropriations. 75th Cong., 3rd Sess. (1937).

Navy Department Appropriation Bill for 1940: Hearings Before the Subcommittee of the House Committee on Appropriations. 76th Cong., 1st Sess. (1941).

Navy Department Appropriation Bill for 1941: Hearings Before the Subcommittee of the House Committee on Appropriations. 76th Cong., 3rd Sess. (1941).

Navy Department Appropriation Bill for 1942: Hearings Before the Subcommittee of the House Committee on Appropriations. 77th Cong., 1st Sess. (1941).

Navy Department Appropriation Bill for 1943: Hearings Before the Subcommittee of the House Committee on Appropriations, 77th Cong., 2nd Sess. (1942).

Nomination of William Franklin Knox: Hearings Before the Senate Committee on Naval Affairs. 76th Cong., 3rd Sess. (1940).

Pearl Harbor Attack: Hearings before the Joint Committee on the Investigation of the Pearl Harbor Attack, Part 17: Joint Committee Exhibits Nos. 111 Through 128. 79th Cong., 2nd Sess. (1946).

Pearl Harbor Attack: Hearings before the Joint Committee on the Investigation of the Pearl Harbor Attack, Part 33: Proceedings of Navy Court of Inquiry. 79th Cong., 1st Sess. (1946).

Problems of American Small Business, Part 30: Navy Yard Subcontracting and the Type C Contract: Hearings Before the Special Senate Committee to Study and Survey Problems of Small Business Enterprises. 78th Cong., 1st Sess. (1943).

Problems of Small Business Enterprises, Part 10: Smaller Concerns in War Production I: Hearings Before the Special Subcommittee to Study and Survey the Problems of Small Business Enterprises. 76th Cong., 2nd Sess. (1942).

Production in Shipbuilding Plants, Part 1: Executive Hearings Before the House Committee on the Merchant Marine and Fisheries. 78th Cong., 1st Sess. (1943).

Proposed Amendments to the Securities Act of 1933 and to the Securities Exchange Act of 1934: Hearings Before the House Committee on Interstate and Foreign Commerce. 77th Cong., 1st Sess. (1941).

Reorganization of the Navy Department and Transfer of the Construction Corps to the Line: Hearings Before the Senate Committee on Naval Affairs on S. 4026 (H.R. 9266) and S. 9450 (H.R. 9450). 76th Cong., 3rd Sess. (1940).

Report of Subcommittee of Committee on Naval Affairs on Private Shipbuilding Companies on the Pacific Coast. 77th Cong., 2nd Sess. (1942).

The Revenue Bill of 1941. Report 673, Part 3: Individual Views to Accompany H.R. 5417 (Robert LaFollette). 77th Cong., 1st Sess., 17 (1941).

Second Deficiency Appropriation Bill for 1938: Hearings Before the Subcommittee of the House Committee on Appropriations. 75th Cong., 3rd Sess. (1938).

Senate Document No. 40. Letter from the Secretary of the Treasury. Statement Relative to Funds under the N.R.A. 74th Cong., 1st Sess. (1935).

Seniority Rights for Employees at Government Navy Yards, Arsenals, Etc.: Hearings Before the Senate Committee on Naval Affairs. 79th Cong., 1st Sess. (1945).

Sundry Legislation Affecting the Naval Establishment 1930–1931: Hearings Before the House Committee on Naval Affairs. 71st Cong., 3rd Sess. (1930).

Sundry Legislation Affecting the Naval Establishment 1941: Hearings Before the House Committee on Naval Affairs. 77th Cong., 1st Sess. (1941).

Sundry Legislation Affecting the Naval Establishment, No. 89: Manpower Utilization in the Navy Yard, New York: A Report of the Johnson Subcommittee of the House Committee on Naval Affairs. 79th Cong., 1st Sess. (1945).

Supplemental Navy Department Appropriation Bill for 1943: Hearings Before the Subcommittee of the House Committee on Appropriations. 78th Cong., 1st Sess. (1943).

Third Supplemental National Defense Appropriation Bill for 1942, Part 2: Hearings Before the Subcommittee of the House Committee on Appropriation on Military and Naval Establishments and Lend-Lease. 77th Cong., 1st Sess., 4 (1941).

To Authorize the Construction of Certain Naval Vessels: Hearings on H.R. 11526 Before the Senate Committee on Naval Affairs. 70th Cong., 1st Sess. (1928).

To Authorize the Construction of Certain Naval Vessels for Replacement and Additions, and for Other Purposes (H.R. 6661 and H.R. 8230): Hearings Before the House Committee on Naval Affairs. 71st Cong., 3rd Sess. (1931).

To Establish the Composition of the United States Navy, to Authorize the Construction of Certain Naval Vessels, and for Other Purposes: Hearings Before the House Committee on Naval Affairs on H.R. 7665 and H.R. 8026. 76th Cong., 3rd Sess. (1940).

To Establish the Composition of the United States Navy, to Authorize the Construction of Certain Naval Vessels, and for Other Purposes: Hearings on H.R. 10100 Before the House Committee on Naval Affairs. 76th Cong., 3rd Sess. (1940).

To Expedite Naval Shipbuilding: Hearings Before the Senate Committee on Naval Affairs on H.R. 9822 to Expedite Naval Shipbuilding, and For Other Purposes. 76th Cong., 3rd Sess. (1940).

To Expedite Naval Shipbuilding: Hearings on H.R. 9822 Before the House Committee on Naval Affairs. 76th Cong., 3rd Sess. (1940).

Walsh-Kaiser Co.: Hearings Before the Subcommittee on Production in Shipbuilding Plants of the House Committee on the Merchant Marine and Fisheries. 78th Cong., 2nd Sess., 20 (1944).

Newspapers and Magazines

Apprentice (Philadelphia Navy Yard)

Brooklyn Eagle

Cramp News

Cramp Ways

Fairplay

Navy Yard Beacon (Philadelphia Navy Yard)

New York Times

Popular Science Monthly
The Shipworker
The Shipyard Worker
Washington Post

Books and Pamphlets

Comstock, John P. *Introduction to Naval Architecture*. Newport News, VA: Newport News Shipbuilding and Dry Dock Company, 1944.

Cramp Shipbuilding Company, Philadelphia, Pennsylvania, 1940–1944. Philadelphia: Cramp Shipbuilding Company, 1944.

Dravo Corporation. *Submerged Shipways: An Account of Pioneer Engineering and Construction of Two Horizontal Shipways of Unique Design at Newport News, Virginia, 1940–1942*. Pittsburg, PA: Dravo Corporation, 1945.

Federal Writers' Project. *New York Learns: A Guide to the Educational Facilities of the Metropolis*. New York: Barrows & Co., 1939.

Ferguson, William B. *Shipbuilding Cost and Production Methods*. New York: Cornell Maritime Press, 1944.

Garyantes, H. F. *Handbook for Shipwrights*. New York: McGraw-Hill, 1944.

Joint Committee of the Shipbuilding Employers' Federation and Shipyard Trade Unions. *Report of Joint Inquiry into Foreign Competition and Conditions in the Shipbuilding Industry*. London: Whitehead Morris, 1926.

Manning, George C. *Principles of Warship Construction and Damage Control*. Annapolis, MD: Naval Institute Press, 1935.

Manning, George C., and T. L. Schumacher. *Principles of Naval Architecture and Warship Construction*. Annapolis, MD: Naval Institute Press, 1924.

McMillin, Lucille F. *The Second Year: A Study of Women's Participation in War Activities of the Federal Government*. Washington, DC: Government Printing Office, 1943.

Mitsubishi Economic Research Bureau. *Japanese Trade and Industry: Present and Future*. London: Macmillan, 1936.

Naval Machinery 1946 Part I. Annapolis, MD: U.S. Naval Academy, 1946.

Naval Machinery Part IV: Marine and Naval Boilers. Annapolis, MD: Naval Institute Press, 1935.

Naval Ordnance: A Text-Book Prepared for the Use of the Midshipmen of the United States Naval Academy. Annapolis, MD: Naval Institute Press, 1921.

Navy Yard Development Association Charleston, SC. *Navy Day*, Oct. 7, 1939.

New York Shipbuilding Corporation. *Annual Reports 1930–1945*. Camden, NJ: New York Shipbuilding Corporation, 1931–46.

———. *Fifty Years*. Camden, NJ: New York Shipbuilding Corporation, 1948.

Newport News Shipbuilding and Dry Dock Company. *Annual Report 1955*. Newport News, VA: Newport News Shipbuilding and Dry Dock Company, 1955.

—. *The Apprentice School*. Newport News, VA: Newport News Shipbuilding and Dry Dock Company, 1935.

—. *The Shipyard in Peace and War*. Newport News, VA: Newport News Shipbuilding and Dry Dock Company, 1944.

Owens, James W. *Fundamentals of Welding Gas, Arc and Thermit: A Textbook for Governmental Engineering Departments, Colleges, Technical Schools, Etc.* Cleveland, OH: Penton, 1923.

Public Papers and Addresses of Franklin D. Roosevelt, 1934. Vol. 3: *The Advance of Recovery and Reform*. New York: Macmillan, 1938.

Public Papers and Addresses of Franklin D. Roosevelt, 1938: The Continuing Struggle for Liberalism. New York: Macmillan, 1941.

Rossell, Henry E. *Riveting and Arc Welding in Ship Construction*. New York: Simmons Boardman Publishing, 1934.

—. *The Training of Shipyard Personnel*. New York: Society of Naval Architects and Marine Engineers, 1941.

Ship Erection: A Manual of Instruction for Pre-Employment and Supplementary Training. Harrisburg, PA: Department of Public Instruction, 1942.

Shipbuilding Shop Fabrication. Harrisburg, PA: Department of Public Instruction, 1942.

Shipfitting Practice: A Manual of Instruction for Pre-Employment and Supplementary Training. Harrisburg, PA: Department of Public Instruction, 1942.

Smith, Edgar C. *A Short History of Naval and Marine Engineering*, 1938; repr. Cambridge, UK: Cambridge University Press, 2013.

Thomas, R. J. *Housing for Defense*. Detroit: United Auto Workers, 1942.

Warren, Glenn B. *Development of Steam Turbines for Main Propulsion of High-Powered Combatant Ships*. New York: Society of Naval Architects and Marine Engineers, 1946.

Welding of Armor in World War II. Watertown, MA: Watertown Arsenal, 1946.

Woodbury, David O. *Battlefronts of Industry: Westinghouse in World War II*. New York: Wiley, 1948.

Articles and Chapters in Books

"$17,500,000 Firm Bid Submitted by Newport News, Lowest Bidder on United States Lines Cabin Ship." *Marine Engineering* (Oct. 1937): 553.

"$3,861,053,312 for Naval Construction: Navy Department Places Contracts for Two-Hundred Combatant Ships." *Marine Engineering* 46 (Oct. 1940): 110–12.

"American Engineers Plan Cargo Ship Without Rivets." *Marine Engineering* 25 (Aug. 1920): 701.

"Arc-Welded Tanker J.W. Van Dyke." *Marine Engineering* 43 (1938): 166–71.

Arnott, David. "Welding in Shipbuilding." *Journal of the American Society for Naval Engineers* 53 (Jan. 1941): 211–27.

Atkins, L. M. "The Manufacture of Marine Propellers." *Journal of the American Society for Naval Engineers* 47 (May 1935): 229–40.

Atsushi Oi. "Why Japan's Anti-Submarine Warfare Failed." U.S. Naval Institute *Proceedings* 78 (June 1952): 587–90.

"Baldwin Acquires Cramp-Morris Properties." *Marine Engineering* 36 (1931): 303.

Bennett, William. "Recent Developments in Special Quality Steels for Shipbuilding." *Transactions of the Society of Naval Architects and Marine Engineers* 39 (1931): 63–84.

"Bethlehem and Sun Ship Submit Low Bids for Building Export Ships." *Marine Engineering* (June 1938): 294.

"Bethlehem Ship." *Fortune* 32 (Aug. 1945): 222.

"Birth of a Propeller." *Marine Engineering* 64 (Mar. 1940): 61.

"Boiler Tube Failure—Metallographic Examination." *Bulletin of Engineering Information* 13 (May 1924): 26–27.

Brierly, R. C. "The Development of B. & W. Boilers for Naval Vessels: Test of Four Boilers at the Fuel Oil Testing Plant." *Journal of the American Society for Naval Engineers* 41 (1929): 634–55.

Brooks, W. A. "The Building and Inspection of a Boiler." *Journal of the American Society for Naval Engineers* 43 (1931): 43–53.

Burkhart, John E. "The Present Trend in Marine Engineering in the United States of America." *Journal of the American Society for Naval Engineers* 50 (1938).

Chantry, Allan J. "Launching of USS 'New Jersey' and USS 'Wisconsin.'" *Transactions of the Society of Naval Architects and Marine Engineers* 52 (1944): 391–438.

Chapman, Lawrence B. "University Education in Ship Construction and Marine Transportation." *Transactions of the Society of Naval Architects and Marine Engineers* 28 (1920): 1–19.

"Charles N. Boylan." *Transactions of the Society of Naval Architects and Marine Engineers* 64 (1956): 642.

Charlton, Alexander M. "From General Board to Trial Board: The Evolution of a Man-of-War." *Journal of the American Society for Naval Engineers* 42 (1930): 39–71.

Cleary, F. J. "The Material Laboratory, U.S. Navy Yard, New York." *Journal of the American Society of Naval Engineers* 43 (1930): 54–104.

"Cord into Ships." *Time*. Aug. 14, 1933. 43.

Culliton, James. "Economics and Shipbuilding." In *The Shipbuilding Business of the United States of America*. Vol. 1, edited by Frederick G. Fassett Jr., 1–13. New York: Society of Naval Architects and Marine Engineers, 1948.

Diergarten, Hans H. "German Ship Builders Use Arc Welding Extensively." *Metal Progress* 22 (July 1932): 60.

"Enters Equipment Field." *Marine Review* 61 (Nov. 1931): 63.

"Ernest H. Rigg." *Transactions of the Society of Naval Architects and Marine Engineers* 64 (1956): 648.

Esler, Jay K. "U.S.S. Northampton, U.S.S. Chester, U.S.S. Houston: Construction, Description, and Official Preliminary Acceptance Trial Data." *Journal of the American Society for Naval Engineers* 42 (1930): 651–60.

Faerman, W. L. "Electric Welding Installation and Organization in Shipyards." *Transactions of the Royal Institution of Naval Architects* 79 (1937): 306–20.

"The Fate of the Former Imperial German Naval Yards." *Shipbuilder* 24 (Jan. 1921): 33–34.

Ferguson, Homer L. "Newport News Shipbuilding and Dry Dock Company," in *Historical Transactions, ed. Society of Naval Architects and Marine Engineers* (New York: Society of Naval Architects and Marine Engineers, 1943), 221.

Fish, E. R. "The Characteristics of Modern Boilers." *Journal of the American Society for Naval Engineers* 40 (1928): 107–11.

Fisher, Charles W. "Industrial Organization of Navy Yards." *U.S. Naval Institute Proceedings* 48 (May 1922): 761–87.

"Four Shipbuilders Submit Tenders on Panama Railroad Steamship Passenger Vessels." *Marine Engineering* (May 1937): 289.

Fox, Sea, and Frederick Lykes. "Turbine-Drive C-3 Cargo Ships." *Marine Engineering* 45 (May 1940): 54–61.

François, Charles. "Notes on Some Researches and Tendencies of Contemporary Naval Construction." *Transactions of the Royal Institution of Naval Architects* 73 (1931): 264–80.

"The Germanischer Lloyd Regulations for Electric Welding." *Marine Engineer and Motorship Builder* 55 (1932): 116–17.

Goldsmith, Lester M. "The High-Pressure, High-Temperature Turbo-Electric Tanker J.W. Van Dyke." *Marine Engineering* 43 (1938): 548–58.

Grassnick, A. J. "New Ingalls Shipyard." *Marine Engineering* 45 (Jan. 1940): 38–53.

Greenhalgh, James, and Angus D. MacDonnell. "The Mold Loft's Place in Production." *Marine Engineering* 47 (Mar. 1942): 122–23.

———. "The Mold Loft's Place in Production II." *Marine Engineering* 47 (Apr. 1942): 189.

———. "The Mold Loft's Place in Production III." *Marine Engineering* 47 (May 1942): 128–32.

Henley, E. K. "Propulsion Machinery in the Process of Construction." *Marine Engineering* 48 (Sep. 1942): 214–18.

Hodge, James C. "Marine Boiler Drums of Fusion Welded Construction." *Journal of the American Society for Naval Engineers* 45 (1933): 149–64.

———. "The Welding of Pressure Vessels." *Journal of the American Society for Naval Engineers* 48 (1936): 498–522.

Homer, Arthur B. "Shipyard Organization. Section 1. Standard Yards." In *The Shipbuilding Business of the United States of America*. Vol. 1, edited by Frederick G. Fassett Jr., 256–60. New York: Society of Naval Architects and Marine Engineers, 1948.

Howard, Herbert S. "What the Naval Building Program Means to Design." U.S. Naval Institute *Proceedings* 54 (Oct. 1928): 878–82.

Hunter, James B. "Some Effects of Welding on Ship Construction." *Transactions of the Society of Naval Architects and Marine Engineers* 45 (1937): 9–12.

"The Huntington Dynasty." *Fortune* 14 (Nov. 1936): 73–75, 190.

Hutchins, John G. B. "History and Development of Shipbuilding 1776–1944." In *The Shipbuilding Business of the United States of America*. Vol. 1, edited by Frederick G. Fassett Jr., 14–60. New York: Society of Naval Architects and Marine Engineers, 1948.

"Improving Power Endurance of Naval Warships." *Bureau of Ships Journal* 6 (Apr. 1958): 11.

Karsten, A. "Die röntgenographische Feinstruktur-Untersuchung und ihr Wert für die Schiffbautechnik." *Schiffbau, Schifffahrt und Hafenbau* 37 (June 1936): 204–6.

Kielhorn, C. "Die ersten schnellen Motorfrachtschiffe für den Liniendienst um die Erde Teil I." *Werft—Reederei—Hafen* 8 (Feb. 1927): 58–61.

King, J. H. "Marine Boilers for Higher Pressures and Temperatures and Their Contribution to Greater Economy." *Journal of the American Society for Naval Engineers* 40 (1928): 238–55.

Küchler, Paul. "Die Lichtbogenschweißung in Schiffbau." *Schifffbau, Schifffahrt und Hafenbau* 34 (Jan. 1933): 8–10.

"Labor Requirements for the Shipbuilding Industry." *Service Bulletin on Defense Training in Vocational Schools* 8 (Feb. 1941): 1–8.

Lamb, Carl L. "The Effect of Disarmament and Treaty Limits Upon Naval Engineering." *Journal of the American Society for Naval Engineers* 42 (1930): 641–50.

Lemler, Arthur. "Multiple Yards: Record and Prospect." In *The Shipbuilding Business of the United States of America*. Vol. 1, edited by Frederick G. Fassett Jr., 225–55. New York: Society of Naval Architects and Marine Engineers, 1948.

Lottmann, Herrmann, Paul Küchler, and Herrmann Burkhardt. "'Heute weiß ich, daß der Versuch scheitern mußte': Drei Originalberichte aus den Anfängen der Lichtbogenschweißtechnik in der deutschen Kriegsmarine und der Handelsschiffahrt." *Schiff und Zeit* 13 (1981): 45–47.

Mann, Charles S. "New Seattle-Tacoma Shipyard." *Marine Engineering* 46 (Mar. 1941): 54–64.

"Marine Welding Advanced." U.S. Naval Institute *Proceedings* 57 (Aug. 1931): 1,108.

Metten, John F. "Shipyard Layout. Section 1. Standard Yards." In *The Shipbuilding Business of the United States of America*. Vol. 1, edited by Frederick G. Fassett Jr., 201–11. New York: Society of Naval Architects and Marine Engineers, 1948.

Michel, R. "Factor of Safety and Working Stresses of Marine Propulsion Shafting." *Journal of the American Society for Naval Engineers* 54 (Feb. 1942): 50–57.

Mitchell, Donald W. "What Our Warships Cost." *The Nation*. Sep. 23, 1939. 320–22.

Mochel, Norman L. "Ten Years of Welding Development." *Journal of the American Society of Naval Engineers* 48 (1936): 455–75.

Montgomerie, James "Shipbuilding Practice Abroad." *Transactions of the North-East Coast Institution of Engineers and Shipbuilders* 54 (1938): 153–76.

Moore, Galen H. "Welded Machinery Foundations for Ships." *Journal of the American Welding Society* 10 (1932): 38–41.

Moss, L. Q. "Navy Yard Apprentice Training." *Marine Engineering* 40 (Oct. 1935): 372–79.

"Navy Department Awards Ship Contracts of $130,000,000 to Private Yards—Allocation of Ships to Navy Yards." *Marine Engineering* 38 (Sep. 1933): 6.

"Navy to X-Ray Vital Parts of Fleet." *Marine Engineering* 44 (Jan. 1939): 22.

"New York Shipbuilding Corporation Awarded Contract for a Battleship." *Marine Engineering* 44 (Jan. 1939): 28.

"New York Shipbuilding Corporation Gets $23,000,000 Naval Contract." *Marine Engineering* (Nov. 1938): 540.

"Newport News and Bethlehem Yards Awarded Contracts for a Battleship." *Marine Engineering* 43 (Dec. 1938): 588.

"Newport News Low Bidder on All Alternate Designs for Two Matson Cargo Ships." *Marine Engineering* (July 1936): 419.

"Personal." *Marine Engineering and Shipping Review* 44 (Oct. 1939): 495.

"Pity the Welder." *Marine Engineering* (Mar. 1939): 124–25.

Powell, Joseph W. "Labor in Shipbuilding." In *The Shipbuilding Business of the United States of America*. Vol. 1, edited by Frederick G. Fassett Jr., 271–94. New York: Society of Naval Architects and Marine Engineers, 1948.

Purvis, Frank P. "Japan's Contribution to Naval Architecture." *Transactions of the Royal Institution of Naval Architects* 67 (1925): 27–40.

Raper, R. G. "Main Machinery: How Do We Stand?" *Papers on Engineering Subjects* 7 (Sep. 1946): 66–76.

"Ready to Begin 'Iowa.'" U.S. Naval Institute *Proceedings* 66, no. 7 (July 1940): 1,033.

"Replacement Shipbuilding in Japan." *Far Eastern Review* 30 (Aug. 1934): 379–82.

Rigg, Ernest H. "Design and Construction of Passenger Steamers." *Transactions of the Society of Naval Architects and Marine Engineers* 29 (1921): 270–302.

Rock, George H. "Education of Naval Constructors and Naval Architects." *Transactions of the Society of Naval Architects and Marine Engineers* 40 (1932): 196–215.

Ronay, Bela. "The Fundamentals of Electric Arc Welding." *Journal of the American Society of Naval Engineers* 46 (1934): 21–30.

Roop, W. P. "Features of Practice Affecting Design." *Transactions of the Society of Naval Architects and Marine Engineers* 44 (1936): 335–37.

Ross, A. A. "Gears for U.S. Defense and Trade." *Marine Engineering* 44 (Dec. 1940): 62–67.

Rossell, Henry E. "Types of Naval Ships." In *Society of Naval Architects and Marine Engineers, Historical Transactions 1893–1943*, 248–329. New York: Society of Naval Architects and Marine Engineers, 1945.

Russell, B. A. "Welding as Viewed by the Shipbuilder." *Marine Engineering* 44 (July 1939): 316–20.

Schade, Henry. "German Wartime Technical Developments." *Transactions of the Society of Naval Architects and Marine Engineers* 54 (1946): 84–90.

Schoenmaker, P., and G. DeRooy. "More Modern Methods and Steels in Welded Ship Construction." *Welding Journal* 18 (May 1939): 273–76.

Schrader, W. O. "Progress of Electric Welding in Shipbuilding." *Marine Engineering* (Sep. 1936): 500–506.

Schuster, L. W. "The Effect of Contamination by Nitrogen on the Structure of Electric Welds." *Journal of the American Society for Naval Engineers* 43 (Feb. 1931): 140–47.

"Shipbuilder Urges Replacement Program." *Marine Engineering* 37 (Apr. 1932).

"Shipbuilding Declines During 1932 in United States Shipyards." *Marine Engineering* 38 (Jan. 1933): 310–11.

"Shipping Men Honor Professor L. B. Chapman." *Pacific Marine Review/The Log* 47 (July 1952): 24.

"Ships on the Ways." *Fortune* 14 (Nov. 1936): 67–72.

Silverman, Morris. "Lt. Comdr. Gokey Instructs Future Shipbuilders." *The* [Philadelphia Navy Yard] *Apprentice* 7 (Mar. 1937): 2.

Smith, H. Gerrish. "Shipyard Statistics." In *The Shipbuilding Business of the United States of America*. Vol. 1, edited by Frederick G. Fassett Jr., 61–200. New York: Society of Naval Architects and Marine Engineers, 1948.

Solov, Abraham. "Scheduling the Work of the Drafting Room: The Application of Scheduling in the Design Section of the Brooklyn Navy Yard." *Journal of the American Society of Naval Engineers* 57 (Aug. 1945): 317–23.

Stevens, E. A., Jr. "The Hull and its Screw Propeller." *Journal of the American Society for Naval Engineers* 54 (Aug. 1942): 372–406.

Stiles, L. C. "Welding of LST's at Seneca, Ill." *Journal of the American Welding Society* 24 (Nov. 1945): 1,053–60.

Sykes, W. E. "Methods Used in Producing Marine Gearing." *Transactions of the Society of Naval Architects and Marine Engineers* 43 (1935): 170–200.

"T. H. Bossert." *Marine Engineering* 40 (Feb. 1940): 75.

"T. L. Schumacher." *Transactions of the Society of Naval Architects and Marine Engineers* 60 (1952): 655.

"Thomas B. Richey." *Transactions of the Society of Naval Architects and Marine Engineers* 57 (1949): 596.

Walker, R. J., and S. S. Cook. "Mechanical Gears, of Double Reduction, for Merchant Ships." *Transactions of the Institution of Naval Architects* 63 (1921): 69–92.

Wallin, Homer N., and Henry A. Schade. "The Design and Construction of an Arc Welded Naval Auxiliary Vessel." In *Designing for Arc Welding: Second Lincoln Arc Welding Prize Competition Papers*, edited by A. F. Davis, 149–94. Cleveland, OH: Lincoln Electric Company, 1933.

Warriner, Robert. "Reduction Gear for Ship Propulsion." *Transactions of the Society of Naval Architects and Marine Engineers* 29 (1921): 13–21.

Watson, A. W. "Corvettes and Frigates." *Transactions of the Institution of Naval Architects* 89 (1947): 165–85.

Wetherbee, Charles P. "High Pressure and Superheat Aboard Ship." *Transactions of the Society of Naval Architects and Marine Engineers* 43 (1935): 225.

"William H. Collins." *Transactions of the Society of Naval Architects and Marine Engineers* 56 (1948): 578–80.

"William W. Smith, Comment on E. H. Rigg, 'Design and Construction of Passenger Steamers.'" *Transactions of the Society of Naval Architects and Marine Engineers* 29 (1921): 295.

Wilson, J. Lyell. "Ship Welding." *Marine Engineering* (Nov. 1936): 634–36.

Secondary Sources
Books

Adams, Cernida W. *Collis Porter Huntington*. Vol. 2. Newport News, VA: Mariners' Museum, 1954.

Alden, John D. *The Fleet Submarine in the U.S. Navy: A Design and Construction History*. Annapolis, MD: Naval Institute Press, 1979.

Amato, Ivan. *Pushing the Horizon: Seventy-Five Years of High Stakes Science and Technology at the Naval Research Laboratory*. Washington, DC: Naval Research Laboratory, 2001.

Amortization of Defense Facilities. Chicago: Machinery and Allied Products Institute, 1952.

Asada, Sadao. *From Mahan to Pearl Harbor: The Imperial Japanese Navy and the United States*. Annapolis, MD: Naval Institute Press, 2006.

Ashworth, William. *Contracts and Finance*. London: Her Majesty's Stationery Office, 1953.

Baer, George W. *One Hundred Years of American Sea Power: The U.S. Navy. 1890–1990*. Stanford, CA: Stanford University Press, 1996.

Baker, R. Scott. *Paradoxes of Desegregation: African American Struggles for Educational Equity in Charleston, South Carolina, 1926–1972*. Charleston: University of South Carolina Press, 2006.

Ballantine, Duncan S. *U.S. Naval Logistics in the Second World War*. Reprint, Newport, RI: Naval War College Press, 1998.

Barnett, Correlli. *The Audit of War: The Illusion and Reality of Britain as a Great Nation*. London: Papermac, 1987.

Barnhardt, Michael A. *Japan Prepares for Total War: The Search for Economic Security, 1919–1941*. Ithaca, NY: Cornell University Press, 1987.

Bennett, Geoffrey. *Naval Battles of World War II*. Barnsley, UK: Pen & Sword, 2003.

Black, Frederick M. *Charlestown Navy Yard, 1890–1973*. Vol 1. Boston: Boston National Historical Park, National Park Service, U.S. Department of the Interior, 1988.

Blair, Clay. *Hitler's U-Boat War: The Hunters, 1939–1942*. New York: Random House, 1996.

———. *Hitler's U-Boat War: The Hunted, 1942–1945*. New York: Random House, 1998.

Boniface, Patrick. *Loch Class Frigates*. Lodge Hill, UK: Maritime Press, 2013.

Borgeson, Griffith. *Errett Lobban: His Empire, His Motorcars: Auburn, Cord, Duesenberg*. Princeton, NJ: Automobile Quarterly, 1984.

Bowen, Harold G. *Ships, Machinery, and Mossbacks: The Autobiography of a Naval Engineer*. Princeton, NJ: Princeton University Press, 1954.

Boyd, Andrew. *The Royal Navy in Eastern Waters: Linchpin of Victory*. Barnsley, UK: Seaforth Publishing, 2017.

Branfill-Cook, Roger. *Torpedo: The Complete History of the World's Most Revolutionary Naval Weapon*. Barnsley, UK: Seaforth Publishing, 2014.

Brooke, G. Clymer. *Birdsboro: Company with a Past Built to Last*. New York: Newcomen Society, 1959.

Brown, David K. *Atlantic Escorts: Ships, Weapons & Tactics in World War II*. Barnsley, UK: Seaforth Publishing, 2007.

———. *A Century of Naval Construction: The History of the Royal Corps of Naval Constructors, 1883–1983*. London: Conway, 1983.

———. *The Design and Construction of British Warships 1939–1945: The Official Record*. Vol. 1: *Major Surface Vessels*. Annapolis, MD: Naval Institute Press, 1996.

———. *The Design and Construction of British Warships 1939–1945: The Official Record*. Vol. 2: *Submarines, Escorts and Coastal Forces*. Annapolis, MD: Naval Institute Press, 1996.

———. *Nelson to Vanguard: Warship Design and Development 1923–1945*. Barnsley, UK: Seaforth Publishing, 2000.

Brown, Ken. *U-Boat Assault on America: Why the U.S. Was Unprepared for War in the Atlantic*. Annapolis, MD: Naval Institute Press, 2017.

Burr, Laurence. *US Fast Battleships 1936–1947: The North Carolina and South Dakota Classes*. Oxford, UK: Seaforth Publishing, 2010.

Buxton, Ian. *Swan Hunter Built Warships*. Cornwall, UK: Maritime Books, 2007.

———. *Warship Building and Repair During the Second World War*. Glasgow, UK: Centre for Business History in Scotland, 1998.

Buxton, Ian, and Ian Johnston. *The Battleship Builders: Constructing and Arming British Capital Ships*. Barnsley, UK: Seaforth Publishing, 2013.

Carew, Michael. *Becoming the Arsenal: The American Industrial Mobilization for World War II, 1938–1942*. Lanham, MD: University Press of America, 2010.

Carlisle, Rodney P. *Where the Fleet Begins: A History of the David Taylor Research Center. 1898–1998*. Washington, DC: Naval Historical Center, 1998.

Clarke, Joseph F. *Building Ships on the North East Coast: A Labour of Love, Risk, and Pain*, Part 2: *C 1914–C 1980*. Whitley Bay, UK: Bewick Press, 1997.

Colletta, Paolo E. *American Secretaries of the Navy*. Vol. 2. Annapolis, MD: Naval Institute Press, 1980.

Connery, Robert H. *The Navy and the Industrial Mobilization in World War II*. Princeton, NJ: Princeton University Press, 1951.

Cook, James F. *Carl Vinson: Patriarch of the Armed Forces.* Macon, GA: Mercer University Press, 2004.

Cressman, Robert J. *USS Ranger: The Navy's First Flattop from Keel to Mast, 1934–1946.* Washington, DC: Brassey's, 2003.

Dallek, Robert. *Franklin D. Roosevelt and American Foreign Policy, 1932–1945.* New York: Oxford University Press, 1995.

Darling, Kev. *Fleet Air Arm Carrier War: The History of British Naval Aviation.* Barnsley, UK: Pen & Sword, 2009.

Davidson, Joel. *The Unsinkable Fleet: The Politics of the U.S. Navy Expansion in World War II.* Annapolis, MD: Naval Institute Press, 1996.

De La Pedraja, René. *The Rise and Decline of U.S. Merchant Shipping in the Twentieth Century.* New York: Twayne Publishers, 1992.

Doepgen, Peter. *Die Washingtoner Konferenz, das Deutsche Reich und die Reichsmarine: Deutsche Marinepolitik 1921 bis 1935.* Bremen, Germany: Hauschild, 2005.

Dorwart, Jeffrey M. *The Philadelphia Navy Yard from the Birth of the U.S. Navy to the Nuclear Age.* Philadelphia: University of Pennsylvania Press, 2001.

Doyle, David. *USS Yorktown: From Design and Construction to the Battles of Coral Sea and Midway.* Atglen, PA: Schiffer Publishing, 2017.

Düffler, Jost. *Weimar, Hitler und die Marine: Reichspolitik und Flottenbau 1920–1939.* Düsseldorf, Germany: Droste, 1973.

Duscha, Julius. *Arms, Money, and Politics.* New York: Ives Washburn, 1965.

Edgerton, David. *Britain's War Machine: Weapons, Resources, and Experts in the Second World War.* New York: Oxford University Press, 2011.

Elliott, Peter. *Allied Escort Ships of World War II: A Complete Survey.* Annapolis, MD: Naval Institute Press, 1977.

Evans, David C., and Mark R. Peattie. *Kaigun: Strategy, Tactics, and Technology in the Imperial Japanese Navy, 1887–1941.* Annapolis, MD: Naval Institute Press, 1997.

Franklin, Bruce H. *The Buckley-Class Destroyer Escorts.* Annapolis, MD: Naval Institute Press, 1999.

Franklin, George. *Britain's Anti-Submarine Capability, 1919–1939.* London: Frank Cass, 2003.

Friedman, Norman. *The British Battleship: 1906–1946.* Annapolis, MD: Naval Institute Press, 2015.

———. *British Destroyers and Frigates: The Second World War and After.* Barnsley, UK: Seaforth Publishing, 2006.

———. *U.S. Aircraft Carriers: An Illustrated Design History.* Annapolis, MD: Naval Institute Press, 1983.

―――. *U.S. Amphibious Ships and Craft: An Illustrated Design History*. Annapolis, MD: Naval Institute Press, 2002.

―――. *U.S. Battleships: An Illustrated Design History*. Annapolis, MD: Naval Institute Press, 1985.

―――. *U.S. Cruisers: An Illustrated Design History*. Annapolis, MD: Naval Institute Press, 1987.

―――. *U.S. Destroyers: An Illustrated Design History*. Annapolis, MD: Naval Institute Press, 2004.

Fukasaku, Yukiko. *Technology and Industrial Growth in Pre-War Japan: The Mitsubishi-Nagasaki Shipyard 1884–1934*. London: Routledge, 1992.

Gardiner, Robert, ed. *Conway's All the World's Fighting Ships, 1922–1946*. Annapolis, MD: Naval Institute Press, 1984.

Garzke, William H. *Battleships: Axis and Neutral Battleships in World War II*. Annapolis, MD: Naval Institute Press, 1985.

Goldman, Emily O. *Sunken Treaties: Naval Arms Control Between the Wars*. University Park: Pennsylvania State University Press, 1994.

Gordon, Gilbert A. H. *British Seapower and Procurement Between the Wars*. Annapolis, MD: Naval Institute Press, 1988.

Greenway, Ambrose. *Cargo Liners: An Illustrated History*. Barnsley, UK: Seaforth Publishing, 2011.

Gropman, Alan L. *Mobilizing U.S. Industry in World War II: Myth and Reality*. Washington, DC: National Defense University, 2001.

Hamer, Fritz P. *Charleston Reborn: A Southern City, Its Navy Yard and World War II*. Charleston, SC: History Press, 2005.

Heinrich, Thomas. *Ships for the Seven Seas: Philadelphia Shipbuilding in the Age of Industrial Capitalism*. Baltimore, MD: Johns Hopkins University Press, 1997.

Heinrichs, Waldo. *Threshold of War: Franklin D. Roosevelt and American Entry into World War II*. New York: Oxford University Press, 1990.

Hendrickson, David H. *The Patrol Frigate Story: The Tacoma-Class Frigates in World War II and the Korean War 1943–1953*. Jacksonville, FL: Fortis, 2011.

Herman, Arthur. *Freedom's Forge: How American Business Produced Victory in World War II*. New York: Random House, 2012.

Herwig, Holger H. *Politics of Frustration: The United States in German Naval Planning, 1889–1941*. Boston: Little, Brown, 1976.

Holley, Irving B., Jr. *Buying Aircraft: Materiél Procurement for the Army Air Forces*. Washington, DC: U.S. Army Center for Military History, 1964.

Holwitt, Joel I. *"Execute against Japan": The U.S. Decision to Conduct Unrestricted Submarine Warfare*. College Station: Texas A&M University Press, 2009.

Hone, Thomas C., Norman Friedman, and Mark D. Mandeles. *American and British Aircraft Carrier Development, 1919–1941*. Annapolis, MD: Naval Institute Press, 1999.

Hume, John R., and Michael S. Moss. *Beardmore: The History of a Scottish Industrial Giant*. London: Heinemann, 1979.

Hyde, Charles K. *Arsenal of Democracy: The American Automobile Industry in World War II*. Detroit, MI: Wayne State University Press, 2013.

Irwin, Manley R. *Silent Strategists: Harding, Denby, and the U.S. Navy's Trans-Pacific Offensive, World War II*. Lanham, MD: University Press of America, 2013.

Johnman, Lewis, and Hugh Murphy. *British Shipbuilding and the State Since 1918*. Ithaca, NY: Regatta Press, 2002.

———. *Scott Lithgow Dejá Vu All Over Again! The Rise and Fall of a Shipbuilding Company*. Liverpool, UK: Liverpool University Press, 2017.

Johnston, Ian. *Ships for All Nations: John Brown & Company Clydebank. 1847–1971*. Annapolis, MD: Naval Institute Press, 2015.

Jordan, John. *Warships after Washington: The Development of Five Major Fleets 1922–1930*. Barnsley, UK: Seaforth Publishing, 2011.

Kiesel, Wolfgang. *Der Bremer Vulkan: Aufstieg und Fall*. Bremen, Germany: Kurze-Schönholz und Ziesemer, 1997.

Kinch, Anton. *Charge it to the Navy*. Milwaukee, WI: A. Kinch, 1945.

King, Ernest, and Walter M. Whitehill. *Fleet Admiral King: A Naval Record*. New York: Norton, 1952.

Koistinen, Paul A. C. *Arsenal of World War II: The Political Economy of World War II, 1940–1945*. Lawrence: University of Kansas Press, 2004.

Koop, Gerhard, and Klaus-Peter Schmolke. *German Destroyers of World War II: Warships of the Kriegsmarine*. Barnsley, UK: Seaforth Publishing, 2003.

Koop, Gerhard, Kurt Galle, and Fritz Klein. *Von der Kaiserlichen Werft zum Marinearsenal: Wilhelmshaven als Zentrum der Marinetechnik seit 1870*. Munich, Germany: Bernard & Graefe, 1982.

Kuckuk, Peter. *Die Ostasienschnelldampfer Scharnhorst, Potsdam und Gneisenau des Norddeutschen Lloyd: Ein Beitrag zur Schiffbau- und Schiffahrtsgeschichte des Dritten Reiches*. Bremen, Germany: Hauschild, 2005.

Kuehn, John T. *Agents of Innovation: The General Board and the Design of the Fleet that Defeated the Japanese Navy*. Annapolis, MD: Naval Institute Press, 2008.

———. *America's First General Staff: A Short History of the Rise and Fall of the General Board of the Navy, 1900–1950*. Annapolis, MD: Naval Institute Press, 2017.

Lane, Frederic C. *Ships for Victory: A History of Shipbuilding under the U.S. Maritime Commission in World War II*. Baltimore, MD: Johns Hopkins University Press, 1951.

Levy, James P. *The Royal Navy's Home Fleet in World War II*. New York: Palgrave Macmillan, 2003.

Lott, Arnold S. *A Long Line of Ships: Mare Island's Century of Naval Activity in California*. Annapolis, MD: Naval Institute Press, 1954.

MacDougall, Philip. *The Chatham Dockyard Story*. Rochester, UK: Rochester Press, 1981.

Mahnken, Thomas G. *Uncovering Ways of War: U.S. Intelligence and Foreign Military Innovation, 1918–1941*. Ithaca, NY: Cornell University Press, 2002.

Maiolo, Joseph. *The Royal Navy and Nazi Germany, 1933–39: A Study in Appeasement and the Origins of the Second World War*. London: Macmillan Press, 1998.

Marolda, Edward J. *The Washington Navy Yard: An Illustrated History*. Washington, DC: Naval Historical Center, 1999.

Marriot, Leo. *Treaty Cruisers: The First International Warship Building Competition*. Barnsley, UK: Pen & Sword, 2005.

Maryland in World War II: Industry and Agriculture. Baltimore, MD: Maryland Historical Society, 1951.

Matloff, Maurice, and Edwin M. Snell. *Strategic Planning for Coalition Warfare, 1941–1942*. Washington, DC: Government Printing Office, 1980.

McBride, William M. *Technological Change and the United States Navy, 1865–1945*. Baltimore, MD: Johns Hopkins University Press, 2000.

McComb, Dave. *U.S. Destroyers 1934–45: Pre-war Classes*. Oxford, UK: Osprey Publishing, 2010.

Mertelsmann, Olaf. *Zwischen Krieg, Revolution und Inflation: Die Werft Blohm & Voss 1914–1923*. Munich, Germany: C. H. Beck, 2003.

Meyhoff, Andreas. *Blohm & Voss im "Dritten Reich": Eine Hamburger Großwerft zwischen Geschäft und Politik*. Hamburg, Germany: Christians, 2001.

Miller, Christopher W. *Planning and Profits: British Naval Armaments Manufacture and the Military-Industrial Complex, 1918–1941*. Liverpool, UK: Liverpool University Press, 2018.

Miller, John A. *Men and Volts at War: The Story of General Electric in World War II*. New York: Bantam Books, 1948.

Milner, Marc. "Anglo-American Naval Co-operation in the Second World War, 1939–1945." In *Maritime Strategy and the Balance of Power: Britain and America in the Twentieth Century*, edited by John B. Hattendorf and Robert S. Jordan. New York: St. Martin's Press, 1989.

Mitchell, C. Bradford. *Every Kind of Shipwork: A History of Todd Shipyards Corporation, 1916–1981*. New York: Todd Shipyards Corporation, 1981.

Mitsubishi Zōsen Kabushiki Kaisha. *Naval Vessels 1887–1945: Mitsubishi Zosen Built*. Tokyo: Nippon Kobo, 1956.

———. *Nihon no shosen 1887–1958/Brief Shipbuilding History of the Company*. Tokyo: Mitsubishi Zōsen Kabushiki Kaisha, 1960.

Moon, John E. *Confines of Concept: American Strategy in World War II*. Vol. 2. New York: Garland, 1988.

Moore, George. *Building for Victory: The Warship Building Programmes of the Royal Navy 1939–1945*. Gravesend, UK: World Ship Society, 2002.

Mooney, James, ed. *Dictionary of American Naval Fighting Ships*, 7 vols. Washington, DC: Navy Department, Naval History and Heritage Command, 1959–1981.

Morison, Samuel E. *History of United States Naval Operations in World War II: The Battle of the Atlantic, September 1939 to May 1943*. Boston: Little, Brown, 1947.

Moss, Michael S. *Shipbuilders to the World: 125 Years of Harland and Wolff, Belfast 1861–1986*. Belfast, UK: Blackstaff Press, 1986.

Newman, Brian. *Materials Handling in British Shipbuilding, 1850–1945*. Glasgow, UK: Centre for Business History in Scotland, 1996.

Nishiyama, Takashi. *Engineering War and Peace in Modern Japan, 1868–1964*. Baltimore, MD: Johns Hopkins University Press, 2014.

O'Hara, Vincent P. *Struggle for the Middle Sea: The Great Navies at War in the Mediterranean Theater, 1940–1945*. Annapolis, MD: Naval Institute Press, 2009.

———. *The U.S. Navy Against the Axis: Surface Combat 1941–1945*. Annapolis, MD: Naval Institute Press, 2007.

Overy, Richard. *Why the Allies Won*. New York: Norton, 1995.

Palmer, David. *Organizing the Shipyards: Union Strategy in Three Northeast Ports, 1933–1945*. Ithaca, NY: Cornell University Press, 1998.

Parillo, Mark P. *The Japanese Merchant Marine in World War II*. Annapolis, MD: Naval Institute Press, 1993.

Pearl Harbor as History: Japanese-American Relations 1931–1941. Edited by Dorothy Borg and Shumpei Okamoto. New York: Columbia University Press, 1973.

Peebles, Hugh. *Warshipbuilding on the Clyde: Naval Orders and the Prosperity of the Clyde Shipbuilding Industry, 1889–1939*. Edinburgh, UK: John Donald, 2000.

Pelz, Stephen E. *Race to Pearl Harbor: The Failure of the Second London Naval Conference and the Onset of World War II*. Cambridge, MA: Harvard University Press, 1975.

Polmar, Norman P., and Edward Whitman. *Hunters and Killers*. Vol. 1: *Anti-Submarine Warfare from 1776 to 1943*. Annapolis, MD: Naval Institute Press, 2015.

Prados, John. *Combined Fleet Decoded: The Secret History of American Intelligence and the Japanese Navy in World War II*. Annapolis, MD: Naval Institute Press, 1995.

Pratt, Fletcher. *Sea Power and Today's War*. New York: Harrison-Hilton Books, 1939.

Preston, Anthony. *The World's Worst Warships: The Failures and Repercussions of Naval Design and Construction, 1860–2000*. Annapolis, MD: Naval Institute Press, 2002.

Reid, Alastair J. *The Tide of Democracy: Shipyard Workers and Social Relations in Britain*. Manchester, UK: Manchester University Press, 2010.

Richardson, James O. *On the Treadmill to Pearl Harbor: The Memoirs of Admiral James O. Richardson*. Washington, DC: Government Printing Office, 1973.

Robins, Nick. *Wartime Standard Ships*. Barnsley, UK: Seaforth Publishing, 2017.

Roehrs, Mark D. *World War II in the Pacific*. Armonk, NY: M. E. Sharpe, 2004.

Roscoe, Theodore. *United States Submarine Operations in World War II*. Annapolis, MD: Naval Institute Press, 1949.

Roskill, Stephen W. *Naval Policy Between the Wars*. Vol. 2: *The Period of Reluctant Rearmament 1930–1939*. Annapolis, MD: Naval Institute Press, 1976.

———. *The War at Sea, 1939–1945*. Vol. 1: *The Defensive*. London: Her Majesty's Stationery Office, 1954.

———. *The War at Sea, 1939–1945*. Vol. 3, *Part II: The Offensive*. London: Her Majesty's Stationery Office, 1961.

Rössler, Eberhard. *Die deutschen Uboote und ihre Werften: Eine Bilddokumentation über den deutschen Ubootbau von 1935 bis heute*. Munich, Germany: Bernhard & Graefe, 1990.

———. *Geschichte des deutschen Ubootbaus*. Munich, Germany: J. F. Lehmann, 1975.

Runyan, Timothy J., and Jan M. Copes. *To Die Gallantly: The Battle of the Atlantic*. Boulder, CO: Westview Press, 1994.

Salewski, Michael. *Die deutsche Seekriegsleitung 1935–1945*. Vol. 1: *1935–1941*. Frankfurt, Germany: Bernard & Graefe, 1970.

Schiffbautechnische Gesellschaft. *75 Jahre Schiffbautechnische Gesellschaft 1899–1974*. Hamburg, Germany: Schiffbautechnische Gesellschaft, 1974.

Schmelzkopf, Reinhart. *Die deutsche Handelsschifffahrt 1919–1939*. Vol. 1: *Chronik und Wertung der Ereignisse in Schifffahrt und Schiffbau*. Oldenburg, Germany: Stalling, 1974.

Schulze-Wegener, Guntram. *Die deutsche Kriegsmarine-Rüstung 1942–1945*. Hamburg, Germany: Mittler, 1997.

Scott, John D. *Vickers: A History*. London: Weidenfeld & Nicolson, 1963.

Scranton, Philip. *Endless Novelty: Specialty Production and American Industrialization, 1865–1925*. Princeton, NJ: Princeton University Press, 1997.

———. *Proprietary Capitalism: The Textile Manufacture at Philadelphia, 1800–1885*. Philadelphia: Temple University Press, 1987.

Showell, Jak M. *Hitler's Navy: A Reference Guide to the Kriegsmarine 1935–1945*. Annapolis, MD: Naval Institute Press, 2009.

Simpson, B. Mitchell. *Admiral Harold R. Stark: Architect of Victory, 1939–1945*. Columbia, SC: University of South Carolina Press, 1989.

Skulski, Janusz. *Battleships Yamato and Musashi*. London: Bloomsbury, 2017.

Snow, Ralph L. *Bath Iron Works: The First Hundred Years*. Bath, ME: Maine Maritime Museum, 1987.

Snow, Richard. *A Measureless Peril: America in the Fight for the Atlantic, the Longest Battle of World War II*. New York: Scribner, 2010.

Sparrow, Bartholomew H. *From the Outside In: World War II and the American State*. Princeton, NJ: Princeton University Press, 1996.

Sparrow, James T. *Warfare State: World War II Americans and the Age of Big Government*. New York: Oxford University Press, 2011.

Stern, Robert C. *The Battleship Holiday: The Naval Treaties and Capital Ship Design*. Barnsley, UK: Pen & Sword, 2017.

Stille, Mark E. *Imperial Japanese Navy Antisubmarine Escorts 1941–45*. Oxford, UK: Osprey Publishing, 2017.

———. *Imperial Japanese Navy Destroyers, 1919–45: Asashio to Tachibana*. Oxford, UK: Osprey Publishing, 2013.

———. *The Imperial Japanese Navy in the Pacific War*. Oxford, UK: Osprey Publishing, 2014.

———. *U.S. Navy Light Cruisers, 1941–1945*. Oxford, UK: Osprey Publishing, 2016.

———. *USN vs IJN Destroyer: The Pacific 1943*. Oxford, UK: Osprey Publishing, 2012.

Sumner, Gregory D. *Detroit in World War II*. Charleston, SC: History Press, 2015.

Sumrall, Robert F. *Iowa Class Battleships: Their Design, Weapons and Equipment*. Annapolis, MD: Naval Institute Press, 1988.

Swaine, Robert T. *The Cravath Firm and Its Predecessors, 1819–1948*. Volume 2: *The Cravath Firm Since 1906*. New York: Ad Press, 1948.

Tazewell, William L. *Newport News Shipbuilding: The First Century*. Newport News, VA: Mariners' Museum, 1986.

Technikgeschichte des industriellen Schiffbaus in Deutschland. Wiefelstede, Germany: Oceanum, 1994.

Thiel, Christopher. *Der Deutsche U-Bootkrieg im 2. Weltkrieg*. Berlin, Germany: Epubli, 2016.

Thiesen, William H. *Industrializing American Shipbuilding: The Transformation of Ship Design and Construction, 1820–1920*. Gainesville: University Press of Florida, 2006.

Tompkins, Tom. *Yokosuka: Base for an Empire*. Novato, CA: Presidio, 1981.

Tooze, Adam. *The Wages of Destruction: The Making and Breaking of the Nazi Economy*. New York: Penguin, 2007.

Two Hundred & Fifty Years of Shipbuilding by the Scotts at Greenock. Greenock, UK: 1961.

Ujifusa, Steven. *A Man and His Ship: America's Greatest Naval Architect and His Quest to Build the S.S. United States*. New York: Simon & Schuster, 2012.

Vandermeulen, Jacob. *Building the B-29*. Washington, DC: Smithsonian Museum Press, 1995.

Vatter, Harold G. *The U.S. Economy in World War II*. New York: Columbia University Press, 1985.

Verband der Deutschen Schiffbauindustrie. *100 Jahre Verbands-und Zeitgeschehen*. Hamburg, Germany: Storck, 1984.

Walton, Francis. *Miracle of World War II: How American Industry Made Victory Possible*. New York: Macmillan, 1956.

Watterson, Rodney K. *32 in '44: Building the Portsmouth Submarine Fleet in World War II*. Annapolis, MD: Naval Institute Press, 2011.

Watts, Anthony J. *Japanese Warships of World War II*. New York: Doubleday, 1967.

Weir, Gary E. *Building American Submarines, 1914–1940*. Washington, DC: Naval Historical Center, 1991.

———. *Forged in War: The Naval-Industrial Complex and American Submarine Construction, 1940–1961*. Washington, DC: Naval Historical Center, 1993.

White, Gerald. *Billions for Defense: Government Financing by the Defense Plant Corporation During World War II*. Tuscaloosa: University of Alabama Press, 1980.

Williams, David L., and Richard P. de Kerbrech. *J. Samuel White & Co. Shipbuilders*. Stround, UK: History Press, 2012.

Williams, William J. *The Wilson Administration and the Shipbuilding Crisis of 1917: Steel Ships and Wooden Steamers*. Lewiston, NY: Edwin Mellen, 1992.

Wilson, Alastair, and Joseph F. Callo. *Who's Who in Naval History: From 1550 to the Present* London: Routledge, 2004.

Wilson, Daniel M. *Three Hundred Years of Quincy. 1625–1925: Historical Retrospect of Mount Wollaston, Braintree, and Quincy*. Boston: Wright & Brown, 1926.

Wilson, Mark R. *Destructive Creation: American Business and the Winning of World War II*. Philadelphia: University of Pennsylvania Press, 2016.

Yerxa, Donald A. *Admirals and Empire: The United States Navy and the Caribbean, 1898–1945*. Columbia: University of South Carolina Press, 1991.

Articles and Chapters in Books

Arendt, Kurt, and Heinrich Oelfken. "Die Baumethoden der deutschen U-Boote 1935–1945." In *100 Jahre Verbands- und Zeitgeschehen*, edited by Verband der Deutschen Schiffbauindustrie e. V. 66–72. Hamburg, Germany: Storck, 1984.

Atsushi Oi. "Why Japan's Anti-Submarine Warfare Failed." U.S. Naval Institute *Proceedings* 78 (June 1952): 587–90.

Barlow, Jeffrey G. "Roosevelt and King: The War in the Atlantic and European Theaters." In *FDR and the U.S. Navy*, edited by Edward J. Marolda, 173–93. New York: St. Martin's Press, 1998.

Brown, David K. "Early Welding for the Royal Navy." *Journal of Naval Engineering* 34 (Dec. 1992): 220–22.

Buckley, Thomas. "The Icarus Factor: The American Pursuit of Myth in Naval Arms Control, 1921–36." *Diplomacy and Statecraft* 4 (1993): 124–46.

Buell, Thomas B. "Roosevelt and Strategy in the Pacific." In *FDR and the U.S. Navy*, edited by Edward J. Marolda, 163–72. New York: St. Martin's Press, 1998.

"Building the Iowa Class Battleships." *Jerseyman* 6 (Oct. 2007): 8–9.

Buxton, Neil. "The Scottish Shipbuilding Industry Between the Wars: A Comparative Study." *Business History* 10 (July 1968): 101–20.

Calhoun, Gordon. "Design and Construction of USS Wisconsin." *Daybook* 6 (Summer 2000): 6–15.

Cernuschi, Enrico, and Vincent O'Hara. "Italy: The Regina Marina." In *On Seas Contested: The Seven Great Navies of the Second World War*, edited by Vincent P. O'Hara, W. David Dickson, and Richard Worth, 123–56. Annapolis, MD: Naval Institute Press, 2010.

Deist, Wilhelm. "Die Aufrüstung der Wehrmacht." In *Das Deutsche Reich und der Zweite Weltkrieg*. Vol. 1: *Ursachen und Voraussetzungen der deutschen Kriegspolitik*, edited by Wilhelm Deist et al., 371–532. Stuttgart, Germany: Deutsche Verlags-Anstalt, 1979.

Dulin, Robert O., William H. Garzke, et al. "The Loss of the USS Yorktown (CV 5): A Forensics Analysis." *Transactions of the Society of Naval Architects and Marine Engineers* 107 (1999): 5–13.

Dunbabin, J. P. D. "British Rearmament in the 1930s: A Chronology and Review." *Historical Journal* 18 (Sep. 1975): 587–609.

"Ernest H. Rigg." In William S. Myers, *Prominent Families of New Jersey*. Vol. 2, 1,094. New York: Lewis, 1945.

Feagin, Joe R., and Kelly Riddell. "The State, Capitalism, and World War II: The U.S. Case." *Armed Forces and Society* 17 (Oct. 1990): 53–79.

Ferguson, Robert G. "One Thousand Planes a Day: Ford, Grumman, General Motors and the Arsenal of Democracy." *History and Technology* 21 (June 2005): 149–75.

Field, Alexander J. "Technological Change and U.S. Productivity Growth in the Interwar Years." *Journal of Economic History* 66 (Mar. 2006): 203–36.

Fisser, Marc. "Die deutsche Seeschiffahrt am Ende des Ersten Weltkrieges und in der Weimarer Republik." *Deutsches Schiffahrtsarchiv* 13 (1990): 111–42.

Ford, Douglas. "U.S. Naval Intelligence and the Imperial Japanese Fleet during the Washington Treaty Era, c. 1922–36." *Mariner's Mirror* 93 (Aug. 2007): 281–306.

Friedman, Norman. "Naval Strategy and Force Structure." In *At the Crossroads Between Peace and War: The London Naval Conference in 1930*, edited by John Maurer and Christopher Bell, 201–28. Annapolis, MD: Naval Institute Press, 2014.

Gordon, Gilbert A. H. "The British Navy 1918–1945." In *Navies and Global Defense: Theories and Strategies*, edited by Keith Nelson and Elizabeth J. Errington, 161–80. Westport, CT: Praeger, 1995.

Grove, Eric. "A War Fleet Built for Peace: British Naval Rearmament in the 1930s and the Dilemma of Deterrence versus Defence." *Naval War College Review* 44 (1991): 82–92.

Haight, John V., Jr. "Franklin D. Roosevelt and a Naval Quarantine of Japan." *Pacific Historical Review* 40 (May 1971): 203–26.

Heinrich, Thomas. "Jack of All Trades: Cramp Shipbuilding, Mixed Production, and the Limits of Flexible Specialization in American Warship Construction, 1940–1945." *Enterprise and Society* 11 (June 2010): 275–315.

———. "'We Can Build Anything at Navy Yards': Warship Construction in Government Yards and the Political Economy of American Naval Shipbuilding, 1928–1945." *International Journal of Maritime History* 16 (Dec. 2012): 155–80.

Heinrichs, Waldo. "FDR and the Admirals: Strategy and Statecraft." In *FDR and the U.S. Navy*, edited by Edward J. Marolda, 115–29. New York: St. Martin's Press, 1998.

———. "The Role of the United States Navy." In *Pearl Harbor as History: Japanese-American Relations 1931–1941*, edited by Dorothy Borg and Shumpei Okamoto, 197–23. New York: Columbia University Press, 1973.

Hone, Thomas C. "The Evolution of the U.S. Fleet, 1933–1941: How the President Mattered." In *FDR and the U.S. Navy*, edited by Edward J. Marolda, 65–114. New York: St. Martin's Press, 1998.

———. "USA: The United States Navy." In *On Seas Contested: The Seven Great Navies of the Second World War*, edited by Vincent P. O'Hara, W. David Dickson, and Richard Worth, 209–52. Annapolis, MD: Naval Institute Press, 2010.

Hooks, Gregory, and McLauchlan, Gregory. "The Institutional Foundation of Warmaking: Three Eras of U.S. Warmaking, 1939–1989." *Theory and Society* 21 (Dec. 1992): 757–88.

Ingram, Paul, and Arik Lifschitz. "Kinship in the Shadow of the Corporation: The Interbuilder Network in Clyde River Shipbuilding, 1711–1990." *American Sociological Review* 71 (Apr. 2006): 334–52.

Johnman, Lewis, and Hugh Murphy. "Welding and the British Shipbuilding Industry: A Major Constraint?" In *The Royal Navy, 1930–2000: Innovation and Defence*, edited by Richard Harding, 89–116. London: Frank Cass, 2005.

Jolliff, James V., and Kenneth B. Schumacher. "The Declining Years (1922–1932)." In *Naval Engineering and American Sea Power*, edited by Randolph W. King and Prescott Palmer, 119–58. Baltimore, MD: Nautical & Aviation Publishing Company of America, 1989.

Jordan, John. "France: The Marine Nationale." In *On Seas Contested: The Seven Great Navies of the Second World War*, edited by Vincent P. O'Hara, W. David Dickson, and Richard Worth, 1–38. Annapolis, MD: Naval Institute Press, 2010.

Kaen, Fred R. "World War II Prime Defence Contractors: Were They Favoured?" *Business History* 53 (Dec. 2011): 1,044–73.

Keitsch, Christine. "Krise und Konjunktur: Die Flensburger Schiffbau-Gesellschaft von der Weltwirtschaftskrise bis zum Ende des Zweiten Weltkrieges." *Deutsches Schiffahrtsarchiv* 28 (2006): 135–96.

Kennedy, Paul M. "The Tradition of Appeasement in British Foreign Policy 1865–1939." *British Journal of International Studies* 2 (Oct. 1976): 195–215.

Koistinen, Paul A. C. "Mobilizing the World War II Economy: Labor and the Industrial-Military Alliance." *Pacific Historical Review* 42 (Nov. 1973): 443–78.

Kuckuk, Peter, and Hartmut Pophanken. "Die A.G. 'Weser' 1933 bis 1945: Handels- und Kriegsschiffbau im Dritten Reich." In *Bremer Großwerften im Dritten Reich*, edited by Peter Kuckuk, 11–103. Bremen, Germany: Edition Temmen, 1993.

Lambert, Andrew. "Seapower 1939–1940: Churchill and the Strategic Origins of the Battle of the Atlantic." In *Seapower: Theory and Practice*, edited by Geoffrey Till, 86–108. Ilford, UK: Frank Cass, 1994.

Lee, Joong-Jae. "Defense Workers' Struggles for Patriotic Control: The Labor-Management Contests over Defense Production at Brewster, 1940–1944." *International Labor and Working Class History* 66 (Oct. 2004): 136–54.

Lengerer, Hans, and Tomoko Rehm-Takahara. "The Aircraft Carriers of the Shōkaku Class." *Warship* 37 (2015): 90–109.

———. "Japanese 'Kaibokan' Escorts, Part I." *Warship* 30 (Apr. 1984): 124–34.

———. "Japanese 'Kaibokan' Escorts, Part II." *Warship* 31 (July 1984): 171–84.

Little, Branden. "An Evolving Navy of Great Complexity." In *In Peace and War: Interpretations of American Naval History, 1775–1978*, 30th Anniversary Edition, edited by Kenneth J. Hagan, 182–202. Westport, CT: Greenwood Press, 1984.

Lobdell, George H. "Frank Knox." In *American Secretaries of the Navy*. Vol 2: *1913–1972*, edited by Paolo E. Coletta, 677–727. Annapolis, MD: Naval Institute Press, 1980.

MacCutcheon, Edward M. "World War II Development and Expansion (1942–1945)." In *Naval Engineering and American Sea Power*, edited by Randolph W. King and Prescott Palmer, 207–55. Baltimore, MD: Nautical & Aviation Publishing Company of America, 1989.

Maiolo, Joseph. "Did the Royal Navy Decline between the Two World Wars?" *Royal United Services Institute Journal* 159 (Aug. 2014): 18–24.

Major, John. "The Navy Plans for War." In *In Peace and War: Interpretations of American Naval History, 1775–1978*, 250–51. Westport, CT: Greenwood Press, 1984.

McBride, William M. "Powering the U.S. Fleet: Propulsion Machinery Design and American Engineering Culture, 1890–1945." In *New Interpretations in Naval History: Selected Papers from the Sixteenth Naval History Symposium Held at the United States Naval Academy, 10–11 Sep. 2009*, edited by Marcus O. Jones, 51–68. Newport, RI: Naval War College Press, 2016.

———. "Strategic Determinism in Technology Selection: The Electric Battleship and U.S. Naval-Industrial Relations." *Technology and Culture* 33 (Apr. 1992): 248–77.

McVoy, James L., Virgil W. Rinehart, and Prescott Palmer. "The Roosevelt Resurgence (1933–1941)." In *Naval Engineering and American Sea Power*, edited by Randolph W. King and Prescott Palmer, 161–200. Baltimore, MD: Nautical & Aviation Publishing Company of America, 1989.

Milanovich, Kathrin. "Hosho: The First Aircraft Carrier of the Imperial Japanese Navy." *Warship* 30 (2008): 9–25.

Miles, Paul L. "Roosevelt and Leahy: The Orchestration of Global Strategy." In *FDR and the U.S. Navy*, edited by Edward J. Marolda, 147–62. New York: St. Martin's Press, 1998.

Miller, Nathan. "The American Navy, 1922–1945." In *Navies and Global Defense: Theories and Strategies*, edited by Keith Nelson and Elizabeth J. Errington, 139–60. Westport, CT: Praeger, 1995.

Mitchell, Alan C. "Requiem for a Royal Dockyard." *Marine Engineers Review* (Apr. 1984): 18–21.

Muir, Malcolm. "Rearming in a Vacuum: United States Navy Intelligence and the Japanese Capital Ship Threat, 1936–1945." *Journal of Military History* 54 (Oct. 1990): 473–85.

Murphy, Hugh. "'From the Crinoline to the Boilersuit': Women Workers in British Shipbuilding During the Second World War." *Contemporary British History* 13 (Dec. 1999): 82–104.

———. "The Health of Electric Arc Welders and the Adoption of Arc Welding in the British Shipbuilding Industry, 1930–1951." *International Journal of Maritime History* 17 (June 2005): 69–90.

O'Brien, Phillips P. "Politics, Arms Control and U.S. Naval Development in the Interwar Period." In *Technology and Naval Combat in the Twentieth Century and Beyond*, edited by Phillips P. O'Brien, 148–64. London: Frank Cass, 2007.

Peattie, Mark. "Japan: The Teikoku Kaigun." In *On Seas Contested: The Seven Great Navies of the Second World War*, edited by Vincent P. O'Hara, W. David Dickson, and Richard Worth, 157–208. Annapolis, MD: Naval Institute Press, 2010.

———. "Japanese Naval Construction, 1919–41." In *Technology and Naval Combat in the Twentieth Century and Beyond*, edited by Phillips P. O'Brien, 93–108. London: Frank Cass, 2007.

Peters, Dirk J. "Deutsche Werften in der Zwischenkriegszeit (1918–1939): Teil 1." *Deutsches Schiffahrtsarchiv* 28 (2005): 95–134.

———. "Deutsche Werften in der Zwischenkriegszeit (1918–1939). Teil 2: Symptome der Krise, Stilllegungen Schließungen, Fusionen und Innovationen (1924–1934)." *Deutsches Schiffahrtsarchiv* 32 (2009): 173–222.

Pfliegensdörfer, Dieter, and Jörg Wollenberg. "Die Werftenkrise der zwanziger Jahre: Ein Lehrstück für heute." In *"Stell dir vor, die Werften gehören uns": Krise des Schiffbaus oder Krise der Politik?* edited by Heiner Heseler and Hans Jürgen Kröger, 167–71. Hamburg, Germany: VSA, 1983.

Rahn, Werner. "German Naval Strategy and Armament, 1919–39." In *Technology and Naval Combat in the Twentieth Century and Beyond*, edited by Phillips P. O'Brien, 109–27. London: Frank Cass, 2007.

"Reviews of Olaf Mertelsmann, Zwischen Krieg, Revolution und Inflation. Die Werft Blohm & Voss 1914–1923 with a Response by Olaf Mertelsmann." *International Journal of Maritime History* 16 (Dec. 2004): 265–308.

Rice, Richard. "Economic Mobilization in Wartime Japan: Business, Bureaucracy, and Military in Conflict." *Journal of Asian Studies* 38 (Aug. 1979): 689–706.

Ristuccia, Cristiano A., and Adam Tooze. "Machine Tools and Mass Production in the Armaments Boom: Germany and the United States, 1929–44." *Economic History Review* 66 (2013): 953–74.

Robb-Webb, Jon. "'Light Two Lanterns, the British Are Coming by Sea': Royal Navy Participation in the Pacific, 1944–1945." In *British Naval Strategies East of Suez, 1900–2000: Influences and Actions*, edited by Greg Kennedy, 128–53. London: Routledge, 2003.

Roberts, Stephen S. "U.S. Navy Building Programs During World War II." *Warship International* 18 (1981): 223–27.

"Robinson, Samuel Murray." *Cyclopædia of American Biography*. Vol. G: *1943–1946*, 293–94. New York: James White & Co., 1946.

Roder, Hartmut. "Der Bremer Vulkan im Dritten Reich (1933–1945)." In *Bremer Großwerften im Dritten Reich*, edited by Peter Kuckuk, 129–53. Bremen, Germany: Edition Temmen, 1993.

Russell, Richard A. *Project Hula: Secret Soviet-American Cooperation in the War against Japan*. Washington, DC: Naval Historical Center, 1997.

Saville, Allison. "Claude Augustus Swanson." In *American Secretaries of the Navy*. Vol II: *1913–1972*, edited by Paolo E. Coletta, 655–67. Annapolis, MD: Naval Institute Press, 1980.

Schenk, Peter. "Germany: The Kriegsmarine." In *On Seas Contested: The Seven Great Navies of the Second World War*, edited by Vincent P. O'Hara, W. David Dickson, and Richard Worth, 39–79. Annapolis, MD: Naval Institute Press, 2010.

Scranton, Philip. "Diversity in Diversity: Flexible Production and American Industrialization, 1880–1930." *Business History Review* 65 (Spring 1991): 27–90.

Shiba, Takao. "Succeeding Against Odds, Courting Collapse: How Mitsubishi Shipbuilding and Kawasaki Dockyard Managed the Post–WWI Slump." *Japanese Yearbook on Business History* 2 (Jan. 1986): 100–18.

Simonson, G. R. "The Demand for Aircraft and the Aircraft Industry, 1907–1958." *Journal of Economic History* 20 (Sep. 1960): 361–82.

Slaven, Anthony. "Self-Liquidation: The National Shipbuilders Security Ltd and British Shipbuilding in the 1930s." In *Charted and Uncharted Waters: Proceedings of a Conference on the Study of British Maritime History*, edited by Sarah Palmer and Glyndwr Williams, 125–47. London: Queen Mary College, 1983.

———. "A Shipyard in Depression: John Browns of Clydebank." *Business History* 19 (July 1977): 192–217.

Sparr, Arnold. "Looking for Rosie: Women Defense Workers in the Brooklyn Navy Yard, 1942–1946." *New York History* 81 (July 2000): 313–40.

Stegemann, Bernd. "Die erste Phase der Seekriegsführung bis zum Frühjahr 1940." In *Das Deutsche Reich und der Zweite Weltkrieg*. Vol. 2: *Die Errichtung der Hegemonie auf dem europäischen Kontinent*, edited by Klaus A. Maier et al., 159–85. Stuttgart, Germany: Deutsche Verlags-Anstalt, 1979.

———. "Die zweite Phase der Seekriegsführung bis zum Frühjahr 1941." *Das Deutsche Reich und der Zweite Weltkrieg*. Vol. 2: *Die Errichtung der Hegemonie auf dem europäischen Kontinent*, edited by Klaus A. Maier et al., 345–61. Stuttgart, Germany: Deutsche Verlags-Anstalt, 1979.

Strohmeier, Daniel D. "A History of Bethlehem Steel Company's Shipbuilding and Ship Repairing Activities." *Naval Engineers Journal* 75 (May 1963): 259–79.

Sumida, Jon. T. "British Naval Procurement and Technological Change." In *Technology and Naval Combat in the Twentieth Century and Beyond*, edited by Phillips P. O'Brien, 148–64. London: Frank Cass, 2007.

Utley, Jonathan G. "Franklin Roosevelt and Naval Strategy, 1933–1941." In *FDR and the U.S. Navy*, edited by Edward J. Marolda, 47–64. New York: St. Martin's Press, 1998.

Warren, Kenneth. *Steel, Ships and Men: Cammell Laird, 1824–1993*. Liverpool, UK: Liverpool University Press, 2011.

Watson, Bruce A. *Atlantic Convoys and Nazi Raiders: The Deadly Voyage of HMS Jervis Bay*. Westport, CT: Praeger, 2006.

White, Graham. *Allied Aircraft Piston Engines of World War II: History and Development of Frontline Aircraft Piston Engines Produced By Great Britain and the United States during World War II*. Warrendale, PA: Society of Automotive Engineers, 1995.

Wilson, John R. "The Quaker and the Sword: Herbert Hoover's Relations with the Military." *Military Affairs* 38 (Apr. 1974): 41–47.

Winkler, David F. "The Construction of USS Atlanta and the Navy Seizure of Federal Shipbuilding." *Northern Mariner* 14 (Apr. 2014): 135–52.

Wragg, David. "Great Britain: The Royal Navy." In *On Seas Contested: The Seven Great Navies of the Second World War*, edited by Vincent P. O'Hara, W. David Dickson, and Richard Worth, 80–122. Annapolis, MD: Naval Institute Press, 2010.

Zeitlin, Jonathan. "Flexibility and Mass Production at War: Aircraft Manufacture in Britain, the United States, and Germany, 1939–1945." *Technology and Culture* 36 (Jan. 1995): 46–79.

Theses and Research Papers

Barrett, John M. "An Analysis of the Causal Factors Behind the United States Navy's Warship-Building Programs from 1933 to 1941." Master's thesis, U.S. Army Command and General Staff College, 2005.

Camp, Joe H. "Birch Rod to Arsenal: A Study of the Naval Ordnance Plant at South Charleston, West Virginia, and the Search for a Government Industrial Policy." PhD dissertation, West Virginia University, 2002.

Dubose-Simons, Carla. "The 'Silent Arrival': The Second Wave of the Great Migration and Its Effects on Black New York, 1940–1950." PhD dissertation, City University of New York, 2013.

McWiggins, Dan P. "Sunrise in the East, Sunset in the West: How the Korean and British Shipbuilding Industries Changed Places in the 20th Century." PhD dissertation, University of Texas at Austin, 2013.

Muir, Malcolm. "The Capital Ship Program in the United States Navy, 1934–1945." PhD dissertation, Ohio State University, 1976.

O'Neil, William D. "Interwar U.S. and Japanese National Product and Defense Expenditure." CNA Analysis & Solutions, Center for Naval Analyses, 2003, available at https://apps.dtic.mil/docs/citations/ADA596762. Accessed May 14, 2019.

Price, Scott T. "A Study of the General Board of the U.S. Navy, 1929–1933." Master's thesis, University of Nebraska, 1989.

Pyke, Justin Z. "Blinded by the Rising Sun? American Intelligence Assessments of Japanese Air and Naval Power, 1920–1941." Master's thesis, University of Calgary, 2016.

Walter, John C. "The Navy Department and the Campaign for Expanded Appropriations, 1933–1938." PhD dissertation, University of Maine, 1972.

INDEX

NOTE: page numbers with *f, n, p,* or *t* indicate figures, notes, photographs, or tables respectively.

ABOUT THE AUTHOR

Thomas Heinrich is professor of U.S. business and naval history at Baruch College, City University of New York. Born and raised in Germany, he received his PhD from the University of Pennsylvania and is the author of *Ships for the Seven Seas: Philadelphia Shipbuilding in the Age of Industrial Capitalism* and *Kimberly-Clark and the Consumer Revolution in American Business*.